BTEC
Level 3

edexcel
advancing learning, changing lives

PERFORMING ARTS LEVEL 3

BTEC National

Sally Jewers | Carolyn Carnaghan | Paul Webster

A PEARSON COMPANY

Published by Pearson Education Limited, a company incorporated in England and Wales, having its registered office at Edinburgh Gate, Harlow, Essex, CM20 2JE. Registered company number: 872828

www.pearsonschoolsandfecolleges.co.uk

Edexcel is a registered trademark of Edexcel Limited
Text © Pearson Education Limited 2010

First published 2010

13 12 11 10

10 9 8 7 6 5 4 3 2 1

British Library Cataloguing in Publication Data
A catalogue record for this book is available from the British Library

ISBN 978 1 846906 787

Copyright notice

Development editing by Althea Brooks
Designed by 320 Design Ltd
Produced by Pearson
Illustrations by Pearson
Cover design by Visual Philosophy, created by eMC Design
Index by Read Indexing
Cover photo/illustration Press Association Images / AP / Vadim Ghirda
Back cover photos Getty Images: intst (left); Pearson Education Ltd: Ken Wilson-Max (right); Gareth Boden (thumbnail)
Printed and bound in Great Britain at Scotprint, Haddington

There are links to relevant websites in this book. In order to ensure that the links are up to date, that the links work, and that the sites are not inadvertently linked to sites that could be considered offensive, we have made the links available on the following website: www.pearsonhotlinks.co.uk. When you access the site, search for either the title BTEC Level 3 Performing Arts or the ISBN 978 1 846906 787.

Disclaimer

This material has been published on behalf of Edexcel and offers high-quality support for the delivery of Edexcel qualifications.

This does not mean that the material is essential to achieve any Edexcel qualification, nor does it mean that it is the only suitable material available to support any Edexcel qualification. Edexcel material will not be used verbatim in setting any Edexcel examination or assessment. Any resource lists produced by Edexcel shall include this and other appropriate resources.

The suggested activities in this book which involve practical work and exposure to hazards must be risk assessed and supervised by a qualified staff member.

Standards are current at the time of publication but may be subject to change during the life of the book. Please check with the relevant standards organisations.

Copies of official specifications for all Edexcel qualifications may be found on the Edexcel website: www.edexcel.com

Every effort has been made to contact copyright holders of material reproduced in this book. Any omissions will be rectified in subsequent printings if notice is given to the publishers.

Contents

Credits

Alamy Images: Photos 12 139, 171, 286, Photos 12 139, 171, 286, Photos 12 139, 171, 286, alam 179, Images of Birmingham 259, Tibor Bognar 168, DigitalVues 211, Paul Doyle 98, 113, Paul Doyle 98, 113, Rebecca Erol 216, Jeff Greenberg 39, Colin Hawkins 274, Jeremy Hoare 47, UpperCut Images 193, Richard Levine 32, Geraint Lewis 41, 44, 87, 249, 250, 257, 301, Geraint Lewis 41, 44, 87, 249, 250, 257, 301, Geraint Lewis 41, 44, 87, 249, 250, 257, 301, Geraint Lewis 41, 44, 87, 249, 250, 257, 301, Geraint Lewis 41, 44, 87, 249, 250, 257, 301, Geraint Lewis 41, 44, 87, 249, 250, 257, 301, Lebrecht Music and Arts Photo Library 94, 148, Lebrecht Music and Arts Photo Library 94, 148, IML Image Group Ltd 10, David Lyons 219, Dennis MacDonald 103, 271, Dennis MacDonald 103, 271, dov makabaw 21, Gunter Marx 264, mediacolor's 221, Trinity Mirror / Mirrorpix 231, 275, 278, Trinity Mirror / Mirrorpix 231, 275, 278, Trinity Mirror / Mirrorpix 231, 275, 278, keith morris 65, Alastair Muir 239, Jeremy Pembrey 245, B&Y Photography 261, Mark Hodson Stock Photography 262, SV Photography 177, paul prescott 243, Zefa RF 295, RichardBaker 110, RubberBall 283, Eitan Simanor 207, Kumar Sriskandan 78, Perov Stanislav 285, StudioSource 155, Ferenc Szelepcsenyi 123, John Terence Turner 238, Arch White 9, Kunz Wolfgang 158, **Vlad Zisser** 288; **Jenny Court:** 151l, 151r; **Getty Images:** ALFRED EISENSTAEDT 5; **Sarah Glenny:** 281; **iStockphoto:** Pavel Aleynikov 143, Mike Bentley 56, Dan Brandenburg 159, Claudia Dewald 293, hulya-erkisi 63, intst 141, Franky De Meyer 209, Bruno Passigatti 225, Reuben Schulz 195, Alexander Yakovlev 173; **Red Ladder:** 4; **Brian Lobel:** Belinda Lawley 19; **Pearson Education Ltd:** www.imagesource.com. Alamy 164, Martin Beddall 89, Gareth Boden 30, 289, 297, Photodisc. Getty Images 25, Ken Wilson-Max 1, 2, 6, 16, 60, 67, 76, 82, 115, 153, 161, 167, 175, 197, 236, 240tl, 240tc, 240tr, 240l, 240c, 240c/2, 240cl, 240cr, 240r, 240bl, 240bc, 240br, 252, 273, 290, Ken Wilson-Max 1, 2, 6, 16, 60, 67, 76, 82, 115, 153, 161, 167, 175, 197, 236, 240tl, 240tc, 240tr, 240l, 240c, 240c/2, 240cl, 240cr, 240r, 240bl, 240bc, 240br, 252, 273, 290, Ken Wilson-Max 1, 2, 6, 16, 60, 67, 76, 82, 115, 153, 161, 167, 175, 197, 236, 240tl, 240tc, 240tr, 240l, 240c, 240c/2, 240cl, 240cr, 240r, 240bl, 240bc, 240br, 252, 273, 290, Ken Wilson-Max 1, 2, 6, 16, 60, 67, 76, 82, 115, 153, 161, 167, 175, 197, 236, 240tl, 240tc, 240tr, 240l, 240c, 240c/2, 240cl, 240cr, 240r, 240bl, 240bc, 240br, 252, 273, 290, Ken Wilson-Max 1, 2, 6, 16, 60, 67, 76, 82, 115, 153, 161, 167, 175, 197, 236, 240tl, 240tc, 240tr, 240l, 240c, 240c/2, 240cl, 240cr, 240r, 240bl, 240bc, 240br, 252, 273, 290, Ken Wilson-Max 1, 2, 6, 16, 60, 67, 76, 82, 115, 153, 161, 167, 175, 197, 236, 240tl, 240tc, 240tr, 240l, 240c, 240c/2, 240cl, 240cr, 240r, 240bl, 240bc, 240br, 252, 273, 290, Ken Wilson-Max 1, 2, 6, 16, 60, 67, 76, 82, 115, 153, 161, 167, 175, 197, 236, 240tl, 240tc, 240tr, 240l, 240c, 240c/2, 240cl, 240cr, 240r, 240bl, 240bc, 240br, 252, 273, 290, Ken Wilson-Max 1, 2, 6, 16, 60, 67, 76, 82, 115, 153, 161, 167, 175, 197, 236, 240tl, 240tc, 240tr, 240l, 240c, 240c/2, 240cl, 240cr, 240r, 240bl, 240bc, 240br, 252, 273, 290, Ken Wilson-Max 1, 2, 6, 16, 60, 67, 76, 82, 115, 153, 161, 167, 175, 197, 236, 240tl, 240tc, 240tr, 240l, 240c, 240c/2, 240cl, 240cr, 240r, 240bl, 240bc, 240br, 252, 273, 290, MindStudio 23, 43, 181, 233, 247, 300, MindStudio 23, 43, 181, 233, 247, 300, MindStudio 23, 43, 181, 233, 247, 300, MindStudio 23, 43, 181, 233, 247, 300, MindStudio 23, 43, 181, 233, 247, 300, MindStudio 23, 43, 181, 233, 247, 300, Studio 8. Clark Wiseman 269, Nigel Riches / www.imagesource.com 108, Nigel Riches. www.imagesource.com 163; **Photostage Ltd:** Donald Cooper 50t; **Press Association Images:** AP 121; **Punchdrunk:** 50b; **National Theatre of Scotland:** 77; **Gabriela Vieru:** 126, 307

All other images © Pearson Education

We are grateful to the following for permission to reproduce copyright material:

Screenshots
Screenshot on page 187 from The Monster under the bed, www.polkatheatre.com, © Polka Theatre; Logo on page 214 from polka Theatre, www.polkatheatre.com, © Polka Theatre

About the authors

Carolyn Carnaghan is an External Verifier for BTEC and a Principal Moderator for A Level Drama and Theatre Studies. Carolyn has written several books about the arts and the teaching of dance and drama. She has also worked on the development of a number of arts qualifications and has many years of teaching experience. Carolyn has performed as a professional dancer and in 1988 she founded and ran her own dance consortium, The Dance Workshop. She also created a dance ensemble called Splitz. She has worked as a performer/choreographer on stage, in schools and colleges.

Sally Jewers has over 20 years experience of the delivery and assessment of BTEC performing arts programmes and is currently a Senior Verifier for BTEC Performing Arts and Music programmes and Senior Examiner for the Level 2 Creative and Media Diploma. Sally leads national and centre based training events as well as offering guidance as part of the 'Ask the Expert' service. She is an experienced author and has written to support both BTEC and Diploma. Sally has also produced a range of interactive whiteboard resources for Boardworks including their *KS4 Music Resource* and is a regular contributor to *Teaching Drama Magazine*.

Paul Webster has been involved in the new BTEC Entry, Level 1, Level 2 and Level 3 qualifications in Performing Arts, and has contributed to the support materials.

He wrote the BTEC First Performing Arts: A Practical Handbook (with Sally Jewers and Rob East) for Edexcel Limited in 2007 and contributed to BTEC in a Box for Nationals in Performing Arts.

He has led the training and standardization of external verifiers, and provided support to teachers delivering the BTEC Firsts and Nationals in Performing Arts, Music and Media.

Previous to this work he has held the post of Drama, Performing Arts and Art lecturer and manager in schools and FE colleges between 1996–2004. He also worked as a professional performer, director and designer from 1994–1997.

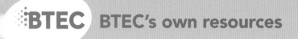

About your BTEC Level 3 National Performing Arts book

Choosing to study for a BTEC Level 3 National Performing Arts qualification is a great decision to make for lots of reasons. This qualification will allow you to look into different areas of the Performing Arts, leading you into a whole range of professions and sectors and allowing you to explore your creativity in many different ways.

Your BTEC Level 3 National in Performing Arts is a vocational or work-related qualification. This doesn't mean that it will give you all the skills you need to do a job, but it does mean that you'll have the opportunity to gain specific knowledge, understanding and skills that are relevant to your chosen subject or area of work.

What will you be doing?

The qualification is structured into **mandatory units** (ones that you must do) and **optional units** (ones that you can choose to do). How many units you do and which ones you cover depend on the type of qualification you are working towards.

Qualifications	Credits from mandatory units	Credits from optional units	Total credits
Edexcel BTEC Level 3 Certificate	10	20	30
Edexcel BTEC Level 3 Subsidiary Diploma	10	50	60
Edexcel BTEC Level 3 Diploma	30	90	120
Edexcel BTEC Level 3 Extended Diploma	60	120	180

Pathways

Qualifications	Credits from mandatory units	Credits from optional units	Total credits
Edexcel BTEC Level 3 Certificate Acting Dance Physical Theatre Musical Theatre	10	20	30
Edexcel BTEC Level 3 Subsidiary Diploma Acting Dance Physical Theatre Musical Theatre	20	40	60
Edexcel BTEC Level 3 Diploma Acting Dance Musical Theatre	40	80	120
Edexcel BTEC Level 3 Extended Diploma Acting Dance Musical Theatre	70		180

How to use this book

This book is designed to help you through your BTEC Level 3 National Performing Arts course. It has two sections:

- A **skills and knowledge** section with chapters covering each of the mandatory units in depth giving detailed information about each of the learning outcomes and including helpful advice for your assessments.

- A **projects** section with chapters covering a number of units. Each chapter guides you through the relevant learning outcomes to complete the project and includes activities to polish your skills and advice on evidence and assessment.

Introduction

These introductions give you a snapshot of what to expect from each unit – and what you should be aiming for by the time you finish it!

Credit value: 10

14 Musical Theatre Performance

Musical theatre is an extremely popular and enduring form of drama. It has the ability to appeal to a wide-ranging audience many of whom might not consider visiting the theatre to watch other forms of drama.

From its origins in the music hall and operetta of the 19th century to the large-scale musical productions of the 21st century, the musical has continually developed and reinvented itself. In the late 20th century, for example, the jukebox musical brought musical theatre to a new audience of pop and rock fans via stage and screen versions of *Mamma Mia!*, based on the music of ABBA. Traditional musicals also continue to be popular with revivals of classic musicals such as *Guys and Dolls*, *Oliver!* and *The Sound of Music* drawing large audiences in London's West End.

For the performer, musical theatre presents a range of challenges. The genre combines singing, movement and acting skills, and the performer is often expected to be a master, not just a jack, of all these trades. This unit will allow you to develop skills in these three areas as well as exploring the ways in which all three interact in performance. You will have the opportunity to investigate and research roles from specific musical theatre repertoire, and develop the technical skills needed to realise these roles. You will also have the opportunity to use the skills and knowledge you develop in the rehearsal and performance of a musical theatre work or extract.

Learning outcomes

After completing this unit you should be able to achieve the following learning outcomes:

1. Understand a role or roles in a musical theatre work
2. Be able to apply the appropriate performance skills
3. Be able to rehearse for a role in a musical
4. Be able to perform a role in a musical

87

Assessment and grading criteria

This table explains what you must do to achieve each of the assessment criteria for each unit. For each assessment criterion, shown by the grade button **P1**, there is an assessment activity.

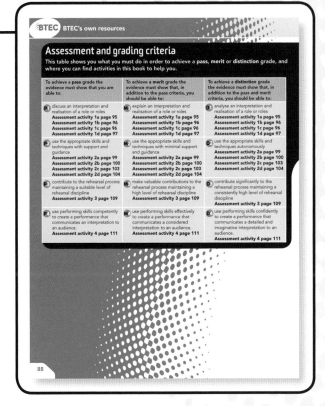

BTEC BTEC's own resources

Assessment and grading criteria

This table shows you what you must do in order to achieve a **pass**, **merit** or **distinction** grade, and where you can find activities in this book to help you.

To achieve a pass grade the evidence must show that you are able to:	To achieve a merit grade the evidence must show that, in addition to the pass criteria, you should be able to:	To achieve a distinction grade the evidence must show that, in addition to the pass and merit criteria, you should be able to:
P1 discuss an interpretation and realisation of a role or roles Assessment activity 1a page 95 Assessment activity 1b page 96 Assessment activity 1c page 96 Assessment activity 1d page 97	**M1** explain an interpretation and realisation of a role or roles Assessment activity 1a page 95 Assessment activity 1b page 96 Assessment activity 1c page 96 Assessment activity 1d page 97	**D1** analyse an interpretation and realisation of a role or roles Assessment activity 1a page 95 Assessment activity 1b page 96 Assessment activity 1c page 96 Assessment activity 1d page 97
P2 use the appropriate skills and techniques with support and guidance Assessment activity 2a page 99 Assessment activity 2b page 100 Assessment activity 2c page 103 Assessment activity 2d page 104	**M2** use the appropriate skills and techniques with minimal support and guidance Assessment activity 2a page 99 Assessment activity 2b page 100 Assessment activity 2c page 103 Assessment activity 2d page 104	**D2** use the appropriate skills and techniques autonomously Assessment activity 2a page 99 Assessment activity 2b page 100 Assessment activity 2c page 103 Assessment activity 2d page 104
P3 contribute to the rehearsal process maintaining a suitable level of rehearsal discipline Assessment activity 3 page 109	**M3** make valuable contributions to the rehearsal process maintaining a high level of rehearsal discipline Assessment activity 3 page 109	**D3** contribute significantly to the rehearsal process maintaining a consistently high level of rehearsal discipline Assessment activity 3 page 109
P4 use performing skills competently to create a performance that communicates an interpretation to an audience. Assessment activity 4 page 111	**M4** use performing skills effectively to create a performance that communicates a considered interpretation to an audience. Assessment activity 4 page 111	**D4** use performing skills confidently to create a performance that communicates a detailed and imaginative interpretation to an audience. Assessment activity 4 page 111

88

Assessment

Your tutor will set **assignments** throughout your course for you to complete. These may take the form of projects where you research, plan, prepare, make and evaluate a piece of work, sketchbooks, case studies and presentations. The important thing is that you evidence your skills and knowledge to date.

Stuck for ideas? Daunted by your first assignment? These learners have all been through it before…

Activities

There are different types of activities for you to do: **Assessment activities** are suggestions for tasks that you might do as part of your assignment and will help you develop your knowledge, skills and understanding. **Grading tips** clearly explain what you need to do in order to achieve a pass, merit or distinction grade.

There are also suggestions for **activities** that will give you a broader grasp of the industry, stretch your imagination and deepen your skills.

Activity: Different dance styles

Find out about each of the styles listed below:

- Jazz
- Hip-hop
- Rock 'n roll
- Folk
- Tap
- African
- South Asia
- Latin.

Consider the following questions:

1 What are the main features of these styles?
2 Are there any you need a dancing partner to take part in?
3 Where do they come from?
4 Who dances them?
5 Do they have a social purpose, such as getting to know other people or celebration?

Select your favourite dance style from those listed above and make up a short sequence in that style.

Now, working with a partner:

- dance it as a street piece with some isolated head and shoulder twitches and rolls, spins and hand gestures
- take out all the gestures, and dance it smoothly and fluently like a piece of contemporary jazz ballet.

Ask your partner to assess how you are doing.

Personal, learning and thinking skills

Throughout your BTEC Level 3 National Performing Arts course, there are lots of opportunities to develop your personal, learning and thinking skills. Look out for these as you progress.

Functional skills

It's important that you have good English, maths and ICT skills – you never know when you'll need them, and employers will be looking for evidence that you've got these skills too.

Key terms

Technical words and phrases are easy to spot. You can also use the glossary at the back of the book.

WorkSpace

Case studies provide snapshots of real workplace issues, and show how the skills and knowledge you develop during your course can help you in your career.

There are also mini-case studies throughout the book to help you focus on your own projects.

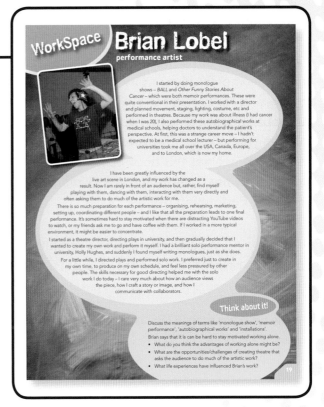

WorkSpace **Brian Lobel**
performance artist

I started by doing monologue shows – *BALL and Other Funny Stories About Cancer* – which were both memoir performances. These were quite conventional in their presentation. I worked with a director and planned movement, staging, lighting, costume, etc and performed in theatres. Because my work was about illness (I had cancer when I was 20), I also performed these autobiographical works at medical schools, helping doctors to understand the patient's perspective. At first, this was a strange career move – I hadn't expected to be a medical school lecturer – but performing for universities took me all over the USA, Canada, Europe, and to London, which is now my home.

I have been greatly influenced by the live art scene in London, and my work has changed as a result. Now I am rarely in front of an audience but, rather, find myself playing with them, dancing with them, interacting with them very directly and often asking them to do much of the artistic work for me.

There is so much preparation for each performance – organising, rehearsing, marketing, setting up, coordinating different people – and I like that all the preparation leads to one final performance. It's sometimes hard to stay motivated when there are distracting YouTube videos to watch, or my friends ask me to go and have coffee with them. If I worked in a more typical environment, it might be easier to concentrate.

I started as a theatre director, directing plays in university, and then gradually decided that I wanted to create my own work and perform it myself. I had a brilliant solo performance mentor in university, Holly Hughes, and suddenly I found myself writing monologues, just as she does.

For a little while, I directed plays and performed solo work. I preferred just to create in my own time, to produce on my own schedule, and feel less pressured by other people. The skills necessary for good directing helped me with the solo work I do today – I care very much about how an audience views the piece, how I craft a story or image, and how I communicate with collaborators.

Think about it!

Discuss the meanings of terms like 'monologue show', 'memoir performance', 'autobiographical works' and 'installations'. Brian says that it is can be hard to stay motivated working alone.
- What do you think the advantages of working alone might be?
- What are the opportunities/challenges of creating theatre that asks the audience to do much of the artistic work?
- What life experiences have influenced Brian's work?

Just checking

When you see this sort of activity, take stock! These quick activities and questions are there to check your knowledge. You can use them to see how much progress you've made or as a revision tool.

Edexcel's assignment tips

At the end of each chapter, you'll find hints and tips to help you get the best mark you can, such as the best websites to go to, checklists to help you remember processes and really useful facts and figures.

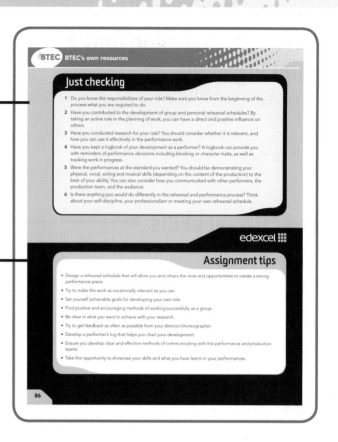

Have you read your **BTEC Level 3 National Study Skills Guide**? It's full of advice on study skills, putting your assignments together and making the most of being a BTEC Performing Arts learner.

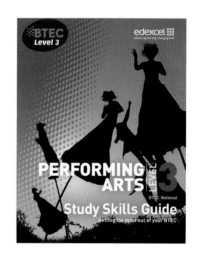

Ask your tutor about extra materials to help you through your course. The **Tutor Resource Pack** which accompanies this book contains interesting videos, activities, presentations and information about the Performing Arts sector.

Your book is just part of the exciting resources from Edexcel to help you succeed in your BTEC course.

Visit:

- www.edexcel.com/BTEC or
- www.pearsonfe.co.uk/BTEC 2010

1 Performance Workshop

This unit is about creating performance work. It will allow you to explore the process of making theatre and to try out different ideas in practical workshop situations.

You may decide to create work that combines a number of performing arts disciplines, such as acting, dance and music performance, or you may prefer to work in a single area. You might decide to experiment with multimedia, such as video and audio, or work in a more traditional manner.

Whatever you decide to do, this unit gives you the opportunity to try out ideas, take risks and create work that you have ownership of. You will take part in sessions where you explore and interpret different ideas for performance work. You will then develop chosen ideas and shape them into two separate performance pieces, which will be performed in a workshop setting. You will also have the chance to review your ideas and the pieces created in light of the performances undertaken.

For the purposes of this unit, a workshop is an informal performance, perhaps for an invited audience, that is designed to allow performers to try ideas out in a supportive setting. It may use only minimal costumes and items of set.

Learning outcomes

After completing this unit you should be able to achieve the following learning outcomes:

1 Be able to interpret ideas for performance material
2 Be able to apply ideas creatively
3 Be able to take part in workshop performances
4 Understand the workshop process in light of performance.

Assessment and grading criteria

This table shows you what you must do in order to achieve a pass, merit or distinction, and where you can find activities in this book to help you.

To achieve a **pass** grade the evidence must show that you are able to:	To achieve a **merit** grade the evidence must show that, in addition to the pass criteria, you are able to:	To achieve a **distinction** grade the evidence must show that, in addition to the pass and merit criteria, you are able to:
P1 show a response to source material through research and practical workshops, recognising obvious possibilities as performance material **Assessment activity 1 page 7**	**M1** show considered responses to source material, exploring its more creative possibilities as performance material with insight and attention to detail **Assessment activity 1 page 7**	**D1** show a range of detailed responses to source material, in which the possibilities as performance material are explored in a perceptive and comprehensive manner **Assessment activity 1 page 7**
P2 develop and shape workable ideas **Assessment activity 2 page 14**	**M2** develop and shape the most workable ideas **Assessment activity 2 page 14**	**D2** develop and shape the most creative ideas **Assessment activity 2 page 14**
P3 perform with a level of skill appropriate to the chosen medium showing engagement with the material and communicating ideas to an audience **Assessment activity 3 page 15**	**M3** perform with a level of skill that shows a degree of control in the handling of the chosen medium, and a degree of engagement with the material, communicating ideas to an audience in a focused manner **Assessment activity 3 page 15**	**D3** perform with a sense of flair, confidence and assured control of the chosen medium, showing consistent focus and engagement with the material and clear and responsive communication to an audience **Assessment activity 3 page 15**
P4 evaluate the potential of the work in artistic, professional and vocational terms with recognition of the strengths and weaknesses of the work. **Assessment activity 4 page 18**	**M4** evaluate the potential of the work in artistic, professional and vocational terms, with considered judgements about what worked well and/or less well. **Assessment activity 4 page 18**	**D4** evaluate the potential of the work in artistic, professional and vocational terms with strengths and weaknesses clearly identified and judgements fully justified and thoughtfully expressed. **Assessment activity 4 page 18**

How you will be assessed

This unit will be assessed by an internal assignment that will be designed and marked by the staff at your centre. You will be assessed on your ability to:

- respond to different starting points and source material
- develop and shape workable ideas for performance pieces
- perform the pieces developed
- assess the success and potential of work in light of performances.

The evidence you produce during your work on this unit may include:

- a process portfolio
- video clips/sequences of practical work, rehearsals and workshop performances
- a written or oral evaluation of the work created.

Effie, 17-year-old drama learner

This unit was really interesting and the things we did were very diverse. It made me think about how performances are developed and how they can grow out of very different starting points.

Before we began working we formed ourselves into a performance company. We talked about the kind of performance work we would undertake and decided on some overall aims for the work.

The first piece we developed was based around a series of sounds. We thought of ways to interpret the sounds with body movements and created a piece of physical theatre. I wasn't sure at first but I stuck with it and after a while I began to feel more comfortable with the work. We decided to create a piece that allowed the audience to move around and come and go as they wished. In the end we were really pleased with the results. Some of the audience loved it, some weren't so sure, but I am really glad to have had the experience of creating something so different to anything I'd been involved with before.

The second piece was much more traditional. We worked on an extract from *Oh, What a Lovely War*. Although this is a piece based on World War I, we wanted to make the work relevant to the many conflicts that are going on in the world at the moment. We did a lot of research into World War I and much of what I discovered was really shocking.

At the end of the unit we assessed the success of the two performance pieces and we voted on which we would like to develop into a full scale performance. *Oh, What a Lovely War* was chosen and we are now going to put on a full production for Unit 14: Musical Theatre Performance. I think this musical tackles some really important issues and I am really looking forward to working on it again.

Over to you

- What is your experience of developing performances from different starting points (ie in previous drama or dance courses you have undertaken or in out of school/college activities)?
- What kind of starting points are good for creating drama or dance pieces?

1.1 Be able to interpret ideas for performance material

Warm up

Forming your own performance company

During this unit, you will be required to work as a performance company. Before you begin, discuss as a group the things your company hopes to achieve and, with the help of your tutor, compile a short list of aims and objectives. For example, your company might wish to create work which "educates as well as entertains".

Use your list of aims and objectives to come up with an artistic policy or mission statement. You may also like to come up with a name for your company.

1.1.1 Sources

Where does the process of creating a piece of theatre begin? A scripted piece may begin with an idea by a writer. Although the director and the performers will have an important input into the interpretation of the piece, the writer's original concept will generally remain unchanged. If a piece of theatre has been devised, it will have been developed by a company of performers working with a director.

Whether a piece of theatre is written by a playwright sitting alone at a computer or is devised by a group of performers working in collaboration, many of the processes they will go through are the same. However a piece of theatre is created, it has to begin somewhere. It has to have a starting point.

The initial idea or source material for a piece of theatre must be strong. It must present a range of possibilities to those working on the piece. It should inspire and intrigue. It could be shocking, memorable or simply suggest a possible story.

Case study: Issue-based theatre

Many performance companies use political and social issues as a basis for their work.

Red Ladder is a company founded over 40 years ago. The company's aim is to create theatre that contributes to social change and global justice.

Age Exchange creates reminiscence performance work. The themes of the plays that they create are related to the connection between past and present and the exchange of values, culture and knowledge between generations.

Cardboard Citizens is a company that aim to change the lives of people without a home through exposure to theatre and performing arts.

For more information on these companies, go to the Hotlinks section on page ii and follow the instructions there.

Over to you

- In small groups, undertake some further research into the work of these companies and/or any other issue-based performance companies you can find.
- Investigate the type of work they create (eg drama, dance, multimedia) and the issues their productions have addressed.
- Share your findings with the others in your class through an informal presentation.
- As a class, brainstorm ideas for a piece of theatre to tackle a current issue.

Themes

Sometimes the starting point for a piece of performance may be a theme, subject or issue that a writer or a theatre company wishes to explore. For example, a company may decide to examine the place of rituals in modern Western society. From this starting point, the members of the company will undertake research. They may gather a range of source material that has relevance to the subject – for example, information about birth and death rituals in comparative religions, stories about ritualistic behaviour by the young (such as stag and hen parties), music used in ceremonies, etc.

Textual

Sometimes the starting point for a performance may be a piece of text, which is used as source material. This could be a traditional script, a musical score or a piece of dance notation. However, other forms of written source material could be used, such as a poem, a short story, a biography or a news article. For example, a company might use a letter written by a soldier from the front line in World War I as a starting point for a piece of theatre that explores what life is like for those at home when soldiers go to war.

V-J Day in Times Square

Visual

Visual starting points for performance pieces can inspire many different types of work. A company may begin with a photograph, painting or piece of sculpture.

In 1937 the German Luftwaffe attacked the Spanish town of Guernica. The massive air raid killed and injured hundreds of civilians and became a major incident of the Spanish Civil War. Pablo Picasso began painting his mural, *Guernica*, two weeks after the attack. The piece examines the tragedies that war inflicts on ordinary people and has become an iconic anti-war symbol.

Victory over Japan Day, also known as V-J Day marked the surrender of Japan towards the end of World War II. During the celebrations in New York on 14th August 1945, photo journalist Alfred Eisenstaedt captured an image that was to become one of the most iconic of the 20th century. Often known as *V-J Day in Times Square*, the photograph is of an American sailor kissing a young woman during the celebrations.

In 1945 American troops captured the island of Iwo Jima from Japan. The battle, in which over 20,000 Japanese soldiers died, was immortalised by photographer Joe Rosenthal who received a Pulitzer Prize for his picture *Raising the flag on Iwo Jima*, which shows marines raising the American flag on Mount Suribachi. The photograph was later used as the model for the US Marine Corps Memorial at Arlington National Cemetery.

Activity: Images of War of the Mid 20th Century

Divide into three groups and select one of the images: *Guernica*, *V-J Day in Times Square* or *Raising the flag on Iwo Jima*. Discuss the view of 'war' depicted/explored in the image.

- Develop a silent dramatic sequence in response to your chosen image. The piece should be constructed from a series of still images, at least one of which must reflect an aspect of the visual stimulus used. You should consider how to move from one image to the next.

- Share and discuss your sequence with the class.

For more information on this topic, go to the Hotlinks section on page ii and follow the instructions there.

Aural

Music, sound and media can be used to very good effect when developing dance and drama work. Music or sound recordings could be used to develop ideas for movement based pieces. A documentary on an issue or historical event might be used as the starting point for a piece of drama.

Activity: Traffic Sounds

In small groups, choreograph a short dance or physical theatre piece on the theme of transport.

Begin by finding a 'soundtrack' for your piece. You could make a recording of traffic noise, use a sound effects CD or download a sound file from the internet. Use travelling and turning as your main movement actions.

Share and discuss your piece with the class.

The final pose

1. 1. 2 Exploration

Potential source material for performance work needs to be explored to test its viability for development into a piece of dance or drama. Performers can employ several methods to explore and test materials:

- Improvisation can be used to test the possibilities of potential source material.
- Carrying out some research to find out more about an issue, historic story or theme being explored.
- Producing a visual mind map of your thoughts and ideas is an excellent way of exploring a number of possibilities and comparing them.

Activity: Finding source material

Divide into pairs and do some research to find a piece of source material that you feel presents opportunities for dramatic exploration. As a class, you may decide to focus on materials linked to a particular theme or simply allow each pair a free choice. However, you should make sure that materials gathered include at least one item from each of these categories:

- textual material – for example, a piece of creative writing (poetry or prose), a letter, a diary entry, an historical account of an event or a newspaper article
- visual material – for example, a painting, photograph, piece of sculpture, artefact or piece of costume
- aural material – for example, a piece of music or a sound effect.

Remember, the source material needs to be interesting and intriguing. Don't settle for something that doesn't inspire you. Keep looking!

Once you have completed your search present your choice of source material to the class.

Explain your reasons for choosing one type of material over another. Now, thinking about the source materials you have selected, respond to the following questions:

- What do you think is interesting and/or memorable about the material?
- Does the material suggest a particular time, place and/or character(s)?
- What potential stories come to mind?

- If a script, musical score or piece of dance notation is being considered, the performers will need to try out the material to assess its suitability.
- Discussions will be vital at each stage of the exploration process to consider the potential of ideas presented to the group.

Activity: The bag

This is an activity that will demonstrate how a piece of source material can be explored to provide ideas for a story or short piece of drama.

Your tutor will give you a bag, explaining the circumstances in which it was found.

Divide into groups and examine the bag and its contents.

Consider these questions:

- Who owns the bag?
- How did it come to be separated from its owner?
- Where is the bag's owner now?

Use improvisation to construct a brief story, which ends at the point at which the bag was separated from the owner.

Activity: Memoir

Consider ideas for a monologue based on a memory you have from your childhood. It could be your first day at school, attending a family wedding, or maybe a holiday or school trip.

Develop your idea into a short monologue or movement piece lasting for a maximum of two minutes.

Share and discuss your piece with your class.

Assessment activity 1

Take part in activities to explore a range of source material in order to get some ideas that you can develop further into performance work.

Activities may include:

- discussion
- improvisation
- research
- trying out materials.

Evidence

- a process log
- your tutor's observation record.

Grading tips

M1 You should consider a number of possibilities for the development of the source material and will be able to do so in a creative way.

D1 You should explore the source material in a detailed and insightful way. You will be able to show that they have considered a number of possibilities and will not be afraid of rejecting ideas that are not viable. You should also explain the reasons for your choices.

PLTS
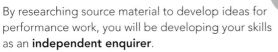

By researching source material to develop ideas for performance work, you will be developing your skills as an **independent enquirer**.

By developing and shaping ideas for performance work, you will be developing you skills as a **creative thinker** and **self-manager**.

Functional skills

ICT: By researching potential source material for performance work, you are using your ICT skills to **find and select information**.

English: By discussing ideas for performance work and evaluating the potential of workshop performances, you are using your **speaking and listening** skills.

1.2 Be able to apply ideas creatively

Once ideas have been explored, a company will need to begin to shape and develop the work that will later form a performance.

Development

If a narrative piece is being created, ideas will need to be developed into a coherent form, called the plot. This might be done by:

- deciding where the audience joins the story
- outlining what happens at each stage of the plot
- considering how and when information will be revealed to the audience.

Activity: The structure of a narrative piece

Consider the material you are working on. If it is a narrative piece (ie it tells a story), identify the key moments of the piece (exposition, rising action, climax, falling action, resolution).

Write the story down as a series of brief bullet points.

Under the direction of your tutor, review your work and consider movement ideas that could be combined and developed into a longer piece.

If the piece does not tell a story, for example, a non-narrative dance piece, then the overall structure of the piece will still need to be considered. A company might begin to develop the structure of a movement piece by:

- using **canon**
- adding answering phrases to contrast with the original movement phrases
- adding new material to create an A – B – A structure, where the original idea/material (A) is followed by a different idea/material (B). The A section is then repeated.

Form and style

The company will also need to make decisions regarding the form and style of the piece. It will need to take into account the potential audience. The nature of the space in which the piece is to be performed will also have a bearing on the form and style of the piece. A **black box studio** allows a totally blank canvas, and a company could decide for the piece to be performed in the round or as a promenade performance. If the piece is to be performed in a more traditional **proscenium arch theatre**, this will present more constraints.

Some companies use the space itself as the stimulus for the development of the piece. **Site-specific** theatre uses the resources of a given space – be it a disused factory, a river bank or a shopping centre. In fact, it can be any space other than a traditional theatre. The choice of site/space has a particular effect on the public, as it used to enhance and inform the production. In site-specific theatre, the conventions of the 'traditional stage', including the separation of audience and performer, are broken down to create a very different experience for everybody who is involved.

Case study: Grid Iron Theatre Company

This company specialises in presenting shows in unusual locations. Its first major production, *The Bloody Chamber*, was based on a book by Angela Carter. Staged as a promenade production in vaults under Edinburgh's Royal Mile, the audience were led through the underground passages by torchlight. Another of their productions, *Roam*, was performed in an airport.

Key terms

Black box studio – a large square room with black walls and a flat floor

Proscenium arch theatre – a performance space with a stage set behind an arch which acts like a picture frame

Canon – movements that are repeated by other dancers, sometimes simultaneously, sometimes following one another

Site-specific – a performance made specially for a particular venue or place that utilises its features in performance

Activity: External factors

How will external factors influence the form and style of the performance work you are planning to create?

Discuss the following factors:

- the characteristics of the potential audience
- the performance space
- time constraints
- financial constraints.

During this stage of the work it will be important to explore the meaning of the material being developed and consider how the meaning will be communicated to the audience.

Forms and techniques

If you are developing a piece of theatre, you may wish to use and apply different drama forms and techniques. For example:

- *thought-tracking* – allowing a character to speak their thoughts out loud at a key moment in the piece
- *narrating* – speaking a commentary over a scene
- *cross-cutting* – inserting flash-forward or flash-back moments
- *hot-seating* – exploring a character in more detail through questioning.

Forum Theatre

Forum is an interactive theatre form developed by Augusto Boal, a Brazilian artist whose work is also concerned with activism. Forum breaks down the barriers between performer and audience. Everyone is encouraged to participate and an audience member may join the actors on the stage to change the actions of a particular character and, therefore, affect the outcome of the piece.

When developing work, this technique can also be used as a method of exploring possibilities and stimulating debate.

A street performer interacting with a member of the audience

Applying the chosen medium and/or media

The work a company is creating may be based purely within one performance medium eg dance or drama. However, many performance companies use a number of different media to bring their work to life.

Case study: Music, movement, drama and other

Here are some examples of how some companies use different media:

- **Dreamthinkspeak**

The company gives equal emphasis to the use of space, light, image, film, sound and text when creating live performance.

- **Green Ginger**

This company expresses a very clear commitment to puppetry and make use of various tools and effects when performing to audiences. Their performances aim to recreate the surreal and the absurd.

- **Dodgy Clutch**

Dodgy Clutch produce new work on visual theatre. They do this by combining music, dance performance, mime and puppetry in a new way.

Visit the sites of these companies to find out more about their work. To do this, go to the Hotlinks section on page ii and follow the instructions there.

Discuss your own experience of the ways in which music, dance, drama, and other media, such as sound or video recording, can be combined in performance.

Think of productions you have taken part in or seen recently (such as musical theatre productions, concerts, plays and visual arts installations). How were the different media combined? What was the overall effect?

Combining dance and music alongside drama in performance work is nothing new. There is a long tradition of musicals in Western theatre, which have their roots in the **operetta** of the late 19th and early 20th century. Brechtian theatre makes use of music in a different way, with clearly defined songs that comment on the story rather than adding weight to the action and/or emotions of the characters.

In more recent years, video, film and recorded sound have made an impact on theatre, with companies using video projections alongside traditional scenery. For example, XL Video worked with the *Little Britain Live* production team to create video backdrops for its stage show. The use of projected backdrops rather than conventional stage sets allowed for quick and seamless transitions between locations. The company has also produced projections for West End productions of the musicals *The Woman in White* and *Sunday in the Park with George*.

For more information on XL Video go to the Hotlinks section on page ii and follow the instructions there.

Key terms

Operetta – a short, amusing opera

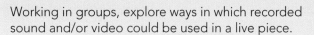

Activity: Experimenting with recorded material

Working in groups, explore ways in which recorded sound and/or video could be used in a live piece.

Experiment with using sound or video in one of the pieces you are currently working on. If you have the facilities, you could record sound or images for your piece. If not, try sourcing some pre-recorded material.

A lot of inspiration comes only from watching TV

1.2.2 Rehearsal

As the work being developed begins to come together, a company will move into the rehearsal stage of the project. A positive and focused rehearsal period is vital to the success of any performing arts work. The basic skills required for either a scripted or a devised piece are largely the same.

> **See Unit 5&7: Rehearsing and Performing for more information about how to make the most of your rehearsal process and technique.**

Each rehearsal is likely to have a similar overall structure, beginning with some kind of warm-up and usually ending with the sharing and reviewing of work – making a decision. What happens in-between may vary greatly from company to company and from rehearsal to rehearsal.

Simon McBurney is one of the co-founders of experimental theatre company Complicite. In an interview on the company's website Simon notes that Complicite's rehearsals sometimes lack structure, while at the same time having some sort of unplanned discipline. For more information and to read the full interview, please go to the *Hotlinks* section on page ii and follow the instructions there.

Rehearsal etiquette certainly demands self-discipline on the part of the actor. Company members should always arrive on time, and they should learn lines and moves by required deadlines. Other rules may include a neutral dress code.

Trust and mutual respect is also vital in the rehearsal room. Performers must feel able to exercise creativity without fear of failure or embarrassment. The rehearsal process often involves trying out ideas and taking risks. Therefore, performers must be honest with each other and be able to take direction and criticism. Professional relationships within the company must be encouraged, so that members do not feel that they are in competition with each other but rather they are working together towards a common goal.

Activity: The director and the performers

As a class, consider these questions.
- What is the role of the director?
- What is the role of the performer?
- How do these roles differ when working on a devised or scripted piece?

Identifying and applying the required skills

The process of rehearsal requires a number of skills on the part of the performer. There are the more obvious performance skills that will need to be applied to the work being rehearsed, but there are also other skills and qualities, such as trust and reliability, which are just as important.

Activity: Rehearsal skills and rules

Working in pairs, discuss what you think the required skills are for a performer in rehearsal.

Make a list of skills you feel are most important.

Share your conclusions with the rest of the class, collating all of your lists as a large mind map.

Afterwards, draw up a list of rehearsal room rules for the company.

Distribute the list so every company member has a copy and post a large copy on the rehearsal room wall.

Did you know?

Most theatre companies treat the rehearsal period as an intensely private process and rarely, if ever, let observers in.

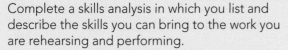

Activity: Your own skills analysis

Complete a skills analysis in which you list and describe the skills you can bring to the work you are rehearsing and performing.

Begin by thinking of the performance skills you have to offer, such as acting, dance or music performance skills.

Try to be detailed in your descriptions – you could write things like "as an actor I have strong vocal skills".

Also think about 'soft skills', such as reliability, the ability to listen and establish good relationships with others, being able to come up with ideas, etc. Also list and describe skill areas you would like to develop.

When you have completed your skills analysis, share it with a partner. Does your partner agree with your views about yourself?

When performers are in rehearsal for a particular piece of theatre, they may need to develop new skills. These might include:

- learning to speak with a different regional accent
- learning a new physical skill, such as riding a unicycle or stilt walking
- learning a new dance style, such a tap
- learning to work with props, such as puppets
- learning stage combat techniques.

It is vital that any new skills are identified early in the rehearsal process to allow performers time to develop and perfect them.

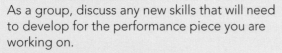

Activity: New skills

As a group, discuss any new skills that will need to develop for the performance piece you are working on.

Identify what these skills are and which performers will need to perfect them.

Practising and refining skills

The rehearsal period is a time for practising, improving and refining the performance skills required for the piece the company is working on. If this involves a performer having to practise a new skill, time will need to be set aside to allow them to work on it. Specialist practitioners may be drafted in to work with the performers.

A good way to organise the time that is available to develop new skills and refine existing ones is to set a series of targets for improvement.

Any targets set should be SMART. This means they should be:

S – Specific: targets should be designed to address specific skills that need to be developed and improved.
M – Measurable: the performer should design targets in a way that will allow them to measure their progress towards them and their eventual achievement.
A – Achievable: targets should be achievable. It is important that the performer is realistic about what can be achieved in the time available.
R – Relevant: targets should be relevant to the skills that have been identified.
T – Time bound: appropriate, specific timescales should be set for the achievement of the skills.

Activity: Personal action plan

Devise a personal action plan for the rehearsal period that identifies:

- new skills or techniques that need to be practised
- existing skills that need to be improved and refined.

Set yourself SMART targets that will help you to complete the work in time for the performances.

Learning lines and/or moves

A secure knowledge of the material is vital for a successful performance. Making sure lines and/or moves are learnt is an essential requirement of the rehearsal process.

Learning lines

Many performers worry about not being able to remember lines. However, there are a number of tips for the memorisation of text:

- repeating lines out loud – saying the lines over and over out loud is better than reading and repeating in your head
- practising with a partner – ask a partner to 'play the other parts'
- breaking it down – break long scenes into smaller sections and practise a section at a time
- thinking about the meaning – ensure you fully understand what you are saying.

Learning moves

Reproducing movement phrases accurately is a skill that performers must master. There are a range of methods that will help you remember moves and reproduce them:

- using word and phrases – eg giving names to different types of movements, counting, using dialogue or the lyrics of a song to provide you with cues
- watching – observing closely as someone else performs a movement phrase then copying and repeating the phrase a number of times
- feeling – remembering how a movement feels in the body.

Giving and taking instructions

It is important that each rehearsal ends with a discussion and target-setting for the next rehearsal. Depending on the style of piece being rehearsed this may be a formal process, with the director or choreographer giving notes or a more informal session, in which company members share their thoughts and discuss how the work is progressing.

Activity: Responding to feedback

It is vital that you use the rehearsal process to refine the work and make adjustments in the light of your own and others' views.

At the end of each rehearsal, record all the notes relevant to your role in the piece. Next to each of the relevant points, write the things you need to do to act on these notes.

Time management

Rehearsals will always head towards a specific performance date or opening night that cannot be moved. It is essential, therefore, that the time available for rehearsal is organised to ensure that the show will be ready for the first public performance.

Time management during the rehearsal period should address:

- the way in which time is used in each individual rehearsal
- the way in which time is used over the whole rehearsal period.

Each rehearsal should have:

- defined aims and objectives
- a clear structure, beginning with a warm-up and ending with a review of the work undertaken
- an overall structure drawn up to ensure that all sections of the piece are ready by the end of the rehearsal period.

Remember

The more warmed-up you are, the more effective your rehearsal will be.

Activity: Rehearsal Schedule

As a group, draw up a rehearsal schedule for the production you are working on, ensuring that time is used effectively.

Assessment activity 2   P2 M2 D2

Take part in activities to develop and shape ideas for a performance.

You should:

- consider different forms and media that could be used
- think of ways to develop a structure for the piece
- consider skills and techniques that will be needed in performance
- be part of the rehearsal process.

During these activities identify any constraints and problems that are likely to be encountered and consider ways of resolving them.

Evidence

- your tutor's observation record
- your notes in a process log diary.

Grading tips

M2 Your contribution to the development process will show that you understand the medium in which you are working, eg drama, dance or physical theatre and can apply your understanding of the medium to the shaping of the work. You will also show some foresight in the consideration of practical constraints you are likely to come across.

D2 Your contribution will show that you can work in a creative and thoughtful way of working. You will be able to identify problems, suggest viable alternatives and work through problems to find workable solutions.

PLTS

By researching source material to develop ideas for performance work, you will be developing your skills as an **independent enquirer**.

By developing and shaping ideas for performance work and solving problems undertaken in the development process of the work, you will be developing you skills as a **creative thinker** and **self-manager**.

By working as a performance company to develop and shape ideas for performance work, you will be developing your skills as a **team worker**.

Functional skills

English: By discussing ideas for performance work and evaluating the potential of workshop performances, you are using your **speaking and listening** skills. If you use texts as a starting point for performance work, you will be using your **reading** skills.

Activity: Gathering responses to your work

As you approach the time when you will present your work, you should begin to think about how you will evaluate the success of your workshop performances.

You could:

- design an audience questionnaire
- arrange a focus group meeting with members of the audience
- ask a professional practitioner to attend one of your workshops and give you feedback afterwards.

As a group, you could:

- discuss ideas for gathering responses to your work
- devise any materials required eg questionnaires.

1.3 Be able to take part in workshop performances

1.3.1 Presentation

The work undertaken in this unit will lead to two separate workshop presentations of the work developed and rehearsed. Your workshop performances may include solo and **ensemble** work. They may involve live presentations of your work, as well as recorded elements. They may also involve singing, dancing and/or acting.

Key terms

Ensemble – the performing group

1.3.2 Performance skills

As with any other performance workshop, you will have to make use of and apply a number of performance skills appropriate to the medium you are working in.

Use of body

Whether a performer is taking part in a dance, a piece of physical theatre or performing an acting role in a play, the use of movement, facial expression and gesture is likely to be central to the success of the performance. It is essential to use the body as an expressive instrument to communicate with the audience. In a drama piece, the body is used to physically bring to life the character. In a dance piece, you will use your body to perform accurate and expressive movements.

Vocal work

Using your voice in a confident manner will be a vital element in many types of performance. Performers must make sure they project words accurately and that they can be clearly heard by the audience. Vocal work, whether spoken or sung, must be expressive in order to communicate the meaning of the material.

Communication with an audience

Communication with the audience is central to the success of any performance piece. In all performances clear communication will be essential to the audience making sense of what they see and hear. In some types of performance, where the barriers between audience and performer are less obvious, performers may also need to interact with members of the audience.

Communication with other performers

An actor, dancer or singer must always be aware of relationships with other performers. In dance work, this will include the use of spatial awareness. In drama work, verbal and physical communication with other characters in the piece will be required.

Assessment activity 3

P3 M3 D3   BTEC

Take part in workshop performances of the work developed and rehearsed, demonstrating performance skills appropriate to the medium and an engagement with the material.

Evidence

- the recordings of the performance

Grading tips

M3 Your work during the workshop performances should show control in the handling of the performance skills you use. You should also show a good level of commitment to the performance work being undertaken.

D3 Your work during the workshop performances should show a confident use of skills, and should also be well focused.

PLTS

By taking part in performances, you will be developing your skills as a **team worker**.

Functional skills

English: If the workshop piece(s) you perform involves the performance of lines, you will be using your **speaking and listening** skills.

1.4 Understand the workshop process in light of performance

The work created in this unit will be performed in a workshop situation. The workshops will provide your company with the opportunity to try out pieces in front of a live audience. Professional shows often go through changes as a result of preview performances. In the case of workshop performances, the review and evaluation process will determine how the piece might be developed into a full-scale performance piece. Sometimes, the decision might be made not to develop the piece further.

Cathie Boyd is the artistic creator of Theatre Cryptic. In an interview published on the company's website, she describes how Theatre Cryptic adopts a three-stage approach to the creation process. She explains that the director and the visual artists, composers and performers spend up to four weeks talking, reviewing ideas and consulting on different aspects of a project. At the end, they record an agreed version of the performance, but only for their internal use. For more information on this topic and to read the full interview, go to the Hotlinks section on page ii and follow the instructions there.

Reviewing and evaluating work is a vital part of the creative process. Learning to do this objectively and dispassionately is a skill all performers must develop, just as they must work on their ability to take criticism professionally, rather than personally.

The art of constructive criticism does not merely involve a statement of what went well or less well. Where a problem is identified, the reviewer should try to provide insights that can take the work forward. For example, saying "scene three was boring, I didn't see the point of it" does not provide any useful information for the performers or the director.

In contrast, the following feedback presents a number of possibilities that could be explored: "Scene three seemed to drag. Some of the speeches were very long and complicated and I think this is why the actors had difficulty keeping the momentum going. I think this may be why the audience found it difficult to follow."

In reviewing your work, you will need to examine the processes of creation and rehearsal undertaken, as well as the final pieces. Audience responses to the work may be judged by reactions during the workshop performances, and through discussions and/or questionnaires.

Remember

Taking constructive criticism on board will help to make your performance better. Listening to constructive criticism gets easier the more you do it.

Do you think they like what they hear?

Activity: The journey

As a class, discuss the 'journey' your performance company has been on while working on this unit.

What have been the highs and the lows?

Did the company manage to achieve its aims and objectives?

Use your discussions to create an advice sheet for learners undertaking this unit in the future. Try to include as many ideas of things that would work in the future and, similarly, other things that might not work.

1. 4.1 Artistic and professional

When reviewing the workshop process you should consider the following artistic and professional aspects of the work you have undertaken.

A company might begin to evaluate their work by considering the following:

Effectiveness

How effectively did the company work during the development and rehearsal stages?

How effective were the final performance pieces?

Creativity

How imaginative were your ideas and those of the group?

How creatively did you interpret the ideas for performance work?

Clarity of interpretation

How clearly were the ideas, themes and/or issues addressed in the performance work interpreted during the performances?

Execution of vocal and physical performance skills

How effectively were vocal and physical performance skills used during performance?

Fulfilment of objectives

To what extent did the work presented achieve its aims and objectives

Audience response

How did the audience respond to the work?

Was the response as expected?

Working relationships

How well did the company work as a team during rehearsals and performances?

Management of time and tasks

How well did the group use the time allowed for development, rehearsal and performance?

Activity: Audience response

Collate the responses of audience members from completed questionnaires and focus group meetings. Analyse and discuss your findings.

Activity: Word bank

In groups, create a bank of useful words and phrases that can be used when writing an evaluation of a production or process.

1. 4. 2 Vocational application

One of the purposes of undertaking a performance workshop is to consider the viability of performance work in terms of development into a full scale piece.

Here are a few points to take into consideration:

Target audience

- Was the work suitable for its target audience?
- Did the target audience respond positively to the work?

Potential for further development

- Could the source materials be further developed?
- Does the work have potential for development into a full-scale performance piece?

Nature of work and possible markets

- Would there be a market/audience for a full scale production of the work?

Economic viability

- What might the cost of a full-scale production of the work be?
- Would a full-scale production be financially viable?

Activity: Personal action plan review

Review your personal action plan and consider the following questions:

- How have you personally developed as a performer? What skills did you develop and/or improve?
- What were your contributions as a member of the company?
- Draw up a further action plan for your development over the next 3-6 months.

Assessment activity 4

Take part in a de-brief meeting for each workshop performance undertaken.

You should discuss the strengths and weaknesses of the work and its potential for further development.

After the meeting, you should complete a written evaluation that assesses the viability of the work in artistic, professional and vocational terms.

Evidence

* your log diary with your own evaluation.

Grading tips

M4 Your evaluation should discuss the potential of the work, making reference to specific examples from the work produced.

D4 Your evaluation will need to weigh up the potential of the work and make judgements about its feasibility in terms of further development. Comments you make will be fully supported by well-chosen examples from the work.

PLTS

By considering strengths and weaknesses of the work produced and the potential of performance work for future development, you will be developing your skills as a **reflective learner**.

Functional skills

English: By evaluating the potential of workshop performances, you will be using your **writing** skills.

WorkSpace

Brian Lobel
performance artist

I started by doing monologue shows – *BALL* and *Other Funny Stories About Cancer* – which were both memoir performances. These were quite conventional in their presentation. I worked with a director and planned movement, staging, lighting, costume, etc and performed in theatres. Because my work was about illness (I had cancer when I was 20), I also performed these autobiographical works at medical schools, helping doctors to understand the patient's perspective. At first, this was a strange career move – I hadn't expected to be a medical school lecturer – but performing for universities took me all over the USA, Canada, Europe, and to London, which is now my home.

I have been greatly influenced by the live art scene in London, and my work has changed as a result. Now I am rarely in front of an audience but, rather, find myself playing with them, dancing with them, interacting with them very directly and often asking them to do much of the artistic work for me.

There is so much preparation for each performance – organising, rehearsing, marketing, setting up, coordinating different people – and I like that all the preparation leads to one final performance. It's sometimes hard to stay motivated when there are distracting YouTube videos to watch, or my friends ask me to go and have coffee with them. If I worked in a more typical environment, it might be easier to concentrate.

I started as a theatre director, directing plays in university, and then gradually decided that I wanted to create my own work and perform it myself. I had a brilliant solo performance mentor in university, Holly Hughes, and suddenly I found myself writing monologues, just as she does.

For a little while, I directed plays and performed solo work. I preferred just to create in my own time, to produce on my own schedule, and feel less pressured by other people. The skills necessary for good directing helped me with the solo work I do today – I care very much about how an audience views the piece, how I craft a story or image, and how I communicate with collaborators.

Think about it!

Discuss the meanings of terms like 'monologue show', 'memoir performance', 'autobiographical works' and 'installations'.

Brian says that it is can be hard to stay motivated working alone.

- What do you think the advantages of working alone might be?
- What are the opportunities/challenges of creating theatre that asks the audience to do much of the artistic work?
- What life experiences have influenced Brian's work?

Just checking

1 For what purposes are workshop performances used?

2 List and describe some of the sources that might be used as a starting point for a piece of performances work.

3 What is 'issue-based theatre'?

4 Describe some of the methods that can be used to develop an idea for a performance piece.

5 How would a company begin to develop the structure of a narrative piece?

6 Describe the external factors that might influence the form and style of a performance.

7 How would recorded media be used in live performance work?

8 What are SMART targets?

9 Why is time management important when developing and rehearsing a performance piece?

10 Why do performance companies gather responses to their work from audiences?

Assignment tips

- This unit requires you to develop, rehearse and perform in two different workshop performances. This means you can use the skills and experience you gained in the first project to improve your work for the second project.

- Complete your process log regularly. After each session, if possible.

- When writing up work undertaken, remember to explain why decisions were made and how they might impact on the work being developed.

- Teamwork is a vital component of this unit. Be considerate to other team members, listen to and respect their opinions.

- Good levels of motivation will be required in this unit. To do well you must contribute fully to the tasks that have been set, demonstrating that you are fully committed to the work. In group work, make sure you make a full contribution. Don't sit back and let others do the work.

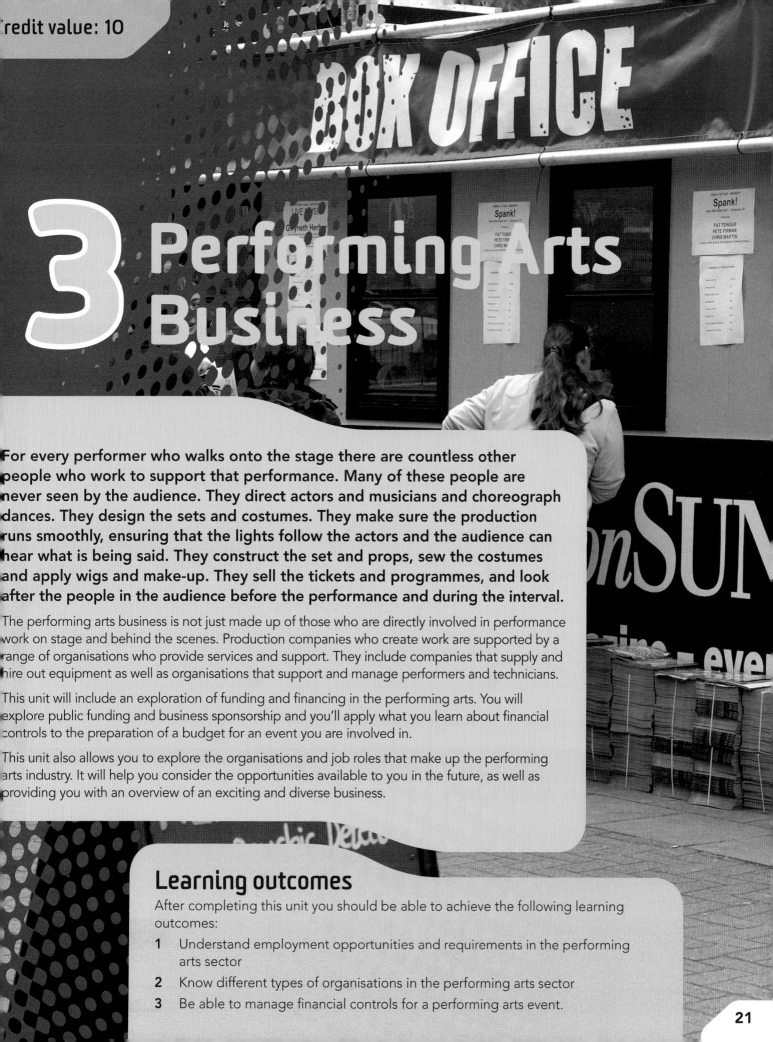

3 Performing Arts Business

For every performer who walks onto the stage there are countless other people who work to support that performance. Many of these people are never seen by the audience. They direct actors and musicians and choreograph dances. They design the sets and costumes. They make sure the production runs smoothly, ensuring that the lights follow the actors and the audience can hear what is being said. They construct the set and props, sew the costumes and apply wigs and make-up. They sell the tickets and programmes, and look after the people in the audience before the performance and during the interval.

The performing arts business is not just made up of those who are directly involved in performance work on stage and behind the scenes. Production companies who create work are supported by a range of organisations who provide services and support. They include companies that supply and hire out equipment as well as organisations that support and manage performers and technicians.

This unit will include an exploration of funding and financing in the performing arts. You will explore public funding and business sponsorship and you'll apply what you learn about financial controls to the preparation of a budget for an event you are involved in.

This unit also allows you to explore the organisations and job roles that make up the performing arts industry. It will help you consider the opportunities available to you in the future, as well as providing you with an overview of an exciting and diverse business.

Learning outcomes

After completing this unit you should be able to achieve the following learning outcomes:

1 Understand employment opportunities and requirements in the performing arts sector

2 Know different types of organisations in the performing arts sector

3 Be able to manage financial controls for a performing arts event.

Assessment and grading criteria

This table shows you what you must do in order to achieve a **pass**, **merit** or **distinction** grade, and where you can find activities in this book to help you.

To achieve a **pass** grade the evidence must show that you are able to:	To achieve a **merit** grade the evidence must show that, in addition to the pass criteria, you are able to:	To achieve a **distinction** grade the evidence must show that, in addition to the pass and merit criteria, you are able to:
P1 discuss a variety of employment opportunities and functions in the performing arts **Assessment activity 1 page 29**	**M1** explain in detail a variety of employment opportunities and functions in the performing arts **Assessment activity 1 page 29**	**D1** critically comment on a variety of roles, responsibilities and functions in the performing arts providing explanations of how they interrelate **Assessment activity 1 page 29**
P2 identify the training requirements and experience for a career path and prepare application material **Assessment activity 2 page 31**	**M2** research the most appropriate training requirements and experience for a career path and prepare suitable application material **Assessment activity 2 page 31**	**D2** research a comprehensive range of training requirements and experience and prepare application material to a professional standard **Assessment activity 2 page 31**
P3 describe the services provided by a range of organisations in the performing arts **Assessment activity 3 page 34**	**M3** explain the services provided by a range of organisations in the performing arts and how they interrelate with other areas of the industry **Assessment activity 3 page 34**	**D3** critically comment on the services provided by a range of production organisations in the performing arts analysing what they offer and how they interrelate with other areas of the industry **Assessment activity 3 page 34**
P4 prepare a production budget for a performing arts event that addresses the essential areas of income and expenditure **Assessment activity 4 page 36**	**M4** prepare a production budget for a performing arts event that addresses relevant areas of income and expenditure with realistic figures **Assessment activity 4 page 36**	**D4** prepare a budget for a performing arts event that is comprehensive and accurate based on careful research **Assessment activity 4 page 36**
P5 describe a range of different methods of funding and financing performing arts events. **Assessment activity 5 page 38**	**M5** explain the different private and public methods of funding and financing performing arts events. **Assessment activity 5 page 38**	**D5** critically comment on various private and public methods of funding and financing performing arts events. **Assessment activity 5 page 38**

How you will be assessed

This unit will be assessed by an internal assignment that will be designed and marked by the tutors at your centre. You will be assessed on your ability to:

- investigate employment opportunities in the performing arts industry, including training requirements and application procedures
- investigate the work of a range of organisations in the performing arts industry
- prepare a budget for a performing arts event
- investigate the funding and financing of the performing arts industry.

The work you produce during your work on this unit may include:

- research notes
- presentations of research findings
- application materials for a chosen career path
- a budget for a performing arts event
- a report into the funding of the arts.

Erin, a performing arts learner

Before I started working on this unit I had no idea how wide ranging the performing arts industry is. I suppose, like most people thinking of a career in the theatre, I was planning to be a performer. I didn't give much thought to other types of careers.

That has changed now. I have begun to think about other possibilities. I really enjoyed researching different backstage roles during this unit and some of them seem really interesting and challenging.

I may still decide to pursue a career as a performer, but if I do I will never take the work of all the other people who work in the industry for granted. I now understand how other organisations and job roles relate to those of performers and appreciate that everyone is vital to the success of a piece of theatre.

I enjoyed the research work for this unit, but found the working on the budget a bit daunting at first (maths has never been my strong point). We got lots of opportunities to practice the skills of budgeting and I soon realised that the maths skills needed aren't that difficult. When I eventually came to completing the assignment I sailed though the budgeting task.

Over to you

- What area/s of performing arts interest you most at the moment?
- Are there other jobs that you'd like to explore?

3.1 Understand employment opportunities and requirements in the performing arts sector

Job opportunities in the performing arts roughly fall into three areas:

- performers and those working directly with performers
- production roles
- arts administration roles.

Warm up

How many people does it take...?

Choose a theatre production you've seen recently. How many people do you think were involved in bringing that production to the stage?

Divide into groups of three or four and make a list of all the different jobs you think people might have undertaken on the production.

Remember to include those people whose jobs involved work during rehearsals and preparations, as well as those working during the actual show.

Come together as a class and collate your ideas into a master list.

3.1.1 Performers

Performers are the people we are most aware of when we go to the theatre or watch a film or TV drama.

Working as an actor

Working as a professional actor is tough. There is fierce competition for a relatively small number of jobs and the financial rewards for the vast majority of jobbing actors are often not that satisfying. As of April 2010, the **Equity minimum rate** for theatre performers is £385 per week (Source: Equity). For more information, go to the Hotlinks section on page ii and follow the instructions there.

Actors have to work long, unsociable hours and are often away from home for weeks at a time. Many actors leave the profession because of difficulty in finding work and most take on other forms of employment such as teaching or taking a casual job while they are not working on a performance or just taking a break.

Working as a dancer

Being a professional dancer is a physically demanding career choice. Competition for jobs is tough, particularly for women, and many dancers supplement their earnings by teaching or doing other work. Dancers are rarely employed on a full-time basis, so most professionals work from one short-term contract to the next. Their career could have a short lifespan and they often need to ensure they are prepared for this with other career choices, often in dance teaching or arts management.

Did you know?

In a musical theatre production one of the members of the dance ensemble needs to fulfil the role of the dance captain. They work closely with the choreographer and provide support to the other dancers, running extra rehearsals if necessary.

Key terms

Equity minimum rate – the minimum rate of pay set by the actors trade union Equity.

You can find much more guidance on dance in **Unit 38: Dance Performance** and **Project 5: Contemporary Dance Showcase.**

Working as a singer or musician

Many musicians earn a living in the performing arts business (rather than the music industry). Singers working in musical theatre also combine their singing with acting and/or dance skills. Some singers may specialise in a particular genre of music e.g. opera or rock whilst others try to be as versatile as possible.

For musicians, playing in the band for a West End or touring musical can represent a steady income, at least for a while. As with other performance roles, musicians and singers work in a competitive profession where high levels of skill and motivation are required.

Typical work activities of a performer				
	Actor	Dancer	Singer	Musician
Looking for work and promoting self	✔	✔	✔	✔
Preparing for and attending auditions	✔	✔	✔	✔
Attending rehearsals	✔	✔	✔	✔
Learning and practicing material for performances	✔	✔	✔	✔
Undertaking role research and character development work	✔	✔*	✔*	
Performing in live and/or recorded events	✔	✔	✔	✔
Undertaking personal development work e.g. learning new skills and improving existing ones	✔	✔	✔	✔
Maintaining musical instrument(s)				✔
Administration activities e.g. keeping records of income for tax purposes	✔	✔	✔	✔

*some character research and development work may be required in certain dance and musical theatre pieces.

You can find much more guidance on musical performances in Unit 14: Musical Theatre Performance.

Singing is just one useful skill for an aspiring performer

The director's team

Depending on the type of production being staged, performers will work under the guidance and instruction of a creative team. This team may include:

- a director, who will have overall responsibility for the artistic content of the production
- a choreographer, who will oversee the dance and movement elements
- a musical director, who will be responsible for singing and other music elements.

The precise duties carried out by the creative team can vary depending on the type of production being staged. The table on the next page sets out their typical responsibilities at various stages of the production process.

	Director	Choreographer	Musical director
Before rehearsals begin	Lead pre-production meetings with other members of the creative and production team Audition performers Cast the show Draft rehearsal schedule	Attend pre-production meetings Audition dancers Agree to the rehearsal schedule Come up with choreographic ideas for dances Hire a rehearsal pianist	Attend pre-production meetings Audition singers Agree to the rehearsal schedule Check the availability of the score Organise and hire members of the band
During rehearsals	Attend production meetings Lead main rehearsals	Choreograph dances and lead dance/movement rehearsals Liaise with director	Lead singing rehearsals Lead band rehearsals Liaise with director
During the run of the production	Provide director's notes to performers Keep in contact with stage manager in case of problems	Provide notes to the dancers	Lead the band

Case study: Paul Bridge – Musical Director

I have been working as a Musical Director, or MD, on and off for the last five years. I began playing keyboards for local amateur and professional productions and got my big break when I was invited to put a band together for a touring production of the musical *Cabaret*. I do a lot of work with a local repertory theatre company, but I don't work for them full-time. I'm contracted on a show-by-show basis. When I am not working with them, I work with touring companies and occasionally undertake contracts playing on cruise ships.

My duties as MD include working with the performers during rehearsals to help them learn the music and to polish up their performances. I sometimes play piano during rehearsals and sometimes we employ a rehearsal pianist.

I work closely with the director of the show along with the choreographer, making any cuts or changes to the music they request. During technical rehearsals I liaise with the sound technicians to ensure that the balance of the music and voices is correct.

As MD I am also responsible for finding the musicians who will play at the performances. For the larger shows I may need to hire a score and band parts. For others I may arrange the music and write the musician's parts myself. I plan rehearsals for the musicians, called band calls, and organise their contracts. During the show, I lead the band and play keyboards.

The musicians we employ are generally members of the Musicians Union (MU). This is a strong union and as a result many people think musicians have the best working conditions of anyone working in the theatre, as their minimum rates of pay are often higher than those for other performers. Even so, because of the casual nature of the work, many of the musicians we hire also coach private pupils or work as visiting instrumental teachers in schools and colleges.

Also, I am part of the company's creative team, which also includes the actors, singers, dancers and musicians, as well as the director and choreographer.

Over to you

- What do you think are the advantages and the disadvantages of being employed as a freelancer taking on short-term contracts?

3.1.2 Production roles

The production elements of a performance can include the sets, lights, sound and costumes. In some productions these elements can be very complex and they need to be designed and managed with skill and care.

The design team

The design team will usually meet with the director of the show very early in the production process. The director may provide a design brief that sets his or her ideas for the 'look' of the show. The designers will then attend subsequent production meetings to present their progress to the director and agree the final design.

In large-scale productions a team made up of separate designers for costumes, the set, lighting, sound and even elements such as props and wigs. In smaller companies these roles may be combined. Like many of the performance roles discussed earlier in the chapter, designers are often employed on a production-by-production basis.

Activity: The 'look' of a show

In small groups, discuss what might be included in a 'design brief' for the costumes for a production.

What information will the designer need before they begin to create the designs for costumes?

Feedback your ideas to the class.

The technical and production team

The production team are vital to the smooth running of a theatrical show. They include people with a diverse range of skills and responsibilities, from the technicians that ensure lighting effects work as they should to the stage crew who move scenery on and off the stage.

The production team may be divided into several sub-groups, each of whom have a specific function eg the technical manager's team is responsible for light, sound and other technical effects. The wardrobe manager's team looks after the costumes and is made up of staff such as cutters, who make the costumes and dressers, who look after the dressing rooms and help actors in and out of their costumes.

The production team in a medium sized producing theatre may look like this:

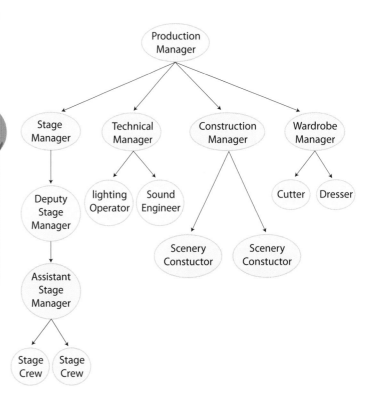

3.1.3 Arts administration

Like any other area of business, the performing arts industry relies on a range of administrative staff. They are the people whose responsibilities include ensuring tickets are sold, the audience is looked after and performers and production staff are paid.

In a theatre, the administration staff will look after:

- **the marketing of productions** – producing appropriate publicity materials to ensure audiences know about future productions
- **the front-of-house areas** – these are the areas of the theatre where the audience go and include the box office, foyer and auditorium, as well as any bars or cafes
- **the finances of the theatre** – finance staff must ensure wages and bills are paid, as well as looking after money that comes in via ticket sales, grants and sponsorship.

The admin team in a typical theatre may look like this :

The Producer

The producer is usually the person who starts and coordinates the production of a new show and they have a vital role in doing so. They coordinate the business and financial aspects of the production as well as appointing key personnel, such as the director for the show. One of the most prolific theatre producers of recent years is Sonia Freidman. She has produced a range of shows in the West End and on Broadway including *Legally Blonde*, *La Cage Aux Folles* and *Boeing Boeing*.

Activity: Before, during and after

Divide into pairs and choose a job role from the production team.

Undertake some research into the function of the job. Then compile a list of responsibilities for that role taking into consideration the different phases of the production process.

For example:

Before: in the planning, development and preparation phases

During: on the first night and during the run of the show

After: the last performance

Share and discuss your findings with others in your class.

Suggestions of useful websites for this activity can be found in the Hotlinks section on page ii.

Activity: Collaboration

Working in the performing arts involves a great deal of collaboration. Divide into small groups and choose one of the following job roles that usually work as a pair. Discuss how they might they need to collaborate with each other during the production/rehearsal period of a show and during the run.

- Box Office Manager and Finance Officer
- Director and Deputy Stage Manager
- Costume Designer and Choreographer
- Set Designer and Scenery Constructor
- Stage Manager and Assistant Stage Manager
- Lighting Designer and Technical Manager
- Marketing Manager and Director
- Assistant Stage Manager and Performers

Share and discuss your findings with the class.

Assessment activity 1

Create a research file that includes information on a variety of employment opportunities and functions in the performing arts.

Include at least two job roles from each of the three areas (performing, production and administration) you have examined in this chapter.

Evidence

- a log book of job descriptions
- completed questionnaires from interviews with practitioners
- profiles of individual jobs
- annotated extracts from newspapers or magazines

Grading tips

M1 Your research file will need to include detailed explanations of a range of employment roles. Research should be extensive and results drawn from several different sources e.g. websites and journals.

D1 Your research file should include comprehensive coverage of different types of roles in employment. Make sure you also include details of how certain roles are linked and how someone starting on those particular roles might progress during their career.

PLTS

By describing a range of employment opportunities and functions in the performing arts, you are using your skills as an **independent enquirer**.

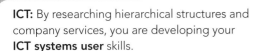

Functional skills

ICT: By researching hierarchical structures and company services, you are developing your **ICT systems user** skills.

English: By writing a report or keeping a log book, you will be using your **writing** skills.

3.1.4 Training

Many of the employment roles discussed in the previous section require specialist training. Some of those who work in the theatre might learn these skills while on the job, by many others require specific qualifications in order to enter the profession.

There are many colleges, universities and other training providers that offer specialist courses for those aspiring to a career in the performing arts industry.

Activity: Drama schools and Dance Conservatoire

Divide into pairs/small groups and choose a training provider from the list below:

- Arts Educational Schools London
- Rambert School of Ballet and Contemporary Dance
- Birmingham School of Acting
- Bristol Old Vic Theatre School
- Central School of Ballet
- Central School of Speech & Drama
- East 15 Acting School
- London Contemporary Dance School (LCDS)
- Guildhall School of Music & Drama
- The London Academy of Music and Dramatic Art (LAMDA)
- Mountview Academy of Theatre Arts
- Royal Academy of Dramatic Art (RADA)
- Royal Scottish Academy of Music and Drama
- Laban
- Royal Welsh College of Music & Drama

Find out about:

- the range of courses they run eg type, level, available specialisms
- the entry requirements.

Share your findings with the class.

Activity: Universities and higher education colleges

Working on your own, search for two universities and/or higher education colleges offering courses in an area of the performing arts you are interested in e.g. dance, acting, performing arts, production and/or technical theatre.

- Find one course that offers your chosen area as a single subject and another that allows students to combine it with another subject.
- Make a note of the type of course they are offering eg degree or Higher National Diploma.
- Find out about the entry requirements.

Keep all information in a log book.

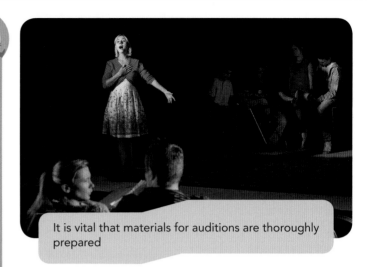

It is vital that materials for auditions are thoroughly prepared

3.1.5 Application procedures

When preparing to apply for a training or educational course, there are certain materials that may need to be prepared. Most applications to training and education courses begin with the completion of an application form. The form is the first line of communication with a college, university or training provider. It must therefore be completed with care and attention to detail.

If an application is being made through UCAS, the University and Colleges Admissions Service, a personal statement will need to be included. This is an opportunity to tell the university or college why you are suitable for the course. A personal statement should include information on:

- why you want to go to college/university
- why you have chosen a particular type of course
- how your current skills and experience relate to the course
- activities you have undertaken that demonstrate your interest in the course.

Many acting, dance and musical theatre courses will require the applicant to undertake an audition. Many have very specific requirements in terms of the number and type of pieces that should be chosen and the length of each piece. It is important that these instructions are considered carefully to ensure appropriate pieces are prepared.

Did you know?

Often in auditions you don't get to perform your whole piece. Sometimes the panel will stop you halfway through, or may ask you to start from somewhere in the middle.

Some production and/or technical theatre courses require applicants to prepare a portfolio of work to demonstrate their skills and experience. Portfolios might contain designs for sets, costumes and/or props. You can submit photos, videos or drawing.

Activity: Application procedures

Choose two courses from those you investigated during the previous activities. Find out about the application procedures for each course.

- How would someone apply?
- Are there any audition requirements?
- Do applicants need to produce a portfolio? If so, what should it include?

Keep the information in a log book.

You can find out more general information on auditions in Project 10: Moving On, page 295.

A vital tool for the performer looking for work is an up-to-date Curriculum Vitae (commonly called CV) and photograph. This is often expected when a job application is made. Many casting agencies promote their clients by including their CVs and photos on their websites. Photos can be black and white and they are often studio photographs, also called **headshots**. A snapshot taken at home is not appropriate.

Key terms

Headshot – a photograph of the head and shoulders only.

Activity: Developing a CV

Visit the websites of some casting agencies to see what the CVs of the performers they represent look like.

Look at a selection of CVs for male and female performers.

Consider the way in which the CVs and photos are presented.

Develop a 'template' for use when writing a CV.

For more information on CVs for performers, check the *Hotlinks* section on page ii.

Assessment activity 2

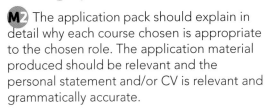 **P2** **M2** **D2** BTEC

Choose a career path that interests you.

Prepare an application pack that:

- identifies the training requirements for the specific role that you have in mind, including information of specific courses that can help you progress to that role
- includes application materials appropriate to the chosen career path eg a CV or personal statement, details of appropriate audition materials and/or examples of work for inclusion in a portfolio.

Evidence

- the application pack with appropriate materials

Grading tips

M2 The application pack should explain in detail why each course chosen is appropriate to the chosen role. The application material produced should be relevant and the personal statement and/or CV is relevant and grammatically accurate.

D2 The application pack should show evidence of wide ranging research that considers factors such as relevance and costs. Application material should be produced to a professional standard.

PLTS

By identifying the training requirements and experience for a career path and producing application material, you will be using your skills as a **self-manager**.

Functional skills

ICT: By using the UCAS site and researching appropriate courses, you are using your skills for **finding and selecting information**.

English: By writing a personal statement or writing a CV, you are using your **writing** skills.

3.2 Know different types of organisations in the performing arts sector

The performing arts industry is made up of a range of different companies and organisations. In this section of the unit we will look at what these different types of organisations do and how their work interrelates.

3.2.1 Services

A service company is an organisation that supplies equipment, materials and services to other organisations.

Activity: Solving problems

You are the musical director of a show. You've put together your cast and the orchestra have been engaged ready for rehearsals. Where will you get the scores from?

You're an actor, and the producer/director is not sticking to the terms of your contract. Who can you talk to in order to solve the situation?

Theatres, production and touring companies rely on other specialised companies to provide particular services. These may be:

- the hire of lighting or sound equipment to theatres or touring companies
- the hire of costumes, props or scenic equipment for use in theatrical productions
- the hire of scores and scripts
- the supply of materials such as make-up, construction materials and fabric
- video and music recording facilities for companies
- the sale of tickets through booking agencies online and in city centre ticket booths
- transport for touring companies.

Service companies come in many sizes from the small fancy dress shop that provides costumes for amateur productions to national transport and logistics companies that move large touring productions from city to city.

This ticket booth in Times Square, New York has provided half price tickets to Broadway since October 2008

Activity: Service companies

Find out about service companies in your region by looking in the Yellow pages directorate and/or the internet.

Make a list of companies you find with details of the services they provide. You may need to make phone calls/send emails to get in touch with these companies and find out what they really offer.

You can share your results with your colleagues in class, where you can present in groups the different types of services you have found.

3.2.2 Employment related organisations

The performing arts industry employs a large number of people from performers to technicians and administrators. Like any industry, it has unions and associations which represent and look after the interests of their members. These associations generally advocate for general working conditions such as pay, hours worked, breaks, health and safety and other such issues.

Unions

There are four main trade unions/associations operating within the performing arts industry:

- Equity
- The Musicians Union (MU)
- Broadcasting Entertainment Cinematograph and Theatre Union (BECTU)
- Theatrical Management Association (TMA).

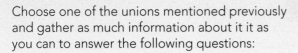

Activity: Unions

Choose one of the unions mentioned previously and gather as much information about it it as you can to answer the following questions:

- What type of people does the union represent?
- What does the union do for its members?
- How does someone join?
- What do you think is the advantage of being a member of a union or association?

To find out which websites to access to get information on this topic, check the Hotlinks section on page ii.

Agencies

Many performers and writers also have agents. A theatrical or casting agency will find work for the performers it represents by liaising with organisations such as theatre, film and television companies. The agent then takes a percentage of the performers fees. Literary agencies perform a similar service for performing arts writers, playwrights writers or screen writers.

3.2.3 Production companies

A production company is an organisation that is directly involved in the creation of film and/or performing arts performances or products. The term refers to performance companies of all sizes, from small touring companies to large national organisations such as the Royal Shakespeare Company. A production company may develop the concept for a certain project, fund or commission it, manage it, as well as employ the creative team. The company may bear ultimate responsibility for the success or failure of the project that it is responsible for.

Production companies create work in a range of styles including:

- Educational outreach work and community arts projects

From full scale Theatre in Education performances to workshops by individual practitioners and community-based work, this is an important area of the performing arts industry.

- Festivals

Festivals are becoming increasing popular in the summer months, but there are others for different periods of time in the rest of the year. Some festivals concentrate on a particular type of performing arts activity, such as film or music, whilst others are organised as forms of celebration.

- Circus performances

Circus has been a popular form of entertainment for centuries, but newer companies, such as Cirque du Soleil, have reinvented the genre.

- Pop and rock concerts

Although part of the music industry, live music events rely on the skills of technical and production staff as well as dancers and musicians.

- Film and TV work

The film and TV industry is an important branch of the performing arts business, producing a wide range of drama, music and dance productions each year.

- Receiving theatres and other venues

Some companies serve as a host, rather than create performing arts productions. Most West End theatres, for example, are receiving theatres. This means they offer the space for the work of production companies. Entertainment complexes and arts centres work in a similar way.

Activity: Production companies

Divide into groups and gather information about a chosen production company. Later create a profile of each organisation.

You could choose from the following production companies or look for other examples:

- Royal Shakespeare Company
- Birmingham Royal Ballet
- Royal Opera House
- Rambert Dance Company
- Royal National Theatre
- Kneehigh Theatre
- Walk the Plank

- The Dream Engine
- Stephen Joseph Theatre
- Northern Stage

For your chosen company find out about:

- the kind of performance work they create
- the venues they perform in
- the size of the company
- how they are funded
- the types of audience their work attracts.

Share the information gathered with the class.

Assessment activity 3

Create a database of services provided by a range of organisations in the performing arts to include service companies such as those specialising in lighting, sound, props and scenic equipment hire, employment related organisations such as Equity and BECTU and production companies.

Write a report in which you should explain how different organisations might interact in their work.

Evidence

- a database produced in an appropriate format eg spreadsheet, a Word document.

Grading tips

M3 The database should provide clear explanations of the work of the organisations including details of how they relate with other areas of the industry eg how a costume hire company might work to supply theatre, TV and film companies.

D3 You should include detailed information on why production organisations do what they do and analyse why their work is so important to the smooth running of other areas of the industry.

PLTS

By describing the services provided by a range of organisations in the performing arts, you will be developing your skills as an **independent enquirer**.

Functional skills

ICT: By creating a database, you will be developing your skills as an **ICT system user**.

3.3 Be able to manage financial controls for a performing arts event

All businesses, no matter what service they provide, must ensure they are financially stable to survive. This means the amount of money the business makes must be at least equal to (but preferably more than) the money it spends. The performing arts industry is no different. Whether you are a financial director for the Royal Shakespeare Company or an administrator for a small touring theatre company, the budget for each production you undertake must balance. In other words, you must have enough money coming in through ticket sales, subsidies etc. to pay for everything that is needed to stage the production.

3.3.1 Production costs

Production costs incurred in the rehearsal and performance of a theatrical production can vary from show to show and company to company. Production costs for the 2007 West End musical *The Lord of the Rings* were said to be £12.5m (for more information, see the Hotlinks section on page ii). At the other end of the scale, some small Theatre in Education companies produce shows on very small budgets. Whatever the size and scope of a production, the costs tend to involve the following areas:

- Wages and fees

In any professional company, people need to be paid regularly. A theatre company may have to pay wages to full-time staff, such as administrators, as well as fees to freelance performers involved in a specific performance.

- Royalties

Each time a play or musical is performed, a royalty fee must be paid to the author or composer. This fee is calculated as a percentage of gross or net sales and it is paid weekly, monthly or quarterly.

- Set design, costumes and props

Materials will need to be bought for sets, costumes and props. Some items may need to be hired.

- Lighting and sound

Lights, sound and other technical equipment may need to be bought or hired.

- Rehearsal and performance spaces

If a company has its own theatre building, the maintenance of the space will be an ongoing expense. For those companies that do not have their own premises, a rehearsal space will need to be hired for the duration of the rehearsal period and fees may need to be paid towards hiring venues in the different locations of a tour.

- Transport

Touring productions will incur costs for the transportation of sets, costumes and other equipment as well as the travelling expenses of the performers and production staff.

- Publicity and marketing

All productions need to have a budget for publicity and marketing to ensure that tickets sell. For small companies, this might be a modest amount spent on posters and leaflets. For larger productions, marketing costs can include money paid for larger advertising campaigns that include television and radio advertisements.

At the beginning of the production process, the different departments involved may be given a budget to cover the costs associated with their area. Staff will then need to ensure they use the money allocated to them in the most cost-effective way. The construction manager of a company may, for example, shop around for the cheapest available timber for the sets that need to be made. Many staff will also have ongoing relationships with service providers, such as hire companies, to ensure they get the best possible deals.

Activity: Production costs

Student productions, like professional productions, also incur some production costs.

Discuss the production costs of the last production staged at your school or college.

Was money spent on any of the areas described above?

Discuss these costs with your tutor and ask about the suppliers your school/college uses.

- workshops e.g. educational events where young people can take part in activities
- special events e.g. back stage tours or talks by the director of the performance.

Many companies also receive money in the form of sponsorship and grants (see the section on Funding on the following page.)

Managing financial controls – the budget

At the beginning of any production, a working budget must be agreed. It will estimate the revenue that is likely to be earned and provide a breakdown of the money allocated to each area of production i.e. the **expenditure**.

A contingency of approximately 5% of the budget is often added to the expenditure to take account of unexpected costs. Balancing the working budget is often difficult and some members of the production team may be disappointed if they do not get the amount of money they wanted for materials or equipment. It is vital that everyone keeps within the budget to minimise the risk of a shortfall, such as the production not making enough money to cover its costs.

3.3.2 Revenue

Revenue is a term used to describe the income of a production. Revenue can be generated from:

- ticket sales
- programme sales
- merchandising e.g. the sale of souvenirs such as T-shirts or mugs
- catering eg the sale of drinks and other refreshments

Assessment activity 4

Create a projected budget for a school/college production that includes:

- areas of expenditure – estimating production costs e.g. by sourcing figures and best prices from catalogues and/or websites on items required for show
- a predicted income – based on likely ticket sales and other forms of revenue that may be generated.

Evidence

- sheet with completed budget

Grading tips

M4 The budget must include a breakdown of income and expenditure for the production. The projected amounts for both income and expenditure must be reasonable.

D4 The budget must address all required areas of income and expenditure, including items such as contingency figures to be used to take care of unexpected costs. The projected amounts you come up with should be based on research into previous productions.

Functional skills

Mathematics: By using estimation and calculation to not overspend on a budget, by completing a budget pro forma, sourcing figures and best prices from catalogues on items required for the show and preparing a forecast on predicted income and expenditure, you will be using your mathematics skills.

ICT: By creating a budget spreadsheet, you are developing, **presenting and communicating information** in ICT.

Key terms

Revenue – the entire amount of income before any deductions are made

Expenditure – the act of spending money for goods or services

3.3.3 Funding

The production costs for a theatrical production can often be very high and many production companies cannot cover these costs only from the revenue obtained by selling ticket and other merchandising. The private and public sectors have always been willing to fund the arts and many companies rely on money donated by the government and/or businesses.

The private sector

Individual producers and groups of producers (known as conglomerates) often work hard to raise funding for productions. Some put up their own money. Others persuade private investors to fund productions in the hope that they will make money on their investment when (or possibly if) the show is a hit. Large national and multi-national companies, as well as smaller organisations, often sponsor production companies. In return they may receive tickets for productions for their clients and employees plus advertising opportunities, as the organisation may be featured in publicity materials, programmes or branded products for the production. An organisation or individual who sponsors a performing arts organisation on a regular basis is often known as a patron.

Case study: Two production companies

Northern Stage

Northern Stage is a production company based in Newcastle-upon-Tyne has a Corporate Sponsorship scheme for regional and national businesses. A local law firm has been supporting the company for almost a decade (for more information about this go to the Hotlinks section, page ii). The company, who are known for their family Christmas performances, stage dedicated performances for the clients and employees of the law firm and their families where children can meet the performers.

The Stephen Joseph Theatre

The Stephen Joseph Theatre in Scarborough is a leading venue as well as a production company. The company raise money each year through a scheme called 'Stephen Joseph Theatre Friends'. For an annual subscription of £20 or a life membership costing £250, friends receive priority booking and money off theatre tickets as well as refreshments.

Over to you

- Check the website for any theatres in your region. Do they have a similar scheme?
- What could you offer to local businesses when staging your school or college productions?

The public sector

Public money, generated by the government from taxation and the National Lottery is also used to fund the arts. The money is distributed to companies and individual practitioners on a national, regional and local level.

The Department of National Heritage and The Arts Councils of England, Wales, Scotland and Northern Ireland tend to fund work that is of national interest. Regional Arts Boards and Local Authorities i.e. City and County Councils fund local and regional work. Money is distributed on a regular basis to organisations such as production companies, orchestras and theatres, as well as in the form of one-off grants for specific projects.

For 2009/10, the Arts Council England has a budget of more than £575m to support the arts (for more information about this go to the Hotlinks section, page ii). Organisations supported on a regular basis include large organisations such as The Royal Shakespeare Company and South Bank Centre, as well as smaller companies such as Dodgy Clutch, a company who specialises in site specific and community theatre.

Go to the Hotlinks section on page ii and follow the instructions to find out what websites are good sources of information on public funding.

Activity: Private funding

Gather posters, leaflets and programmes from venues and companies in your region. Look for evidence of private funding (e.g. company logos, names of patrons).

Collate your evidence and share with the class to produce a list of business sponsors.

Draft a letter to a local business asking them to sponsor an event you are staging.

Activity: Public funding in your region

Investigate public funding for the arts in your region by finding out about your regional arts board and their work.

Visit their website to find out about the companies, individuals and projects they fund.

Investigate how a company might apply for funding.

Assessment activity 5

 **BTEC**

Produce a written report that describes a range of different methods of funding and financing for performing arts events. Suggest ways in which a school/college event might be financed.

Evidence

- funding report

Grading tips

M5 Your report should explain the differences between private and public methods of funding the above event.

D5 Your report should investigate different private and public methods of funding and financing performing arts events and it should suggest innovative ideas for methods of funding the event.

PLTS

By describing a range of different methods of funding and financing a performing arts event, you will be using your skills as an **independent enquirer**.

Functional skills

English: By writing a funding report, you will use your **writing** skills.

Jump to It
Theatre in Education Company

Jump to It
are a small Theatre in Education
Company (TiE) who have been commissioned to
devise a piece for Key Stage 3 children. They have secured
some funding but need to hire a writer to produce a teacher's pack
and an office worker to help to book the tour. They will produce leaflets
for a mail out as well as the teacher's packs.

The company will perform up to eight shows per week. They will charge
£105 per show and £30 for a teachers pack. The mail out is to 127
schools and youth groups. The company will 'break even' if
approximately 25% (32) of the schools and youth groups
book the show with 20 also buying the
teachers pack.

The budget for the project is as follows:

Income		Expenditure	
Grants & Sponsorship		**Fees**	
County Council Grant	£2600	3 Actors @ £350 per week for 6 weeks	£6,300
Transport Police Grant	£2000	Writers Fee for Teachers Pack	£500
Regional Arts Board	£2400	**Hire of Rehearsal Space**	
Sponsorship from		6 days @ £40 per day	£240
"Jamie Hendry Trust"	£400	**Transport**	
Earned Income		Van Hire 5 weeks @ £180 per week	£900
Performance Fees		Petrol	£250
32 @ £105	£3360	**Admin & Marketing**	
Sales of Teachers Pack		General Admin costs including	
20 @ £30	£600	casual office staff	£500
		Marketing, publicity and printing	£1420
		Production Materials	
		Set, props and costume	£570
		Contingency	£550
Total Estimated Income	**£11,360**	**Total Expenditure**	**£11,230**

Think about it!

1 What does break even mean?

2 What will the shortfall be if 25 shows are booked and 15 teachers packs bought if £200 of contingency fund is spent?

3 What will the profit be if 40 shows are booked and 37 teachers packs bought if £450 of the contingency fund is spent?

4 If the show is a real success and the tour is extended by two weeks, what will the increased expenditure be?

Just checking

1 Many people working in the performing arts industry are employed on a freelance basis. What does this mean?

2 What job roles might be included in the design team for a theatrical production?

3 What is the difference between the role of the director and that of the producer?

4 Why is having an up-to-date CV and headshot important for a performer?

5 What does the term *front-of-house* refer to?

6 What is a service company?

7 What is a receiving theatre?

8 What are the names of the four main trade unions for people working in the performing arts industry? What do these unions do?

9 When drawing up a budget for a production would 'ticket sales' be included under income or expenditure?

10 What is the different between public and private funding?

11 What is the Arts Council?

12 Why do some businesses sponsor theatre companies?

Assignment tips

- Undertake some primary research when investigating job roles by arranging interviews with local people who work in the industry.

- Use your careers library to research training requirements for job roles and order a prospectus from any higher education institutions you are considering applying to.

- The UCAS website is an excellent source of advice and information when planning and writing a personal statement. Your *BTEC Level 3 National Performing Arts Study Skills Guide* also includes some valuable advice.

- The *Yellow Pages* is a good place to begin when finding out about performing arts organisations in your region.

- When creating your database of local organisations, remember to categorise them by the type of work they do and/or services they provide.

- Take care when creating your budget. Remember to ensure you take into account all areas of income and expenditure and check your calculations carefully.

- It is a good idea to consider the type of work being produced when investigating possible sources of funding. Are any local businesses likely to be particularly interested in contributing e.g. maybe because the subject of the piece or the target audience is related to the work that they do?

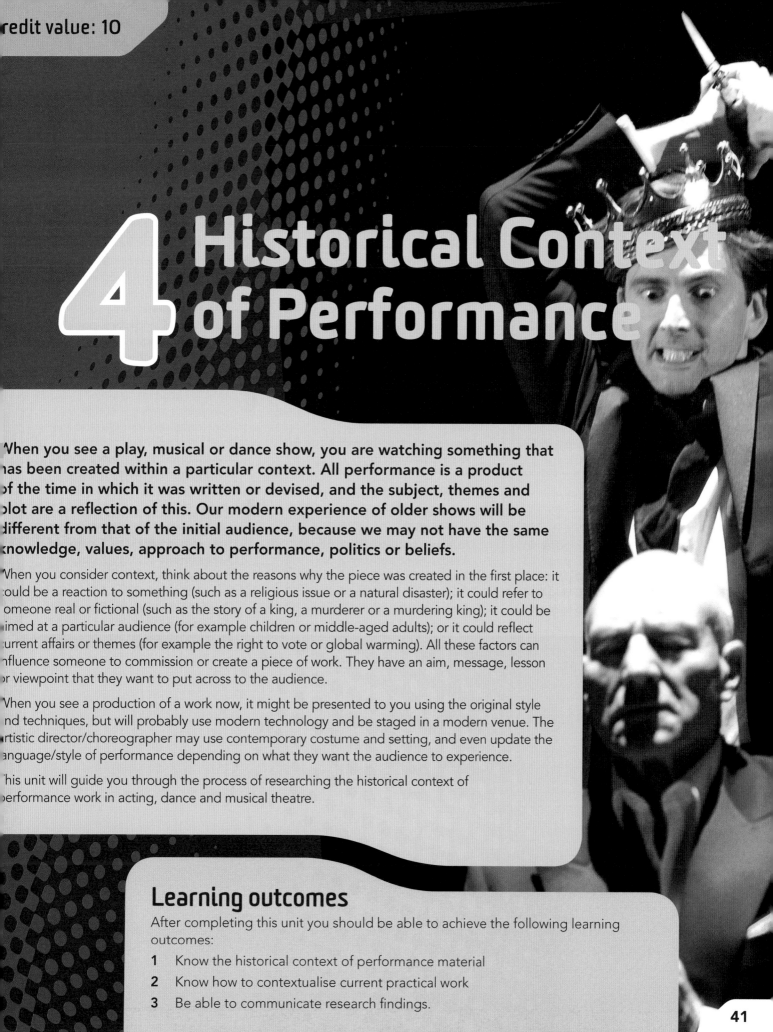

4 Historical Context of Performance

When you see a play, musical or dance show, you are watching something that has been created within a particular context. All performance is a product of the time in which it was written or devised, and the subject, themes and plot are a reflection of this. Our modern experience of older shows will be different from that of the initial audience, because we may not have the same knowledge, values, approach to performance, politics or beliefs.

When you consider context, think about the reasons why the piece was created in the first place: it could be a reaction to something (such as a religious issue or a natural disaster); it could refer to someone real or fictional (such as the story of a king, a murderer or a murdering king); it could be aimed at a particular audience (for example children or middle-aged adults); or it could reflect current affairs or themes (for example the right to vote or global warming). All these factors can influence someone to commission or create a piece of work. They have an aim, message, lesson or viewpoint that they want to put across to the audience.

When you see a production of a work now, it might be presented to you using the original style and techniques, but will probably use modern technology and be staged in a modern venue. The artistic director/choreographer may use contemporary costume and setting, and even update the language/style of performance depending on what they want the audience to experience.

This unit will guide you through the process of researching the historical context of performance work in acting, dance and musical theatre.

Learning outcomes

After completing this unit you should be able to achieve the following learning outcomes:

1 Know the historical context of performance material
2 Know how to contextualise current practical work
3 Be able to communicate research findings.

Assessment and grading criteria

This table shows you what you must do in order to achieve a **pass**, **merit** or **distinction** grade, and where you can find activities in this book to help you.

To achieve a **pass** grade the evidence must show that you are able to:	To achieve a **merit** grade the evidence must show that, in addition to the pass criteria, you are able to:	To achieve a **distinction** grade the evidence must show that, in addition to the pass and merit criteria, you are able to:
P1 outline the background context of performance material, providing some research findings **Assessment activity 1 page 45** **Assessment activity 2 page 46** **Assessment activity 3 page 48** **Assessment activity 4 page 53**	**M1** explain the background context of performance material, providing detailed research findings **Assessment activity 1 page 45** **Assessment activity 2 page 46** **Assessment activity 3 page 48** **Assessment activity 4 page 53**	**D1** provide a comprehensive account of the background context of performance material, providing detailed research findings **Assessment activity 1 page 45** **Assessment activity 2 page 46** **Assessment activity 3 page 48** **Assessment activity 4 page 53**
P2 describe how performance material is contextualised for contemporary use **Assessment activity 5 page 58** **Assessment activity 6 page 61**	**M2** explain how performance material is contextualised for contemporary use **Assessment activity 5 page 58** **Assessment activity 6 page 61**	**D2** comprehensively explain how performance material is contextualised for contemporary use **Assessment activity 5 page 58** **Assessment activity 6 page 61**
P3 communicate the results of research. **Assessment activity 1 page 45** **Assessment activity 2 page 46** **Assessment activity 3 page 48** **Assessment activity 4 page 53** **Assessment activity 5 page 58** **Assessment activity 6 page 61**	**M3** communicate the results of research effectively in an imaginative and coherent manner. **Assessment activity 1 page 45** **Assessment activity 2 page 46** **Assessment activity 3 page 48** **Assessment activity 4 page 53** **Assessment activity 5 page 58** **Assessment activity 6 page 61**	**D3** communicate the results of research in an informed, highly articulate and creative manner. **Assessment activity 1 page 45** **Assessment activity 2 page 46** **Assessment activity 3 page 48** **Assessment activity 4 page 53** **Assessment activity 5 page 58** **Assessment activity 6 page 61**

How you will be assessed

This unit will be assessed through an internal assignment that will be designed and marked by the tutors at your centre. You will be assessed on your research and presentation skills. You will need to show that you can make decisions about how you will develop material written in the past for a 21st-century audience.

The work you produce may include:

- a portfolio of research evidence
- a log book or production diary
- recordings of practical work
- observations from your tutor
- examples of presentation materials such as a written document, handouts of drawings and diagrams, presentation slides.

Jen, 17-year-old musical theatre learner

We were doing a performance of *Into The Woods* by Stephen Sondheim and were asked to produce programme notes about him and the play for the audience. We thought this was important, as most of the audience would be friends and family, and not many of them would know who Stephen Sondheim is.

We worked in small groups; each group had to look at a different aspect of the show. We had to present our work to the rest of the group, and then the best bits would be used in the programme.

The categories were:

- The life of Stephen Sondheim and his other plays and musicals, eg *West Side Story*
- The people he worked with (James Lapine, Oscar Hammerstein)
- Grimm brothers and their fairytales
- *Into The Woods* plot and influences
- Life in the late 1980s (when this musical was first shown).

I was in the last group, and I had to research what life was like in the late 1980s. I used lots of different sources, including the internet, books on the history of musical theatre and visited the V&A Museum. I also interviewed my mum, some of her friends and my sister.

I was never any good at writing essays but my tutor said I could present my work as a speech. This really helped me and I felt more confident doing it this way.

Over to you

- Given the choice, how to present your work? Would you choose a written essay or a presentation?
- What skills do you think you need to do this? What are the benefits and challenges of your choice?

4.1 Know the historical context of performance material

Warm up

Capturing the moment

Imagine you are going to create a performance piece that shows what life is like in your area right now for people of your age. You should make it as relevant as possible.

You can include any combinations of dance, acting and singing.

With a group, discuss the following elements and make a list of the decisions you reach:

- Subject matter and themes – what is important to you?
- How will you ensure that the material is topical?
- Where will you stage it?
- Who is your audience?

- What will be the setting and 'the look' of the show? What about costumes?
- If using music, what will you choose?

Once you have made the major decisions about your performance piece, consider the following with your group:

- When do you think the context of your ideas will go 'out of fashion'?
- How long will it be before the clothing and music becomes outdated?
- How quickly will the topic/subject matter be taken over by other issues?
- If you moved the action ten years back in time, what would you need to change? What could you keep the same?

4.1.1 Performance material

In this unit, you will be studying a play, dance or musical theatre piece. You will look at the work of the person/people who created the piece, that is, the playwright, composer, or lyricist. If a group or production company created the performance material, you may also look at the work of the director, choreographer, performer or group of performers.

The decision to study a particular performance piece will probably be made by your tutor. They might decide to choose a particular work because:

- you are going to stage a performance, or extracts from the work
- there is the opportunity to see a live/recorded production of the work (the original and/or adaptations/interpretations)
- you need to understand a particular period of performance history or genre, to help you develop other projects.

A scene in *Oedipus* by Sophocles

Assessment activity 1

Create an overview of the performance material that has been chosen. You could use this in publicity material, in programme notes or in a presentation to introduce your work to the audience. Include the following:

- The title of the work
- Who created it (for example a playwright, director, choreographer, performance company)
- When it was created (year)
- Where it was created (city, situation)
- A general summary of the performance piece (an outline of the plot, type of dance(s), musical style)
- Performance style (genre of performance, influences)
- Anything that made the work unique or original when it was first shown.

Here are some more specific questions for Performing Arts pathways.

Acting

1 What do you think of the work? Give your first impressions from a read through or from watching a DVD or live performance.
2 Is this work seen as important in theatre history? Why is it important?
3 How would you describe the genre? Does it follow any traditions?

Musical theatre

4 Is it a musical with equal measure of dancing, singing and acting?
5 Does it begin to cross boundaries? Is it a play with songs?

6 Would you want to perform in this work? If so, which role would you take?

Dance

7 What genre is it: classical, contemporary or street?
8 How you would describe it: breathtaking, interesting or relevant?
9 Does it cross boundaries? Does it use styles and techniques from different genres?
10 Is the work included within a musical?

Evidence

- log book of your progress
- presentation/programme notes

Grading tips

M1 Make sure that you provide detailed notes on your research findings. This will help you to explain the background of your performance material.

D1 Explain the context of the work. You could compare the work with other types of performances you have seen, or explain why it is an important historical work.

M3 Experiment with how you communicate your ideas (different formats and styles).

D3 Take inspiration from professional theatre programmes and publicity and adapt them for your work.

PLTS

Researching performance material is an excellent way to demonstrate that you are an **independent enquirer** and **self-manager**.

Functional skills

English: By reading historical performance material, you will be using your **reading** skills.

4.1.2 History

It is important to know the historical background of performance work, as it may affect your understanding of the piece or you may judge the work differently if you know the context. You can enjoy *The Crucible* by Arthur Miller (first seen in 1953) without knowing anything about the context. However, when you understand that the suspicion of witchcraft is a metaphor for the 'witch-hunts' of suspected communists in McCarthy-era America in the early 1950s, you may feel entirely different about it, and watch it again with a new perspective and appreciation. Consider how the contemporary (of that time) audience would have received and understood the work. Could they be objective about its meaning? Can you appreciate the meaning and message of performance work only by considering the time it's set in?

Performance work is created in a particular context, so it is worth finding out about the important and significant events and people of the time. You might be aware of specific periods of history, for example World War II (1939–1945), but the period of simplicity and hardship that followed (1946–1959) might be unknown to you. Therefore, if you were studying a piece from this period, such as *Guys and Dolls* (1953) or *Waiting for Godot* (1955), you would need to research the historical events and background.

Performance conditions

Live performance requires a venue. There must be a space for the audience to watch and appreciate the work, and a space for the performers to work in.

Are you familiar with the following description of a theatre?

1 There is a proscenium arch stage (most, if not all, of the action will take place on the stage behind the curtain line).

2 The audience are all facing towards the stage and are sat in reasonably comfortable seating (although leg room can be a problem).

3 The performers work on a **raked stage**; there are curtains that open to reveal the show, and close when it is over.

4 You can buy a programme, and you can buy an ice-cream during the interval.

5 You are expected to sit in silence during the play (it is accepted that you will laugh if it is funny, clap if something is extraordinary, and applaud at the end of the show).

Assessment activity 2

Create a news report showing the major headlines, news events and developments of the year in which your chosen performance was first shown.

General historical information on the year

- Important events in the year the work was created or first shown
- News headlines including disasters and any scientific discoveries
- Political issues: details of the government and their policies, monarchy, relationships with other countries (pacts and wars)

- Popular music, fashions, and what people wanted and expected for entertainment
- Sporting achievements, advances in art.

You should decide what is important information for your audience and what will help them understand the context of the performance material.

Evidence

- the news article you have written

PLTS

By presenting research into historical performance material, you will be developing your skills as an **independent enquirer**.

Functional skills

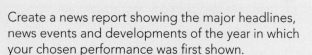

ICT: By using the internet to research historical performance material, you will be using your ICT skills to **find and select information**.

A particular venue may be chosen to stage the performance for one (or more) of the following reasons:

- The venue and the facilities are good.
- The performance piece will work in that venue rather than anywhere else.
- The location/prestige of the venue matters more than the suitability for the work.
- The work has been commissioned for that venue and/or fits into the artistic vision of the venue.
- It is the only venue available.

Here are some more examples of types of performance space and venue that you could investigate:

- Amphitheatre (Greek/Roman)
- Church altar/promenade (medieval)
- Inn-yard/courtyard/thrust (Elizabethan)
- Proscenium arch (Georgian/Victorian)
- Promenade
- Traverse
- In-the-round (20th century).

In Georgian and Victorian theatres the audience is expected to remain generally silent and still as the performance takes place before them

Visual elements of performance

In most productions there are visual elements that support the work of the performers.

The visual elements can provide context: they can help tell the story, progress the plot and indicate the period, time and environment.

The setting: includes the floor, the backdrop or area surrounding the performance space, and any set decoration in the performance space (this includes furniture and objects that are not used by the performers). It can also include projected images.

Props: any object used or held during the performance. Props of realistic objects may need to be remade for the purposes of theatre. For example the audience may not be close to the stage and the prop may need to be designed for viewing at a distance.

Costumes: the clothing, hats, shoes and general attire for each performer. Costumes can represent the age, status, background and lifestyle of characters. They may be designed to highlight or emphasise the shape and physique of the dancer.

Did you know?

Theatre Royal is a popular name for many theatres; there may be one in your area. The name used to be an indication that the theatre was a patent theatre, that is, licensed to perform 'spoken drama' after the English Restoration of Charles II in 1660. If a theatre did not have the license, they were only allowed to show comedy, pantomimes or melodramas.

Aural elements of performance

What we hear during a performance will vary. We need to hear the voice of the actor or singer. Performers are trained to project their voices, but there are times when the voice is artificially amplified. Nowadays, it is standard practice for professional performers in the West End to be wearing concealed microphones (generally in musical theatre). The use of microphones was introduced to live theatre performance in the 1960s, and became more popular in large theatres and in productions that use loud background music and effects.

If there is an orchestra pit in the performance space, there is the opportunity for live music to accompany the performance. Most Victorian theatres have a pit,

as it was expected for most performances to include some form of orchestrated music. Nowadays, not all orchestra pits are used, as not all performances need live music. The high costs of having an orchestra can be cut by using recorded music instead.

Recorded music and sound effects have been standard in theatre performance since the 1950s.

Sound can be used as a backdrop to create **atmosphere**, set the context of the work, describe the environment and setting, and provoke reaction and emotion in the audience (for example, it can scare and shock the audience with volume and content). The music might remind us of a certain time and place, or it could act to underline the action without us really noticing what we are listening to.

Assessment activity 3

Consider what it would have been like to watch your chosen piece when it was first shown.

1 Decide on the year, time of year, the day it is shown on, and the time of performance.

2 Find out about the performance venue: what is it like? Where is it? How do you arrive?

3 First impressions: what other types of audience members are there? Is it an 'occasion'? Are people dressed up?

4 What are the seating arrangements (if any)? Is the audience treated equally? Or do some get a better view, sat in more comfortable seats?

5 Describe the performance.

6 The staging: describe the set, props and costume.

7 What do you hear? Can you hear the performers clearly (if appropriate)?

8 What about the music/sound effects? Are they live or recorded?

9 How does the audience behave during the show, in the interval, and after the show?

Evidence

• your log book

Grading tips

M1 You could add extra detail about your surroundings, the performance and the audience.

D1 You could compare the behaviour and experience of a modern audience with the historical one.

M3 Imagine you are an audience member, and you are telling your friends or family about your experience.

D3 Be imaginative – put yourself in character.

PLTS

By presenting research into historical performance material, you will be developing your skills as a **self-manager**.

Functional skills

English: By presenting research findings, you will be using your **speaking and listening** skills.

Performers

Nowadays, most professional performers are contracted to take part in eight performances per week (six evenings, two matinées), but this has not always been the case. Performers' conditions today have been influenced by a combination of developments and historical factors: union representation; audience demands; social developments; and other art forms, such as television.

Traditionally performers were paid a pittance (sometimes in food or by good favour). Medieval mystery players were paid fairly. In Elizabethan times, many believed that the theatre had a corrupting, subversive influence on its audiences and theatres were located in areas that were at the time outside of the city (for example, the Globe was in Southwark).

In 1931, a trade union was created to represent the employment rights of professional performers. It was called Equity, and it is as important now to those working in the performing arts industry as it was then. Today, performers receive Equity agreed minimum wages for regional and west end professional performances.

Key terms

Atmosphere – the tone or mood of a theatrical performance

Soliloquy – a character speaking thoughts aloud when alone on stage

Aside – a character speaking thoughts directly to the audience when other characters are present

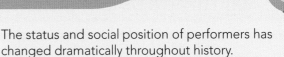

Activity

The status and social position of performers has changed dramatically throughout history.

Investigate the performance conditions and context of the performer for your chosen performance piece:

Include the following:

- Pay (did they need to subsidise with other work?)
- Training and skills development
- Background, social status and lifestyle.

You could also find out how a professional performer in your local area is paid and treated in the workplace, and make a comparison

Audience behaviour and experience

Some theatre companies require the audience to participate and take a role in the show.

In order for the performance to continue, the audience has to take an active role and their reactions have been considered and written into the work.

How did the creators of your performance want the audience to feel? What did they want the audience to experience?

The table below shows some examples of how an audience might be expected to behave:

The silent, stationary audience	The interactive, progressive audience
Proscenium arch theatre	Elizabethan inn-yard
Audience seated, sometimes in split levels (stalls, royal circle, dress circle, boxes)	Audience on three sides, often standing, some sitting on stage
Performers 'ignore' audience, but may still enter their space, eg via a thrust stage, or entrances/exits in the auditorium	Performers acknowledge audience, interacting and talking directly with them (e.g. **soliloquies**, **asides**)
Audience listens and watches silently unless prompted.	Audience communicates with performers to drive the show
Examples include naturalism, Chekhov, Ibsen, melodrama, Stoppard, Kane, Frayn	Examples include Shakespeare, pantomime, commedia dell'arte, Brecht's Epic theatre

Case study: An interactive audience – *Mnemonic* by Theatre De Complicite, 1999

Audience seated, facing proscenium arch stage looks like wide screen cinema, with action taking place behind the cut-out oblong.

Each member of the audience is given a bag containing an eye-mask and a large leaf. The Narrator (in front of the cinema screen performance space) instructs them to put on the eye-mask, and then talks, almost hypnotising them, asking them to imagine themselves as a child, to imagine their ancestors surrounding them, and to do so while feeling the back of the leaf, comparing the structure and relationships of the veins of the object with their own family history and connections.

The audience have an active role, and their experience could have been different if they didn't follow the narrator's instructions.

Over to you

- What do you think about this idea as an opening to the play?

Case study: A participatory audience – *Faust* by Punchdrunk, 2007

The play is set in a disused warehouse. The audience wear full face masks. They are allowed to roam freely through the performance spaces (promenade); performances happen at set times and are not reliant on members of the audience being present. The audience experience can differ from person to person, and the performers adapt their work to suit their needs and to promote interaction with the audience.

Over to you

- How would you feel to be involved as a member of the audience? Do you think that some audience members may be unwilling to participate?

Did you know?

One of the first times that a traditional Victorian theatre had been transformed into a promenade theatre was for the play *Road* by Jim Catwright in 1986. This was an innovative approach to theatre production and audience behaviour at that time. The audience could not sit down and get comfortable as they had to remain alert to switches in the setting.

Influences on the performance work

All performing arts works begin with a creative spark. Artists respond to a variety of influences; they might be inspired by another artist or by real-life events or issues. Here are some examples:

Plays

Accidental Death of an Anarchist (Dario Fo, 1970) is inspired by corruption in the law and police.

The Stephen Lawrence Inquiry – The Colour of Justice (Tricycle Theatre, 1999) is a tribunal play based on the real-life inquiry into the racially motivated murder of a London teenager.

Black Watch (National Theatre of Scotland, 2006) is based on interviews with soldiers from the Black Watch regiment of the British Army during the Iraq war (2004).

Dance

Ghost Dances (Rambert, 1999) is inspired by human rights violations in South America.

Play Without Words (Matthew Bourne, 2002) is a ballet performance based on the 1960s' film *The Servant*.

To Be Straight With You (DV8, 2008) uses interviews as the basis for a dance piece about homophobia.

Musicals

West Side Story (Sondheim, Bernstein, 1957) is an updated version of *Romeo and Juliet*. Set in 1950s New York, it focuses on the same issues (love, cultural clashes, identity, and violence) as the original.

Rent (Larson, 1996) is based on the Puccini opera *La Bohème*, it is a reaction to the AIDS epidemic in New York.

Spring Awakening (Sater, Sheik, 2006) mixes a 19th-century Frank Wedekind story with modern American songs; includes controversial subject matter.

Activity: Internet

Search websites such as YouTube for video excerpts from the performance works above.

Activity: The stimulus or spark for your performance piece

The performance piece may be inspired by any of the following elements:

- A theatre practitioner
- A choreographer
- A play, dance or artistic event
- A social event
- A political theory
- A cultural movement.

How original is your performance piece? Is it heavily influenced by the work of others or is it truly innovative?

An example of mixing and matching influences and styles is the play *East* by Steven Berkoff (1975). The play mixes Elizabethan verse, the techniques and styles of theatre practitioners Antonin Artaud and Bertolt Brecht, mime, contemporary cultural references in language and costumes, and British post-war family traditions.

4.1.3 Society and culture

Some people in Britain today think that theatre and live performance is elitist. That is, it is aimed at, caters for and is made by the rich and educated. Theatre prices in the West End tend to be very high and this can put people off, especially if they are not guaranteed a good time.

Do you agree with this? Can you find examples of theatre that cater for different kinds of audience, for example people your age or people with your tastes?

Nowadays, there are a lot of West End shows that include well-known performers from television, film or music. Do you agree that having a household name in the show (regardless of their experience as a stage performer) can attract people who may not normally go to the theatre?

Activity: A show in your local area

Go and see a show in your local area. Notice the following:

- Who the show is aimed at – analyse the publicity materials (posters, flyers)
- Where the show is staged – in a traditional theatre space, or somewhere unusual?
- How the audience is treated – how do they behave before, during and after the show?
- Whether you can identify a particular 'type' of person in the audience.

Audience attitudes and values

The tastes and beliefs of an audience can vary depending on the context. **Cultural taboos** shift and change.

Some themes and issues will gain controversy more than others and will provoke reactions of intolerance and **bigotry** in the audience, for example aspects of sexuality, violence, religion, race and ethnicity.

A show can become successful and well known for its controversial content and the publicity it gathers, but may not be artistically challenging or progressive.

The play *Saved* by Edward Bond (1965) depicts youths killing a baby by throwing stones and rocks at the pram. It is a shocking and awful act that continues to be as controversial today as it was at that time. Why do you think people want to watch a performance like that?

The musical *Spring Awakening* (2006) deals with child abuse, rape, teenage sexuality and suicide among other issues, but it has been an incredibly successful show on Broadway and in London. This type of show would not have been allowed to be shown up to the late 1960s due to the Stage Licensing Act (see political section 4.1.4, page ii).

But people's attitudes towards certain issues change: for example, the representation of sexuality and sexual acts on stage (*The Romans* includes scenes of male rape); violence with knives to solve disputes and rivalries (*Romeo and Juliet*); a woman's role in society (*Look Back in Anger*). Representations of 'traditional' roles from the 1950s can look outdated now.

Did you know?

Reginald Rose's play *Twelve Angry Men* is now often performed with a mixed cast of twelve angry jurors, or twelve angry women.

The media

Today live performance is included in TV and radio programmes aimed at a minority audience: for example BBC specialist programmes, BBC4, Radio 4 and Sky Arts broadcast recordings of performances.

Stage performers (and those involved in the creative side of the live performance) are generally given respect and relatively high status within the media, especially broadsheet newspapers.

There are professional critics in the media who are employed to review the performance work. This can be an attempt at objective criticism – when the reviewer has a solid knowledge of theatrical history – and sometimes an award of a number of marks or stars is given for the show. There is a tendency for the public to rely on the critic's remarks to judge whether the performance work is worth seeing. Productions will sometimes use extracts from positive reviews to promote the show (including the comments or marks awarded in publicity material).

Key terms

Cultural taboo – Something that a certain cultural group considers to be unacceptable. Some taboos are shared by the majority of cultures, such as the view that intentional murder or cannibalism is wrong, whilst others are more culturally specific, for example in Japan it is seen as a cultural taboo to wear shoes indoors. Taboos can also be specific to a certain era or time period. For example, some things that were once considered taboo in the UK, such as divorce, are now much more widely accepted

Bigotry – the intolerance of a person who does not accept any opinions differing from their own

Zeitgeist – trend; the cultural spirit and mood of a particular time

Assessment activity 4

P1 M1 D1 P3 M3 D3   BTEC

Find any reviews or critiques of the performance work you have chosen (from the original staging or subsequent productions).

1   What do you think is the value of the review?

2   What receives criticism – the content, the themes, the performance style or the performers?

3   Compare the work of critics by looking at the similarities between reviews. Are they in agreement?

4   Can you see any influences on the critic's review, such as cultural values?

5   Write a review of the performance.

Evidence

• your own written review and the researched articles

Grading tips

M1 Try to justify your comments using background information on the work or comparisons with other performances/performance styles.

D1 You will need to provide a clear and balanced argument for your critique.

M3 Write your review as it is to be included in a newspaper and try to stick to a limited word count. If possible, try to watch the play before writing about it.

D3 Compare your work with other learners. Do they have the same opinion on certain issues?

PLTS

By considering performance material in a contemporary play, you be developing your skills as a **reflective learner**.

Functional skills

English: Understanding the critic's review of the performance work will require you to use your **reading** skills.

Fashion

Fashionable elements of life can quickly become outdated: the style and content of language, the clothes we wear, the fashions we follow and the music we listen to.

Some performances capture the **Zeitgeist**, but can quickly seem out of date and old fashioned.

Joe Orton's *Loot* (1965) seems very dated now in terms of the language used, the behaviour of the characters and the attitudes to Christianity and sexuality.

The musical *Hair* (1967) is also in a time warp as the style of music, language, cultural references in the lyrics, the idea of hippies and counterculture, and the reaction to American involvement in the Vietnam War are firmly rooted in the late 1960s (a revival of this musical took place in 2010 in London, with no changes made to the original script).

Styles of performance can be popular sometimes only for a limited period of time. For example, musical theatre with extravagant stage sets and big budgets was trendy in both the 1890s and the 1980s, while jukebox musicals were a hit in the 1990s.

In Elizabethan theatre, the performances of plays and dances doubled up as fashion shows. Because the performers often wore exquisite costumes considered *haute couture*, theatre became a way to display clothes much like the catwalk shows of today. This was usually how performers gained higher status. Fashion trends can sometimes matter more than historical accuracy: Shakespeare's *Anthony and Cleopatra* was originally performed in Elizabethan contemporary high fashion, even though the play is set in 43AD in Egypt.

Communities

Your performance work may have been created and performed by individuals connected with particular minority groups. Or it could be about a minority group, or a particular lifestyle.

Communities can demand particular types of performances and shows.

The Theatre Royal Stratford East in London specialises in work created or produced in-house (by the theatre), and has built a tradition over the last 50 years of providing entertainment (and a voice) for working class communities in the East End.

> **Activity: What would *EastEnders* be like in...?**
>
> Watch the latest episode of the British TV soap opera. Imagine how it would have looked if it had been produced in:
>
> - the 1960s
> - the 1600s.
>
> Consider the differences between now and the given years in terms of:
>
> - language used
> - types of characters
> - the structure of family, work and social relationships
> - cultural references and fashions
> - housing, lifestyles, storylines.

4.1.4 Politics

Censorship and legislation have had a significant influence on the type of performance work that has been allowed to be shown in this country in the past few hundred years.

In 1737, the Stage Licensing Act was introduced because of the outrage caused by satirical plays, such as *The Beggar's Opera*, mocking the ruling establishment.

From 1737 to 1968, the Lord Chamberlain (Chief Officer of the Royal Household) had the power to censor, ban and edit plays before public performance in the West End of London. For example, in 1957 the Lord Chamberlain's office refused to give Samuel Beckett's play *Endgame* a theatrical license because of the following line about God: 'The Bastard! He doesn't exist!'. The line had to be changed to 'The swine!' before it was granted permission to be performed.

Satire

Satire is a historically popular method of commenting on and making fun of leaders and famous members of society. Here are some examples of performance

material that use satire: Dario Fo makes fun of politicians and businessmen in his plays; *Monty Python's Spamalot* is a satire of musicals, and the musical *Avenue Q* is satire of liberal American values and ethics using the style of children's TV shows (*Sesame Street* and *The Muppets*).

Although British theatre has been seen as a medium for uncensored free speech since 1968, there have been recent attempts to censor performance work so as not to offend particular religious groups. This is a result of pressure put on local government through protest, campaigning and media representation. *Jerry Springer: The Opera* saw protests outside theatres during a national tour, and a failed attempt to prosecute the BBC in 2005 after a recording of the stage performance was broadcast on television.

> **Did you know?**
>
> Female performers in Elizabethan theatre were banned, deemed unacceptable by audiences and ruling classes. Their roles were played by boys aged 8–12 years dressed in women's clothing.

Current events

Some current events and news items seem trivial; others have a longer lasting effect and influence. Sometimes it is only with hindsight and the passing of time that we can see what was important.

David Hare wrote the play *Stuff Happens* in 2004. The title is inspired by US Secretary of Defence Donald Rumsfeld's response to widespread looting in Baghdad during the Iraq war:

'Stuff happens and it's untidy, and freedom's untidy, and free people are free to make mistakes and commit crimes and do bad things.' (April 11, 2003).

The politician's words compelled the playwright to create the work and the play was showing within a year of the speech being made.

> **Discussion point**
> **Does your play comment on current affairs and events of a particular time?**

4.1.5 Economic

Private funding

Nowadays money is put forward by a producer or a performance is commissioned by a private organisation. Many West End productions are privately funded.

The producers must make a profit as well as cover the cost of the production to fund subsequent productions. This can affect the casting (a 'star' name might attract audiences), the type of show (guaranteed popular shows/adaptations of films), how long the show will run to make the profit or to break even, and the cost of tickets.

There are some production companies that rely on the patronage of fans to help subsidise the work.

Public funding

Currently the UK government provides money for performances through charitable organisations, for example the Arts Council. Public funding is dependent on a number of factors, such as the international reputation of the performance company, the expenditure of government departments and the economic climate.

Established institutions such as Royal National Theatre and the Royal Opera House particularly rely on public funding, as they are seen as 'flagship' organisations for arts provision in the UK. Other arts organisations receive funding according to their status, position, location and the work they produce.

Public-funded organisations are not necessarily run for profit and can afford to take risks with the content and style of performances.

Resource costs

The costs involved in producing a show will influence the style and content of work. If the production company is not reliant on **sponsorship** or public or private funding, it will have to cover the production costs. It may give the company artistic license to perform, but it may be hampered by inhibitive costs.

Throughout history, productions have been influenced by financial constraints. Regional theatres may not get much private or public funding and have a small production budget.

A large budget can result in expensive sets, extravagant costumes, star names and large casts. It can also extend the length of a production run even if the show is not attracting huge audiences.

For more information on funding and resources check Unit 3: Performing Arts Business, page 21.

Activity: Funding

Find out who produced the original production of your chosen performance, and how much it cost.

It may have been commissioned by royalty, or it may have been subsidised by the government and private donations.

Investigate how much it cost an audience member to see it. Or was it by invitation only?

Key term

Censorship – examination by an authorised person or organisation of publications, theatrical work, films, letters, and so on, in order to suppress those considered obscene or politically unacceptable

Satire – a literary technique of writing or art which principally ridicules its subjects

Sponsorship – to provide support (usually financial) to a person, object, activity or company

Did you know?

One of the most expensive productions ever was The Lord of the Rings (which ran at the Theatre Royal, Drury Lane from June 2007 to July 2008); it cost approximately £12 million to create and run the show. Some of the costs were spent on a cast of over 50 performers and sophisticated hydraulic staging.

4.1.6 Stage technology

It was not until the 1880s that electrical lights were introduced into theatres. Gas lighting had been used to illuminate stage performances during the 18th century; oil lamps and candles were used from the 15th century to the 1700s.

Lighting has a big impact on the modern audience experience as it can do the following:

- it creates mood, atmosphere and environments.
- it indicates time and space, and emphasises or replaces storytelling and description.
- it focuses, guides and highlights the action.
- it projects still and moving images.

The use of technology in live performance has increased significantly in recent years. For example, artists use microphones to amplify the voice rather than vocal skills and technique.

Amplifying sound and music is now taken for granted.

Here are some advantages of recorded sound and music on stage:

- music recording and playback can be made using a variety of sources and recordings
- producers do not need to pay for live musicians (only music licensing rights)
- the volume and content can be easily controlled and manipulated
- sounds and effects can be mixed together.

Did you know?

In the 19th century, curtains became very important in live performance to hide the movement of scenery. As the setting (and the change-overs of set) became more sophisticated, the Stage Manager job was created.

Activity: Stage technology

Find out what kind of stage technology was available for the original staging of the performance work you have chosen.

You might want to focus on the following:

- flying techniques
- traps
- trucks (for moving scenery)
- special effects (such as, snow, rain).

Was it very different from what is available today?

If it was, do you think the work would have been improved by the new technology?

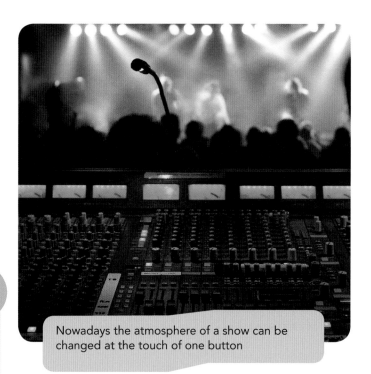

Nowadays the atmosphere of a show can be changed at the touch of one button

Key terms

Jacobean tragedy – a play with a tragic theme written in the Jacobean period (1603 – 1625)

Practitioner – someone who creates performance work and a theoretical context for the work

Choreography – sequences of steps or movements for a dance performance

Form – the design, structure and arrangement of performance work

4.2 Know how to contextualise current practical work

Warm up

You are going to explore the performance material chosen to see how it might be performed to a 21st-century audience.

You could experiment with ideas for showing the work to a contemporary audience through:

- discussion
- practical ideas and exercises
- writing (or recording) your ideas.

4.2.1 Performance material

If you are going to create a modern version of the performance material you have chosen, you should decide how you will update and contextualise the work.

You might use the original performance style or you might experiment with adapting the work to incorporate different performance techniques and genres. For example, by:

- incorporating contemporary dance technique into a classical ballet
- using modern songs and references in a musical from the 1960s
- adapting a **Jacobean tragedy** to include modern references in the text, setting and costumes.

Activity: Experimenting with the work

In workshops and rehearsals, you could try performing the original material using different styles and techniques. These may include:

- using the exercises and approach of a particular **practitioner**, such as Sergei Diaghilev or Peter Brook
- performing in the style of a particular performer, such as Steven Berkoff or Elaine Stritch
- directing or **choreographing** using a certain style or technique, for example naturalism or contemporary
- experimenting with **form** and structure, such as cutting and pasting scenes together from different performance work.

As an example, you could take a scene from a well known classical play, such as *Romeo and Juliet*.

You could make suggestions for modernising costume, setting, props and music and consider updating some of the scenarios and references. How would you make the audience think the play is set now in contemporary Britain, rather than Elizabethan England?

You might choose to modernise some of the language, as we do not usually speak in verse, you might decide to keep the same characters and interaction between them, but make the language more contemporary. Make sure that you understand the meaning of what is being spoken in the original text.

You might wish to keep the idea of speaking in verse, and perform in rhyming couplets (use hip hop as an example).

4.2.2 Context

The artistic director or choreographer will usually provide a concept for the production. That is, the aims and objectives of the work, what they want the audience to see, hear and experience.

The director or choreographer will communicate their ideas to the production team, including the producers, the performers and the designers. Sometimes the artistic vision for a production is developed collaboratively.

4.2.3 Knowledge

In the previous section we explored the various elements of performance that should be considered firstly in the original context, and then in the modern version. These elements include:

- the visual and aural elements of the performance
- the audience and how they interact with the performance

- the social, cultural and historical influences on the performance material
- the impact of economic and technological factors
- the performance practitioners – the writers, directors, choreographers and performers.

When adapting the work for a contemporary audience, you should refer to all of the above.

Assessment activity 5

Create your own context for your performance work. You may have explored your ideas in practical exercises and workshops; this activity can be completed with or without these explorations.

Your version can be imaginary, that is, you have an unlimited budget, any performers you want and it can be produced in any venue.

Or you may wish to make it a more realistic experience, and consider how you would stage it within your local area, with a small budget and a cast of classmates.

The following questions might help you:

1 Do we perform this material as the original audience would have seen it?
2 Does this material have anything to do with modern life?
3 Who is the production aimed at?
4 How do we get an audience to come and see it?
5 How much are we going to modernise the original material?

6 How much should we cut?
7 How far can we take this?

You might also want to consider the following elements in your modern version:

- the performance technique and **conventions**
- the original performance venue compared with your ideal or actual performance venue
- the use of performance space
- setting, costumes and props
- the use of sound, lighting and technology.

Grading tips

M2 You must explain clearly what you want to achieve, demonstrating imagination in your approach to staging.

D2 You should give much detail about your intended update, and be highly creative with your ideas.

PLTS

Planning your modern performance with a cast of classmates will allow you to demonstrate that you are a **team worker**.

Functional skills

English: Taking part in the group discussion will allow you to use your **speaking and listening** skills.

Key term

Conventions – doing things in generally agreed upon ways

4.3 Be able to communicate research findings

Now that you have researched the historical context of the chosen performance piece, and considered how it could be performed to a modern audience, you need to be able to communicate all of the things that you have learned.

If you do research, you carry out an investigation to establish facts and information. Use the following ideas to help you research effectively.

4.3.1 Primary sources

You do the research yourself and make notes and observations. You can do this in a variety of ways: you make observations of the performance style; you visit performance spaces; you interview performers and anyone who can help you with your research – teachers, family and friends or theatre staff.

4.3.2 Secondary sources

You use other people's articles, reviews and thoughts to develop your ideas. You can find material in books, magazines, television programmes articles on the internet, recorded interviews and even your notes taken in class.

4.3.3 Research skills that you can use

- Note taking – knowing how to write in shorthand (create your own) during lectures and demonstrations
- Visual recording – on camera
- Editing the materials you find – isolating suitable clips to include in your presentation
- Analysis – reading research material with set objectives for use
- Compiling – putting together relevant information into one folder
- Structuring – selecting the relevant quotations from interviews and giving them order and status.

4.3.4 Presentation

Your tutor should provide you with the overall theme of your presentation. It could be for a particular purpose (for example, to create programme notes for the performance) or for a particular audience (for example, to create a five minute presentation on the choreographer that will take place before the performance). If in doubt, ask your tutor what is required.

Hints and tips on giving an effective presentation

- A presentation is a performance that needs practice and rehearsal. If you are working with other people, you need to rehearse to ensure you all know your cues and responsibilities (changing slides, giving handouts, introducing each other, and so on). Do not let it look like you have just met each other and this is your first attempt!
- Your voice should be clear, you should sound confident. You might need to do a warm-up beforehand to ensure your performance will be smooth.

You should be following a script, or an outline script, and you can use prompt cards, or use the slides as a prompt.

- Make eye contact with your audience.
- If you do not understand something, find out what it means, or do not use it. It will be obvious to your audience if you are just repeating someone else's words without understanding the meaning, and it could put you in an embarrassing position if you are questioned.
- Tell the audience things they do not know, and do it in an interesting way. Try not to be boring.
- If you are using presentation slides, do not read from them; the slides must be a summary of your speech. They are highlights and should use big, bold font. The audience does not want to read from them. A slide normally takes three to four minutes explanation. Use a maximum of four bullet points. Use words rather than sentences.
- The audience can look at detailed images and diagrams easier on a handout than on a projected screen. Give them copies of the slides if you want them to make notes.
- If you are using DVD extracts and links to the internet for clips, they should be cued and rehearsed. No one wants to wait in a presentation; the audience might lose interest and you could lose the rhythm and flow.

- If you are using aural recordings, ensure sound clips are played at a comfortable volume (especially if you are going to talk whilst they are playing), and that they are introduced properly and rehearsed.

Activity: Practice makes perfect

Practise your presentation skills with friends.

Ask them to give feedback on your presentation skills, and whether they have any suggestions for improvement.

Voice: are you clear enough? Do you say 'er' or 'um' a lot? Are you speaking in a monotone (one tone), which could sound boring?

Movement: do you look comfortable or are you fidgeting with your hands, or with your notes? Are you swaying as you stand?

Medium and format

If your tutor allows you to choose the format you want to use to present your research findings, here are some questions and answers for a variety of presentation methods:

Written document

How much should I write?

You need to provide a comprehensive overview of all aspects of the performance work, including detailed information on the background context of the original work and your ideas for the interpretation. There is no word limit as such; it is more important that you can demonstrate you have thoroughly researched the material, are able to communicate your ideas effectively and clearly, and have applied imagination and creativity to your work.

Should I include illustrations and photos?

Be as creative as you want to be; if the images are relevant and will help to communicate your ideas, include them.

Lecture

Can I use notes?

Yes, you can use prompt notes. You should try to make eye contact with the audience, or at least look at the audience, during the lecture. The notes are reminders of the next topic or the key points you want to make.

How long should the lecture last?

There is no minimum or maximum time length for a lecture, but at this level you could aim to speak for between five and ten minutes depending on the nature of the work and the vocational context.

Demonstration or performance

Can I get others to help me?

Yes, it is fine to have other learners supporting your work.

Do I have to perform, or can I direct or choreograph others?

No, you can do a presentation or lecture and introduce other performers. They might perform an extract that you could pause and discuss with the audience. There are lots of interesting performance ideas to explore in this context.

Discussing ideas for performance

Audio or video presentation

Can I record my work?

Yes, you might make a film on location (for example in a performance space), or record an interview with a performer or designer.

If I use an extract from a performance, how much should I use?

It depends on the nature of the performance, and the context; if you are giving a 15-minute presentation and you use a three-minute clip of a performance, that would be acceptable.

CD-ROM or website/blog

How much information should I include?

There are no limits to the amount of research you should include (for example the blog could contain detailed progress notes on practical experiments and workshops). If you demonstrate good communication skills by including information that is all relevant and clear, you should be able to gain the targeted grading criteria.

Assessment activity 6

Your tutor may instruct you to present your work to a particular type of audience; for example the information is to be included in a theatre programme, or you are to lead a presentation to an invited audience of learners and tutors. If you are not provided with a specific context, present your research findings to an audience in a format of your choice. Make sure that you use primary and secondary sources of information in the development of your work.

Evidence

- your notes for the presentation

Grading tips

M2 You will need to explain clearly what you want to achieve in your research.

D2 You should demonstrate that you have covered the chosen topic thoroughly, and can explain your findings with confidence.

PLTS

By presenting research you have done for this activity, you will be developing your skills as an **independent enquirer**.

Functional skills

English: By presenting your research findings, you will be using your **speaking and listening** skills.

References and sources

Make sure that you provide details of where you found your facts and information. If you fail to do this, you may be accused of plagiarism (passing someone else's ideas off as your own), and will lose marks. Making a note of the references as you go along will make the task easier.

Harvard referencing is the accepted format for providing this information. Follow this structure:

Surname, initial – title of book (publisher, year published), page reference.

Supporting evidence

Putting all your research findings, notes and log book in one folder will help your tutor when assessing your work.

Conclusions

There are a number of conclusions to be drawn, and this process could be completed through discussion with your tutor.

Evaluating the work you are doing (or have completed) can be useful for future projects. It might identify good practice, or stop you from wasting time.

Consider the following questions:

- Has your research been successful? Did it help you understand the performance material?
- Have you met the targeted grading criteria?
- Would your ideas for a contemporary performance be successful? What kind of feedback did you receive?

Sam Cahill
Artistic Director

Sam Cahill is working on a contemporary version of *The Bacchae* by Euripides with Servants of the Light theatre company.

The artistic policy is to bring ancient stories to life, putting a new spin on classical tales, and making them relevant to a young audience.

The ancient Greeks were the masters of storytelling; they used words to conjure up images of unknown lands of gods and monsters, to describe epic battles, and to provide moral lessons to the audience.

We begin every production we do by asking ourselves a series of questions about what we want to achieve, and how we are going to do it.

1   Do you perform this as the original audience would have seen it?

We don't live in a particularly warm climate and most of our performance spaces are indoors. We don't live how the ancient Greeks did, and our cultural references are completely different. To stage the play in 'traditional' costume might distance the audience and they might see it as a museum piece, rather than an exciting and relevant story. Therefore, we are going to update it.

2   Does this story have anything to do with modern life?

There are many similarities between life in 400 BC (when the play was written) and now – although we live in a technologically advanced world, the fundamental issues of being human still remain. We haven't changed much in over 2000 years – we still feel envy, we are still tempted by power and lust, we seek revenge and redemption. These are some of the themes of the play, and these are why we feel it is worth staging.

3   Who is the production aimed at?

We want everyone to see this play, and experience something new, especially young people. We had a lot of ideas – changing the title, where we would perform it, what we can tempt them in with. We had the idea of giving away a free glass of wine with every ticket (Dionysus being the god of wine), but that might not be a good idea for those under 18!

We have tried to communicate in a way that people are used to, so we have designed the ticket to look like a flyer for a gig, and we advertise the show using flyposters, the ones you see on abandoned buildings. We try to keep the costs as low as we can for tickets, and we offer special two for one deals.

5 How much are we going to modernise the original play?

In the play Dionysus is a powerful, enigmatic, attractive young man/god, but quite camp and androgynous, too, so he isn't threatening to women and acts as a catalyst for them to go wild. So we have updated him to be a pop /film star kind of character; the action is set in a night club in Brighton on a Saturday night, but it could be any town. He is doing a PA (personal appearance) and the Bacchae are his fans.

Music plays a big part in the show. It is a powerful method of bringing people together and helps them lose their inhibitions (the ancient Greeks knew this very well). There is a constant rhythm, but not in a way that detracts from the storytelling.

There are moments when it goes absolutely crazy, and it is really exciting to see the reaction from the audience.

Euripides' storytelling is very powerful and we didn't want to lose it; the characters are narrating most of the time, with long passages of description of action that has happened, so we have some of the scenes being re-enacted around/ below them. We also use technology as much as we can, and try to be as innovative as we can be with our budget and resources. We create backdrops by using projected images and films, which we made ourselves.

6 How far can we take this?

We want to push the boundaries of what is accepted as theatre. We use modern clothing, we set it in a nightclub, we make it a promenade performance, with the audience moving around the action. We use a box theatre, a small adaptable space. No seats, with audience required to move, walk and dance.

There are lots of opportunities for the performers and audience to interact and use the same spaces.

Think about it!

- What are the challenges of getting young people to watch a performance of a historical play in a traditional set?
- How much do you think it matters that a performance is presented in an unusual space. Does that change the message of the performance in any way?

Just checking

1 Do you understand the historical background of the original performance material? When researching your work, make sure you use as many sources of information as you can, including: textbooks on theories and practice; the original playtext or score; information on the playwright, director, musical director, choreographer, performers and musicians; performance programmes; critical reviews.

2 What was the stimulus or spark for the original work? Understanding the social, historical and cultural background for the original performance work can have a significant impact on your appreciation of the work. Find out as much as you can about why the work was created, and who it was aimed at.

3 What were the performance conditions for the original material? If it is possible to visit the original performance space, or a similar venue, it might help you understand the performance conditions better. It could also help you with your modern interpretation.

4 What changes have you made to the original work to make it suitable for a modern audience? Have you experimented with different styles of performance? Have you modernised the language or adapted the work to include modern references or sound? If you perform your modernised work to an audience, try to get feedback on what they think is successful, and what may need further work.

5 Can you communicate your research findings effectively? It is important that you feel comfortable presenting your work to your audience, so take time to choose a suitable style and format for your presentation. If you are doing a presentation, why not practise in front of your friends and family? Ask them for honest feedback as to how you might improve your presentation technique.

edexcel ▦

Assignment tips

- Research the background of the performance piece thoroughly.
- You must make decisions about what research is valuable, and what information is irrelevant and can be discarded.
- Use your imagination to put yourself in the position of an audience member, watching the performance piece in the original context.
- Find out what it was like to be a performer in the original work.
- Decide on the important elements to include in your critique of the performance material.
- Be creative with your modern interpretation ideas, and consider what a contemporary audience will want to see.
- Present your ideas and findings in the clearest way you can.

5&7 Rehearsing & Performing

All professional companies go through intensive rehearsal processes before showing their work to audiences.

This unit will guide you through the process of taking part in a professional production, from an initial casting and audition through to the curtain call. It will focus on how to contribute effectively to the rehearsal process; how to select and apply appropriate rehearsal and performance skills; how to develop self-discipline and a professional attitude, and how to perform with skill, confidence and commitment.

You will learn and develop a professional attitude that will include time management, personal responsibility, collaboration and negotiation with other company members, and exploratory work outside of rehearsals.

The experience you have when studying this unit should reflect the working environment of a professional company rehearsing towards public performance. You will have an opportunity to use and develop the skills and performance techniques developed in other units.

You will be assessed on your development as a performer; there is no expectation that you will be ready to perform from the start of the project.

Learning outcomes

After completing this unit you should be able to achieve the following learning outcomes:

Unit 5: Rehearsing for Performance

1. Be able to contribute to the rehearsal process
2. Be able to select and apply appropriate rehearsal and performance skills
3. Be able to progress rehearsal and performance skills/techniques in response to feedback and evaluation.

Unit 7: Performing to an Audience

1. Be able to undertake a performance role for a live audience
2. Be able to interpret performance material for an audience
3. Be able to perform a role, communicating meaning to an audience
4. Be able to work with discipline within an ensemble.

Assessment and grading criteria

This table shows you what you must do in order to achieve a pass, merit or distinction, and where you can find activities in this book to help you.

To achieve a **pass** grade the evidence must show that you are able to:	To achieve a **merit** grade the evidence must show that, in addition to the pass criteria, you are able to:	To achieve a **distinction** grade the evidence must show that, in addition to the pass and merit criteria, you are able to:
Unit 5: Rehearsing for Performance		
P1 identify key rehearsal tasks appropriate to the role **Assessment activity 1 page 72** **Assessment activity 2 page 74** **Assessment activity 3 page 76** **Assessment activity 5 page 80**	**M1** describe and prioritise key rehearsal tasks appropriate to the role **Assessment activity 1 page 72** **Assessment activity 2 page 74** **Assessment activity 3 page 76** **Assessment activity 5 page 80**	**D1** explain and prioritise key rehearsal tasks, with insight, foresight and confidence **Assessment activity 1 page 72** **Assessment activity 2 page 74** **Assessment activity 3 page 76** **Assessment activity 5 page 80**
P2 complete designated rehearsal tasks, so that a valid contribution is made to the rehearsal process **Assessment activity 2 page 74** **Assessment activity 3 page 76** **Assessment activity 5 page 80**	**M2** complete designated rehearsal tasks with attention to detail, so that a significant contribution is made to the rehearsal process **Assessment activity 2 page 74** **Assessment activity 3 page 76** **Assessment activity 5 page 80**	**D2** complete designated rehearsal tasks with considerable attention to detail, so that an outstanding contribution is made to the rehearsal process **Assessment activity 2 page 74** **Assessment activity 3 page 76** **Assessment activity 5 page 80**
P3 develop and apply research for the role **Assessment activity 4 page 78** **Assessment activity 5 page 80**	**M3** develop and apply research for the role, employing findings constructively and progressively during the rehearsal process **Assessment activity 4 page 78** **Assessment activity 5 page 80**	**D3** develop and apply research for the role, employing findings in a constructive, progressive and imaginative way during the rehearsal process **Assessment activity 4 page 78** **Assessment activity 5 page 80**
P4 select and use rehearsal and performance skills appropriate to the role **Assessment activity 3 page 76** **Assessment activity 5 page 80**	**M4** select and employ rehearsal and performance skills appropriate to the role, in an effective, controlled and considered way **Assessment activity 3 page 76** **Assessment activity 5 page 80**	**D4** select and employ rehearsal and performance skills appropriate to the role, demonstrating strong command and insight **Assessment activity 3 page 76** **Assessment activity 5 page 80**
P5 develop and improve rehearsal and performance skills in response to feedback. **Assessment activity 3 page 80** **Assessment activity 5 page 81**	**M5** demonstrate commitment to the development and improvement of rehearsal and performance skills with positive and constructive responses to feedback. **Assessment activity 3 page 80** **Assessment activity 5 page 81**	**D5** demonstrate outstanding commitment to the development and improvement of rehearsal and performance skills, with detailed responses to feedback. **Assessment activity 3 page 80** **Assessment activity 5 page 81**
Unit 7: Performing to an Audience		
P1 apply the required performance skills appropriately, with some attention to detail **Assessment activity 8 page 84**	**M1** apply the required performance skills in a controlled and considered way **Assessment activity 8 page 84**	**D1** apply the required performance skills showing a strong command of these skills, handled with confidence, ease and fluency **Assessment activity 8 page 84**
P2 present an interpretation of a role that is considered, logical and consistent **Assessment activity 8 page 84**	**M2** present an interpretation of a role that is thoughtfully and carefully considered, showing creativity and spontaneity **Assessment activity 8 page 84**	**D2** present an interpretation of a role showing energy, commitment, insight and confidence, making a significant impression in the overall performance **Assessment activity 8 page 84**

P3 perform a role, communicating meaning to an audience **Assessment activity 8 page 84**	**M3** perform a role, communicating meaning to an audience in an integrated, responsive way, maintaining focus and engagement with the work and audience **Assessment activity 8 page 84**	**D3** perform a role, communicating meaning to an audience with consistent focus and engagement, showing imagination, flair and commitment to the work **Assessment activity 8 page 84**
P4 demonstrate self-discipline during the performance process. **Assessment activity 3 page 76** **Assessment activity 7 page 83**	**M4** demonstrate consistent self-discipline during the performance process. **Assessment activity 3 page 76** **Assessment activity 7 page 83**	**D4** demonstrate a high standard of self-discipline throughout the performance process. **Assessment activity 3 page 76** **Assessment activity 7 page 83**

How you will be assessed

This unit will be assessed through an internal assignment that will be designed and marked by the tutors at your centre. You will be assessed on your rehearsal and performance skills. You will need to show that you are fully committed to all rehearsal and performance tasks.

Kaysha, 18-year-old performing arts learner

Our performance company staged a production of *The Wizard of Oz*. We took the performance on tour to primary schools.

I was cast as the Wicked Witch of the West. I had to do an audition to get the role – I was up against six other girls (and one boy!), so I had to prepare well. I really liked the role, especially as I had recently seen *Wicked* the musical – I realised that the character of Elphaba is quite complex.

We had to create a rehearsal schedule for the group, and then one for ourselves. It was a ten-week schedule, and we were rehearsing every day, and some evenings. When it got to production week, we spent about 12 hours a day in the theatre. It was exhausting and hard work.

The first performance was good, but there were a few hitches – the Tin Man's arm fell off and he couldn't stick it back on again; Toto got lost backstage (he was hidden under a blanket) and there were major issues with the finale. We had to work hard the next day, to tighten up some of the scenes, as it looked sloppy in places.

By the third performance, we all felt that the show was finally working, and we got a standing ovation! Everyone performed with real dedication and purpose. The feedback was brilliant. The kids really liked it, especially in the scenes where they joined in as Munchkins.

Over to you

- What skills do you think you need to be able to rehearse effectively as part of a performance group?
- If you were asked to take part in a long running show as a performer, what difficulties do you think you might face?

5.1 Be able to contribute to the rehearsal process

Professional production

Think back to the last professional performance you went to see; it could have been a play, a musical or a dance piece.

If you have the opportunity, look at the performance programme, note the size of the company, including the cast, the artistic team, the technical team, and front of house.

Think about the overall quality of the production, focusing on the performance skills. Did anyone impress you? What kind of skills and techniques were demonstrated? How long do you think you would need to rehearse?

Over to you

Make a list of things you would need to do if you had been involved in this production. Here are some suggestions:

- Learn the material: the movements, the songs or words
- Develop and practise new skills
- Work as an ensemble
- Own the stage: perform and communicate with confidence
- Meet a high standard of performance in every show.

Creating a performance/ production company

To meet the requirements of Unit 5: Rehearsing for Performance and Unit 7: Performing to an Audience, you must be involved in the development of a large-scale production.

Your tutor(s) will decide how best to organise the production, but will probably create and run a performance company. The performance company should emulate a professional company in terms of structure, personnel, responsibilities and timescales. You will need to consider the following:

What roles are available to tutors and learners? Possible roles might include:

- tutor as director/choreographer/producer
- hiring artistic director/choreographer in residence for the rehearsal period
- learners responsible for directing/choreographing the show.

Do you have a performance budget? You may need money for:

- using a suitable performance venue
- acquiring performing rights or a license
- hiring, buying or making costumes and props
- designing and building the set and furniture
- writing, creating and obtaining the rights for music
- technical and production support
- publicity, marketing and front of house requirements.

Activity: What's your name?

Professional companies have an identity; a name that describes their work, their status and their approach. Think about the kind of identity you could adopt. It might reflect your centre, the work you are doing, or the kind of performers you are.

A group or company name can instil harmony and focus, together with the ethos and artistic direction of your work. Referring to the name throughout the production process can help refocus the work.

Artistic policy

Artistic policy defines what you want to achieve through your performance. You might say, for example, that you want your work to be:

- entertaining
- instructing or educating, for example TiE and outreach
- targeting a particular type of audience
- performed at a particular time of year, or time of day, such as summer solstice, or for a religious celebration
- performed in a particular venue (perhaps special or unusual) or taken on tour concerned with the work of a particular artist, playwright, choreographer, director or performer
- contributing to larger project, such as an arts festival
- offering equal opportunities to all performers (cast on talent and ability, not looks).

Selecting performance material

Your performance material could be any, or a combination of the following:

- An interpretation of an existing play, musical, ballet or dance piece: you might be given the opportunity to make a decision, or choose from a selection. In most cases, your tutor(s) will decide because there are certain elements that must be taken into consideration, such as the size of the group, the performance budget and available performance venue(s)
- An adaptation of existing work: this might be an adaptation of a film, a television show or a book
- A devised piece: the work might be in response to stimuli, such as a piece of music, a painting, a poem or a news story
- A compilation of extracts from one genre or mixture of work
- A variety show: including circus performance, stand-up, mime, singing or talent show.

Activity: The performance company

As a group, decide on the following:

- The purpose of the performance
- Company identity and name
- Company members, roles and responsibilities
- Artistic policy
- Performers' contract
- Logo designed for publicity, programme, T-shirts, and so on.

Casting

The casting of a production is very important; if you are telling a story, you will not want the audience to be confused by 'miscasting' a role. If the performance is a showcase for demonstrating particular skills, you will want the audience to be impressed, not misled.

A vocational training course like a BTEC can offer opportunities to those who may not get them in the professional industry. When casting, you need to find a balance between what is fair and offers equal opportunities, and what would confuse or affect the audience, experience/understanding of the work.

Activity: Defining your role

It is a good idea to define what is required for each role. Take each character and work out what the performer will need to do.

Example: Sally Bowles, Cabaret

- Lead vocals in four songs
- Lead dancer in four routines
- Acts in ten scripted scenes

There is a requirement to perform some scenes in revealing costumes; also, a romantic scene with another character.

If the analysis of the roles is provided before the show is cast, it will help in preparing audition material and deciding on the suitability of the role.

If you are working in a large group, you could:

- choose a performance that offers a lot of roles
- cast more than one person in a particular role
- have two casts; for example, cast A and cast B (this can help in rehearsals as there will be an understudy in case of absence, and the two performers can help each other develop the role).

Auditioning

Advertising the roles available imitates real practice in the performing arts industry. Performers identify the role(s) they want to audition for.

Auditioning can be time/resource-consuming for the tutors and panel and potentially stressful for the performers (some will not get the parts they auditioned for).

Those auditioning will need to prepare a speech, dance or song (which could be an extract from the chosen performance work), or prepare their own choice of audition material.

Auditioning offers further opportunities to prepare and practise audition speeches.

See Project 10: Moving On, for more guidance on auditioning, page 295.

Workshops

A workshop can consist of a variety of exercises and activities, such as taking part in exploratory exercises, improvising and performing different characters, dance styles, songs or performance styles.

Workshops can give the director/choreographer an opportunity to experiment with casting, use different performers for the same role, and improvise with themes, characterisation, performance styles and music.

Workshop performers might be asked to develop work. For example, they might be choreographed in a number of different dances, or rehearse and learn a short extract or a set dance.

Workshops can give the participants a clearer understanding of the performance work, provide focus and direction for the performance style, and challenge preconceived ideas about the work.

Blind casting

Blind casting is a radical method of casting, with roles cast at random (for example, performer names are pulled out of a hat).

Blind casting offers equal opportunities to learners. It offers the chance to 'stretch and challenge' some learners, who may rise to the challenge offered in the particular performance role.

There is the chance that blind casting could lead to confusing the audience. Some performers may be intimidated with the level of responsibility provided, or there may be missed opportunities to showcase particular individuals' skills.

Multi-casting

Multi-casting is allocating more than one performer per role.

This is useful for sharing the responsibilities of research, working together to develop and rehearse the role, providing understudies. It is especially useful in a big group (performances of the same show with different casts).

Activity: Casting your show

Make a list of the positive and negative aspects of blind casting and multi-casting for you as a performer. Which type of casting do you think your group should use?

5.1.1 Requirements of the rehearsal process

Blocking/positioning

Defining the performance space, entrances and exits, audience space and 'back stage' is an important starting point in the rehearsal process. The performance space will need to be 'marked out' (normally by the deputy stage manager – DSM).

Decisions will need to be made on the position of the setting, entrances and exits, stage furniture, and so on.

Blocking tends to refer to the general positioning and movement within the scene: entrances and exits of the performers, relationship of performers to audience and positioning on the stage.

The DSM normally records blocking and positioning decisions that are made during rehearsals. As a performer, you should also keep a record. It can be helpful to have your own records if a lot of decisions are being made, and you are rehearsing alone.

Off book or learnt material rehearsals

In acting and musical theatre performance, it is difficult to physically explore the material with a script in your hand; therefore it is useful to learn your lines as soon as you can.

Some performers like to learn the material with all the emotion and understanding cemented; most tend to learn the lines and moves and then focus on developing the role.

Running scenes or sequences

Rehearsing scenes in isolation can be confusing and misleading for the performers and director/choreographer. Once a number of scenes and sequences have been blocked and rehearsed, it is helpful to do a 'run' in order to get a better understanding of how they work together. Issues with continuity, storytelling, character development, and set and costume changes can be identified and amended.

Final rehearsal period

This is the time to finish, polish and refine performance work. It may include costume fittings, working with dummy props (if the actual props are not ready or are hired for a limited period), and rehearsing on set.

A non-dress run gives the director/choreographer a chance to view the performance as a whole.

In musical theatre, the singers sing with the orchestra. This rehearsal is called the **Sitzprobe**. The focus is on ensuring the two groups are integrated and work together successfully.

Key terms

Sitzprobe – a seated rehearsal where the singers sing with the orchestra, focusing attention on integrating the two groups

Technical rehearsals

The technical (lighting and sound) elements of the performance are plotted and set. These rehearsals will normally take place in the performance venue (unless touring).

If the production has lots of lighting and sound cues, the technical rehearsal may take a long time to perfect. Lights have to be set and focused, lighting states created and sequences programmed.

Technical rehearsals can test the patience of the most dedicated performer; there will probably not be an opportunity to perform the piece as a whole, nor run a scene or sequence in its entirety. The technical crew will require the performers to hit cue changes rather than running the show; time will be spent ensuring the lighting states are right (so that the performers are lit according to the needs of the director or the projection cues are set), the sound levels are suitable (so that the audience can hear and understand the amplified sound), and the technical operators can meet the cues. Performers must appreciate how difficult technical rehearsals can be and should prepare themselves mentally and physically. It can be a good opportunity to revise your lines and movements, motivations or characterisation. You might also find that watching the process of bringing the production elements together enhances your understanding of performance.

Dress rehearsals

These are performances as they will be shown to the audience, that is, on set, in costume and with full technical support. These rehearsals usually avoid any stopping and starting unless absolutely necessary – for example a safety issue. The creative team takes notes to give to the performers and production team at the end of the rehearsal.

Preview performance

You may get the opportunity to do a preview performance. In professional theatre this is a performance(s) offered to the audience at a cheaper cost, and is an opportunity to iron out any problems with the show, whether they are technical or performance-based.

Previews are followed by press night (when the show is reviewed by professional critics).

Other requirements of the rehearsal process

Other deadlines to consider for your show include:

- set and props designed and built or hired, installed and tested
- costumes designed and made, bought or hired, delivered and fitted
- sound and music designed or sourced and delivered
- programme designed, written and printed
- performance venue(s) booked and prepared
- publicity materials designed and distributed
- tickets sold and distributed
- front of house team hired and trained
- technical team hired and trained.

Assessment activity 1

Unit 5 **BTEC**

The timescale for your rehearsal period will probably be determined by your tutor(s). There will be important factors to consider, such as the budget (how much money you have to stage the work), and the availability of the venue(s) for your performance(s).

Once the timescale is provided, for example 15 hours of rehearsing per week for eight weeks, and one week of performances, you will need to decide and plan the following:

- location(s) of the rehearsal space(s)
- preparatory rehearsals, such as, read-through(/s), exploratory workshops, 'on the floor' workshops, preparatory visits, research and presentations

- call times for individual and group rehearsals
- performer deadlines for research, workshops, read-through(s) and exploratory work.

Evidence

- a rehearsal schedule

Grading tips

M You should provide detailed information on the tasks for each rehearsal.

D You must explain why you prioritised particular tasks and deadlines for the group.

PLTS

Creating and contributing to a rehearsal schedule will use your skills as a **self-manager**.

Functional skills

English: By producing a rehearsal schedule, you will be using your **writing** skills.

Here is an example of a rehearsal schedule.

Rehearsal details	Location	Week/date/day	Times
Acting Workshop	Hall	1 22/2 Wednesday	9am–12.30pm
Singing Workshop	Hall	1 23/2 Thursday	1pm–4.30pm
Dance Workshop	Hall	1 24/2 Friday	9am–12.30pm
Auditions	Drama studio	1 27/2 Monday	2pm–6pm
Auditions	Drama studio	2 1/3 Wednesday	9am–12.30pm
Auditions	Drama studio	2 2/3 Thursday	1pm–4.30pm
Act I: cast	Hall	3 6/3 Monday	2pm–6pm
Act I: cast	Hall	3 8/3 Wednesday	9am–12.30pm
Act II: cast	Hall	3 9/3 Thursday	1pm–4.30pm
Prod meeting (design): cast, crew	Hall	3 10/3 Friday	9am–11.30am
Act II: cast	Dance studio	4 13/3 Monday	2pm–6pm
Act I: Scenes 1, 2 leads	Drama studio	4 15/3 Wednesday	9am–12pm
Act I: Scenes 1, 2 leads	Dance studio	4 16/3 Thursday	1pm–4pm
Prod meeting: cast, crew	Hall	4 17/3 Friday	9am–12.30pm
Act II: Scene 3 leads	Drama studio	5 20/3 Monday	2pm–6pm
Act II: Scene 3 see info board for cast details	Drama studio	5 22/3 Wednesday	9am–12.30pm
Act II: Scene 4 leads	Drama studio	5 23/3 Thursday	1pm–5pm
Prod meeting (costumes): cast, crew	Hall	5 24/3 Friday	9am–12.30pm
Act II: Scene 4	Hall	6 27/3 Monday	2pm–5.30pm
Act I: cast	Hall	6 29/3 Wednesday	9am–12pm
Act I: see info board	Dance studio	6 30/3 Thursday	1pm–4.30pm
Prod meeting: crew	Hall	6 31/3 Friday	9am–12.30pm
Act II: cast	Drama studio	7 3/4 Monday	2pm–5.30pm
Act II: cast	Dance studio	7 5/4 Wednesday	9am–12pm
Run full show: cast, crew	Hall	7 6/4 Thursday	1pm–4.30pm
Prod meeting (set, props): cast, crew	Hall	7 7/4 Friday	9am–12.30pm
Run full show: cast, crew	Venue	8 10/4 Monday	1pm–10.30pm
Tech: cast, crew	Venue	8 11/4 Tuesday	9am–6pm
Tech: cast, crew	Venue	8 12/4 Wednesday	10am–6pm
Dress: cast, crew	Venue	8 14/4 Friday	10am–10.30pm
Performance: cast, crew	Venue	9 17/4 Monday	1pm–9.30pm (perfs: 3pm, 7.30pm)
Performance: cast, crew	Venue	9 18/4 Tuesday	1pm–10.30pm (perf: 7.30pm)
Performance: cast, crew	Venue	9 19/4 Wednesday	5pm–10.30pm (perf: 7.30pm)
Performance: cast, crew	Venue	9 19/4 Thursday	1pm–10.30pm (perfs: 3pm, 7.30pm)
Performance: cast, crew	Venue	9 21/4 Saturday	1pm–10.30pm (perfs: 3pm, 7.30pm)

5.1.2 Exploration of rehearsal material

As a performer, you must contribute to the development of the performance work. Working in collaboration with the production and performance team, you should make decisions on how to develop the performance material. Here are some examples of how you might contribute and explore through rehearsing:

Experimenting with ideas, material and rehearsal techniques

Experimenting in rehearsals can involve: trying out new styles of performance; developing new working relationships with others; finding new ways to explore performance material; taking performance risks – making mistakes and getting things wrong (in order to get things right).

Elaborating meaning

If you are using scripted or published material, you will be required to understand and interpret the intentions of the people who created the work originally. Bringing ideas to life and making them accessible to the audience is a fundamental element in the rehearsal process.

Developing performance material

There are times during rehearsal when the work needs to develop beyond how movements are blocked; the performers are responsible for following instructions of the director/choreographer to bring the work to life, and for showing initiative and developing work themselves. This might mean finding an appropriate piece of music to accompany the scene, or delivering the lines with a new motivation.

Evaluating the process

You should update your performer's log regularly during the rehearsal process. You will receive feedback from your tutor(s) and your peers, but most importantly you will be actively involved in charting the progress and development of your work.

PLTS

By producing your own rehearsal schedule, you will be developing your skills as a **self-manager**.

Functional skills

English: By completing a character profile sheet, you will be using your **writing** skills.

Assessment activity 2

Unit 5 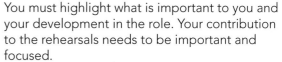 **BTEC**

As well as the group rehearsals, you must organise your own preparation and practice time to develop your performance work.

Produce your own individual rehearsal schedule. You will have to set your own deadlines and prioritise your tasks, according to your performance role. Your tasks could include:

- preparatory research, including skill development
- learning performance material, including lines and movements
- practising skills and technique, such as, accent, singing style, movement, physical expression and using specialist props.

Evidence

- regular updates in your performer's log

- improvements in your performance skills and technique

Grading tips

You must highlight what is important to you and your development in the role. Your contribution to the rehearsals needs to be important and focused.

Grading tips

You should confidently prioritise the tasks that will have a significant impact on your improvement. Your contribution to the rehearsal process needs to be thorough and extremely positive.

Here is an example of an individual's rehearsal schedule. Josie has the role of Ilse in *Spring Awakening*. There are two casts: Josie is in cast B. As well as performing, Josie is the deputy stage manager for the production.

Josie's individual responsibilities

Background research:
- Spring Awakening productions (reviews, programme notes)
- Life for teenagers in 19th-century Germany/Bohemian lifestyle.

Text/song analysis:
- annotate script.

Character development: work with Katrin (cast A)
- character decisions
- observations
- present character analysis to group
- keep performer's log up-to-date.

Character profile

Singing rehearsals with Katrin:
- 'The Dark I Know Well', 'Don't Do Sadness', 'Song of Purple Summer'
- Choreograph songs.

Singing rehearsals with Katrin, Mike, Jon, Liza, Mel, Sasha, Corey

Blocking/off book explorations

DSM responsibilities:
- marking out
- blocking notes
- prompting.

Production meetings:
- As DSM – prepare notes and updates
- Write notes during meetings
- Complete meeting action points.

Lead vocal warm ups rehearsal Weeks 4 and 8.

Lead physical warm ups rehearsal Week 6 and dress.

Lead in four songs, ensemble/chorus in six songs.

Write biography for programme notes.

Final rehearsals:
- Dress
- Techs.

Eight performances.

The rehearsal space

Rules must be set regarding behaviour and conduct during the rehearsal process. General rules of conduct might include:

- Arriving at rehearsals ten minutes before starting time

- Following instructions
- Showing respect to other performers: for example, keeping noise to a minimum during rehearsals.

It is very important to observe health and safety requirements in the rehearsal and performance space. These might include:

- Removing jewellery during rehearsals of physical performance
- Not eating or drinking in the rehearsal and performance space (which could cause spillages)
- Ensuring the performance space is kept clear of bags, coats, and so on
- Wearing suitable clothing and ensuring hair is tied back during physical performance
- Not touching or using electrical equipment unless instructed to do so
- Not playing or tampering with the set, costumes or props.

A performer's contract

You might create a performer's contract to ensure that all members of the performance company understand the importance of cooperation, respect and focus during the rehearsal period.

Here are some examples of a performer's roles and responsibilities during the rehearsal period and performance run.

- Self-discipline and time management: punctual, excellent attendance record, meets deadlines, keeps to schedules, takes part in warm-ups, and occasionally leads
- Energy: focused and ready to work, determined to progress and succeed, contributes to development of the work through creative input
- Professional manner: supportive of others, provides constructive feedback, positive attitude
- Health and safety conscious: dresses and behaves appropriately, keeps the rehearsal space clear of clutter
- Takes responsibility: will lead in directing/choreographing, volunteers to help others, responsible for creating and leading a warm-up, lets others lead and does not dominate.

Assessment activity 3

Unit 5  P1 M1 D1 P2 M2 D2 P4 M4 D4

Unit 7 P4 M4 D4

 BTEC

Create your own performer's contract for your production. As a group, discuss this in your first production meeting. You could ask everyone to agree to it, and sign it.

It might help to offer an incentive or a punishment if a performer breaks the rules of the contract; for instance, they might have to put the chairs away at the end of the rehearsal.

Evidence

• performer's contract

Grading tips Unit 5/Unit 7

M1 M2 M4 You should make a positive and effective contribution to the creation of the contract and to following the contract in practice.

D1 D2 D4 You should propose and fulfil effective rehearsal and performance skills that have a positive effect on the group work.

PLTS

Creating your performer's contract will demonstrate your skills as an **effective participator**.

Functional skills

English: Discussing your performer's contract with your group will allow you to practise your **speaking and listening** skills.

Case study: Mark, 17-year-old, acting learner

We started on a really exciting project – we were going to stage a production of *Marat/Sade*, do a small tour, then take it to the Edinburgh Festival in the summer.

When we started rehearsals, it became obvious that some people were not taking it as seriously as others – turning up late to rehearsals, not paying attention, messing around, missing deadlines. So we decided to make a performer's contract, which stated that if someone breaks the rules, they would be handed a yellow card. If you got three yellows, you would get a red, and would be thrown out of the show. It seemed a bit harsh, but if someone had a good excuse, they wouldn't get a yellow.

It was a really good thing to do – when people got a yellow, they realised how easy it would be to get kicked out, and made them take the rehearsals much more seriously.

As well as having the card system, we also had rewards – we did things outside of rehearsals as a group, like we went bowling, and became much closer because of it.

5.1.3 Research

The performance work you choose to do must include elements of research. The research you undertake can be applied at any point in the rehearsal process and development of the work.

Informing performance material

You should research and investigate the following:

- the historical, cultural and social context of the performance work
- theatre and/or dance practitioners (ideas, rehearsal practice, performance techniques)
- playwrights and/or songwriters, choreographers and/or theatre directors
- the themes and issues of the particular piece
- professional performers, organisations and groups, such as, charities, women's groups and other support groups.

Investigating social, cultural and historical contexts

Look at Unit 4 Historical Context of Performance page 41 for ideas and suggestions on researching the background of performance work.

Identify procedures and rehearsal techniques practised by professional practitioners

You can research the work of a current (or historical) practitioner or company. For example, you might investigate the rehearsal processes of theatre director Simon McBurney and use his ideas and techniques to develop your work. Alternatively, you could find out about the choreographer Martha Graham and incorporate some of her style and technique into your own work.

See Unit 14 Musical Theatre Performance, page 87, Unit 38 Dance Performance, page 161 and Project 6: Performing in a Contemporary Play, page 245 for more information on individual practitioners and techniques.

Sharing, application and review of research findings

When you have researched your chosen area, you should share this information with your group. For example, if you have researched the skills and techniques of a chosen practitioner, you could:

- practise and rehearse using the skills and techniques found
- keep notes in your rehearsal/performer's log of your findings, your experiments with style and content, and how others have responded.

Case study: Vicky Featherstone, Artistic Director

Vicky Featherstone is the Artistic Director of the National Theatre of Scotland.

The company created a performance piece titled *365* in 2008. The work was based on real experiences of young people in care.

The actors were required to research and create a back story for the characters, including information on their childhood, where they were born, schools they attended and what family contact they had.

Vicky is sometimes cynical about the process of developing a back story. She says that if the audience are not going to know it, why waste time on it? However, for this play she thought it was important to create characters that were really active, and reactive in the moment, in a very extreme way.

The director and actors conducted interviews with young people who had lived in care homes and invited them to workshops. Actors produced a lot of research themselves and the director created an atmosphere that allowed experimentation with ideas.

Assessment activity 4

Unit 5 · P3 M3 D3

Have clear objectives for your research. For example:

- I want to find out about the political background of Dario Fo.
- I need to investigate the performance work of Akram Khan.

Once you have conducted your research, think about how you can use it. For example:

- It might provide your group with a greater understanding of the work.
- You can use some of the techniques in your rehearsals.
- You can give your audience some background information in the programme notes.

If you are going to use an existing work(s), try to experience a performance of it.

If you are lucky, there might be an opportunity to see a live production of the show.

You may be able to get a recording of the play (or extracts), on DVD/video, or TV or radio recordings of the work.

The National Theatre has recordings of all productions shown in the three theatres for the past few years; you can book a place to view chosen work.

The V&A Museum has a performance section including materials and recordings for viewing, and lots of online resources.

Explore websites of actors and performance companies. Youtube is an excellent source of excerpts and clips.

If you are devising or adapting work, find examples of performers or performance companies who have successfully attempted this kind of activity. Watch their work, make notes on what decisions they made, what they created and changed, and how they did it.

Evidence

- collate your findings in a performer's log

Grading tips

M3 You will keep notes in your performer's log, highlighting how your research findings could be used in the rehearsal process.

D3 You will keep your performer's log up-to-date with regular details of how your research has developed and enhanced the performance work.

PLTS

By planning and carrying out research into skills required for rehearsal, you will be developing your skills as an **independent enquirer**.

Functional skills

ICT: By exploring, extracting and assessing the relevance of information from websites which contain significant creative ideas, images or text, you will be using your skills of **finding and selecting information** using ICT.

You might find that your local library has a helpful DVD section

5.2 Be able to select and apply appropriate rehearsal and performance skills

5.2.1 Performance skills

Unit 5: Rehearsing for Performance and Unit 7: Performing to an Audience give you the opportunity to demonstrate the skills you have acquired and developed in other units, for example contemporary dance, classical theatre performance and singing techniques for actors and dancers.

Communication

As well as vocal, physical, creative and intellectual skills, you must show you can communicate, work as part of a team, and collaborate with others to develop a performance. Make sure you are able to:

- respect others in production meetings and rehearsals
- take responsibility for the development of your own role
- manage discussions to reach agreements, achieve results and progress, and develop work
- communicate effectively with fellow performers, production team and crew
- maintain a professional attitude throughout the creative process.

When working with the director/choreographer, you will:

- share creative ideas
- listen to instructions
- work as part of a team
- show patience in the development of work
- be reliable and responsible.

5.2.2 Rehearsal skills

You are part of a team, and being a reliable and cooperative member of the company is very important. Others will be relying on you to meet all your deadlines, as they may not be able to progress further. For example, you are going to rehearse a very physical scene that will take a lot of time to perfect. All the performers must practise the moves carefully, repeatedly, over a long rehearsal period. All performers must learn their words and moves before

the rehearsal, as it will be impossible to develop physical movements. What problems could occur if one of the learners does not learn the lines or moves? What effect could it have on the rehearsal schedule, or on the morale of the other performers?

Personal management

When working as part of a team, being able to manage yourself is essential to making a positive contribution. Personal management skills include the following:

- Attending and being punctual (on time) for rehearsals
- Being focused and ready to work during rehearsals
- Taking part in warm-ups, relaxation/vocal/musical/breathing exercises (as appropriate)
- Meeting specific deadlines: research, learning lines and moves
- Physical preparation: a healthy diet, avoiding late nights, regular exercise
- Mental preparation: focus, concentration, determination, a positive attitude, group spirit, self-discipline, not being afraid to make mistakes
- When working with others: being trustworthy and supportive (some performances can deal with personal and potentially uncomfortable subject matter – a reliable and cooperative team can be very helpful to a performer), helping others, communicating ideas effectively
- Completing a performer's log: charting progress, planning, capturing important information and guidance from others, recording own thoughts
- Responsibilities: you may be required to find or look after your own costume and props, apply your own make-up, set your own props (if required)
- Health and safety: behaving in a responsible manner in rehearsals and performances.

Working as part of a group in a large-scale production requires each performer to have certain skills. Here is some guidance to help you:

- Be able to accept direction; listening to the ideas and guidance of others (and put into practice), requires trust and patience on your part.

- Show creative flexibility and generosity: there may be times when ideas (even the ones you think have potential), cannot be used or are not considered. Due to the flowing nature of creative work, you will have to accept that not all ideas can be developed, and good ideas are not always acknowledged.

- Use rehearsal exercises and technique effectively: throughout the rehearsal process there will be opportunities to explore the text, characterisation and relationships (depending on your performance material) using particular exercises and techniques. You must demonstrate that you can pay attention and respond to the scenarios, techniques and developments you are asked to take part in. Do not be afraid to ask for clarification; sometimes you might need a demonstration before you grasp it.

- Be supportive within the group: make yourself heard, but make sure everyone gets a chance to express how they feel. When working in a big group, it is easy to lose some opinions when rehearsals are developing at a quick pace. Take time to give everyone a chance to have an input.

- Responding positively to feedback: it is not always easy to take criticism, especially if you have been working hard. Learn to take feedback as it will help you develop your work. Trust the director/choreographer to help you; they are acting as the audience, describing to you what the audience will experience.

Memorising

The size and scale of the production can mean that the actor is required to remember a lot of information, such as:

- the lines for their character, and other characters
- their positions on stage, blocking, dance or fight sequences
- entrances and exits
- the order of scenes
- the positioning and use of props
- any set changes
- costume changes
- the order of the curtain call (the bows at the end of the performance need rehearsing).

Assessment activity 5

Unit 5 — P1 M1 D1 P2 M2 D2 P3 M3 D3 P4 M4 D4 P5 M5 D5 **BTEC**

Capture evidence of your contribution to the rehearsal process in a performer's log book.

Your work could include the following:

Exercises and explorations of themes, ideas and research

Regular diary-style updates of the work in progress, including setting and amending targets for development

Evidence of research, such as themes, history, performance styles, practitioners

A record of achievements and progress, for example blocking/choreography moves, warm-ups and exercises to practise

Your reflections on rehearsals

Character/role development

Notes on changing role/responsibilities/non-performance responsibilities

Feedback on your work from your tutor, director, choreographer or musical director

Feedback and comments from other performers.

Evidence

- performers log book

Grading tips

M1 M2 M3 M4 M5 The notes you keep in your log book should be detailed to help you make progress.

D1 D2 D3 D4 D5 Your log book demonstrates that you understand its importance and relevance; you should record the progress you have made as a performer clearly.

5.3 Be able to progress rehearsal and performance skills/techniques in response to feedback and evaluation

5.3.1 Selection of creative ideas

As a performer, you will have many opportunities to select and implement creative ideas. Although you may be directed and advised how to develop your role, there are decisions that you must make yourself. Do your ideas have potential for development? Are they relevant to the project or production? Here are some suggestions for creative ideas and input:

Your performance

- Make suggestions about physicality, gestures, movement, appearance and costume.
- Experiment with non-verbal communication, blocking, positioning, entrances and exits.
- Make decisions on the use of your voice – tone, volume and accent (if appropriate).

The production

- Contribute ideas for artistic elements including design, appearance, colours, textures, positioning of furniture, audience, and music.
- Communicate your creative ideas through discussion and consultation with your director/ choreographer and your fellow performers.
- Listen to and accept others' points of view, and understand that not all your ideas will be suitable or considered for the work.

Editing and refining

Adapting, adjusting and amending your performance is a necessary element of the rehearsal process; there are a number of factors that could affect this, including the needs of others in the group, or the changing demands and requirements of the production. Most importantly, there is the feedback on your performance skills from your director/choreographer, and sometimes your peers or members of the production team, such as the stage manager (SM).

You may be corrected on your physical expression and posture, how you deliver a song, or how you vocalise a particular speech or emotion. You could receive specific support or guidance, such as extra dance lessons or a series of vocal exercises that you must practise. It is vital that you are able to accept criticism and do whatever is necessary to improve your technique.

5.3.2 Self-evaluation

As well as receiving feedback from others, you should also evaluate your own work.

Assessment activity 6

Unit 5   BTEC

The reflective performer will set goals throughout the project as they want to improve and achieve perfection.

Working as a group or as an individual, set yourself some goals. Keep notes in your performer's log, recording whether or not you completed your goals, and what you need to do to progress.

Evidence

- performer's log book

Grading tips

M5 The notes you keep in your log book, and discussions with your tutor, should demonstrate how you are developing your performance technique.

D5 Your log book and discussions will clearly show how committed you are to the improvement of your own technique.

Here are some examples of reflective questions:

Is my idea effective?

Problem: I want to use a favourite piece of music instead of the original song for the opening scene, but does it actually work? Do I think it works because I know the song so well?

Solution: Ask for the honest opinions of others, and accept the response.

Tip

If you are unsure about the success of a particular idea, or feel that your performance technique is lacking, you need to work out why.

Discuss your ideas with others, and request their thoughts and opinions. You are inviting feedback on your own work.

Do I have the skills to perform this role successfully?

Problem: I am losing projection and clarity towards the end of songs.

Solution: Practise vocal exercises to increase vocal capacity, modulation and diction, and phrasing.

Tip

Make a list of the skills needed to do justice to your role.

Give yourself marks out of ten for each skill. If you score below ten, think about what exercises, techniques and rehearsals you can do to improve?

How can I respond in a positive way to critical feedback?

Problem: I take it personally when I get criticism on my performance.

Solution: Stop taking it personally. This is not about you, it is about the audience. The criticism is so that the work makes sense to the audience.

Tip

Keep notes on the feedback received. Consider what you need to do to improve. Rehearse and develop your work. Ask for further feedback according to the changes made.

How do I provide criticism without making it personal?

Problem: I need to tell another performer that she is out of sync and needs to speed up, as it is affecting everyone else's performance.

Solution: Be honest. Consider how you would feel to receive this type of criticism; you would want someone to tell you straight, but maybe not in front of everyone else. Do not be angry, but be supportive.

Tip

Work out what the problem is. Look at it from your own perspective and how you would want to be treated. You can discuss the issue with your director/ choreographer, who may wish to deal with the issue themselves.

Is my performance technique effective?

Problem: My shoulder hurts when I am doing lifts.

Solution: Do thorough warm-ups, and practise lifting outside rehearsals. You might want to visit your GP for a check-up if the shoulder still hurts.

What do I do if I disagree with the adjustments I've been told to make?

Problem: I don't think that there is anything wrong with the movements I choreographed.

Solution: Think about your situation; is it pride that is stopping you from making the suggested adjustment? If you think you have reason to disagree, you can discuss it sensibly with your choreographer, stating your case.

Feedback sessions are part of good professional development

7.4 Be able to work with discipline within an ensemble

You will be expected to take a professional attitude in all aspects of the production, but especially in the final stages.

The technical rehearsal

Technical rehearsals provide the production team (stage management, and lighting and sound crews) with the opportunity to prepare, test and set (or fix) the technical and non-performance elements. The performers will be required to attend the technical rehearsals and perform aspects of the work to help the technical team focus lighting states, input preset lighting and sound cues, set props, prepare and run scene changes, clear the stage, and so on. The performers may be requested to run through entrances and exits, verbal and visual cues or the first and last lines of speeches.

The technical rehearsal can include long and complex series of technical instructions and manual operations; it is important that the performers are aware of this, and prepare themselves mentally for the process. The worst thing that could happen is for the performers to complain because they are bored; the production team are not bored during the technical rehearsal, and may be offended by the insensitivity of such remarks.

The dress rehearsal

Dress rehearsals are full performances without an audience. All the elements of the production are in place, that is, the performers and all production requirements. The dress rehearsal allows the director/choreographer to see the show in its final stage, it provides the stage management and technical crews the opportunity to test and run the production elements, and it gives the performers the chance to perform in the whole show.

The importance of maintaining a professional manner before, during and after dress rehearsals cannot be understated. The director, choreographer and musical director will take the opportunity to provide notes and feedback after the dress rehearsal. Listening to and absorbing this feedback is vital to the success of the show and your development as a performer.

Assessment activity 7   Unit 7   P4 M4 D4   BTEC

Consider your role and contribution during:
- the technical rehearsal
- the dress rehearsal(s).

How can you ensure that you are demonstrating self-discipline? What are the qualities you should be showing to others?

Evidence
- tutor observations
- performer's log book

Grading tips

M4 You must ensure that you can maintain a disciplined and professional attitude throughout the process.

D4 You should lead by example, taking responsibility for ensuring that you and others are focused and disciplined at all times.

PLTS

By maintaining a professional attitude throughout a creative process, you will be developing your skills as an **effective participator**.

Functional skills

English: By maintaining a performer's log, you will be using your **writing** skills.

7.4.1 Discipline

Preparing yourself for your performance can involve simple exercises and techniques. Some performers like to visit a new performance venue, and get used to the performance space without the presence of an audience.

Before the show, you should prepare yourself mentally and physically. Here are some tips:

- You might do a relaxation exercise, focusing on visualisation or breathing exercises. Depending on how much space you have, and the time available, you might do exercises where you are lying down, sitting on a chair, or even standing up.

- If you are doing a vocal performance, you will need to do a vocal warm-up either on your own or in a group.

- Your voice is an instrument, and you need to tune it to get it ready for performance. See Project 10: Moving On for specific vocal exercises, but your vocal tutor or musical director may lead a comprehensive vocal warm-up with the group.

- Your physical warm-up (solo) could consist of stretches or short dance moves.

- If you are in a group, you might want to play a very short game of tag or keepy uppy with balloons or a beach ball. Exert a bit of energy, but not too much – you do not want to exhaust yourself before the performance.

- A group motivational speech beforehand can really focus the mind: it might consist of positive thoughts, a reminder of the hard work you have put in, praise for your abilities, group responses to questions or statements, and it should prepare you psychologically for the performance.

Assessment activity 8   Unit 7   P1 M1 D1 P2 M2 D2 P3 M3 D3   **BTEC**

Presenting your work to the audience is the final part of the process. It is what you have been rehearsing for: the culmination of research, skills development, exploration of performance material and developmental rehearsals.

The performance must show, at the very least, that you are able to communicate meaning to the audience, and that you have interpreted a role that is clear and consistent. It will demonstrate one or more of the following:

- physical skills
- vocal skills
- acting skills
- musical skills.

Evidence

- recording of live performances
- tutor observation reports

Grading tips

M1 M2 M3 You must show you have been creative in your interpretation of the role, communicating your work with focus and engagement.

D1 D2 D3 You must demonstrate your energy and confidence, engaging with the audience and showing them your commitment and flair in performance.

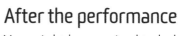

PLTS

Presenting your work to the audience will allow you to demonstrate that you are a **team worker**.

After the performance

You might be required to help with tidying up the set or the backstage, but you should always seek an opportunity to get feedback from the director/choreographer and from the DSM. Also, you must evaluate your own work and not rely on others to tell you if anything needs amending or adjusting.

Natalie Best
professional performer

Natalie Best was a BTEC National in Performing Arts learner before graduating from Mountview Theatre School.

'When I finished drama school, my first job was on TV; I was a guest lead on an episode of *Holby City*. After this I went straight into theatre work. I have been very lucky to have performed in a range of different shows including *Hairspray* in the West End, *The Icarus Girl* at the Arcola Theatre, or *The Life of Galileo* at the National Theatre and *Jack and the Beanstalk* at the Lyric Hammersmith.

Everyone has different methods for preparing and developing a character.

I believe a good writer tells you a lot about the character. I usually start by writing down everything my character says about themselves, what the other characters say about me, what I say about the other characters and finally what facts the writer has given me about my character. I can then begin to get a sense of what this character is about, what they believe in, how they feel … I might then begin to physicalise.

Before each performance, I do a vocal warm-up routine. I have tongue twisters that I use. I like to sing as well before I go on stage even if it is not a musical performance. It warms me up best!

To achieve the same level of performance every night, stamina is very important. I drink plenty of water and do a good physical warm-up to prepare my body for what is ahead. Every time I feel tired or exhausted, I would just remind myself of how lucky I am to be doing the show and I'd also remember the amount of money people pay to see the show. They deserve an excellent performance from you every night.

Performing is an exceptional job and an excellent profession, but you have to be 100 per cent dedicated to your craft. Be prepared to work very hard, but it is important for your sanity to live life to the fullest; it will actually make you a better performer.

Think about it!

1 What kind of professional performance work would you like to do?
2 What is important to you when developing a role for performance?
3 Do you have any favourite warm-ups and preparatory exercises?

Just checking

1 Do you know the responsibilities of your role? Make sure you know from the beginning of the process what you are required to do.

2 Have you contributed to the development of group and personal rehearsal schedules? By taking an active role in the planning of work, you can have a direct and positive influence on others.

3 Have you conducted research for your role? You should consider whether it is relevant, and how you can use it effectively in the performance work.

4 Have you kept a log book of your development as a performer? A log book can provide you with reminders of performance decisions including blocking or character traits, as well as tracking work in progress.

5 Were the performances at the standard you wanted? You should be demonstrating your physical, vocal, acting and musical skills (depending on the content of the production) to the best of your ability. You can also consider how you communicated with other performers, the production team, and the audience.

6 Is there anything you would do differently in the rehearsal and performance process? Think about your self-discipline, your professionalism or meeting your own rehearsal schedule.

edexcel :::

Assignment tips

- Design a rehearsal schedule that will allow you and others the time and opportunities to create a strong performance piece.

- Try to make the work as vocationally relevant as you can.

- Set yourself achievable goals for developing your own role.

- Find positive and encouraging methods of working successfully as a group.

- Be clear in what you want to achieve with your research.

- Try to get feedback as often as possible from your director/choreographer.

- Develop a performer's log that helps you chart your development.

- Ensure you develop clear and effective methods of communicating with the performance and production teams.

- Take the opportunity to showcase your skills and what you have learnt in your performances.

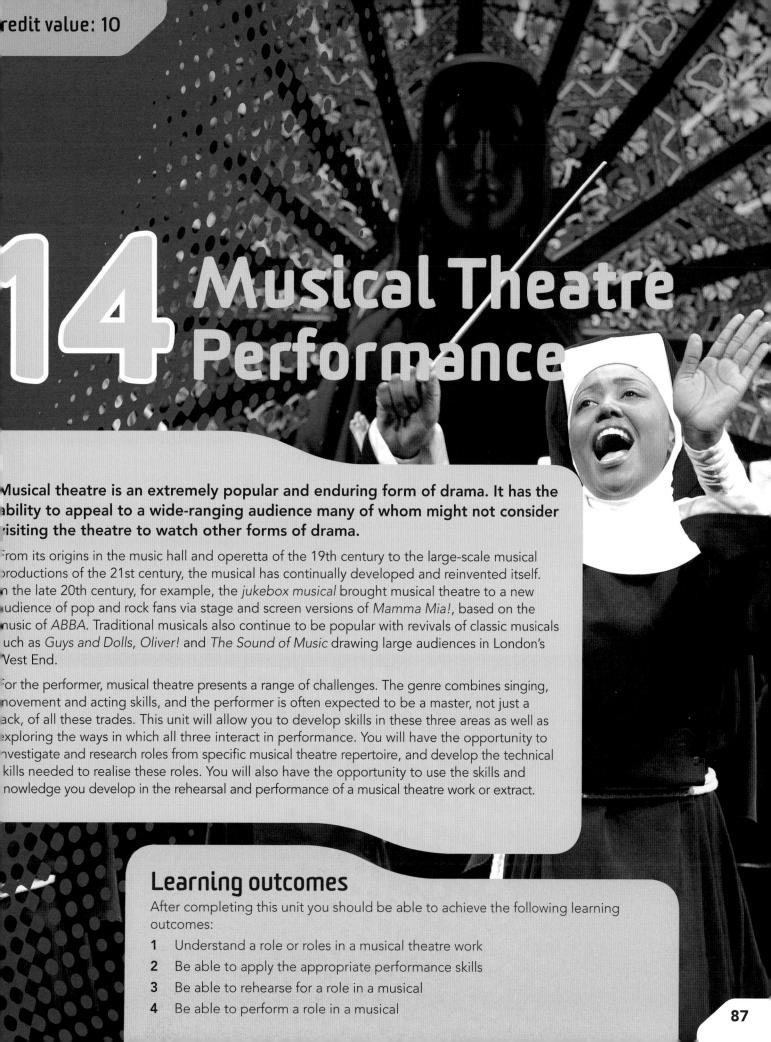

14 Musical Theatre Performance

Musical theatre is an extremely popular and enduring form of drama. It has the ability to appeal to a wide-ranging audience many of whom might not consider visiting the theatre to watch other forms of drama.

From its origins in the music hall and operetta of the 19th century to the large-scale musical productions of the 21st century, the musical has continually developed and reinvented itself. In the late 20th century, for example, the *jukebox musical* brought musical theatre to a new audience of pop and rock fans via stage and screen versions of *Mamma Mia!*, based on the music of *ABBA*. Traditional musicals also continue to be popular with revivals of classic musicals such as *Guys and Dolls*, *Oliver!* and *The Sound of Music* drawing large audiences in London's West End.

For the performer, musical theatre presents a range of challenges. The genre combines singing, movement and acting skills, and the performer is often expected to be a master, not just a Jack, of all these trades. This unit will allow you to develop skills in these three areas as well as exploring the ways in which all three interact in performance. You will have the opportunity to investigate and research roles from specific musical theatre repertoire, and develop the technical skills needed to realise these roles. You will also have the opportunity to use the skills and knowledge you develop in the rehearsal and performance of a musical theatre work or extract.

Learning outcomes

After completing this unit you should be able to achieve the following learning outcomes:

1 Understand a role or roles in a musical theatre work
2 Be able to apply the appropriate performance skills
3 Be able to rehearse for a role in a musical
4 Be able to perform a role in a musical

Assessment and grading criteria

This table shows you what you must do in order to achieve a **pass**, **merit** or **distinction** grade, and where you can find activities in this book to help you.

To achieve a **pass** grade the evidence must show that you are able to:	To achieve a **merit** grade the evidence must show that, in addition to the pass criteria, you should be able to:	To achieve a **distinction** grade the evidence must show that, in addition to the pass and merit criteria, you should be able to:
P1 discuss an interpretation and realisation of a role or roles **Assessment activity 1a page 95** **Assessment activity 1b page 96** **Assessment activity 1c page 96** **Assessment activity 1d page 97**	**M1** explain an interpretation and realisation of a role or roles **Assessment activity 1a page 95** **Assessment activity 1b page 96** **Assessment activity 1c page 96** **Assessment activity 1d page 97**	**D1** analyse an interpretation and realisation of a role or roles **Assessment activity 1a page 95** **Assessment activity 1b page 96** **Assessment activity 1c page 96** **Assessment activity 1d page 97**
P2 use the appropriate skills and techniques with support and guidance **Assessment activity 2a page 99** **Assessment activity 2b page 100** **Assessment activity 2c page 103** **Assessment activity 2d page 104**	**M2** use the appropriate skills and techniques with minimal support and guidance **Assessment activity 2a page 99** **Assessment activity 2b page 100** **Assessment activity 2c page 103** **Assessment activity 2d page 104**	**D2** use the appropriate skills and techniques autonomously **Assessment activity 2a page 99** **Assessment activity 2b page 100** **Assessment activity 2c page 103** **Assessment activity 2d page 104**
P3 contribute to the rehearsal process maintaining a suitable level of rehearsal discipline **Assessment activity 3 page 109**	**M3** make valuable contributions to the rehearsal process maintaining a high level of rehearsal discipline **Assessment activity 3 page 109**	**D3** contribute significantly to the rehearsal process maintaining a consistently high level of rehearsal discipline **Assessment activity 3 page 109**
P4 use performing skills competently to create a performance that communicates an interpretation to an audience. **Assessment activity 4 page 111**	**M4** use performing skills effectively to create a performance that communicates a considered interpretation to an audience. **Assessment activity 4 page 111**	**D4** use performing skills confidently to create a performance that communicates a detailed and imaginative interpretation to an audience. **Assessment activity 4 page 111**

How you will be assessed

This unit will be assessed by an internal assignment that will be designed and marked by the tutors at your centre. You will be assessed on your ability to:

- investigate a role or roles from a musical theatre work
- apply and combine singing, movement and acting skills within the rehearsal and performance of a musical theatre work
- rehearse for a role in a musical theatre work
- perform a role in a musical theatre work.

The work you produce during your work on this unit may include:

- a performer's portfolio
- DVDs/videos of rehearsals and performances.

Marlon, 20 year-old musical theatre learner

My first experience of the theatre was being in the chorus of *Joseph and the Amazing Technicolor Dreamcoat*. I was only nine, but I can still remember it like it was yesterday. I was completely overwhelmed by the experience and I loved every minute of the rehearsals and performances. I remember crying my eyes out after the last performance because it was all over. After that I was pretty much hooked. The junior theatre group I was a member of did productions every year, and when I was 12, I was lucky enough to be cast as Oliver in the musical of the same name.

When I was 16, I joined a BTEC National in Performing Arts course at my local college. The course allowed me to develop my skills as a musical theatre performer by improving my singing, acting and dance skills. I am now half-way through a BA Hons course in Musical Theatre and I am hoping to eventually earn my living as a musical theatre performer.

Musical theatre is hard work and there are highs and lows to deal with. It can be disappointing when you don't get a role you have set your heart on and the long hours of rehearsal and practice often don't leave much time for socialising. It is worth it however when you are standing in the wings on the opening night of a new production.

Over to you

- What experience do you have of musical theatre performance, e.g. in school or college productions?
- Do you enjoy taking part in and/or watching musical theatre?

14.1 Understanding roles in a musical theatre

Before you set foot on the stage, it is important that you understand the nature of the work you are to perform and the characters you will portray. In this part of the unit we will explore typical musical theatre roles. We will consider how these roles function within the structure of a musical, and explore ways of interpreting a role.

Warm up

On 20th December 1927 a show opened in New York that is now considered the first true example of a classic American musical, i.e. a 'dramatic' play with music.

Show Boat by Oscar Hammerstein and Jerome Kern is a seminal work, which includes many features that are now synonymous with the musical theatre genre.

It has a plot that spans over 47 years and requires numerous sets including a Mississippi theatre boat and a nightclub in Chicago.

Based on a novel by Edna Ferber, it tells the story of the highs and lows of a romance between a riverboat gambler and the daughter of the owner of a theatre boat (the Show Boat).

Show Boat continues to be performed professionally and by amateur groups to this day. In 2006 it became the first musical to be performed at London's Royal Albert Hall where it was staged in the round.

Over to you

- What do you think are the essential features of a musical?
- Divide into pairs or small groups and come up with a list of essential features (e.g. 'memorable songs').
- Share and discuss your ideas with the whole group.
- Illustrate your ideas by producing a list of essential features or a mind map.

14.1.1 Form and structure

Before a performer can begin to consider an interpretation of a role in a musical theatre work, it is important that they understand the form and structure of the piece as a whole. The musical is a type of theatre that includes a range of different genres, each with its own particular style and theatrical conventions. We will begin this section by considering a range of typical examples.

Key terms

Revue – a variety show

Style and genre of a musical theatre work

'The musical' is a term used to describe a number of different genres and styles of performance. Its origins lie in entertainment genres of the late 19th century when music hall, vaudeville and operetta were popular in Britain and the USA.

British Music Hall and its American counterpart, Vaudeville, was a form of variety entertainment that included singing, dance routines, comedy and speciality acts. This form of entertainment developed in the mid to late 19th century as a form of entertainment for the population that had moved into towns and cities as a result of the Industrial Revolution. In America, Vaudeville shows in the early 20th century led to a form of musical and dance revue known as 'Follies'. Follies were musical **revues** with elaborate sets and lavish costumes which were more high class than previous vaudeville shows. The most famous example were the Ziegfeld Follies, a series of shows that were staged on New York's Broadway. The shows were directed by Florenz Ziegfeld, who later went on to direct the 'first' American musical called *Show Boat*.

Operetta or Light Opera is a form of musical theatre that borrows some of the conventions of opera and treats them in a lighter, more popular manner. Operettas of W.S. Gilbert and Arthur Sullivan set the blueprint for the genre. During the late 19th and early 20th century, Gilbert and Sullivan wrote numerous operettas such as *The Pirates of Penzance*, *The Mikado*, *HMS Pinafore* and *The Yeomen of the Guard*, which were successful on both sides of the Atlantic. Many follow a formula as follows:

- a comic central plot involving a pair of young lovers
- two acts with one continuous scene/setting per act
- a range of supporting characters including a comic role for a middle-aged/elderly male
- a range of musical numbers including solos, duets, small ensembles and rousing chorus pieces.

The operettas remain popular with audiences to this day and since being out of copyright from the early 1960s have become popular performance pieces for amateur dramatic groups. *The Pirates of Penzance* gained a second life in the 1980s when American theatre producer, Joseph Papp, revived and updated the show in a Broadway production and a subsequent film.

The mid 20th century could be described as the golden age of the musical. In America 'classic' musicals such as *Oklahoma!*, *The King and I*, *South Pacific*, *Guys and Dolls*, *My Fair Lady*, *Annie Get Your Gun* and *Kiss Me Kate* were performed on stage and developed into films. The American musical might be seen as a development of the operetta as examples include many of the key features of the operetta.

Operetta	Mid 20th-century American musical
Comic central plot involving a pair of young lovers	The central plot of most musicals written at this time involves the fortunes of a pair of young lovers.
Two acts with one continuous scene/setting per act	Most musicals have two acts. However these may be broken down into several scenes, and more than one setting is often used in an act.
A range of supporting characters including a comic role for a middle-aged/elderly male	Musicals also include a range of supporting characters, some of which will be comic characters providing a lighter sub-plot.
A range of musical numbers including solos, duets, small ensembles and rousing chorus pieces	Musicals generally include all these features.

The American musical also owes much to the Follies tradition in which dance was an important feature. Many musicals written in the mid 20th century include dance routines, and some feature extended narrative dance pieces. In *Oklahoma!*, for example, Laurey's feelings for Curly are explored though a dream sequence that was choreographed by Agnes de Mille.

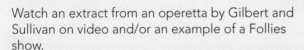

Activity: Operettas and Follies

Watch an extract from an operetta by Gilbert and Sullivan on video and/or an example of a Follies show.

Discuss the style of the piece(s) in relation to the 'essential features' of a musical you identified in the earlier activity.

If you are able to watch both extracts, compare and contrast the features of each.

The following DVDs will be useful for this activity:

Pirates of Penzance, 1982, Universal Picture UK

Ziegfeld Follies, 1946, Warner Home Video.

Activity: *Oklahoma!*

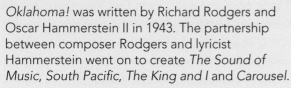

Oklahoma! was written by Richard Rodgers and Oscar Hammerstein II in 1943. The partnership between composer Rodgers and lyricist Hammerstein went on to create *The Sound of Music*, *South Pacific*, *The King and I* and *Carousel*.

Based on the play *Green Grow the Lilacs* by Lynn Riggs, *Oklahoma!* is set at the turn of the century and tells the story of Laurey and the two rivals for her affections: Curly, a cowboy and Jud, a farm hand.

Building on the conventions and features that were established in Show Boat in 1927, *Oklahoma!* is a typical example of the American musical genre, i.e. a musical play in which the songs and dance pieces are fully integrated into the plot.

Although the plot of *Oklahoma!* includes a good deal of frothy comedy, some of the underlying themes are serious ones. The way in which Jud is treated because he is a hired hand rather than a land-owner is explored, as is the conflict between cowboys and cattlemen.

Watch a production of *Oklahoma!* and note how the musical and dance numbers are integrated into the plot.

The following DVDs will be useful for this activity:

Oklahoma!, 1955, 20th Century Fox Home Entertainment (2004)

Oklahoma!, 2004, Universal Pictures (National Theatre Production).

Did you know?

The songs and dance pieces in a musical are usually referred to as 'numbers', because they are each given an identifying number in the musical score.

In the mid to late 20th century the musical continued to develop on both sides of the Atlantic. Andrew Lloyd Webber has been prominent in the development of British musical theatre since the1970s. He initially worked with lyricist Tim Rice. Their early collaboration on *Joseph and the Amazing Technicolor Dreamcoat* was followed by success in the West End and on Broadway with *Jesus Christ Superstar* and *Evita*. Many

of Lloyd Webber's musicals are 'through sung', that is, there is no spoken dialogue. This is similar to the tradition of the opera where a form of singing which mimics dialogue, known as 'recitative', is used to link the more lyrical songs (arias) in the score.

Whilst the American musicals of the mid 20th century touched on serious issues, many musicals of the late 20th century aimed to tackle them head on. *Evita* is the story of Eva Perón at the time of her husband's rise to power in Argentina. *Blood Brothers*, the 1988 musical by Willy Russell, explores the theme of nature versus nurture through the story of twins separated at birth. These musicals do not include an uplifting chorus number with a dance routine at the end of the show when everything is resolved. *Blood Brothers*, for example, ends in a very operatic manner with a mother grieving over the bodies of her two sons.

In 1989 *Return to the Forbidden Planet* opened in the West End. It had a plot loosely based on a 1950s science fiction movie of the same name, which was in turn based loosely on Shakespeare's *The Tempest*. The show was directed by Bob Carlton and rather than including musical numbers especially composed the piece used existing pop and rock songs from the 1950's and 60's. The script included passages of dialogue taken from a range of Shakespeare plays.

The show was one of the first examples of what has been described as a songbook or jukebox musical. It was a high-energy production, which required the cast to sing and play the songs live on stage. *Return to the Forbidden Planet* also drew from the pantomime tradition, including a good deal of audience participation. The show was a huge success in the

Activity: *Evita*

Watch an extract from *Evita* by Andrew Lloyd Webber and Tim Rice.

Discuss the different singing styles used in the extract, noting the through sung style of the piece.

How does this compare with other examples you have seen where the music stops for dialogue sections?

The following DVD will be useful for this activity:

Evita, 1999, Entertainment in Video.

West End and on Broadway and subsequently toured both nationally and internationally for many years. It opened the way to a new style of musical that now includes *Mamma Mia!*, *We Will Rock You*, *Jersey Boys* and *Daddy Cool*.

The book, the lyrics and the music

A musical is a combination of three elements: the book, the song lyrics and the music. Different people often create these elements. One person, for example, may write the book and the lyrics, whilst another composes the music. These elements must combine together seamlessly to create a successful piece of theatre and partnerships between writers and composers have been responsible for many successful musicals.

The book

The book is also known as the 'libretto' (from the Italian word 'libro' which means book). Like a script for a play, the book contains the spoken dialogue for the musical along with stage directions. As with any piece of drama, the dialogue needs to communicate the plot in a clear manner.

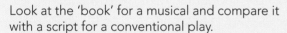

Activity: The book

Look at the 'book' for a musical and compare it with a script for a conventional play.

Note how the musical numbers are referenced in the book.

Discuss the similarities and differences between the book and the script.

The lyrics

The lyrics are the words within the musical that are set to music. The lyrics are often (but not always) written by the person who created the dialogue for the book. The relationship between the lyrics and the music, and therefore between the lyricist and the composer of the music, is a close one. Many partnerships continue over many years and many musicals.

The music

Musical numbers in a musical might include a few:

- solo songs

Solos are a key feature of many musicals and the leading characters will often have at least one solo song to deliver. Solo songs are often used to allow a character to share their thoughts and feelings with the audience. 'Hopelessly Devoted to You' sung by Sandy in *Grease* and 'Soliloquy' sung by Billy in *Carousel* are examples of this type of solo.

- duets

Duets are songs for two people and are found in many examples of musical theatre. The romantic duet between the two leading characters is a common feature of the musical. Examples include 'People Will Say We're in Love' from *Oklahoma!* and 'All I Ask of You' from *Phantom of the Opera*. Comedy duets such as 'Brush Up your Shakespeare' from *Kiss me Kate* are also featured in many musicals. Duets can be used to allow two characters to have a conversation. 'Marry the Man Today' from *Guys and Dolls*, for example, involves a conversation between two female characters, Adelaide and Sarah, in which they decide to marry their partners and then try to change them.

- small ensemble pieces, e.g. trios, quartets

Whilst ensemble songs for three or more characters are not as common in musicals as they are in operettas, examples can be found in many musicals. 'Fugue for Tinhorns' from *Guys and Dolls*, for example, is a trio sung by three gamblers, Nicely, Rusty and Benny at the opening of the show, and it sets the scene for what is to come.

- **chorus** pieces

Many musicals feature a chorus. The musical song and dance numbers that feature the chorus are often the **show stoppers** of the piece. Many chorus pieces also feature one or more of the leading characters of the musical. Memorable musical numbers that feature a chorus include 'Sit Down, You're Rockin' the Boat' from *Guys & Dolls* and 'Big Spender' from *Sweet Charity*.

Key terms

Chorus – an ensemble of singers and dancers

Show stopper – a musical number received by the audience with prolonged applause that literally stops the show until it dies down

- instrumental pieces for the band or orchestra

The band or orchestra will usually have more to do than accompanying the singers in the musical numbers. Most musicals begin with an overture, which is an introductory piece of music made up of segments of the most popular songs from the show. *Gypsy* (with music by Jule Styne) includes a classic example of the musical overture as it is made up of a range of extracts from the musical to whet the audience's appetite for what is to come.

Some musicals may include an **entr'acte** and a play-out is often performed at the end of the show as the audience leaves. Incidental music, played over dialogue can also be used in musicals.

The function of the roles within the work

Roles within musical theatre works generally fall into two categories: leading roles and supporting roles. When preparing to play a role from a musical theatre work, it is important that you understand the function of the role within the piece.

Leading roles

Many classic musical plots centre around a love story between two characters known as the romantic leads. In Frank Loesser's musical *Guys and Dolls*, the romantic leads are Sarah and Sky. Their story is typical of the 'girl meets boy, boy loses girl, boy and girl are finally reunited' plot that is found in many shows. The character of Sarah is typical of the sweet and innocent female romantic lead, whilst Sky ticks all the boxes for a romantic male lead as he is suave and sophisticated with just a hint of danger. Famous Sky-type characters include Marlon Brando in the 1955 film version and Ewan McGregor in the 2005 West End revival.

Not all leading roles in musicals are 'romantic leads'. In Lerner and Loewe's *My Fair Lady*, for example, the leading male character is Professor Higgins who has a purely platonic relationship with his pupil, Eliza, the leading lady of the musical. The love story between Eliza and Freddy is more of a sub-plot to the main business of Eliza's transformation from a cockney flower girl to a lady.

Guys and Dolls: many musicals revolve around a love story between the two leading characters

Supporting roles

Musicals generally include a range of supporting roles for performers of all ages.

For example, supporting roles might include:

- The 'second' couple with an existing relationship, e.g. Nathan and Adelaide in *Guys and Dolls*; Ado Annie and Will Parker in *Oklahoma!*
- The father/mother figure, e.g. Nettie in *Carousel*; Madame Dubonnet in *The Boyfriend*; Aunt Eller in *Oklahoma!*
- Comic roles, e.g. Ali Hakim in *Oklahoma!*; Nicely-Nicely Johnson in *Guys and Dolls*.

Supporting characters are essential to the success of a show. They put the meat on the bones of the story. They sometimes provide a comic sub-plot that balances with the more serious story of the leading characters. Many of the most memorable moments in the musical theatre repertoire have been provided by supporting characters, for example the Mother Abbess persuading Maria to follow her heart and return to Captain von Trapp in *The Sound of Music* by singing 'Climb Evr'y Mountain'.

Key terms

Entr'acte – a short piece of music played between an act or scene

14.1.2 Interpretation

For a performer preparing to undertake a role in a musical theatre work, the process they go through should be approached in a similar way to that of any work written for the theatre. The performer must carefully study the text (the book), the lyrics and the musical elements. They will need to analyse the context of the show through research to find out about the setting (time and place) and any historical or social issues. They will need to analyse and research the role in which they have been cast so that they develop an understanding of their character's journey through the plot of the show and their relationship with others in the cast. In this way, the performer will develop a full and detailed understanding of the role through a combination of their understanding of the text and personal research into the work.

Role development through research

Preparation to play a role must begin with the text. The script is the only text a performer needs to consider for a play. In musical theatre, the performer must think about the book and the score.

As we have already seen, the book includes the dialogue and stage directions. The score includes the musical numbers and song lyrics. Like many performers working in musical theatre, you will learn the musical material you are required to perform by ear (that is, by listening and repeating), but it is nevertheless essential that you are able to understand how a score for a musical is set out. Although reading by sight from a score (known as 'sight singing') is a difficult skill that takes time to master, being able to use a score to work on a melody you are being taught by ear is not so difficult.

Assessment activity 1a

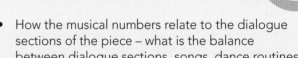

When preparing to play a role in a musical theatre piece, it is vital that you begin with a good understanding of the show as a whole.

You should start by reading the book and looking at the score. This is important even if you are familiar with the work. Remember that the film versions you may have seen may not be the same as the original stage versions.

Depending on the genre and style of the musical you are studying, you might consider some or all of the following:

- How the show opens – how is the scene set for the audience, how do they know where and when the show is set?

- How the musical numbers relate to the dialogue sections of the piece – what is the balance between dialogue sections, songs, dance routines, etc.?

- The high-energy moments of the piece – where are the big show stopping numbers to be found?

- Moments of tension or crisis – where are these to be found and how are they resolved?

- The end of the show – are all the loose ends of the plot resolved, does the show have a big high-energy ending?

PLTS

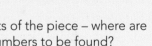

Researching the context of a show is an excellent opportunity to develop your personal, learning and thinking skills by working as an independent enquirer.

During your work in this activity you should show that you can:

- analyse and evaluate information, judging its relevance and value.

Once a performer has gained an understanding of the plot of the show the next task is to consider the context of the piece.

Many musicals are set in particular places at specific times in history. For example, *Guys and Dolls* is set in New York in the Prohibition era of the 1920s and 1930s. *Phantom of the Opera* is set in Paris at the beginning of the 20th century. Both these are examples of musicals that have been developed from other media. The plot of *Guys and Dolls* was developed from two short stories by Damon Runyon whilst *Phantom of the Opera* is based on a novel by Gaston Leroux.

Assessment activity 1b

Getting to know the show through an examination of the text is only the beginning. You should now try to immerse yourself in the work of the show.

You should do this by:

- undertaking research into the place in which the show is set
- investigating the period in which the action takes place
- finding out about the origins of the story, i.e. the book, play or historical event the show is based on (if applicable)
- considering the work in the context of the musical theatre in general.

Response to dialogue, direction, lyrics and choreography

As soon as a performer is familiar with the show and its context, they will begin to investigate the role they are playing. Getting inside the skin of the role is vital to a believable interpretation of the character. Researching a character to play a role in a musical is much the same process as a performer in a play would undertake. They will need to consider what happens to the character during the piece, and also what has happened before we meet them.

This exploration will be guided by the dialogue sequences in each of the scenes the character is involved in. The performer will also need to take into consideration the director's vision of the character. A discussion with the director of the show will provide valuable information as to how the character fits into the director's overall vision of the show. If the role involves dance routines, the choreographer will also be a source of information and support.

The songs the character sings will be key to a performer's understanding of the role. Solos, for example, are often used to allow a character to express their thoughts and feelings.

Assessment activity 1c

Now that you have investigated the show and its context, you should investigate how your character fits into the piece, and make decisions about how the role you will play might be interpreted and realised.

Research

You should begin this process by undertaking some or all of the following activities:

- create a role that is off the wall for your character.
- write out the lyrics of any songs your character sings using double spacing. Take notes about the thoughts and feelings of the character above the relevant lyrics.
- write a character biography, e.g. a diary entry, 'a day in the life' extract, or a monologue about some aspect of your character's background.

Rehearsals and other preparations

- During rehearsals and other preparations, you should make notes about any decisions made regarding the interpretation of your role.

Further guidance and activities for researching, exploring and developing a role are included in Unit 1: Performance Workshop, pages 1–20.

Reaction and relationship to other roles within the piece

The way that a character relates to others in the piece and how they react in exchanges with others, will provide very important clues for the performer in terms of interpretation.

The performer should study dialogue sequences and consider how and why the character reacts to others in the piece. Duets and ensemble pieces may also provide information about a character's status within a group and their relationship to others.

Assessment activity 1d

You should investigate your character's relationship with other characters in the piece.

Research

You should begin this process by undertaking some or all of the following activities:

- create a mind map that illustrates your character's relationship with other characters at the beginning of the piece
- consider how these relationships change during the piece
- analyse dialogue sections to explore your character's reactions to the actions of others in the cast.

Rehearsals and other preparations

Use improvisation to explore your character's relationships with other characters in the piece; explore events that happen 'off stage', eg before we join the action.

Evidence for Assessment Activities 1a, 1b, 1c, 1d

Your performer's portfolio – section 1

- your research notes in a log book

Grading tips for Assessment Activities 1a, 1b, 1c and 1d

M1 The entries in your performer's portfolio – section 1 should explain your role (or roles), giving reasons for the decisions you have made about interpretation, and referring to your examination of the text, your research and the work you have done during the rehearsal process. You should explain how you have arrived at your decisions about your role (or roles).

D1 The entries in your portfolio will show that you have carried out relevant research into your role (or roles) using the text, as well as secondary sources which you have analysed to inform your interpretation. Decisions you make about the role (or roles) should be fully supported by a reasoned argument based on evidence from the text, your intuition as a performer and other sources.

PLTS

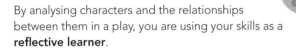

By analysing characters and the relationships between them in a play, you are using your skills as a **reflective learner**.

Functional skills

English: By writing documents, including extended writing pieces, communicating information, ideas and opinions, effectively and persuasively, you will be using your **writing** skills.

14.2 Be able to apply the appropriate performance skills

Some musical theatre performers consider themselves to be actors who sing and dance, some might describe themselves as dancers who sing and act, whilst others might feel that they are musicians who dance and act. Whilst most performers will admit that they are more skilled in one area than another, they do need to be able to use all their skills in a way that is appropriate to the role they are playing.

14.2.1 Selection and practice of skills

Matching own abilities to the role

Different roles require different skills, and preparation for a role in a musical theatre piece may begin with the matching of your existing skills to those required by the role. Whilst many musical theatre roles require a performer with acting, singing and dance skills, the extent to which these skills are required, and the balance between the three, differs from role to role.

Chicago by Kander and Ebb is a high-energy musical which, since its opening on Broadway in 1975, has been performed in theatres across the world. The West End production opened in 1997 and ran for nine years in the Adelphi Theatre before transferring to the Cambridge Theatre. The show requires a cast with a range of skills plus an ensemble who can both sing and dance.

Case study: Josefina Gabrielle

Josefina Gabrielle is probably best known for her Olivier Award-nominated role as Laurey in the National Theatre's 1998 production of Oklahoma! Josefina trained at Arts Educational in London and later joined the National Ballet of Portugal.

When casting Laurey, director, Trevor Nunn and choreographer, Susan Stroman were looking for a performer who could also perform in the dream ballet sequence (a section of the musical usually undertaken by a dancer in the role of 'dream Laurey'). Josefina Gabrielle's acting, singing and dance skills made her perfectly matched to the role.

Speaking in an interview for a theatre-goers website in 2001, she reflected on her dance skills in relation to musical theatre performance:

"My dancing has been a huge asset to my work in musicals. My first musical was *Carousel* at the National Theatre, which was choreographed by Kenneth MacMillan. I had just left the National Ballet of Portugal (where I was a soloist), so dance was my strongest discipline at that time. That meant I was lucky enough to join the cast of *Carousel* as a dancer. Being surrounded by all that talent every night, it was easy to be inspired to get back into class and reawaken the rest of my training."

Over to you

- What do you think your main strengths are in terms of the different skills required for musical theatre performance?
- Which skill(s) are you least confident about?
- How might you improve the skill(s) that need improvement?

Role	Skills required	Famous examples
Velma Kelly	This high-energy role requires a performer who can act, dance and sing to a high level.	Ute Lemper Leigh Zimmerman Ruthie Henshall
Roxie Hart	This role requires an all-rounder with good acting, singing and dance skills.	Jill Halfpenny Denise van Outen Jennifer Ellison Suzanne Shaw
Mama Morton	This role requires a performer with a big voice and good acting skills.	Alison Moyet Kelly Osbourne Brenda Edwards
Billy Flynn	This suave character needs a performer with good singing and acting skills as well as an ability to dance.	Darius Danesh Duncan James John Barrowman
Amos	This character requires a performer with good acting and singing skills.	Les Dennis Nigel Planer Joel Grey

- **Which of these roles would you be most suited to play?**

Assessment activity 2a

Consider the role (or roles) you will be playing in the musical theatre piece you are preparing.

- What skills does the role require?
- What is the balance between acting, dance and singing skills?
- How well do your present skills match the skills required by the role?
- What are your current feelings about your ability

to play the role and the work that needs to be done? (For example, are you confident, apprehensive or excited?)

Evidence

- your performer's portfolio – section 2. Add your answers to the questions above to section 2 of your performer's portfolio.

PLTS

Considering your own skills against the requirements of a role in a musical is an excellent opportunity to develop your personal, learning and thinking skills by working as a reflective learner.

During your work in this activity you should show that you can:

- assess your skills, identifying opportunities for improvement and achievements to date.

Functional skills

ICT: By presenting information in ways that are fit for purpose to an audience, you are using your ICT skills.

The principal roles in the West End production have been played by a range of performers.

Developing vocal and physical mannerisms appropriate to the role

When preparing to play a role in a musical, you will need to consider the vocal and physical **mannerisms** that will be appropriate to the character.

Many actors build a character from the ground up and begin with the walk. The way a character moves can say a lot about the type of person they are. When developing a role, the performer must consider how the character moves and any physical mannerisms they might exhibit.

The way a character talks (and sings) is also part of who they are. Many musicals are set in the USA, and therefore a good American accent will be vital. Home-grown musicals may require the performer to adopt an accent that is not their own. In addition to getting the accent right, a performer must consider the manner in which the dialogue is delivered, so that the meaning of the text is clear and the motives behind what is being said are fully communicated to the audience.

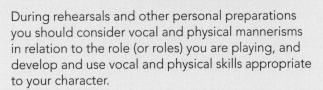

Assessment activity 2b

 P2 M2 D2 BTEC

During rehearsals and other personal preparations you should consider vocal and physical mannerisms in relation to the role (or roles) you are playing, and develop and use vocal and physical skills appropriate to your character.

Evidence

- your performer's portfolio – section 2. Make notes in your performer's portfolio about decisions made in relation to vocal and movement work.

- you tutor will observe your work in rehearsals and other activities, and assess your ability to develop and use appropriate vocal and physical skills.

Key term

Mannerism – a trait; a behavioral attribute that is distinctive and peculiar to an individual

Casting – the process by which the creative team decides who will undertake the principal roles in a show

Did you know?

When practising and rehearsing, it is important to consider the shoes the character would wear. If you are playing a traditionally glamorous woman, for example, you will need to find an appropriate pair of elegant shoes. Practising in trainers will make it difficult to move in an appropriate manner.

Further guidance and activities for developing vocal and physical mannerisms appropriate to a role are included in Unit 5&7: Rehearsing and Performing, page 65.

Developing and learning appropriate styles of singing, dancing and acting

As we have already seen, the musical can encompass a wide range of different styles and genres of theatre. This means the performer must be familiar with, and able to use a range of different acting, singing and dance styles.

Did you know?

The creative team in a musical

Rather than working with a single director, performers in musicals often work in rehearsals with a creative team consisting of:

- a director who oversees the creative concept of the whole show, and directs the action in dialogue and musical sections of the show
- a musical director who works with the singers and the musicians
- a choreographer who works with the dancers and creates the dance routines.

Although the style of acting used in a musical will be largely the choice of the director, the style and genre of the show is likely to suggest a particular approach. Many musicals, for example, require a naturalistic style of acting to be adopted, that is, where a 'normal' view of people in a dramatic or comedic situation is presented. Trevor Nunn's production of *Oklahoma!*, for example, was a largely naturalistic piece.

Some musicals, however, may require a more stylised approach to acting similar to that used in melodrama or pantomime. The jukebox musical *Return to the Forbidden Planet* is a highly stylised piece that requires a more exaggerated style of acting typically found in pantomime.

Further guidance on different styles of acting is included in Unit 19: Principles of Acting, page 113.

Musicals can require a range of singing styles from light classical through to jazz and pop. Many of the leading roles in mid 20th-century American musicals, such as Emile in *South Pacific* and Eliza in *My Fair Lady*, require a singer with some degree of classical training. Many musicals written in the late 20th century require singers who can perform in a pop or rock style, for example Judas in *Jesus Christ Superstar* or Sandy in *Grease*. Musicals such as *Chicago* and *Cabaret* require a jazz style of singing. Some performers are accomplished singers who can successfully manage all of these styles, however in amateur and learner productions the vocal abilities of performers will be taken into account when **casting** a show.

Dance styles within musicals can vary. Jazz dance is widely used in the musical, and the work of choreographers such as Bob Fosse has meant that as a style Jazz dance tends to be strongly associated with musical theatre. Other styles of dance are found in musicals too. Tap, for example, is found in *42nd Street* and *The Boyfriend*. More lyrical styles of dance can also be found in musicals. The dream sequence in *Oklahoma!* is in ballet style, and the opening sequence of *West Side Story* is an extended narrative dance sequence that tells of the rivalry between the Sharks and the Jets.

Further information on different styles of dance can be found in Unit 38: Dance Performance, page 161.

Activity: Acting, singing and dance styles

Watch extracts from a range of musicals and discuss the styles of acting, singing and dance used.

Points for discussion:

- How is movement used? (For example, are naturalistic gestures and mannerisms used or are they exaggerated?)
- How is dialogue delivered? (For example, is there variation in sound, pace, rhythm and timing?)
- Is a recognisable style of acting, dance and/or singing being used in the extract?
- How appropriate is the style to the work being performed?
- Where a particular style is employed, do all the performers use this style?

The following DVDs will be useful for this activity:

Oklahoma!, 2004, Universal Pictures (National Theatre Production)

Chicago, 2002, Walt Disney Studios Home Entertainment

The Boyfriend, 1971, MGM Entertainment (VHS)

South Pacific, 2004, 20th Century Fox Home Entertainment

Jesus Christ Superstar, 2005, Universal Pictures UK.

Following a practice regime

A performer must ensure that they are fully prepared to play the role or roles in which they are cast. Musicals require high levels of skill as well as stamina, and following a well-structured practice regime is the best way to prepare for what is to come.

Depending on the role being prepared, practice might include:

1 Vocal work to:
- perfect an accent
- improve technical skills, such as projection, tone, attack and breath control
- improve the placement of the voice when singing
- increase a vocal range when singing
- improve intonation when singing.

2 Movement work to:
- improve strength, posture, alignment, balance and flexibility
- improve stamina and general fitness.

A practice session should always begin with an appropriate warm-up, and should include exercises designed to improve techniques as well as work on specific songs, routines and/or dialogue sequences. Your singing, dance and/or acting tutor may suggest these exercises.

Setting personal targets and meeting them

Designing a personal action plan is an excellent way to track your progress as a result of practice and rehearsal. An action plan should always include a set of achievable targets.

Targets set should be **SMART**. This means they should be:

- **S**pecific: your targets should be designed to address specific skills that need to be developed and improved.
- **M**easurable: you should design your targets in a way that will allow you to measure your progress towards them.
- **A**chievable: your targets must be achievable. Small steps are best.
- **R**elevant: the targets you set should be relevant to the role you are preparing for.
- **T**ime-bound: your targets should be time-bound, ie you should set appropriate timescales for their achievement.

Key term

Off book – able to perform the dialogue from memory

Note-bashing – a rehearsal where the musical director teaches a song to performers by bashing the melody out on the piano

Assessment activity 2c

Step 1: Consider the skills needed for the role (or roles) you are playing.

You identified these in Assessment activity 2a. Revisit the notes you made for this activity.

Step 2: Assess your current level of skill against the skills required to play the role.

Make a list of those skills you are confident about and those you need to improve. Where skills need improvement, seek advice from the relevant tutor to ensure you have a range of exercises that you can follow.

Step 3: Draw up a personal action plan.

Make sure your targets are SMART. This will ensure that the work you do is correctly focused.

Step 4: Plan and undertake a practice regime.

Decide when and where you will practise, draw up a structured plan for your practice regime, and keep a record of what you do.

Step 5: Review your personal action plan at regular intervals.

Keep an eye on your progress towards the targets you set. Ask for feedback from the relevant tutor as well as your peers.

Make adjustments to your actions plan where necessary.

Evidence

- your performer's portfolio – section 2. Make notes in your portfolio as you undertake your five step plan. Keep a copy of your personal action plan in your portfolio

- tutor observations – your tutor will monitor your progress, and assess your ability to manage the development of the skills you need to undertake your role

PLTS

By considering your own skills against the requirements of a role in a musical, you will use your skills as a **reflective learner**.

14.2.2 Memorisation

To deliver a successful performance in a musical, you must know the role (or roles) inside out. This means memorising lines, vocal singing parts and choreographed movements.

Dialogue sections of the show need to be memorised as quickly as possible. The director may provide a date by which performers need to be **off book** and it is vital that this deadline is met. Performers learn lines in various ways from recording and listening back to them, to reading and rereading.

The musical director will lead early singing rehearsals

Songs are normally taught to performers in **note-bashing** sessions round the piano, which are led by the musical director. Accuracy is vital in these sessions and the performer must develop their listening skills to ensure they can correctly pick up the melody and rhythm of a vocal line.

The choreographer teaches the performers the dances. Dance routines are broken down into phrases which the choreographer demonstrates and the performers copy.

Repetition is generally the best way of memorising something, and when a performer is practising, they must always make sure that they are repeating the correct movement, line or melody. A performer must use their eyes and ears to identify and make corrections as required. An overlooked mistake can be difficult to undo if it has been repeated a number of times. It is important that the performer responds to instructions from the director, choreographer or musical director who will give feedback in terms of accuracy, and provide corrections where necessary.

During the rehearsal process, all these elements will need to be combined and it is not unusual for changes to be made. A dance routine may need to be altered to take into account the positioning of scenery of rostra, for example. At this stage, new information, such as stage positioning, entrances and exits will need to be taken in and memorised. The performer must therefore remain alert and deal with changes as they happen.

Assessment activity 2d

During rehearsals and individual practice sessions you should memorise the lines, songs, movement sequences and dance routines you are taught taking care with accuracy and responding to corrections and any changes that are necessary.

Evidence

- your performer's portfolio – section 2. Make notes in your performer's portfolio on the work you do to memorise material
- tutor observations – your tutor will monitor and assess your ability to memorise material for your role

Grading tips for Assessment activities 2a, 2b, 2c and 2d

M2 During preparations, you should show that you can apply the skills you already possess to new contexts, for example, using dance skills developed in jazz classes for choreography learnt for the musical. You should be able to follow instructions, ask questions when required and undertake practice with only a small amount of guidance from your tutors. You should also be able to organise your time effectively outside class time in order to consolidate new learning.

D2 You should use skills confidently and independently, and show that you are able to find the right gesture, tone of voice, dance move, rhythm and pitch of a note and apply them to the context of the work at hand. When questioning a tutor, you should demonstrate that you understand the work you are undertaking, and make suggestions about style and interpretation.

14.3 Be able to rehearse for a role in a musical

The rehearsal period for a musical can often be longer and more complex than that of a play or dance performance. The merging of the various elements takes time and requires the collaborative skills of the director, the musical director and the choreographer.

- The musical director will lead music rehearsals and will ensure the principals and chorus know the musical numbers.
- Performers will rehearse dialogue sequences separately with the director.
- The choreographer will hold dance rehearsals.
- The director and choreographer will often work in collaboration on any sections of the piece that need musical staging.
- These processes will lead to an initial stagger through in which all the elements come together for the first time.
- Further rehearsals will need to be undertaken to refine and polish material.
- These lead to technical rehearsals in which the show is run in 'real time' to allow the technical team to rehearse lighting, sound and other cues.
- The rehearsal period finishes with the dress rehearsal(s).

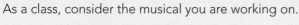

Activity: The rehearsal schedule

As a class, consider the musical you are working on.

Devise a rehearsal schedule for the show remembering to include:

- initial rehearsals for songs, dance routines and dialogue sequences
- the initial stagger through
- subsequent rehearsals to refine and polish material
- technical rehearsal(s)
- dress rehearsal(s)
- the opening night.

Post a copy of the schedule on the wall of your rehearsal room and distribute copies to the cast and creative team.

14.3.1 Rehearsal techniques

We have already established that the musical theatre performer needs to use and combine dance, singing and acting skills in their work. In rehearsal, the musical theatre performer must employ a range of more general skills and techniques to ensure the performance is ready for the opening night.

Time management

Poor timekeeping is perhaps the biggest enemy of the rehearsal process. Time in the rehearsal room is precious. Even a few minutes missed at the beginning of each session because the cast is waiting for someone to arrive can add up to a lot of valuable time wasted. In the professional theatre, call sheets are used to provide performers with details of rehearsals for the day. Members of the cast must ensure they know when and where they are needed and arrive in good time for the rehearsal.

Focus, concentration and self discipline

In rehearsal, the performer needs to focus their attention on what is required of them. Rehearsals can be lengthy and performers may be asked to go over a passage of dialogue, a dance phrase or section of a song several times. The performer must, therefore, maintain their concentration throughout to ensure directions are taken on board and corrections made as necessary. This requires a good deal of self-discipline. Rehearsals often include periods of inactivity, for example, when a performer is not directly involved in the action. It is important that they do not engage in disruptive behaviour when others are rehearsing, for example, by talking or sending text messages on a mobile phone.

Cooperative attitude and approach

Performers must display a positive attitude to the work being rehearsed. This includes being supportive of other performers and responding appropriately to direction. In the theatre, what the director says goes – a performer must never answer back or argue. It is important to remember that the director's job is to help the performers create the best possible performance they can. Performers must respond to corrections positively and should never take criticism personally.

Preparation

A performer demonstrates commitment to work being rehearsed in the way they prepare for rehearsals, for example, by meeting deadlines for line learning and being prepared to undertake practice in their own time. Energy levels in a musical theatre piece will inevitably be high, so it is also vital that the performer is physically fit. Being out of breath after a dance routine is not acceptable if you are required to go straight into a song or dialogue sequence. The performer must therefore be physically prepared for rehearsals and the actual shows.

14.3.2 Vocal requirements

During rehearsals singers will work with the musical director who will teach them the songs and work on their interpretation of the music. Learning a song requires recognition of:

- the pitches of the individual notes
- intervals between individual notes
- the tempo and pace of the song
- the accompaniment, for example, the chords used
- the key of the song.

Activity: The score

Your tutor will introduce you to a score for a song and talk you through the way in which the score is set out, e.g. the vocal line(s) and the piano accompaniment.

Watch the score as it is played or sung. Try to follow the vocal line, looking at the pitches of the notes as well as the lyrics, and noting how they rise and fall with the melody. It may help to think of the melody as a series of steps along a pathway. Note any large leaps where the melody goes suddenly from a low note to a high note or vice versa.

The melody will be written in phrases. Look and listen to see if they are all of equal length or if they differ.

Your tutor will also discuss the directions included on the score, eg the tempo and the **dynamics**.

When you have listened to the piece and followed the score begin the work on the piece, learning it phrase by phrase. Use you ears but also use the information on the score to help you reproduce the melody accurately.

It is vital that a singer always performs songs that are comfortable within their vocal range. This is particularly important for young singers (those under the age of 21) as the voice will continue to develop and change well into adulthood. Voices are typically divided into six types – from soprano, the highest female voice, to bass, the lowest male voice. It is common, however, for young female singers to have a mezzo soprano range (middle C to top G), and for young males singers to have a similar range an **octave** lower which is high baritone.

Work with your tutor to establish your vocal range. You can do this by starting with a mid-range note and singing firstly up, then down the notes of the scale.

An important tip is never strain to get a high note. You could damage your voice.

Correct breathing techniques are important for singers. Breath control is not just about learning to get through long phases without going blue in the face; the breath supports the voice, so the way in which a singer controls the breath will drastically affect the sound and tone quality of their singing voice.

When someone breathes normally they tend to inhale shallowly, that is, they do not fully inflate the lungs. A singer needs to inhale to fully fill the lungs, then exhale in a controlled manner.

Breathing

When you breathe deeply, the lower ribs (which are moveable) expand.

Place your hands on each side of these lower ribs. Breathe deeply and you will feel the ribs and your intercostal muscles moving.

Another muscle which helps you breathe is the diaphragm. It is located below the ribs, but above the stomach. To feel the diaphragm moving, place the flat of your hand just above your stomach and breathe deeply.

Good posture will also help you breathe correctly. Remember to stand upright with your shoulders down and relaxed. Do not allow your shoulders to rise when you inhale.

Key terms

Dynamics – the volume of the piece

Octave – an interval of eight notes

Intonation – tuning

Activity: Preparing a song

Select a song from the musical you are rehearsing.

Prepare the song for a 'performance' that will be videoed, remembering to think about characterisation (vocal and physical).

Watch your performance back and consider how well you:

- maintained your focus and concentration throughout
- communicated the mood and emotion of the song through vocal and physical expression
- performed with good **intonation**.

14.3.3 Movement requirements

During rehearsals, performers in musicals work with the choreographer whose job it is to create the dance routines for the show. Performers must be able to pick up routines quickly, responding to the choreography with rhythmical accuracy.

Some sections of the show may require musical setting. This is where choreographed movement work is used to move the ensemble and/or principals round the stage. Awareness and use of space and other performers is vital during movement work. A busy street scene, for example must be carefully planned and rehearsed to ensure it looks natural.

Activity: Movement accuracy

With a partner, rehearse a short movement sequence you have learned in class.

Perform the sequence to each other and give feedback about accuracy of movement. Practise the sequence together, if possible in front of a mirror.

Do you look the same when you are performing?

Ensemble work is often at the heart of a musical. In early forms of musical theatre, for example operetta, the chorus would primarily be an ensemble of singers with classical training. As the music developed, chorus members had to be increasingly flexible; they had to be competent singers in a number of styles as well as accomplished dancers. The technical ability required in movement and dance sequences in a musical can vary. The 'ensemble' in *Chicago*, for example, are required to sing as well as perform very complex and demanding dance routines.

Activity: Musical setting

Watch an extract of a musical that involves the ensemble.

Discuss the technical aspects of the movement work. Are the ensemble required to perform a complex piece of choreography or is the piece more like a movement sequence set to music?

The following examples may be useful:

The title song from *Guys and Dolls*

Guys and Dolls, 2005, MGM Entertainment

'The Farmer and the Cowman Should be Friends' from *Oklahoma!*

Oklahoma!, 2004, Universal Pictures (National Theatre Production)

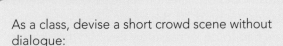
Activity: Crowd control

As a class, devise a short crowd scene without dialogue:

- Decide on a setting, e.g. a busy shopping street on Saturday afternoon or the canteen of a busy office at lunchtime.
- Choose a short piece of incidental music (about two minutes long) to set your crowd scene to.
- Make decisions about who each character is, what they are doing, where they are going, etc.
- Organise some performers into family and/or social groups.
- Use props where appropriate.
- Choreograph the scene so there is always someone on stage and something going on. Use the music to cue entrances and exits.
- If you can, video a 'performance' of your scene. Watch it back and discuss how successful you were in creating a natural-looking scene.

14.3.4 Acting requirements

In rehearsal, actors put their research and character development work into practice under the guidance of the director. The director advises on interpretation and application of appropriate acting styles to suit the show and the director's creative vision of the piece.

The director gives feedback on an actor's performance throughout the rehearsal period. They give instructions about the actor's use of movement and gesture, their vocal work and their interpretation of their character. The actor must take that feedback positively to improve and develop their performance. It is important to remember that the director is not making personal remarks or critiques. They want the actor to give the best performance they possibly can.

During early rehearsals this feedback may happen constantly as a scene is stopped and started, worked and reworked. In later rehearsals, when the director wants the performers to run a larger section of the show without interruption, the director may give notes at the end of the rehearsal. It is important that a performer listens carefully to the director's notes, noting down any feedback that relates to them, and putting instructions into practice during the next rehearsal.

Case study: Jimi – Chorus member

'I am currently a member of the chorus in a touring production of *Guys and Dolls*. This is my first professional job. I completed a Musical Theatre course at university just over a year ago, and I have been working in a shop whilst going to auditions ever since. I was really excited when I finally got my first professional job.

Being a member of the chorus requires a range of skills. There are times when you have to blend into the background, then the next minute you are in the thick of it, taking part in an energetic dance routine. In this production, the director was keen for the chorus members to devise a character for themselves complete with a back-story. I found this really helpful particularly in the crowd scenes as it gave me a sense of purpose.

Being on tour means we perform in a different theatre virtually every week. No two stages are completely alike, so you have to really concentrate to make sure you know where you are in relation to the set and other performers. It also takes a lot of energy to give it your all night after night. I try to think of every performance as an opening night.

Over to you

- What pressures might performing in a long run (a large number of performances) put on a performer?
- How might they keep their performance work fresh?

Activity: Emotional register

Your character may undergo various emotions during the course of the show, for example:

- fear
- excitement
- worry
- anger
- happiness
- frustration

Take a scene from the show and consider the emotional state of your character during the scene.

Consider how the emotion(s) might manifest themselves in the character's behaviour, i.e. in their voice, facial expressions, movements and gestures.

You could do this by thinking back to a time when you felt the same emotion(s), e.g. when you were worried about an exam result, you might have been fidgety and unable to stay still.

Use this memory to inform your work when rehearsing the scene.

PLTS

By taking part in rehearsals for a musical, you will demonstrate your skills as a **team worker**.

Functional skills

English: By making a range of contributions to discussions and making effective presentations in a wide range of contexts, you will be using your **speaking and listening** skills.

Assessment activity 3

Take part in rehearsals for a musical production.

Initial rehearsals may include work on:

- musical numbers
- dance and movement sections
- dialogue sections.

Later rehearsals will require the combining of this work as the show comes together.

You should contribute to all rehearsals you are required to attend, maintaining a suitable level of discipline throughout.

Evidence

- your log book with notes on the work you undertake in rehearsals
- tutor observations monitoring your ability to contribute positively to rehearsals
- recordings of milestone rehearsals on DVD to provide evidence of your contribution

Grading tips

M3 You should focus on tasks during rehearsals and contribute ideas, which make a notable difference to the process, or to the shape and content of a scene, song or musical number.

You should have a good attendance and punctuality record.

You should arrive at rehearsal fully prepared in terms of warming up, having learnt lines, songs and/or moves, wearing the correct clothing, and having carried out any required research.

D3 You should have a professional attitude to rehearsals and be fully focused on the task of interpreting and engaging with the musical theatre material. Throughout the rehearsal process, you should help to energise the creative process and make insightful suggestions that help to move the work on.

You should have an exemplary attendance or punctuality record, and any matters to do with absence or time-keeping must be fully justified and agreed in advance.

14.4 Be able to perform a role in a musical

The opening night of any show, whether in the West End or the theatre of a school or college, is an exciting and nerve-racking time for all involved. It is the culmination of all the hard work that has been undertaken, and the point at which the director, musical director and choreographer must step back and allow the performers to get on with the show.

The opening night is when all the elements of the musical will come together

14.4.1 Physical and vocal expression

An effective and expressive performance of a musical theatre work requires the performer to put into practice the skills and techniques (vocal and physical) that they have practised and rehearsed.

In terms of physical expression, this will include:

- effective control of movement and physical range
- use of balance, poise and dynamics in movement work.

Musical theatre works often include moments of high energy where dynamic physical work is required as well as quieter, more restrained movements.

In terms of vocal expression, this will include:

- effective control of the voice and use of vocal range
- awareness of tone, pitch and intonation in vocal work.

14.4.2 Communication

In the professional theatre, shows often have a long run of performances stretching to months or even years. Whilst the cast may alter from time to time, many performers will stay with a show for countless performances, and they must ensure the show remains as fresh as it was on the opening night. For the cast it may be the 'umteenth' time a show has been performed, but for the audience it is the first time they have seen it. Maintaining focus and concentration throughout the performance is vital.

You will need to think about:

- vocal projection – can the audience hear you?
- physical embodiment of a role – are you effectively using movement, gesture and physical expression to personify the role you are playing?
- communication of mood and emotion – are you effectively communicating the moods and emotions your character is feeling during the piece?
- communication of interpretation – are you effectively interpreting the material you are performing, i.e. songs, dance routines, scripted elements?
- communication with other performers – are you relating and reacting to other performers in the piece in an effective manner?

Performance elements

Final preparations before the opening night of a musical will include technical and dress rehearsals. These rehearsals allow performers to get used to the various performance elements they will be working with.

These are likely to include:

Lighting: Many musicals are staged with lighting and other technical effects. Performers must position themselves correctly to ensure they are lit.

Scenery: Some musicals may have a number of elaborate sets. Performers must ensure they are familiar with the items of scenery, taking particular care when different levels, e.g. rostra and steps, are used.

Sound: Whether working with a live band, keyboard or backing track, the performers' voices need to balance with the accompaniment. Sounds technicians must ensure a correct balance is achieved, and that the performers can hear the accompaniment clearly.

Microphones: With most musicals performed in large theatres, microphones are frequently used to amplify the singers' voices. Small radio microphones known as 'lavalieres' can be attached to the edge of the performers' hairline on the forehead using surgical tape.

Costume: Costumes in musicals can be elaborate or simple. The costume team undertake final fittings before the dress rehearsal, and make any adjustments needed after the dress rehearsal in time for the first night. Performers must be aware of and prepare for any costume changes during the show, particularly those where limited time is available.

Props: Props (also known as 'properties') include set dressings and furnishings that the performers handle during the show. When not in use, they are usually kept on a props table back stage, and performers must collect and return props as necessary. Small 'personal' props that are kept with an actor's costume are the responsibility of the performer.

14.4.3 Integration

The performance of any musical theatre production involves the bringing together of different skills and techniques. The performer combines acting movement and singing skills to produce a successful interpretation of their role. They successfully fit the performance of their own role (or roles) in terms of style to the overall production concept, working with production elements as appropriate. They are responsive in performance, making adjustments as appropriate.

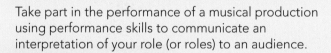

Assessment activity 4

Take part in the performance of a musical production using performance skills to communicate an interpretation of your role (or roles) to an audience.

Evidence

- the recorded performance on DVD

Grading tips

M4 You should produce a performance which is technically secure, and that has aspects to it that are occasionally inspired and/or inventive. Your performance should be consistently watchable with memorable elements. You should demonstrate engagement with the material, and produce an interpretation of your role which works.

D4 You should perform with confidence in everything you do on stage. You should demonstrate the ability to communicate your role (or roles) with a complete sense of ease and commitment.

PLTS

Taking part in the performance of a musical will develop your skills as a **self manager**.

You should show that you can work towards goals, showing initiative, commitment and perseverance.

Functional skills

English: By making a range of contributions to discussions and make effective presentations in a wide range of contexts, you will be using your **speaking and listening** skills.

Just checking

1   What were the key features of a 'follies' show?

2   What features does the Operetta have in common with the classic American musical?

3   What is an Overture?

4   What is a songbook or jukebox musical?

5   What are the meanings of the following terms:
   • Solo
   • Chorus
   • Through Sung
   • Libretto
   • Lyrics?

6   What is the difference between the work carried out by the director, the choreographer and the musical director?

edexcel

Assignment tips

• Research your role (or roles) with care and attention to detail. Use your findings as a way of getting to know your character(s) and inform your interpretation.

• Use some initiative when developing and using the skills and techniques required in this unit. Rehearsal does not have to be led by the director. Work on developing and improving your skills in your own time as well as in the rehearsal room.

• Maintain a good level of discipline in rehearsals. Contribute in a positive manner, being supportive of others and responding to direction in an appropriate way.

• Give your all in performance. Think about your character and how you can communicate imaginatively with the audience.

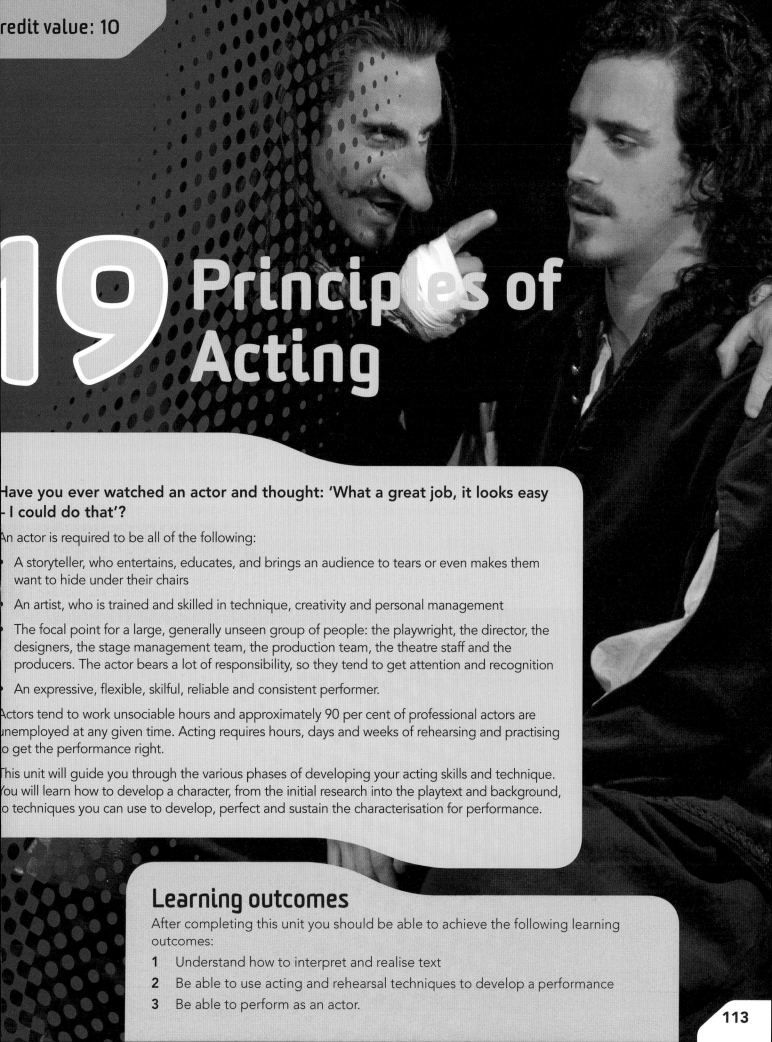

19 Principles of Acting

Have you ever watched an actor and thought: 'What a great job, it looks easy – I could do that'?

An actor is required to be all of the following:

- A storyteller, who entertains, educates, and brings an audience to tears or even makes them want to hide under their chairs
- An artist, who is trained and skilled in technique, creativity and personal management
- The focal point for a large, generally unseen group of people: the playwright, the director, the designers, the stage management team, the production team, the theatre staff and the producers. The actor bears a lot of responsibility, so they tend to get attention and recognition
- An expressive, flexible, skilful, reliable and consistent performer.

Actors tend to work unsociable hours and approximately 90 per cent of professional actors are unemployed at any given time. Acting requires hours, days and weeks of rehearsing and practising to get the performance right.

This unit will guide you through the various phases of developing your acting skills and technique. You will learn how to develop a character, from the initial research into the playtext and background, to techniques you can use to develop, perfect and sustain the characterisation for performance.

Learning outcomes

After completing this unit you should be able to achieve the following learning outcomes:

1. Understand how to interpret and realise text
2. Be able to use acting and rehearsal techniques to develop a performance
3. Be able to perform as an actor.

Assessment and grading criteria

This table shows you what you must do in order to achieve a **pass**, **merit** or **distinction** grade, and where you can find activities in this book to help you.

To achieve a **pass** grade the evidence must show that you are able to:	To achieve a **merit** grade the evidence must show that, in addition to the pass criteria, you are able to:	To achieve a **distinction** grade the evidence must show that, in addition to the pass and merit criteria, you are able to:
P1 interpret and realise texts with an appreciation of performance demands **Assessment activity 1 page 119** **Assessment activity 2 page 124**	**M1** interpret and realise texts demonstrating a sound appreciation of performance demands **Assessment activity 1 page 119** **Assessment activity 2 page 124**	**D1** interpret and realise texts demonstrating a thorough appreciation of performance demands **Assessment activity 1 page 119** **Assessment activity 2 page 124**
P2 develop material for performance through research, rehearsal and characterisation **Assessment activity 3 page 132**	**M2** develop material for performance through competent use of research, rehearsal and characterisation **Assessment activity 3 page 132**	**D2** develop material for performance through confident and imaginative use of research, rehearsal and characterisation **Assessment activity 3 page 132**
P3 perform using vocal and movement skills appropriate to the role **Assessment activity 4 page 136**	**M3** perform demonstrating good control of vocal and movement skills in a thoughtful interpretation of text and character **Assessment activity 4 page 136**	**D3** perform demonstrating vocal and movement skills in an effective and imaginative manner to physically embody character and interpret text with clarity and intelligence **Assessment activity 4 page 136**
P4 communicate with an audience. **Assessment activity 4 page 136**	**M4** communicate with an audience with clarity. **Assessment activity 4 page 136**	**D4** communicate with an audience with complete focus and engagement. **Assessment activity 4 page 136**

How you will be assessed

This unit will be assessed through an internal assignment that will be designed and marked by the tutors at your centre. You will need to show that you have explored a variety of different ways of bringing the characters to life, through research and rehearsal. As you will need to perform your work to an audience, it is important to develop your vocal and physical skills to a sufficient standard.

The work you produce may include:

- an actor's log (including notes on the play(s) and character(s) being studied)
- examples of research material, such as notes on practitioners and styles of acting
- notes on professional performance(s) that you have watched
- audio/visual recordings of rehearsals and performances
- recorded feedback from your tutor(s)
- feedback from audiences, for example a questionnaire.

Philip, 17-year-old acting learner

In our major project we did a play called *Two* by Jim Cartwright. I played two characters: the boy and Kev. Kev was a bigger role than the boy, who only appears towards the end of the play. Kev is one of the most significant roles in the show.

Characterisation

Kev is a nasty and pathetic little character. He is paranoid, over-sensitive, jealous, possessive, cruel and dominating. He constantly attempts to keep a high status, assumes he is popular and well regarded in the pub, and tries to disguise his dysfunctional relationship with his girlfriend. He makes her life awful.

I created reasons for his behaviour; I gave him a back story and thought about what motivated him to behave in this way. It then became a lot easier to build the character – the way I said lines, the looks I gave, how I played with and used personal props. During rehearsals I could feel the tension and stress levels rising inside me; I had to step back from the role and gather distance from Kev's nastiness in the last movement of the scene. I slapped my girlfriend across the face and this made the audience gasp. We had practised the slap to ensure it sounded and looked convincing but didn't hurt her at all. It worked.

Performance

We did eight performances; five in week one, three in week two. I think our performances got better through the run. We got really comfortable with each other, and began to improvise in role during the Kev scene. Our director warned us that although we had the freedom to experiment, we should not 'milk' it, or lose the rhythm of the scene. But the second week was brilliant, and because we knew it was coming to an end, it seemed to make us perform better.

Over to you

- Have you ever taken part in a major production of a show? What kind of role did you play?
- If you did, what difficulties did you face as a performer? If you didn't, what problems do you think you might need to overcome?

115

19.1 Understand how to interpret and realise text

Warm up

Who is your favourite actor?

They can be a male or female performer, working in theatre, film, television or radio.

1 What do you like about their performances? Think about their acting skills. Does anything make them unique?

2 How 'believable' are they in character? Perhaps they seem to be comfortable in the role, and are acting 'naturally' or 'realistically'.

3 Are they emotive? Listen to the voice and notice how they express emotions. Observe how they communicate physically.

4 How is their relationship with other actors? Think about how they relate to other actors in role, whether you believe the relationships, and whether they work well together.

5 Could you act like them? You might be similar physically, or in performance style.

6 Do their looks matter? They might look beautiful, striking or classically handsome.

Write 150 words about your favourite actor. Be precise and clear about their skills and technique. Present your findings to the group. Notice how others describe the qualities of their chosen actors.

19.1.2 Styles and approaches

In order to understand how to interpret and realise text, it is important to know there are many different styles and approaches to performance.

There are historical periods of performance, such as Greek, Medieval, Elizabethan and Restoration, and the plays and performance styles of each can be dictated by:

- the conventions and approaches to style and content by playwrights
- content, themes and issues of the play
- structure, plot, storytelling, language of the writing
- types of characters, relationships
- audience types, tastes and expectations
- performance spaces
- setting, costume, lighting, and so on.

There are styles of performance, such as naturalism, expressionism, farce, melodrama, physical theatre and Theatre of the Absurd.

Further information on acting styles is included in Project 6: Performing in Contemporary Plays, page 245.

Some playwrights' work is influenced by, or in the style of, particular **theatre practitioners**.

There are theories and approaches to performance that have been developed by theatre practitioners. A theatre practitioner may have done one or more of the following:

- Developed a particular approach to theatrical performance and staging
- Written plays
- Directed own plays and/or plays by others
- Created a formula or theory on development and practice
- Had an influence on their contemporary playwrights, directors, actors, designers and future or modern artists.

19.1.1 Research and analysis

The actor is responsible for interpreting and realising the playtext or script for performance.

The first thing to do when staging a play is to read it. You may choose to do this alone, although reading aloud in a group can have advantages: you can hear how others interpret characters, and it can highlight rhythms and meanings.

Some plays are very easy to understand:

- You can read through the text and immediately understand the plot, the types of characters and their relationships.
- The language is straightforward and recognisable; there are no unusual words, terms or references in the text.

There are lots of plays that seem more difficult to understand:

- You might not recognise some of the language used.
- It might be that the plot and storyline are very complicated.
- You might not recognise the references to characters, places or events.

If you are unsure about meaning, ask your tutor, director and fellow actors, or do the research yourself.

Sources for research

The published playscript may contain introductory notes by the playwright or translator (if appropriate). The playwright may include footnotes or a glossary/index to provide further information.

Some plays have supporting published material, because they are used in academic study or included in exam syllabuses.

You may also use general theatre/drama history/theory books and publications, or watch recorded versions of the performances of the play on DVD or internet video/audio resources.

You will need to investigate the social and historical background of a play before you begin rehearsing.

Activity: Researching your play

Choose a play you have discussed or may be using for performance, and research the following:

- The playwright: who they are, why they wrote the play, when and where the play was written
- The social, cultural and historical influences on the playwright
- References within the text that will help you to discover the meaning and subject matter of the play, situation and setting, characters, relationships, and so on
- Your character: fictional or based on real person, or type of person.

Remember: every word in the playtext is important if the playwright has chosen all of them to tell the story.

Did you know?

'Actor' refers to both males and females. The term 'actress' was developed in the early 20th century to differentiate between male and female performers. Nowadays, it is hardly used; some people see the term as old fashioned, unnecessary and sexist. In this unit, we refer to the actor only, meaning both male and female performers.

Key terms

Theatre practitioner – someone who creates theatrical performance and/or writes theoretical ideas and teachings

Psychological insight

Constantin Stanislavski (1863–1938) is the Russian director, actor and writer who founded Moscow Art Theatre and created the 'system': a set of rules, exercises and approaches for acting.

Stanislavski's techniques provide an insight to the character's psychology.

Knowing the psychology of the character (their thoughts and desires, and what motivates them) will be very useful for you as an actor. Analysing the text will help you discover what is happening inside the mind of the character. This can help you make decisions on how you will bring the character to life.

To understand the psychology of the character, you will need to look at what the character says and does. You may want to write down your ideas – and if you have a major role in the play, there might be a lot to analyse. You could pick out key words that sum up your character. You could also note what others say to your character, and about the character (see the example of a character analysis sheet on page 124).

Subtext and motivation

In most plays, you can discover what **motivates** your character, that is, what the character 'wants'.

Each line, or series of lines, will have a subtext. The subtext is the motivation of the person speaking. You can work out the motivation for a line of speech or series of lines (both known as an 'objective'), a whole scene or act, and even the whole play (known as the 'super objective').

Here is an extract of text. Can you work out what the subtext and motivations are?

Ste: I really don't think I want to …

Jane: I knew you were going to say that.

Ste: Well, it's true. I'm tired.

Jane: Go then…

Ste: Oh, don't be like that. That isn't fair.

Jane: God, I hate you when you're like this!

Here is the same text, but this time with added subtext and motivations, showing what the characters want

Ste: I really don't think I want to …
I want to tell you that I don't love you any more.

Jane: I knew you were going to say that.
I want you to know how much I care about you, and don't want to lose you.

Ste: Well, it's true. I'm tired.
I want to have to stop pretending I love you.

Jane: Go then …
I want to test you to prove your love and loyalty.

Ste: Oh, don't be like that. That isn't fair.
I want you to argue with me so I have an excuse to leave.

Jane: God, I hate you when you're like this!
I want you to cuddle me.

Once you have determined the motivations and objectives, you will need to think about how you could perform the lines: the tone of your voice, eye contact, body language, physical contact, standing or moving, and so on. You will need to consider how the audience will perceive your actions: will your acting decisions be understood?

You could try reading through the text again, this time adding extra information; for example underline words that you want to emphasise, or include stage directions that match the subtext or motivation.

Interpretation

The character is created by the words on pages of a script. These words will be interpreted by the actor and director and brought to life. It is the actor's responsibility to grasp the meaning of the words and to create a true, living version of the character.

Understanding the character is essential; knowing *why* the character speaks and behaves in the way they do will allow the actor to develop the performance.

You must understand the original intentions of the playwright before you make your interpretation. Sometimes the actor will use the analysis of the text to determine how the character will be interpreted. Sometimes the playwright will have given very strong guidelines about the setting and behaviour of particular characters, and there is not much room for major shifts in interpretation.

For example, in a play like *Our Country's Good* (written by Timberlake Wertenbaker), the language, the situation and the relationships all determine a particular time and place, that is 1780s on a ship going to an Australian penal colony. These are defined elements, stated by the playwright. Your play (the story, the relationships and the meaning) could be undermined by not understanding this, and by using behaviour, gestures and clothing, that are not authentic. However, there are decisions for the actor to make, such as the eye contact, the gesture or the tone of the voice.

There are plays that allow for flexibility and greater opportunities for artistic freedom in interpretation, for example Shakespeare, or Pinter's *The Caretaker*. The language demands verse speaking, but the action and setting can be manipulated and experimented on. A good example of this is Shakespeare's *Romeo and Juliet*, which has not only been interpreted successfully using settings centuries apart (the film directed by Baz Luhrman in 1996), but also into different cultural settings and styles such as the musical *West Side Story*.

Did you know?

The word 'actor' is derived from the ancient Greek word 'hypokrites' and means 'one who interprets'.

Source: Csapo, E. and Slater, W., *The Context of Ancient Drama*, 1994

Key terms

Motivate – to drive or compel a character to behave, speak, act and react

Assessment activity 1

P1 M1 D1 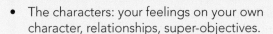 BTEC

Choose one scene from a play you are currently working on. Check with your tutor before you start.

- Decide on the units, objectives and subtext.
- Work out the motivations for each character, and how you think you should express them. Write them down as in the example on the previous page.
- Read through the scene, thinking about the subtext.
- Now read aloud your subtext 'script'.
- Does it influence how you think about the characters?
- Does it have an effect on how you say the lines?
- What about the physical interaction and movement, and body language?

You might be staging the whole piece, or extracts, but there are opportunities to discuss how the play could be interpreted. You might want to discuss the following:

- The setting: realistic, set in a particular time, the staging you will use, the audience

- The characters: your feelings on your own character, relationships, super-objectives.

Evidence

- notes on your findings and thoughts in your log book
- annotated script

Grading tips

M1 You should delve deeper into your analysis and make sure you are grasping the essence of the character.

D1 Your analysis should demonstrate your understanding of the subtext and truth of what the character 'wants'.

PLTS

By considering your own personal development as an actor while reflecting on the scene, you will be developing your skills as a **reflective learner**.

Functional skills

English: Discussing the possible meanings of the play you are studying, will allow you to practise your **speaking and listening** skills.

19.1.3 Preparation and improvisation

Observation

You may be playing a character that behaves or communicates in a particular way. Let's say you will want to act as a barrister in a courtroom. If you want to be convincing, or show a recognisable demonstration to the audience, you will need to conduct some preparatory work. This might involve observing real judges or barristers in action, or watching other actors performing in courtroom scenes.

Remember

You want to observe people behaving 'naturally' in their environment. You should ask for permission to observe them over a set period of time, but not actually let them know exactly when you are going to do it. This way they won't know to change their normal behaviour because they are being observed. Observation should be conducted safely. Do not put yourself in danger when observing with permission.

You may choose to observe the behaviour of:

- Real people, as individuals or within a group. A barrister in a courtroom is 'performing', whereas an elderly person walking to the post office is not. A group of people waiting for a train to arrive in rush hour could all share the same desire: 'I want the train to come now and I want a seat.' This could cause them all to behave in a similar way.
- Professional performers in live or recorded performance. They could be playing the same role as you, or they could be performing a type of character, for example age, physicality, occupation and status.

You might observe people in the following situations:

- sitting on a park bench
- eating lunch at a café in a shopping centre
- waiting at a bus stop
- travelling on public transport
- in a library, art gallery or museum.

Observation can be useful for noticing:

- unusual or extreme behaviour, such as a nervous tic or drunkenness.
- how physicality changes according to situation

- how people create and use personal space; for example, how people maintain distance
- communication with others in physical and verbal ways; for example how people greet one other, create status, or talk to one other
- how older people move and behave
- how physical disabilities can affect how someone stands, walks and behaves in public
- how people behave and interact with others in public spaces; for example, in shops (window shopping, focus, embarrassment, status), at bus stops (comfort, informal/formal queuing system), at a party (status, flirting, intoxication, relaxation), in a theatre audience (status, attitude) or in a football stadium (conformity, masculinity). How do people use and define personal space, eye contact and communication? There are defined spaces, even on a busy train.

When observing people, notice open and closed behaviour; for example hands on hips as opposed to arms crossed. What do these gestures and stances signify? Look for examples of body language that signify:

- confidence and arrogance
- nervousness and embarrassment
- aggression and intimidation
- love and attraction.

You could also observe yourself: recognising your own patterns of behaviour is very important as an actor. You can compare your own behaviour with the character, and whether you share any physical behaviour traits.

Did you know?

Some actors take character observation and preparation to extremes. Daniel Day Lewis and Robert de Niro have both used the techniques of method acting in film performances. Method acting involves the actor immersing themselves in the life of the character. This can involve researching and imitating the behaviour of the character as well as the internal thoughts and emotions of the characters. It might result in the actor 'living' as the character off screen. Both Day Lewis and de Niro trained as boxers for performance roles, gained or lost weight and changed their physical appearances to ensure that the physicality of the characters was realistic and believable.

Activity: Imitation

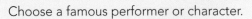

Choose a famous performer or character.

Perform extracts from your play, imitating their vocal style or physicality.

This is an interesting exercise to do, as it can be silly, yet can also develop and focus the characterisation.

Exploration

Constantin Stanislavski developed the 'system', a series of concepts and exercises that actors could use when preparing for performance. This unit contains some of these exercises for you to try.

A good first exercise is when the actor questions why the playwright (or the director) suggests a particular action: why am I entering this room? Why am I looking out of the window?

Naturalistic acting can use 'the given circumstances', which are created by the playwright, and developed and fixed by the director, designers and actors.

The given circumstances are identified by analysing the play, using:

- stage directions
- lines you say about yourself
- lines others say about you.

They can include the following:

- The plot of the play
- Facts about the play: period (century), time of day, geographical location, situation and environment
- Social, cultural and historical information
- Facts about the character: age, physical appearance, accent, class, status and relationships.

You can use the following questions to help you discover facts about your character:

Who am I? Think about identity, status, inner feelings and emotions, how others see you, interact with you, and feel about you.

Where am I? It could be the character's bedroom, on the street, in an enchanted forest, or a courtroom.

When is it? Consider the conditions of the period you are living in, the society, the situation, your clothing and behaviour.

What do I want? Decide your small objectives (for example, 'I want him to tell me the truth'), your super objective (for example 'I want to be free from guilt over my mother's death').

What obstacles do I have to overcome to achieve my aims? Think about the people and situation(s) you have to overcome, such as your own doubts, other people trying to scare you, or your responsibilities.

What effect do I want to make? Consider what you want the audience to think about you.

Who am I talking to? Think about who the other character(s) are, and whether you are talking to yourself or directly to the audience (who may also be 'characters').

You can invent facts and a back-story, filling in the gaps in the life of the character. You will need to be imaginative and use the facts provided within the text. You could use your background research to do this.

Activity: Hot-seat

Hot-seating is a popular and simple exercise that actors and directors use to develop and explore their knowledge and understanding of the character.

Encourage each member of the group to take part.

The director and other cast members (sometimes in character themselves) ask questions about the character. You will be tested on the facts of the play, and you will develop background information for the character, such as relationships, motivations and tastes.

Try to stay in character during hot-seating. This exercise requires focus and concentration; losing characterisation during the exercise can have a negative effect on the performance work of others too.

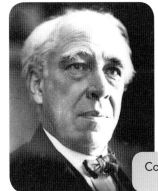

Constantin Stanislavski

Identification

Identifying with the character is important in both naturalistic and non-naturalistic performance. Here are some activities that you can explore to help identify with your character. Depending on the style of performance, you can incorporate these elements into your interpretation.

Activity: Identification

If you are working alone, complete the following tasks.

1 Compare your character with an animal that shares some of the characteristics and traits.

2 Choose a famous person who behaves or talks in ways that you have imagined the character would. Find an image, such as a photograph, a painting, or a still from TV or film.

3 Decide on three adjectives that describe both yourself and your character. No matter how different you think you might be, find some similarities.

If you are working in a group, complete the following tasks.

1 Standing in a straight line, each actor decides on a colour that sums up their character (and can include shades or types of colour, for example sky blue, buttery yellow, oily black). Reposition yourself so the line becomes a 'colour chart'. Everyone gets into position in order from light to dark colours. The line becomes a moral barometer – one end is kind and virtuous, the other end is evil and cruel.

2 Now try the same exercise, this time using status as the barometer; one end is high, the other end of the line is low.

To help the actor identify with the role to be played, Stanislavski developed a technique known as the 'magic if'. The actor must use their imagination when performing. The given circumstances provide the context for the actor, while the *magic if* technique tests the imagination, with questions such as: 'What would happen if …'

You could try the *magic if* theory through off-text improvisations and hot-seating. Here are some examples which you may need to adapt according to the context of the play.

Activity: What would happen if your character …

- … gets stuck in a lift? (worries; sickness; makes friends with others)
- … witnesses a hit and run accident? (feels guilt; helps; runs away; steals wallet)
- … is cooking a special birthday meal and there is a power failure? (cries; drinks wine; goes out)
- … gets a phone call from the police about a local burglary? (panics; guilt; falls asleep)
- … is told that you have six months to live? (turns to drink and drugs; prays)

Through this activity you will make connections with the character; it will 'cement' the given circumstances and your understanding of how the character is motivated. The development of the character should be substantial.

Activity: Improvising in role

Try performing improvisations of situations to 'flesh out' the characterisation with other members of the cast. You could:

- show characters meeting for the first time
- show what happened before and after a particular scene
- develop scenes that the audience does not see, but are referred to in the play.

You can also think about how using your five senses influences or changes the way you are going to experience a situation. You can think about how you are likely to behave if you cannot feel anything when you touch an object; or how your facial expression is going to change if you enter a room where there is a bad smell; or maybe how your eyes will glow if you get served your favourite food; or how would it feel to wear wet clothes.

Feeling and emotional truth

There are two approaches to emotional truth. The first is through the actor's own experiences of a particular emotion, feeling or reaction to something or to a situation. The actor playing the role may not experience murder, extreme violence or living in extreme conditions, but there are some emotional states that most people will experience and think about when developing the role. Empathy is important; you can put yourself in someone else's position and imagine how they would feel, and how you think you would react or respond.

The second approach is through the actor enacting the emotional truth, without having to dredge it up from his or her own experience. Your character's parents might die, for example. You might not have experienced such grief, but you could relate it to your own experiences; you might have experienced loss (it could have been a pet, or an object that was special to you), and you could consider how this made you feel, relating this to the emotions felt by your character.

Concentration and focus

As an actor, it is important to maintain your concentration and focus during rehearsals, and especially during performance. Have you ever been to a performance and noticed an actor lose concentration or be distracted by someone in the audience?

It does not tend to happen in professional theatre, but learner actors can lose concentration. This might happen because:

- the actor might not really understand the play
- the actor might forget about the needs of the audience.

Remember

When you make a mistake on stage, it is always better to keep on going and not to acknowledge the mistake in any way. Sometimes, the audience will not even notice!

How easy would it be for this actor to hide that he has forgotten one line?

Assessment activity 2

P1 M1 D1

Select a character from a play you are currently working on. Create a character profile sheet, using the following headings:

- What the playwright states as facts (age, address and home information, significant relationships, occupation, status)
- What the character says about himself or herself
- What others say about the character
- Character actions and behaviour
- The 'super objective' of the play
- Significant objectives and motivations for your character
- Character relationships (create a family tree)
- Internal emotional states
- Character through-line, from birth to death
- Interpretations (background, tastes, clothing, props).

Create a performance profile, using the following headings:

- Influences on performance (practitioners, styles of performance)
- Similarities to other characters and performers
- Decisions made by director, designer and actor.

You could also keep a record of your decisions in the following way:

Evidence

- your notes in a log book

Grading tips

M1 During preparations, you should show that you can apply the skills you already possess to new contexts. For example, you can use dance skills developed in jazz classes. You should be able to follow instructions, ask questions when required and undertake practice with only a small amount of guidance from your tutors. You should also be able to organise your time effectively outside class time in order to consolidate new learning.

D1 You should use skills confidently and independently, and show that you are able to find the right gesture, tone of voice, dance move, rhythm and pitch of a note and apply them to the context of the work at hand. When questioning a tutor, you should demonstrate that you understand the work you are undertaking, and make suggestions about style and interpretation.

Characteristics	Play reference	Performance interpretation
(Summarising your thoughts and findings, eg violent, affectionate, loving, spiritual, sexist)	(This could be stage direction, lines spoken by character)	(This could be use of voice, gestures, stance, physical relationship with other characters use of props, entrances/exits, etc.)

PLTS

By developing a character, you are using your skills as a **creative thinker**.

Functional skills

English: By discussing possible interpretations of a piece of text, you will be using your **speaking and listening** skills.

19.1.4 Skills and techniques

In this section, we will continue to look at the naturalistic style of performance used by Constantin Stanislavski, Lee Strasberg and Augusto Boal, amongst others. The activities can be used to meet P1, M1, D1, P3, M3 and D3.

Movement

The body is used to express characteristics, age, emotion, status and environment. In a naturalistic play, movement by the actor will be realistic and believable. In a non-naturalistic play, movement might suggest concepts, shapes and objects. These activities ask you to think about how to use your body to express ideas effectively.

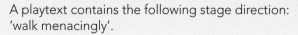

Activity: Movement

A playtext contains the following stage direction: 'walk menacingly'.

Try and do it as naturally as you can. You might find it difficult to do. Did it feel unnatural and unbelievable?

Think of a reason why you might be walking menacingly: are you trying to intimidate someone? Are you frightened and need to pretend you are not?

Now try to 'walk menacingly' with a motivation. It should now be easier to feel, and appear, natural and believable.

This is naturalistic acting, using a realistic situation and performed with a motivation.

Gesture

A gesture is a form of non-verbal communication. Examples include a defiant shrug of the shoulders, a dismissive handshake, or a sympathetic hand resting on the back.

Gestures are usually made to communicate an idea, a feeling or emotion and can be used with words and body language; for example gesturing with the hands to emphasise an argument or idea.

Some performance styles are very open and 'over the top'; for example epic theatre and pantomime.

If the style of performance uses half masks, such as commedia dell'arte, the gestures will probably be exaggerated and larger than life.

No matter how 'realistic' the performance style, the actor must ensure the audience can understand the emotional truth of the character. In most theatre spaces, the actor must amplify the performance; it has to be 'bigger' than real life, purely because of the distance between the audience and the stage.

Physicalisation

We use body language to communicate our feelings, relationships and physical interaction with others, animals, our environment and objects around us.

Elements of physicalisation include:

- posture
- gesture
- facial expression
- movement.

Activity: Physicalisation

Find a scene from a play that has strong emotional themes, for example Shelagh Delaney's *A Taste of Honey*.

Block it, rehearse it, learn lines and perform without using scripts.

Perform without words; say them in your head, but keep the movement and gestures.

Notice how you concentrate on the movements and gestures to express your emotions, as without words they are the only way to communicate.

Perform again with words, but now try to get a balance between how you communicate your emotion and motivations through the words and the movement and gestures.

Further guidance on commedia dell'arte is included in Project 9: Physical Theatre Performance, page 283.

Voice: articulation and tone

Modulation refers to the musical elements of the speaking voice, including pitch, pace, inflection/tone, volume, intensity and pausing.

The following sentences or phrases are known as tongue twisters. They are designed to exercise and prepare the tongue and facial muscles for performance.

- She quickly fetched a new coal scuttle.
- She was inexplicably mimicking him.
- Red lorry, yellow lorry, red leather, yellow leather
- Two tickets to tooting
- Unique New York, New York unique
- You may choose fruit spoons or soup spoons.
- Peggy babcock, babcock Peggy
- Put the kettle by the bottle on the settle.

Soft and hard voice tones are used for different purposes: softer tones can be comforting and develop a sense of relaxation, while harder tones can seem aggressive.

The character's motivation can determine the tone used for a line or speech.

Voice: pace

You can use the speed of speech to indicate particular characteristics.

A fast pace could imply you are confident, demanding, excited, nervous, or attempting to hide something, whereas a slower pace could mean you are controlled, determined, explaining instructions, hesitant or nervous.

Here are some ways you could experiment with pace:

- Notice the speed of your speech when you are feeling particular emotions.

- Find the pace, speed and rhythm of the play, or scenes/moments of the play.
- Do a speed run of the play, speaking the lines (and doing moves) as quickly as possible.
- Try the articulation, pace and tone exercises with your lines, experimenting with sound.
- Emphasise and exaggerate moments of tension, and downplay other sections.

Emotional range and investment

Have you experienced any of the following emotions or emotional states?

- Relief; happiness; joyous ecstasy; overwhelmed; speechless and bewildered
- Envy; jealousy; bitterness; revenge
- Self-satisfaction; delusion; paranoia
- Trapped; physically beaten; mentally beaten
- Loss; sadness; grief; depression
- Unhappiness; anger; violent rage
- Undermined; manipulated; lonely
- Lost; fear; horror; repulsion; sickness.

The character you will perform could experience (or could have experienced) any of these emotional states.

When developing the performance of a particular emotion, try to remember your own experiences, how you felt, how you behaved and acted (for example, how you communicated with others), and how you felt about yourself.

If you have not experienced the emotion, or anything like it, talk to people who have. Use your imagination to develop the performance, or imitate how others look and sound when they are feeling or acting the emotion.

Case study: Thomas Aldridge, actor

Before playing an emotional scene, I will get into a particular frame of mind so I will enter the scene 'ready'. I don't use 'emotional memory' (see section about Feeling and emotional truth, page 123), but will put myself in a certain emotional state. It may be difficult to suddenly switch into the mood when walking on stage, so I find the 'state' backstage. I cannot cry real tears (although there are some actors that can), but I can be extremely sad and tormented if necessary. (See Project 10: Moving On, page 295.)

Inner and outer characteristics

People often judge each other, making decisions based on external characteristics, such as clothing, make-up, behaviour, accent, colour of skin or hairstyle. What we see on the outside, however, may not reflect the internal feelings, emotions and objectives.

Inner characteristics define *who the character is*: their beliefs, emotions, thoughts and attitudes. As an actor, you can determine the internal emotions through your interpretation. In performance, you can feel the emotion (or consider it), and you may use your own experiences to do this.

Outer characteristics demonstrate *who your character appears to be* (and wants to be), and what others think about your character. These are determined by: appearance, friends and associates, situation, job, status and behaviour. As an actor, you can demonstrate the external expression of emotions in your face, your voice (and any vocal sounds like a scream, yelp, grunt), your posture, your gestures and movements.

Did you know?

Looking the part can have a big influence on your performance. Wearing certain clothes or using particular props might reflect inner and outer characteristics (for example, a short skirt, a crucifix or a necklace, or a temporary tattoo).

Interaction and responsiveness

When performing in a naturalistic or realistic way, you must listen to what the other characters are saying, and respond appropriately.

Practise the technique of 'cue biting' (reacting quickly and promptly, verbally and/or physically, to your cue). This will demonstrate that you are attentive and responsive as a performer.

Use of space

The physical space between characters in the performance can signify the state of relationships, levels of status and emotional connections.

Consider a tutor and a group of learners in a classroom; all sitting in a circle feels different from the tutor standing and the learners sitting. Is there a difference in status? Does it affect how they feel about their roles to teach or to learn?

Activity: Use of space

Try experimenting with distances between characters, for example when eating a meal or sitting at the bus stop.

Notice how different it feels to be sat next to each other, than to be 3 metres apart.

Does it change the status, relationships or emotions between the characters?

The concept of 'personal space' can change according to the situation and circumstances. In public spaces, people sometimes surround themselves with invisible barriers. The context will determine how wide the barrier is. Standing close to someone on a crowded train is different from standing close to them on an empty train. Personal space can be claimed and fixed, and it can feel like an invasion if someone moves into this space.

Activity: Filling the space of the stage

Try to balance the performance space with other characters through positioning, distance or height.

Imagine the performance space is on an axis. If there is not an equal distribution of weight, there will be an imbalance. Watch other performers during rehearsals to see if it is possible to maintain balance and equality in the performance space.

Use of time

Each scene will have its own tempo and rhythm depending on the characters, the plot, and the length of the scene. Think about the time it takes to say a line or a speech, and the speed of reaction and interaction with other characters. Experiment with time in performance, for example the length of a pause. Have you noticed the length of silence after an argument, or a heavy storm?

Use of weight

The way an actor uses their physical weight can be referred to as 'centre of personality'; this is the placing of their weight, as if there was a magnet attracting, or string pulling, from different parts of the body. What are the effects on your posture, behaviour and attitude, movements and status?

Activity: Use of weight

Try to capture the following characteristics physically:

- Boredom and laziness: a heaviness in the shoulders, chin, knees and stomach
- Confidence and self-belief: lightness, magnet above the head, nose turned up, chest lifted
- Cruelty and mischief: focus on eyelids, lips, hands.

19.2 Be able to use acting and rehearsal techniques to develop a performance

The actor must:

- Develop skills and technique to respond to the style of the play and performance.
- Make sure the voice and body is effective and ready for the demands of the style of the play and performance.
- Develop techniques to prepare for rehearsal and performance.
- Interpret the character and create a live performance.
- Be assisted by a director, who in turn might be influenced by a practitioner or use a particular style of acting.
- Be responsible for developing the role outside rehearsals as well as with the director (and other actors, if applicable).
- Learn that there is a relationship between them and the audience in live performance.
- Learn how to communicate effectively with the audience using vocal and physical expression.

19.2.2 Personal management

Time management

The actor needs self-discipline to ensure that the performance work is developed to the required standard. Being punctual for workshops, auditions, rehearsals and performances is essential if an actor wants a positive reputation.

Physical preparation

Stanislavski believed actors should be intelligent and have totally expressive bodies that enable them to express what their 'soul' feels. This involves:

- freedom of the body
- relaxation of the muscles.

To achieve this, the actor must be physically prepared for rehearsal and performance. Stanislavski suggested that daily exercise would guarantee the actor the freedom to perform with truth and effectiveness.

Further guidance on time management is included in Unit 5&7: Rehearsing and Performing, page 65.

Here is a suggested programme for daily exercise:

1 General stretches

- 'Centre' your body: imagine you are a puppet, with a piece of string holding you up from the top of your head. Try to achieve symmetry in your body. Bending your knees slightly, flop over from the waist. Your arms should swing loose. Pull back up to standing slowly: imagine that you are placing one vertebra on top of the next. Let your arms rise, then your shoulders, and finally your head.

2 Muscle tension and relaxation

- Walk as stiff as a tin soldier, as floppy as a rag doll, or as wobbly as a monster made of jelly.

- Lie down and support your head with a pillow or a couple of stacked books. Breathe in through your nose, counting to three, and out through your mouth for three counts. Take deep, slow breaths. Imagine lying on a sandy beach after a shipwreck; you are exhausted. As you breathe in, tense each part of your body, beginning with your feet, then relax as you breathe out. Move through the body, tensing your legs, hips, stomach, chest, arms and hands, shoulders and neck, and head. Finally, tense your whole body as you breathe in, then relax as you breathe out.

3 Breathing and vocal exercises

- Massage your face with your hands. Pretend to chew toffee. Blow kisses. Pretend to yawn. Pull faces like a chimpanzee. Make the biggest expression you can, followed by the smallest.

- Resonate: breathe in for five counts; breathe out with short 'huh' sounds. Breathe in for five counts, then out with an 'hmmm' sound. Repeat, changing the 'hmmm' into an 'aaah' sound.

- Tongue twisters: practise two a day.

4 Recital of a song, poem or extract of verse with focus on clarity, projection and rhythm

5 Do a 15 to 20 minute cardiovascular exercise

- Group: you could play a highly physical exercise like captain's coming, dance, scarecrow tag, touch and freeze, knee fights or back fights.

- Alone: skipping, jogging, swimming or cycling.

Activity: Vocal skills audit

Conduct a vocal skills audit. An audit is an assessment and evaluation of the current state of something – in this case, your voice and how you use it in performance.

Select an extract from a well-known poem or verse, such as TS Eliot's *The Wasteland*, Lewis Carroll's *Jabberwocky* or Shakespeare's sonnets.

Practise it, then perform it to your audience in a workshop setting (you do not have to learn it).

With the help of your tutor and members of your group, identify your vocal strengths and weaknesses (see qualities of voice on page 133).

Mental preparation

Before starting rehearsals or performances, it is important to wake up your brain and prepare yourself so you can demonstrate:

- Energy
- Focus
- Discipline
- Cooperation
- Imagination.

A good way to do this is to take part in a game or exercise of strategy or concentration during your warm up.

Use of actor's log

The actor's log is a useful way of keeping track of your character's development. In your actor's log you can keep:

- Notes and research findings
- Observation findings
- Ideas on interpretations – images, photos, extracts
- Director's concept, instructions, suggestions and exercises
- Vocal and physical exercises
- Any independent study or homework
- Important dates, times, locations
- **Blocking** diagrams.

Key terms

Blocking – deciding on the general positions and spatial relationships for the actors on stage

Costume and props

If you are involved in a small-scale production, there may be a tiny or non-existent production budget. You might have to find costume and props for yourself and for others.

Alternatively, you may be presented with the costume and props; in most cases, they are hired for the duration of the latter stages of rehearsals and the performance run.

You may have to be responsible for:

- bringing the costume and props to rehearsals
- making sure they are not damaged
- maintaining them during the hire period by cleaning them and hanging them up
- setting them (putting them on the props table, or on the clothes rail) before and during performances
- storing them safely
- returning them at the end of rehearsals, performances and the end of the production run.

Healthy and safe working practices

It is worth setting some ground rules at the beginning of rehearsals. Here are some common ones:

- The rehearsal space is to be kept free of drinks and food.
- Everyone must take part in a vocal and physical warm-up before rehearsals.
- Jewellery must not be worn during physical rehearsals as it can be dangerous if you are taking part in practical exercises.
- Do not play with the set, props, costumes or any electrical equipment.

Concentration and discipline

If you want to work as a professional actor, it is essential that you are employable so that people will want to work with you. The actor that can remain disciplined and focused is respected much more than the actor who is easily distracted.

To develop positive working relationships with your director and fellow actors, you must listen to instructions, and stay within the performance conditions and guidelines set by the director.

Trust and cooperation

The rehearsal period is a series of exercises and processes that will, at some point, involve failure and rejection of certain ideas. As an actor, you must be prepared to experiment with your performance, trying out ideas and suggestions that may not be successful. You must learn to lose your inhibitions!

Responsibilities

Your responsibilities as a performer must include:

- Respect for others during rehearsals and performance
- Understanding your role and the roles of others
- Shared responsibilities for the success of the performance.

In your performance group, decide on how you can work effectively as a company to rehearse and perform your piece. Make a list of ways you can help each other during the rehearsal process, such as providing each other with feedback on technique, standing in if anyone is absent, acting as prompt, being objective, and providing positive criticism. Record your performance rules and the support provided in a process log.

19.2.3 Listening and response

Taking direction and responding positively to feedback

It is important to remember as a performer not to take criticism personally. The director acts as the eyes of the audience, and helps you to develop the character and tell the story. Understanding this is key to your success as an actor.

Here is an example of a positive and negative response:

Director: You're not getting onto the stage quickly enough in the middle of Scene 2.

Actor (negative response): I'm so rubbish in this show, and I swear the director doesn't like me.

Actor (positive response): I keep forgetting that cue. I'll have to make a note about it, and reread that part of the script a few more times.

Creative flexibility and generosity

Be generous towards yourself and others when rehearsing and performing together. This means giving and taking, and responding to the needs of others. You can do this by:

- accepting that your character does not have the focus in a particular scene, and that you should hold back and give the focus to others
- realising the creative process of a collaborative process; the group is directed, but the individuals will create together
- being prepared to let others lead, and for you to take control too. How the group interacts is very important; the group has a dynamic, a relationship and a set of rhythms that are constantly shifting – if you work against them, for example have a tantrum, everyone can be affected. Effective communication and trust are essential.

Use of rehearsal exercises and technique

The director will provide you with instructions throughout the rehearsal process, and it is vital that you listen carefully to instructions, so that you do not waste time, and undermine your relationship. The more you respect the process and use the advice you are given, the better your performance will be.

19.2.4 Growth and development

Experiment and risk

Experimenting with the role can be a wonderful experience; you can really develop and take the character to places you might not have considered it can go. Do not be scared, let yourself go.

Here are some examples of experimenting and taking risks with your character:

- Play a character that is completely different from yourself; there is a risk of failing (not being convincing, and not grasping all the aspects of the character).
- Perform a scene without using your hands.
- Imagine you have a superhuman power.
- Test the power of silence; see how long you can remain silent in a scene without losing the pace and tension.

Engagement with the role

Engaging with the role means that you find connections with the character as you develop an understanding of what motivates them. You might begin to feel a sense of pride and ownership when developing the role.

Here are some ideas to help you engage with the role:

- Looking the part can be really helpful; wearing a costume, even the right shoes, can help you feel, look, move, sound and behave like the character.
- Find a personal prop, maybe something you keep hidden, that can act as a focus, lucky charm or keepsake.

Character decisions

Some of the decisions you will need to make about your character include how to say particular lines, how to enter the scene, and how to interact with another character.

They can be developed through exercises such as hot-seating, where you improvise in role, and then 'stick' to your decisions. You might decide that your character will always leave a room before anyone else, or that they will chew their nails if they feel any stress. These decisions are made through research, imagination, engagement and risk-taking.

When you capture the essence of the character, you respond in a particular way, that is, you say a line in a manner that perfectly encapsulates the character.

Having achieved this once, you must do it again; you have to be able to capture it, and repeat it, so that your mind and body remember how to do it in performance.

An actor is creative in the way that they can create the character from scratch, making decisions on performance that are exciting and fresh. However, the actor needs technique to be able to repeat, when required, the same level of creativity.

Extension and refinement

An actor needs to be able to sense when to prolong a look or action, and when to hold back. Subtlety in performance is a difficult skill to develop. The actor must experiment by trying out different ways of acting and reacting. The rehearsal process is an organic process; if you act in a certain way, and another character reacts differently from how they did in previous rehearsals, you may reveal an unfound relationship or understanding of the play. Trust the feedback you receive from your director and audience during rehearsals.

Activity

Next time you are rehearsing a scene, choose an action or a moment to extend or emphasise. Notice the effect this has on the scene. Is it too much? Or does it take the scene to the next level? Did it change how the other actors responded and reacted?

Memorising

An essential skill for any actor is the ability to remember lines. It comes more easily to some people than others, but there are techniques you can practise to help you memorise lines, movements and actions, and blocking.

Some actors like to learn their scripts as soon as they can; it allows them to develop the character and relationships without having a book to hold (and focus on).

Although studying the motivations and objectives is useful, it is sometimes only in the rehearsal that you develop an understanding of the 'wants' of the character.

> **Further guidance on memorising skills can be found in Unit 5&7: Rehearsing and Performing, page 65.**

Sustained spontaneity

As you develop as an actor, you might find that you are able to introduce a sense of improvisation during rehearsed scenes and performances. You might feel comfortable enough to make decisions in the scene: it could be a change in movement, or a new way of interacting that does not detract from the play or the story. These changes do not undermine the work in any way, and they do not happen (or should happen) all the time, but are glimpses of actors in control and demonstrating their understanding of the play.

Assessment activity 3

As part of the assessment for this unit it is likely that you will be rehearsing for a performance. Using the techniques and exercises in this unit:

- work successfully as a positive member of the group by listening, trusting and respecting others
- make decisions and experiment with characterisation and relationships
- take on, and fulfil, responsibilities in the rehearsal process, including supporting the work of others.

Evidence

- DVD recordings of your work
- notes in your log book

Grading tips

M2 You should take an active role, developing your own work and contributing to the work of others. You must be a good listener and participant in exercises and the rehearsal process.

D2 You should show how confident and imaginative you can be in the rehearsal process. You should be supportive of others, helping to create strong performance work for yourself and the overall piece.

19.3 Be able to perform as an actor

To be a successful actor, you must evaluate whether you are using your voice and body effectively to communicate the character to the audience.

The actor's 'toolkit' consists of physical elements, (the body and the voice), and the performance techniques for using these elements. These include:

- The body: gesture, movement, physicalisation of the character
- The voice: clarity, expression, modulation, vocalisation of the character
- Knowledge and understanding of the play, the style of performance required, characterisation
- Developing a relationship with other actors and the audience.

19.3.1 Vocal and physical expression

There are different types of performance space, and each will have an impact on your performance. The director will position and block you so that the audience will be able to see and hear you. Here are some types of performance space:

- Proscenium arch or single view: the 'fourth wall' is removed with the audience looking in. Naturalistic acting does not mean you can completely ignore the audience; they need to see your expression and hear your words, otherwise they will not be able to understand the story.
- Traverse: the audience is either side of you.
- In-the-round: the audience is on all sides.
- Promenade: the audience may be surrounding you, above and below you.

Evaluate the range and use of your voice in performance:

- Projection – not shouting (and potentially straining your vocal chords), but ensuring you can be heard throughout the performance space.
- Breathing – having control of your breathing as you talk, not running out of breath halfway through a speech, or faltering as you reach the end of a line.
- Articulation – enunciating, making your words clear and accurate, with the audience able to understand every word spoken.

- Pace (the rhythm and speed of speech) – speaking too quickly may result in not be heard or can imply panic or impatience. Speaking too slowly can result in losing impetus or the meaning of the words, and can imply tiredness or a patronising manner.
- Tone/inflection (the musicality) – using different notes when speaking which maintains the listener's interest. Good use of inflection shows you understand the meaning of the words, as you may be emphasising questions or highlighting key issues in the speech. When explaining something, we might use more inflection to make it more interesting. If we want to sound bored, we speak in a monotone (one note).

I
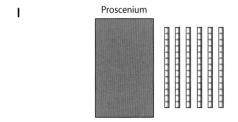
Proscenium

II
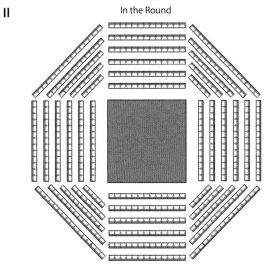
In the Round

III
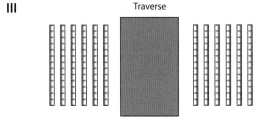
Traverse

A few types of performance spaces

Activity: Vocal projection

These short exercises can help develop vocal projection and breath control. Practise them before performing as part of your warm-up routine.

- Ensure you open and use your diaphragm.

- Centre yourself, stand upright, with your body relaxed and release any tension (shoulders, legs, neck). Imagine a piece of string travels up through your body and out of the top of your head.

- Pat your chest with open hands and open mouth, breathe in and make an 'aaah' sound for five seconds. You should hear the 'aaah' interrupted by each pat of your chest.

- Rub your hands together, then gently massage your nose, cheekbones and jaw.

- Rub your jaw up and down, including the joints around the ears.

- Keep your mouth closed and make a 'mmm' sound for ten seconds. Your lips should tingle and vibrate. Open your mouth, making an 'aaah' for ten seconds (it will be impossible to make the 'mmm' sound with your mouth open).

- Relax your lips and blow out, feeling your lips vibrate and making the sound of a horse.

- Bounce lightly on the spot; when you hit the floor make a 'ha' sound. Get louder each time.

- Lie on the floor with your head supported, knees in the air and soles on the floor.

- Imagine your head is attached to string across the room on the wall.

- Put your hands on ribcage.

- Breathe in for six seconds, and out for six. Do a fake yawn.

- Breathe in for seven seconds. Say 'bar' that lasts for seven seconds.

- Try to raise the ceiling by saying 'A E I O U'. Do not strain or shout, but visualise.

- Do the same with 'ohmmm'.

- Sing 'baa baa black sheep' softly, then in operatic style and then raise the ceiling.

- Slowly rise to your knees, then up to standing.

Did you know?

You will damage your voice if you do not exercise your vocal chords and prepare them for performance; if you are working in a large performance space, you must practise projection and clarity exercises.

Idiosyncrasy

To give your character individuality, you might include habits, tics, and certain types of behaviour in your performance. Think back to the observations you made of people to help develop your character; you may have noticed some unique behaviours that real people have.

Here are some examples of behaviours that you could use (with subtlety if performing in a naturalistic piece): stroking the top of your head; blinking rapidly; pushing your sleeves up; cracking your knuckles; sucking your thumb; hiding your hands up your sleeves; biting the skin around the edge of your nails; nodding your head; folding your arms.

Dialect and accent

If you are performing with a particular dialect or accent, you may need to check whether your pronunciation of any words in the script needs clarity.

When learning new accents and dialects, it is important to hear how they sound. You can do this by:

- listening to recordings with the same accents (there are professional audio recordings of accents and dialects available; you can also identify and use accents and dialects used in television, radio and film)

- writing down the sounds phonetically – breaking down sounds into their vowels and diphthongs.

Posture and gesture

Try to physically inhabit the character. If your performance became a series of freeze-frames, the audience would need to see the essence of your characterisation in every frame. Be as clear as you can be. Use body language to express the emotion and state of the character.

If you were playing an elderly person, their posture might not be as upright and energetic as your own. If you were playing a very quiet and reserved person, using your arms and hands a lot when talking might not be appropriate.

Tempo-rhythm

This term refers to the rhythm of the characters, the scene and the play.

The interpretation of characters determines the speed and beat (rhythm). There might be different **tempo** – rhythms in action within a given scene. For example, the nervous tutor (quick beat) and the higher status learners (slower rhythms). You may only notice the tempo-rhythm after a number of performances; it is sometimes difficult to notice until the actors are 'in the moment'.

Key terms

Tempo – usually a music term, meaning how fast a piece of music is to be played. It also means the pace at which an action or process occurs

Energy

Most actors are energised by nervousness and anticipation before and during the performance. The body is preparing itself for the intense physical and emotional workout you are about to give it. You can harness this energy and use it in the performance by ensuring you are fully prepared, warmed up, focused and determined to succeed in communicating the story to the audience.

Remember

Some actors believe that nerves can help an actor to give a good (energetic and truthful) performance.

19.3.2 Emotional investment

Evaluating your performance skills is important. There should be an ongoing process of evaluating, refining and developing your performance skills and techniques.

If you are involved in a run of performances, evaluating what went well (and not so well) will help to develop your performance for the next show, and iron out any problems.

Commitment on stage

Are you totally committed to telling the story when you are on stage? Are there any moments when you lose concentration?

You might hear a noise or see something that diverts your attention, or start thinking about other things. When does it happen? How can you stop it happening again?

Interaction and response

As an actor, you interact with and respond to both the audience and other actors.

Your performance is not about you as a person; it is about entertaining your audience. They are watching a story being told, not watching you being yourself, so do not let your ego interfere.

A good response is waiting until the audience finish laughing or clapping before the actor says their next line.

A poor response is the actor laughing at the laughter of the audience.

Playing the moment

When you are on the stage, you must be aware of and listen to the audience. For example, if you are playing a comic character, you will get an audible response from the audience. You cannot hide from it; you will hear them laugh (or not!). 'Playing the moment' is recognising that you have the opportunity to extend or heighten a particular action, line or scene. The same applies in a highly emotional scene.

If other actors are playing the moment, you must be generous and allow this to happen.

Playing the moment can also be a feeling you get in a scene; it is spontaneous, it may not happen very often, but it is an opportunity to improvise, to repeat and to extend the moment.

Activity: Public solitude

Stand in the performance space. Imagine a circle around you, and block out everything beyond it. Slowly, allow the circle to expand. Fill this new space with your focus, still blocking everything outside. Expand the circle again.

Has your focus changed? Does it feel clearer? Do you feel less anxious in performance?

Appropriateness and use of emotional range

Work out the emotional range of your character.

Is it a naturalistic or non-naturalistic piece?

Are you upstaging others when it is not appropriate? For example, bursting into tears might demonstrate your talent, but it could be totally unsuitable for the scene.

Did you know?

'Upstage' literally means on, at or to the rear of the stage. Nowadays, however, the term often means drawing attention to oneself or stealing the show.

Assessment activity 4

 BTEC

Using some of the acting skills and techniques you have learned about, perform a chosen piece to an audience. You must agree this with your tutor beforehand. The piece should be 10 to 20 minutes long.

Your interpretation should be appropriate to the role.

Focus on keeping your voice clear and your physicality suited to the character you have researched and interpreted.

Evidence

- DVD recordings of your work

Grading tips

M3 You should be confident when performing; your movements, posture and gestures should be clear and precise, and your voice will demonstrate your grasp of inflection and tone.

D3 You will perform with artistic truth, and demonstrate your understanding of the demands of the role, impressing the audience with your performance. Your performance skills practice will be clear to see (and to hear).

M4 Your aim will be to communicate the character successfully to the audience so that they understand whom you are playing.

D4 You should totally be immersed in the performance of the character.

PLTS

Performing your work to an audience will allow you to demonstrate that you are a **team worker**.

Functional skills

English: By interpreting your work to an audience, you will be using your **speaking** skills.

Gurpreet Singh
Professional actor

Gurpreet Singh completed a BTEC National in Performing Arts and trained at LAMDA.

Gurpreet has worked with the Royal Shakespeare Company and appeared in the West End musical *Bombay Dreams*. His most recent show is *Nation* at the Royal National Theatre (2009–2010).

"In my current play (*Nation* by Mark Ravenhill) all the characters are completely three-dimensional; the research we have done means every character has a complete back story, e.g. this is where I am from, this is my history. As actors, we wrote biographies for the characters.

I would say the performance is generally naturalistic, but we've got flying and there are abstract elements including expressionism.

We begin our rehearsals with an hour of yoga. We are performing on the Olivier Theatre stage and if you are hunched over, no one will believe your particular emotion, so you have to stand in a particular way (upright, chest out).

A typical day in this show: get in at 11 a.m.; notes for an hour, rehearse our singing for three hours, tea break, and then work on a scene. We would have two hours off, and then a vocal warm-up, a music warm up, then the show. That typically finishes at 10.30 p.m.

As a performer, I have faced many difficulties getting to this level. The first few years of drama school were really tough as it's like putting a mirror up to yourself – this is what you are about – and it's kind of scary. I didn't really do that well, as I was quite timid and shy. Something clicked in the final year and I left the school playing leads.

You are judged on what you are and how you look in this industry, whether you are brown, fat, or have three arms. You have to accept how you are and how other people perceive you, and that can be difficult.

I wouldn't be in this play if I didn't have the look the director is going for."

Think about it!

1 What kind of professional performance work would you like to do?
2 What is important to you when developing a role for performance?
3 Do you have any favourite warm-ups and preparatory exercises?

Just checking

1 Have you conducted research into a play and performance type?
2 Are you able to analyse a text and understand the playwright's intentions?
3 Have you completed preparatory work for the development of a character?
4 Have you practised vocal and physical exercises regularly?
5 Did you demonstrate personal management skills in the rehearsal process?
6 Have you kept an actor's log or diary to chart your development?
7 Have you worked well with other actors?
8 If you could change anything about your work in this process, what would you do differently?

edexcel

Assignment tips

- Research the character thoroughly.

- You have to make decisions about the relevance of your research, what to use and what to discard.

- Use your imagination to develop the role; you could use your own experiences and compare how you might react in a given situation.

- Build a substantial character profile, making decisions on background and information that might not be in the playtext.

- Take a positive and active role in the rehearsal process, demonstrating that you can be responsible for developing your work and that of others.

- The more thoroughly you have explored your character's background and motivations, the more convincing you should be in performance.

32 Developing Physical Theatre

Physical theatre is a form based around the way a performer uses their body as the main tool for telling a story or communicating a meaning. Physical theatre performers don't usually rely on external factors, such as set or props. They use themselves to produce an idea of a place and time, a character or group of characters in such a way that people in the audience believe in it.

By developing excellent physical movement skills, facial expression, voice and theatricality, you too can take your audience on a journey without the need to specifically convey place and time.

Physical theatre is a very old form of performance and there are traditional texts that you might use as starting points, such as fairy tales. Traditionally, the storyteller enacts what he or she is telling their audience. Today, many contemporary practitioners prefer to explore new, diverse ways of performing physical theatre.

Your work for this unit will be largely practical. The research you will do exploring working methods and contributions of well-established physical theatre makers will help you develop your own skills and techniques. You will gradually build up your own portfolio.

There will be plenty of chances for you to create your own physical theatre performances based on stimulus material, such as stories, picture themes and ideas. You will refine your ideas and develop ways of expressing them through the medium of physical theatre.

Learning outcomes

After completing this unit you should be able to achieve the following learning outcomes.

1   Understand key influences in physical theatre
2   Be able to develop skills and techniques associated with physical theatre
3   Be able to select, develop and refine materials.

Assessment and grading criteria

This table shows you what you must do in order to achieve a pass, merit or distinction, and where you can find activities in this book to help you.

To achieve a pass grade the evidence must show that you must be able to:	To achieve a merit grade the evidence must show that, in addition to the pass criteria, you must be able to:	To achieve a distinction grade the evidence must show that, in addition to the pass and merit criteria, you must be able to:
P1 explain contemporary developments of physical theatre recognising key features, influences and working methods **Assessment activity 1 page 146**	**M1** explain contemporary developments of physical theatre, making clear and considered judgements about key features, influences, and working methods **Assessment activity 1 page 146**	**D1** analyse contemporary developments of physical theatre, fully justifying all judgements concerning key features, influences and working methods **Assessment activity 1 page 146**
P2 demonstrate the use of physical theatre skills in performance **Assessment activity 2 page 149**	**M2** apply physical theatre skills with confidence and style in performance **Assessment activity 2 page 149**	**D2** apply physical theatre skills with ease, confidence and fluency in performance **Assessment activity 2 page 149**
P3 respond to stimulus material, recognising performance possibilities **Assessment activity 2 page 149** **Assessment activity 3 page 157**	**M3** demonstrate considered responses to stimulus material, recognising performance possibilities **Assessment activity 2 page 149** **Assessment activity 3 page 157**	**D3** demonstrate responses to stimulus material, showing insight and full awareness of performance possibilities **Assessment activity 2 page 149** **Assessment activity 3 page 157**
P4 use ideas, resources, research and materials to find and shape an appropriate form. **Assessment activity 3 page 157**	**M4** develop ideas, resources, research and materials, imaginatively shaping them in an appropriate form. **Assessment activity 3 page 157**	**D4** develop ideas, resources, research and materials indicating the possibilities for performance, in a perceptive and comprehensive manner. **Assessment activity 3 page 157**

How you will be assessed

This unit will be assessed by assignments that will be designed and marked by the tutors at your centre.

You will explore the ideas of established practitioners, from the past or today and you have to take part in at least two workshops/demonstrations/performances organised by your tutors. Your contribution will amount to about five minutes in each.

Your tutors will organise a series of workshops in which. The tutors will start you on the road to understanding this physical theatre by exploring some ideas or work already created. Evidence could come from:

- tutor observations of your work in class and your log book
- tutor observation of you in performance
- Video/DVD recordings of your work in class/performance
- peer assessment.

Kai, 16-year-old acting learner

I took part in a storytelling 'marathon' for some pupils that came to visit the theatre department in our centre.

We worked on our own as well as in small groups and came up with physical theatre performances that we developed from fairy tales and stories.

My team decided to play some clowns who went on a journey to the fairground. We had previously taken part in naïve clowning workshops, so we got inspiration from that. We acted out the story playing all the parts and the rides, so that when I was on the rollercoaster, my partner played both my chair and the bar that held me in.

When we went on the ghost train ride, we each took turns to play the passenger and the ghouls.

We wore clown outfits – baggy pants, vests, big jackets, hats and we had smiles painted on. That was all we had. Everything else we needed, like hankies to use to wipe our eyes when we were laughing and crying at the same time, we made up just by using one another.

The audience feedback was really good – they loved our scenes.

Over to you

- What kinds of stories would you like to develop into the style of physical theatre?
- What would you find challenging about this kind of work?
- Which of the assessment areas do you think Kai's work contributed towards?

32.1 Understand key influences in physical theatre

Getting started

Working with a partner, imagine that you are going shopping to a strange town quite far away. Improvise your shopping trip using voice and movement, making sure lots of crazy things happen to you on the way. Imagine that you will see, hear and smell new things on your trip, as well as experience things that make you feel happy, sad or surprised. You won't have any props or scenery to use, but you might like to choose a couple of pieces of costume you can wear, swap and change around on the way.

Polish up improvisation elements that you want to include at the start, middle and at the end of your trip.

Perform your piece of physical theatre to your group and, at the end, ask them for feedback on the storyline, your characters and whether or not they understood what was happening.

32.1.1 Historic practice and practitioners

The key practitioners of physical theatre are the pioneers that helped shape and develop this form into the highly popular medium it has become. You will need to have a good understanding of their work and the historical forms of physical theatre, in order to really be able to perform well in this theatre form. The following sections offer some key examples to get you started.

Ancient Greece and Rome

The chorus in ancient Greek theatre was an integral part of any play. It was usually made up of 12–15 actors and their purpose was to support the action of the play. They would often help to make the relationship between the main actors easier to understand as they clarified the emotions and thoughts the characters were experiencing. They were seen as representing the audience, 'the people' and their messages were communicated through words, song and physical theatre. Chorus players frequently wore masks and even strapped on body parts to make them larger than life. In comedies, they could be very rude.

Theatre in ancient Rome was developed from Greek forms and also employed a chorus to help tell the story. Roman actors wore masks and, again, in comedies they could be crude and vulgar, but they used mime instead of speech. Roman theatre developed many of the stock characters that were early forms of those we see today in pantomime, like the slave who is witty and clever. We meet this character as the Genie in the story of Aladdin in *1001 Arabian Nights*, or as the character of Buttons from *Cinderella*.

Commedia delle' Arte

This theatre form featured a series of key characters that played out specific roles and only did specific things in the drama. Three examples of these characters are:

1. Columbine   2. Harlequin   3. Buffo

One of the key features of this form of theatre was that it allowed female performers – almost unheard of at that time. There are early records going back to the mid-1500s that talk about women on stage in these comedies. In fact, the form is much older than this and can be traced right back to the Greeks. These plays were improvised, but gradually became more formally structured. They became known as the *Zanni comedies*. Their subject matter was universal, such as love, death and betrayal. Improvised comedy scenes were called *burle* – can you find a similar name for a type of theatre that is popular today?

The key characters mentioned all had particular ways of behaving. Because the work was improvised, it often took inspiration from the local realities where performance was taking place. For example, the actors would mock the town's mayor or other figures of authority.

One of them was *Arlecchino*, who is now called *Harlequin* in English – a very acrobatic character, even though he was a glutton and quite fat. His **antics** were very popular in the 16th century. He was a servant to one of the *innamorato*, the Italian word for lovers, or one of the *vecchio*, the Italian word for elders. He also had a lover, *Columbina* (Columbine in English) and, although he lusted after her, he was always more tempted by the thought of food.

It was the combination of his stupidity and agility that made audiences laugh, along with the ease with which other characters could fool him. For instance, he might have been easily tricked into thinking he was dead. Sometimes he played more formal characters, like a doctor; he would then prescribe ridiculous medicines and remedies.

The tradition of this theatre form still goes on in the work of some writers and directors.

Activity: Researching Dario Fo

See what you can find out about Dario Fo. One of his plays features the character of a mad man, escaped from an asylum. Everyone else in the play thinks he is a judge and the results are chaotic. Find out the name of this play.

Are there any other contemporary practitioners still using commedia dell'arte today? List some of their works.

Key terms

Antic – a ludicrous or grotesque act done for fun or amusement

Raga – traditional Indian melody made up of five or more musical notes usually associated with different parts of the day or various seasons

Kathakali

Kathakali is an ancient Indian tradition of dance-drama from Kerala dating back to the 16th century. It uses very distinct characters, who wear elaborate costumes, masks and make-up. The performances used to last for hours, but are generally shorter these days. The stories are traditional and epic. Music is based on Indian **ragas** and there are 101 classic Kathakali stories that can be told in this theatre form.

More recently, Kathakali has been used to tell other, non-Hindu stories, such as those of Shakespeare and The Bible.

Traditional Kathakali dance costume

Antonin Artaud

Antonin Artaud was born in 1896 and introduced a very new form of theatre. His early work could be described as surrealist but, later on, he directed his thinking towards immersing his audience within the performance – they would be totally unprotected from what might happen. He developed the 'Theatre of Cruelty', designed to expose life's brutal truths in order to make the experience of theatre more thrilling.

Although he suffered greatly from mental illness during his life, his work has been highly influential. For example, he has influenced the work of British theatre directors Peter Brook and Jerzy Grotowski, and actors like Sam Shepard.

> **You will find more information on Artaud in Project 9: Physical Theatre Performance, page 283.**

Did you know?

Antonin Artaud is mainly celebrated for his writing and theatre criticism, rather than for his performances. In his book, *The Theatre and its Double*, he said that he thought theatre was dead and needed to be replaced by something that had no set or script and very little lighting. Actors should wear grotesque costumes and masks. Rather than speaking lines, actors should just create sounds and **dirges**; Artaud said he hated the written word. His own staged works were generally about brutal themes like rape, incest and mass murder.

He has become well known and celebrated through the work of other, later practitioners.

Key terms

Dirge – a song or hymn of mourning composed or performed as a memorial to a dead person

Jacques Lecoq

This theatre practitioner was born in France in 1921. He trained first as a teacher of physical education, but after developing his interests in theatre, he opened a school to train actors in physical theatre, *L'École Internationale de Théâtre Jacques Lecoq*.

He trained a number of famous actors including Geoffrey Rush and Steven Berkoff. He also trained the founder members of what was first called Théâtre de Complicité, and are now just Complicite. Complicite are one of the UK's best known physical theatre companies.

He taught actors to find a sense of neutrality. The actors were to bring nothing into the acting space; no attitudes or pre-conceived ideas. From this neutrality they could then build up true characters.

Activity: Building a character

This is a classic way of starting a physical theatre workshop and develops some of the ideas promoted by Jaques Lecoq.

- Lie down on the floor and empty your mind of all thoughts.
- Relax, from toes up to head, by first tensing a body part, then letting the tension go.
- Slowly get up from the floor and try to walk around the studio, as if seeing everything there for the very first time. You are so new to this place that you can't even speak the language. You have your own language.
- Everything is new, so it might be scary, amazing, funny. React as if it is.
- Say 'Hi!' to another actor, but consider the fact that neither of you can speak English.
- If you like the look of the other character, ask them out on a date; maybe invite them for a coffee.
- See what happens when you go on that imaginary date. Remember that these characters believe that the date is real.
- Discuss the sort of character you become?
- How did you communicate with the other character?
- What happened on the date?

Masks

Lecoq trained a lot of actors to use masks. He would use full-face masks, half-face masks or just noses. By wearing a mask the actor can be whoever he/she wants to be. The idea is that the audience will concentrate far more on the body language of the actor who is wearing a mask than on the actor who isn't wearing one.

> ### Activity: A character with a mask
>
> Use a plain plastic mask, or make one out of cardboard. Re-play the scene in the previous activity (Building a character) using the mask. Perform it in front of the group.
>
> - How did your acting in the scene differ?
> - Ask the audience to describe the differences in the two characters you played in the unmasked and masked activities.
> - What do you think is the purpose of performing characters in mask?

Working with masks is an effective way of performing physical theatre. Masks help an actor to develop the physicality of characters, to play a number of characters within a single scene/play and also to bring to life very different ones from the classic type or characters that they might be expected to play. A good example of each of these factors is:

- where a character has a deformity, or the director wants the character to be physically deformed
- where the actors multi-role, or they play more than one character in a show
- where a female performer plays a male, or a child, a role they do not physically resemble

Masked theatre is well suited to plays that deal with magical characters or have fantastical narratives. It allows performers to take the audience on a journey to places that it would be impossible to visit in reality.

Jerzy Grotowski

Jerzy Grotowski was born in 1933 and dedicated his life to developing a style of physical theatre that was fundamentally about being truthful. He did not want his actors to develop skills and tricks that masked their true natures. His performances involved sitting the audience within the production, encouraging interaction between them and the actors.

The theatre created by Jerzy Grotowski further developed Artaud's ideas. His *Tragical History of Doctor Faustus* was performed with audience members sitting as guests at the table for the feast, whilst the actors played around them. In his performance of *Akropolis*, the actors built a crematorium around the audience during the play.

The influence of his work can be seen today in performances created and directed by many contemporary practitioners. The company *DV8 Physical Theatre* often produce work that places the audience squarely in the centre of the action. *Frantic Assembly* performers often talk directly to their audience and Nigel Charnock, once with *DV8*, now puts on his own shows in which he interacts very closely with the audience.

Assessment activity 1

P1 M1 D1

BTEC

Make a short presentation about a physical theatre artist that you have a particular interest in. You could write a short essay, create a slideshow presentation or work up a short practical demonstration to show your findings. Remember to make a link to anything you have done in the workshop, on your course. You could link your own responses to what you have been taught in a lecture your tutor has delivered or to some personal research you have carried out.

You should make reference to both practitioners from the past and those working today – maybe compare the work of one with another.

Try to refer to the connection between your practitioner's physical training and their work and performances, for example where a dancer uses their training to make their work physically daring and exciting, eg *DV8*.

Give examples from actual works you have seen or researched.

Evidence

- films of the workshop presentation/demonstration and/or performance
- your log book where you record your ideas, responses to criticism and plans for improving your work
- an essay
- a slideshow presentation
- tutor feedback
- peer feedback

Grading tips

M1 Clearly show how your chosen practitioner's work influences other performances in physical theatre. Make sure you demonstrate your opinion in your presentation and support it with examples.

D1 Show that you can analyse your chosen practitioner and that you can make links between their ideas, training and work. Discuss the form and structure of their work, explain your judgements and support it with examples.

PLTS

By carrying out personal research into physical theatre practitioners, you will use your skills as an **independent enquirer**.

By exploring the most effective ways of communicating ideas gleaned from research into practitioners and styles you will be developing your skills as a **reflective learner**.

Functional skills

ICT: By carrying out research into physical theatre practitioners, their styles, working and training methods, history, you are using your skills to **find and select information**. By presenting research into practitioners through discussion, workshops, demonstrations you are developing your **presentation** skills.

English: By researching, and preparing and giving presentations/demonstrations of research into the work of practitioners, you are using your **reading** and **writing** skills.

32.1.2 Contemporary practice and practitioners

Earlier on in this unit you read about the contemporary physical theatre group called *Complicite*, who are influenced by Jaques Lecoq. A broad range of contemporary artists and performance groups have taken influences from historical practitioners. A key part of understanding contemporary physical theatre is seeing their work, either live or recorded.

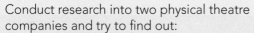

Activity: Research two companies

Conduct research into two physical theatre companies and try to find out:
- Who are the founder members?
- When were they set up?
- Who/what are the key influences for these practitioners?
- What is the key feature of their work that marks them out from other companies?
- What are the names of some of their main performance pieces?
- How did the training of founder members influence the work of the company?

Complicite

Complicite is a successful theatre company founded in 1983 by Simon McBurney, Annabel Arden and Marcello Magni. The company's members are always changing and its style of work evolves, too. They have devised productions that are entirely new and have also re-worked theatre classics.

Most of their work involves physical theatre but they also train actors and directors.

Complicite produce regular performances of a wide variety of plays. It might be possible to see some of these on DVD. The company's website hosts resource packs that are full of exercises you can complete to give you an idea of the company's style.

The approach of the company's director, Simon McBurney, is to keep the action as physical as possible. It can be realistic, stylised, based on music and involve design components. The company is well known for their extraordinary technical feats in their use of

scenery, moving sets and even collapsing stages. For example, in a performance of *The Three Lives of Lucie Cabroll*, the actors ran up and down the back wall of the set, with this wall eventually collapsing at the end of the show. Actors in these shows must be very fit and athletic.

Examples of Complicite's work include:

The Street of Crocodiles

The Three Lives of Lucie Cabrol

The Noise of Time

The Elephant Vanishes

Mnemonic

You can research recordings of these productions through the *Theatre Museum* archive.

Frantic Assembly

Frantic Assembly is a much newer theatre company that has developed its own distinct way of working. This company, set up in the 1990s by Scott Graham and Steven Hoggett, has used texts and improvisation as their basis for drama. They approach ideas and texts in their own unique way, for example they might cut up a play script and re-organise it.

Frantic's directors want their performers to be bold, experimental and not bound by rules, which is why their work is challenging, new and irreverent.

Activity: Pieces of script

Take a page of script, copied from a play.
- Cut up the text, line by line.
- Put the text back together.
- Play the scene in its new form.

How does this affect the meaning of the text?

DV8 Physical Theatre

DV8 Physical Theatre is a dance-drama company set up in 1986. DV8's work is often considered highly challenging and sometimes dangerous for the performers. The company's director, Lloyd Newson, generally works with trained dancers, rather than actors. Much of their work is highly dance-based, but actors have had roles in some performances, for example in a show called *Living Costs*. Sometimes their work is specifically produced for a particular place or space.

DV8's 2003 production (which included some elements from *Living Costs*) was site-specific, having been designed for performance in the London gallery building of the *Tate Modern*. The *Tate Modern* is a huge London art gallery which used to be a power station. This is a play about life today and how we see each other. It involves a series of scenes that take place in different parts of the building. Performers began their show in the massive Turbine Hall on the ground floor. As the show progressed, the audience were directed to scenes taking place in other gallery rooms. The show involved actors, dancers, trapeze artists, and a narrator, who wasn't always present in the building.

This company's work is uncompromising and can even be violent – their main aim is to break down what they perceive as barriers between more conventional forms of dance and drama.

Some physical theatre performances challenge our own perceptions about society

Assessment activity 2

Go on a journey

The brief is to work with a partner to create a piece of children's theatre to be performed at a showcase event in your centre. The piece must be at least three minutes long. You will need costumes, maybe props, and a whistle or squeaker for one of you to use in communicating with the other.

First, decide on which practitioner's ideas you can use to help you develop the work.

Now select two characters that you will play, for example, they could be naïve clowns who have never been anywhere before.

Improvise the drama:

You are going on a journey to somewhere you have never been to before; in fact you have never been anywhere before. You and your partner find yourselves setting off to find a job – you don't have any skills to speak of. One of you cannot speak in sounds, you just blow a whistle, the other can speak in a language, but it isn't English or anything recognisable.

Act out the following sequence of events:

- Start the day
- Get up and get dressed
- You realise you don't have any money so you decide to go out and look for a job
- On the way, various things happen to you
- In the end you don't get a job
- You go home feeling sad
- Suddenly you hear a knock on the door
- You have won the lottery.

Remember to ask for advice from your peers and tutor.

Evidence

- your observations

- your group's observations
- films of the workshop and performance
- your log book where you record your ideas, responses to criticism and plans for improving your work
- tutor feedback.

Grading tips

M2 You need to use the skills you have learnt and developed confidently in performance. This means not forgetting any cues, and moving and speaking confidently so you communicate with the audience.

D2 You need to use what you have learned about the working methods of the practitioners you have studied to improve your own performance. You will need to show you are at ease on stage, working fluently and with a clear driving force or objective, so that your performance has a definite impact on the audience.

M3 You need to show that you can respond to stimuli and get the most out of these stimuli in your performance. You will need to take the key ideas from the brief and shape them to develop your performance material into a successful work.

D3 You need to go beyond what you did for **M3** by trying out lots of ideas to show you are aware of all the different ways that you can interpret your stimulus material. You can then choose the ones with the most potential for a successful performance and develop some of them into the final piece.

PLTS

By using ideas, resources and research to find and shape appropriate forms, you are using your skills as an **independent enquirer**.

By exploring new angles on materials using a range of skills to interpret them, responding to stimulus material and recognising its performance possibilities, you are using your **creative thinker** skills.

Functional skills

By researching the work of physical theatre practitioners, you are using your **reading** skills.

32.2 Be able to develop skills and techniques associated with physical theatre

32.2.1 Physical skills

Your regular classes at school/college will help you to develop your physicality. Refer to Unit 38: Dance Performance, pages 161–178 for tips on how to use class to develop technique, strength, stretch and stamina.

Most serious physical performers will take regular classes in dance skills and often go to the gym to build extra strength. You will need to develop physical control by practising as much as possible in class and this will come as you gain strength. Similarly, balance will improve as you practise skills and become stronger.

In any activity that is physically challenging the way you use your breathing is key. You cannot exert yourself without using special breathing techniques throughout the workout – usually you would need to exhale at the point where you make the most effort.

Did you know?

Poor balance is usually caused by muscles not being strong enough and the fact that you don't fully understand what you are doing. This is why babies fall over so much.

Use of levels and height

Where you place a movement, in terms of height, can give it different meanings at different times. For instance, walking high and proud communicates something about what the character thinks about themselves at that point in time. Walking low or slumping has the opposite meaning. You can explore how this works in the workshop by repeating movements at different levels. Generally, the higher the level, the more you communicate a sense of superiority and elevated self-esteem. Movements low to the floor can communicate low self-esteem and even feelings close to depression.

Lifting, catching, taking and placing weight

These are key skill areas you should try to master in order to become a successful physical theatre performer.

You will be taught to lift others without hurting yourself. Once you master this, it's surprising who you can lift!

The same applies to catching. When your partner is relying on you as support for their moves, you should try your best to be there for them. For example, if you are part of a group carrying a performer, as if they are flying, you must be sure of what your role is and that you are not making a mistake that could cause injury to the person 'flying'. You will need to learn how to place your weight in difficult physical manoeuvres – this will be very beneficial to the success of a performance.

Activity: Playing a sequence

Working with a partner, make a move towards your partner with your torso, then let them catch you and push you back and gently away. Repeat this to put together a slow and careful sequence of movements.

- Give your sequence a title.
- Develop the sequence so it takes you around the studio.
- Put the sequence to music that is appropriate to the style of the piece. Select music with an epic quality if you want to explore some difficult places or something that features 'beach' sounds/music if you want to explore a desert island.

32.2.2 Vocal skills

Vocal skills depend on:

- good posture
- proper breathing.

You must stand straight with your head level, shoulders relaxed and knees soft to allow your voice to work properly.

You should always warm-up your voice before you take a class that involves using it. You should breathe in through the nose and out through the mouth. Pant like your pet dog to warm up your breathing.

See Unit 38: Dance Performance, page 161 for posture tips and activities.

Activity: Vocal warm-up

Try out the following exercises to help you warm-up:

- yawn
- massage your face
- place hands on either side of your ribs to check breathing is using the whole of the chest cavity
- sing a series of vowel sounds – a, e, i, o, u
- sing a series of consonant sounds – cc, ttt, mmm, bbb, www, yyyy.

Vocal range and dynamics

Your range will develop with practise. This will come as you try different plays and performances. The key thing to remember is not to strain your voice by shouting, screaming or screeching. The voice must be warmed up properly before rehearsals and performances.

Vocal dynamics will also develop gradually. If you have already undertaken vocal training, you will have a head start as your vocal chords and mouth might have already developed. Practise speaking extracts of text out loud, eg extracts from Shakespeare or The Bible, where the words used are difficult to pronounce. This will help with **projection** too – your voice will build strength as you practise and learn to control the way you use your breathing with your diaphragm. This is essential to prevent vocal strain.

You can find more about singing and vocal techniques in Unit 14: Musical Theatre Performance, page 87.

Key terms

Vocal dynamics – the range of sounds the voice can make by using the vocal organs (vocal chords, mouth, throat)

Projection – a way of projecting the voice through driving the breath from the lungs (using the diaphragm), over the vocal chords and through the mouth

Physicalising the sound

This is all about moving to demonstrate the meaning of the words being spoken or sung. When physical theatre actors want to create meaning through a range of movements, they often move around the space to reflect the sound itself or the words of a song.

32.2.3 Acting skills

Acting is a highly complex process. This unit will approach some of the acting skills you might use in physical theatre, but you might also use skills learned in the more specialised units, such as Unit 19: Principles of Acting, pages 113–138 or Unit 5&7: Rehearsing and Performing on pages 65–86.

The way you develop a character in physical theatre will depend on the type of work that you are doing. Generally, physical theatre actors do not use naturalism, which would require them to embody or become the person they are playing.

As described in the previous sections of this unit, when interpreting a role as a physical theatre performer, you might not even be playing a classical character - you could be a piece of furniture or a place. However, you might have to find the voice of the role you are playing, and this will be influenced by the type of role you are developing.

Whatever the role, you will almost definitely have to be able to work well with others. The way you interact with other performers will help to add layers of meaning to the work. For example, when trying to convey that two characters are related to one another, it makes sense for them to act as though they are used to being in each other's company.

A physical theatre performance will be constructed so that it has its own rhythm; there will be moments of **climax** and moments of quiet. As you are directed, you will have to keep your work in line with the rest of your group. Similarly, dynamics will need to be maintained so that the work has its rhythm.

Key term

Climax – the highest point of anything conceived of as growing, developing or unfolding

Tableaux – the plural for 'picture' or 'image' in French. They were a popular form of entertainment before radio, film or television.

Tableaux

Tableaux are an interesting way of marking a moment in a drama. A tableaux is like a living picture.

Activity: Recreate a picture

Find your own tableaux to use as stimulus material:
- take a picture from a paper or magazine
- recreate the action in the image with your group
- ask those watching to describe the situation, say who the characters are and what the relationships between them are
- use the tableaux as the starting point for an improvised drama.

Physical comedy

Many physical theatre performances have elements of comedy. Comedy can be created through all kinds of means:
- the script may be funny
- the relationships may be made funny, eg by having characters of very different sizes
- the actions may not fit closely with the lines
- the actors might add movement/facial expressions/ vocal expressions that provide potential comedy.

Activity: Make it funny

Take some lines from a classic text, such as a Shakespeare play, eg the speech from Richard III, beginning with: 'A horse, a horse…'
- play the lines 'straight', with only one intonation or as if you are delivering a sermon
- deliver the lines as if you are a sergeant major, drilling some soldiers
- as you say the lines move around the space, as if your clothes are far too small; then as if your clothes are far too big for you.

Later on ask your partner's opinion on which of these scenarios is funnier.

What does 'physicalising' your lines do to their meaning? What happens to the way we see the character when you make the lines 'explode' from clothes that are too small, or when they are struggling to keep clothes on?

Actors like Lee Evans use the method of dressing their characters in ill-fitting clothes. When their clothes are too tight, the audience feels more sympathetic to them. Why is that?

Mime

Mime is an art form of its own. Many performers spend years learning and perfecting their mime skills. For this unit you will develop some basic mime skills. For example, you might be given lines to mime, rather than speak.

Think about why directors use mime in physical theatre.

If you mime the words rather than speak them, how does this influence the meaning of the piece?

Spontaneity and improvisation

Throughout the unit, you should do your best to go with the flow and try to be spontaneous in your approach to the work in hand. When your tutor asks you for your ideas on playing a scene try to just 'go for it!' Successful physical theatre comes from actors giving away their ideas very generously for the benefit of the piece. This attitude makes improvisation easier.

Improvisation is a way of working that depends on how quickly you can come up with ideas and different ways to express them. When your tutor gives you a task, such as devising a scene to show the relationship between two characters, you should leap straight in. After that, you will often have to develop your first improvised ideas, towards a more polished improvisation.

This is a skill that takes a while to develop but generally involves each member of the working group being bold, generous and positive. A few basic rules are:

- don't be afraid to communicate your ideas and opinions
- be generous to others, don't cut them off or refuse to listen to their suggestions
- instead of criticising or closing down an idea, try to take it a step further
- practise you skills.

Any kind of drama can involve improvisation during its rehearsal process – this is a key way in which directors find out what elements they can introduce in a performance and what things don't work as effectively. There are also plays that leave room for improvisation throughout or just at certain moments, such as most of the works of Dario Fo.

As your work develops, your timing will improve and you will know where other performers around you are. Remember, you are generally not working alone on stage – much performance in this form is group-based.

32.2.4 Physical ensemble

It is essential that you work closely with your group as an ensemble. Through trust and teamwork, cooperation with others and interaction, your work will improve far more quickly than if you look at doing things from an individual, non-inclusive point of view. Most professional physical theatre work involves being part of a group, and even solo artists, like Rowan Atkinson or Lee Evans work, with a director or a producer who helps them think about and try out ideas for their shows.

The ultimate form of cooperation is contact improvisation. Here, two or more performers use each other's bodies and the contact they have with each other to create movement.

A basic technique is to try standing side-by side by with a partner and start by copying the movements they are making. Gradually, you can expand your moves to include call and response, where one person creates a movement and the other responds to it.

The interaction you have with your partner will help develop this style of work; many close contact partnerships lead to performance of spontaneous dance/drama.

Lifting and catching

Your tutor will help you learn the safe ways of taking and giving weight in movement, but there are some key rules you must follow. See page 154 for more guidance.

Remember

Never attempt a lift without a responsible adult present.

Complex dynamic moves should be attempted only after proper training

Activity: Safety in lifting and taking weight

Lifting

- You must be warmed up for any physical session that involves lifts.
- Work with a partner who is roughly similar to you in weight and height.
- The person who is being lifted must 'want' to be lifted – you will never lift a partner who is a dead weight.
- Practise the different ways to hold or support your partner – it helps if the partner being lifted uses their arms/legs to brace their weight against their partner's body to help lever themselves upwards.
- You need some momentum to achieve a lift, so ensure a lift comes in the middle of a movement sequence.
- When lifting, ensure your back is straight, your centre is held firmly, and that your knees are slightly bent.
- Make sure you breathe properly when you are lifting and are being lifted; exhale at the point of most exertion.
- Bend your knees on landing or roll to the floor when you come out of a lift.

Catching

- For catching a partner, make sure you have enough stability in your legs and keep your balance before catching anybody.
- It is a good idea to be prepared for the next move after the catch, so that it looks more natural.

32.2.5 Dynamic quality

You should always try your best so that your contribution in any rehearsal/performance matches the effort of the rest of the group. This will be particularly important when you are working physically and when working on a slow lyrical piece as part of an ensemble. Where movement is needed, you should try to coordinate your efforts in terms of timing and precision, so that you are a good team player and support to your fellow performers.

Activity: Movement sequence

Working in a trio, work out a sequence of leaning, lifting and catching. Start with the first person leaning on to the next one, with the second person then initiating a movement towards the third performer.

- Improvise a sequence of push - react - push. Make sure your pushes are only strong enough to initiate a movement – you're not trying to push your co-performers over.
- Change the dynamics or speed of the sequence; change the direction of the flow; speed it up, then contrast by slowing it all down, slowly and carefully.
- Find some words from a piece of writing: a poem or song lyrics that you find appealing, and speak them as you move through the sequence. Make sure the emotion of the lines comes across in your voice and movements.
- Rehearse your sequence then perform it to the group.
- Evaluate your work – don't forget to ask for the opinions of your audience.

This short exercise will help you develop several skills and techniques in physical theatre and could be used to produce material that you are then able to develop towards a performance.

32.3 Be able to select, develop and refine materials

32.3.1 Stimulus

Your tutor will provide a range of stimulus materials from which you can develop physical theatre workshops and performances. These might be:

• stories	• sculpture
• poetry	• architecture
• random objects	• masks
• random themes	• costume
• music	• paintings
• props	• pictures

This list gives you some idea of the kind of stimulus materials you might use. You will not be asked to produce work in response to all these. From the table above, which stimulus materials have you already used when doing various exercises for performance?

Old brick wall

Key terms

Manipulation – to handle especially skilfully; to manage or influence cleverly

Activity: The old brick wall

Working in a small group, look at the picture of an old brick wall on this page and think about how you can improvise a piece of dance/drama about the wall. You can also take inspiration from a painting called *Man Lying on a Wall*, by LS Lowry. Another good source of ideas is a ballet called *A Simple Man*, which is based around the paintings of LS Lowry and the story of his life.

* Think what the wall represents, who might have built it, what's its purpose?
* Devise a short sequence, adding words, where the idea of the wall is central to the piece.
* Rehearse and perform the piece.
* Review and evaluate the whole creative process and performance.

32.3.2 Manipulation

Whatever way you choose to develop your work from a stimulus, you are always using **manipulation** techniques to transform an idea through your own efforts. The old brick wall activity gave you a taste of how to do that. You used words combined with action and movement. If you think back to the piece, you will probably discover that you changed the tempo, the use of space and the performance dynamics as you developed your work. These were all ways of manipulating the work.

If you are not too sure about lighting technology, ask your tutor or one of the technical crew to show you what different lighting effects can do for your work.

Try to think how some mysterious lighting, eg blue gel in the lights would change the work you did for the old brick wall activity.

How would your old brick wall piece change if you used live sound, recorded sound, or other multimedia, such as video projections?

32.3.3 Development

The activity you worked on in 32.2.5 produced a **motif** – this was the movement sequence you developed at the very start of the activity. In this unit you will often be asked to do this and to then develop this motif towards a performance, or into another piece.

The old brick wall sequence used both a picture and a theme, because you first looked at what the picture might mean, then took the wall idea forward. How you developed the sequence, by adding words, meant you were working up your piece in a very particular physical theatre style. You will undoubtedly have produced work that has elements of what your tutor has taught you, but you will also have started developing your own as well. Overall, you worked:

- through improvisation from a movement-based idea, involving text
- towards a performance of physical theatre.

Key terms

Motif – a sequence of movement that is developed through repetition or change, throughout a piece

32.3.4 Effectiveness of the work

Each piece of work you develop will have its own production values. This is about creating work of quality that meets the needs of its audience and the brief you have been given. In some cases, you will produce physical theatre for a particular, given, audience, such as one made up of parents and friends or the employees of a company. You should consider who will be watching your work – you might want to shock your audience, but you might want to consider what is going to be offensive for them.

Keep going back to the original brief when you are working, ensuring your contributions will be suitable to the type of audience you are performing for.

Sometimes you might be working on your own and it can be hard to find ways of motivating yourself. You may find it helpful to show your ideas to someone else, to get their response and some objective criticism. In any case, you will be assessed by your tutor on your individual contributions to the performance or workshop.

The closer you work as an ensemble, the better results you'll get; it is difficult to create successful work if you are part of a group that argues incessantly and does not get along. This is called group coherence. It is easy to see dynamism on the stage if the group works well together towards achieving the brief they have been set.

The following assessment activity will cross-reference with work you are doing for other units, such as **Unit 39: Choreographic Principles** in Project 5 or **Unit 9: Devising Plays and Unit 10: Theatre in Education** in Project 1.

PLTS

By carrying out personal research into physical theatre practitioners, using skills imaginatively to create work for demonstration and performance and by using ideas, resources and research to find and shape appropriate forms, you will be using your skills as an **independent enquirer**.

By exploring new angles on materials using a range of skills to interpret them and by responding to stimulus material and recognising its performance possibilities, you will be using your **creative thinker** skills.

By working with others to devise, demonstrate and perform work and by using ideas, resources and research to find and shape an appropriate form, you are using your skills as a **team worker**.

Functional skills

English: By researching the work of physical theatre practitioners and giving presentations and demonstrations of your research, you are using your **reading** and **writing** skills.

ICT: By presenting research into practitioners through discussion, workshops, demonstrations, you are developing your skills in **developing, and communicating information**.

Assessment activity 3

The brief

Your group has been asked to create and perform a piece about the dangers of smoking, to be performed in a primary school. The work is to last ten minutes and be suitable for an audience of ten year olds.

The title is: 'Smoking kills, so why does it look so cool?'

Preparation

- Decide on who will be responsible for what: performing, organising, technical, props, costumes.

- Research some key facts you might want to get across, such as the impact of smoking on somebody's health or the fact that smoking is an expensive habit. One of you could interview a few people who used to smoke and get useful insights about how smoking made them feel and why they quit. Think about how you are going to express those feelings.

- Create a timetable of activities with deadlines.

- Visit the venue to check on space and how you can bring in the technical equipment.

- Discuss ideas with the host school for suitability and needs of the audience.

Develop the piece

Explore the theme through physical theatre, using the ideas of at least one of the professional practitioners that you've studied to help with the working method.

- Devise the piece.

- Decide on costumes and set, technical elements such as sound, and possible lighting.

Prepare for performance

- Rehearse and refine the work towards performance.

- Before the performance, do a technical rehearsal in costume etc.

- Devise an audience evaluation sheet.

- Perform.

Feedback

- Ask the audience and the teachers what they liked and what didn't work so well.

Write or record your own review and evaluation of the work. This could be an essay, in your log book, or recorded on audio or visual digital media. Keep copies in paper form or on the centre's Virtual Learning Environmet (VLE), if there is one.

Evidence

- your group's and your own observations

- films of the workshop and performance

- your log book where you record your ideas, responses to criticism and plans for improving your work

- tutor and/or audience feedback.

Grading tips

M3 You should show that you can see potential in your stimulus materials for how they can be developed into a performance. You should take previously used ideas and apply them in the workshop.

D3 Your work needs to explore and develop the original ideas and materials far beyond the starting points. Ensure you apply your understanding of other practitioners' work.

M4 You need to develop the ideas of the group into the final piece. You will need to show imagination in your work, using light, décor and other resources that might help to exploit your work further.

D4 Ensure you explore the ideas of your group, and other materials from several sources. Discard ideas that do not have enough potential and refine those that do. Always keep in mind the effect your ideas will have on your audience.

Here is a way of recording your timetable of activities for Assessment activity 3 to ensure everyone knows what they are doing and what the deadline is:

Activity	People involved	Goals	Resources	Deadline
The venue	Jenni Dave Kenny	• Find out about the needs of the group • Suitability of material • Venue possibilities • Technical aspects	Library information Internet Travel to venue	1 February
Investigate effects of smoking	Roberto Mei	Research facts and ideas to use in piece	Library Internet Two interviews with people who used to smoke	1 February
Costumes etc	Shani Melissa Tarik	Design ideas and outcomes	Library Design notebooks etc Websites about costumes	1 February

If your work on the dangers of smoking was to be produced for a different audience, you might consider using the work of another practitioner to inform the creative process. For example, the work and ideas of Pina Bausch could form the basis of a more grown-up dance/drama.

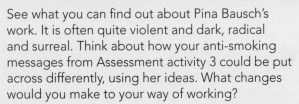

Activity: Research

See what you can find out about Pina Bausch's work. It is often quite violent and dark, radical and surreal. Think about how your anti-smoking messages from Assessment activity 3 could be put across differently, using her ideas. What changes would you make to your way of working?

- You could try out one of the scenes, using and developing Pina Bausch's ideas and methods.

- Show your ideas to the group and canvas their thoughts about the possible success of this development.

- What kind of audience would you invite to watch a new version of this performance?

Pina Bausch worked closely with her dancers to devise modern dance theatre ballet

Alex McNullin
Performing artist

Alex is a young performing artist living in Bristol. He trained at college by taking his BTEC National Diploma in Performing Arts and then went on to Middlesex University, where he took a degree in the same subject.

He performed in many undergraduate productions, a number of which involved physical theatre, which Alex considers his strongest area of skills. He recently auditioned successfully for a production of a new stage version of *Alice Through the Looking Glass*. He got the part and will be playing an ensemble cast member, with roles including a playing card, animals and various magical creatures.

"I am so glad I was successful in my audition. It was really nerve wracking! We had to take a workshop, led by the director, and this involved improvising movement sequences as all kinds of creatures. I thought back to some of my college work and this helped me come up with some great ideas.

I think the best scene I created was as a playing card. In my mind I just kept thinking that I was extremely lucky to be there and I was determined not to fail in anything I did in that audition. The group I was in were supposed to act out a day out to the beach and my role was to pretend that I was having fun and join the rest of the group in the water even though I couldn't swim.

The director was impressed with my skills and I got the job."

Think about it!

1 What sort of work did Alex do for this audition?
2 Did he use any ideas from the practitioners you have been studying?
3 What do you think Alex brought to the audition that others may not have done?
4 What qualities could you bring to your work that might make you successful in further training and education, like Alex?

Just checking

1 Make sure you have explored the work and ideas of more than one practitioner – both past practitioners and those working today.

2 Watch live work whenever possible to help develop your own ideas.

3 Use the ideas of practitioners in your practical work.

4 Be bold – discard ideas that have limited potential; develop those that work better.

5 Always ask your tutor and your peers to watch your work and be critical.

6 Learn through watching others at work in the studio.

7 Be generous in practical work; when improvising make sure you don't cover or undermine the work of others.

8 Work carefully and be safe.

9 Look for ideas in unexpected places; you can find resources on which to base your explorations that way.

10 Be confident in performance.

Assignment tips

• Come to class prepared for whatever activity you are working on, be on time, be focused and have the correct gear.

• Keep an open mind when working so you can explore and experiment.

• It is a good idea to offer to 'go first' when your tutor asks for a volunteer.

• Be brave and take risks with your work.

• Watch others working in your group.

• Keep up your log book so you have a record of your thinking and working.

• Be active in seeing new plays from professional or amateur practitioners of physical theatre.

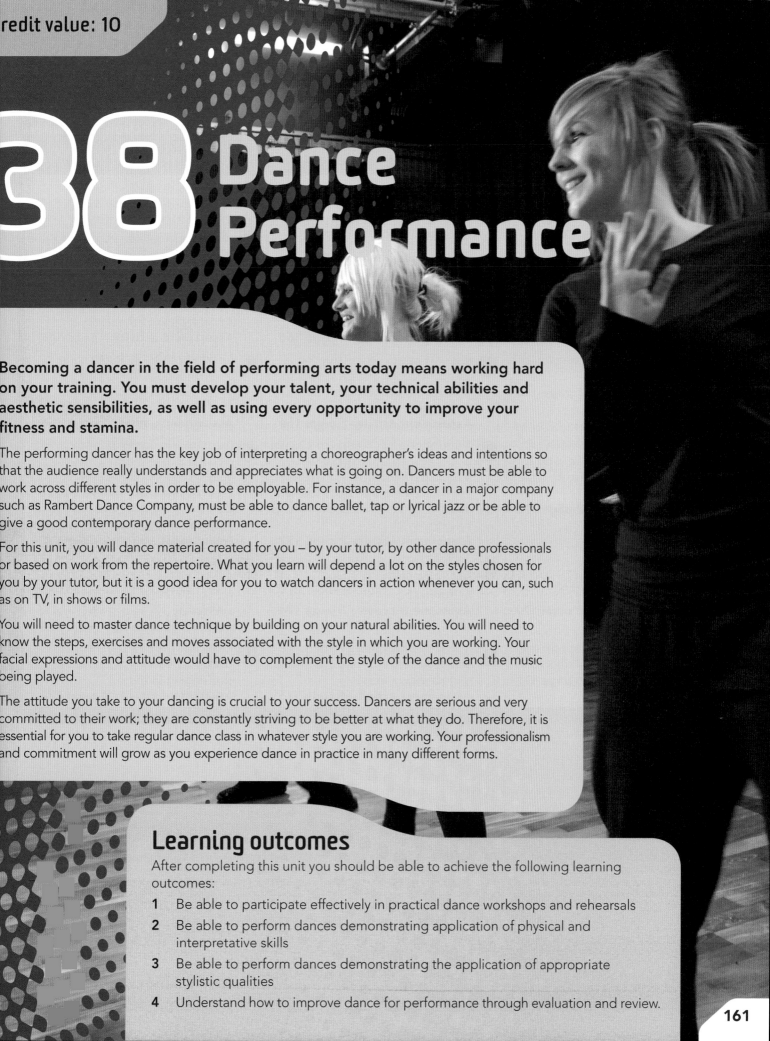

38 Dance Performance

Becoming a dancer in the field of performing arts today means working hard on your training. You must develop your talent, your technical abilities and aesthetic sensibilities, as well as using every opportunity to improve your fitness and stamina.

The performing dancer has the key job of interpreting a choreographer's ideas and intentions so that the audience really understands and appreciates what is going on. Dancers must be able to work across different styles in order to be employable. For instance, a dancer in a major company such as Rambert Dance Company, must be able to dance ballet, tap or lyrical jazz or be able to give a good contemporary dance performance.

For this unit, you will dance material created for you – by your tutor, by other dance professionals or based on work from the repertoire. What you learn will depend a lot on the styles chosen for you by your tutor, but it is a good idea for you to watch dancers in action whenever you can, such as on TV, in shows or films.

You will need to master dance technique by building on your natural abilities. You will need to know the steps, exercises and moves associated with the style in which you are working. Your facial expressions and attitude would have to complement the style of the dance and the music being played.

The attitude you take to your dancing is crucial to your success. Dancers are serious and very committed to their work; they are constantly striving to be better at what they do. Therefore, it is essential for you to take regular dance class in whatever style you are working. Your professionalism and commitment will grow as you experience dance in practice in many different forms.

Learning outcomes

After completing this unit you should be able to achieve the following learning outcomes:

1 Be able to participate effectively in practical dance workshops and rehearsals

2 Be able to perform dances demonstrating application of physical and interpretative skills

3 Be able to perform dances demonstrating the application of appropriate stylistic qualities

4 Understand how to improve dance for performance through evaluation and review.

Assessment and grading criteria

This table shows you what you must do in order to achieve a pass, merit or distinction, and where you can find activities in this book to help you.

To achieve a **pass** grade the evidence must show that you are able to:	To achieve a **merit** grade the evidence must show that, in addition to the pass criteria, you are able to:	To achieve a **distinction** grade the evidence must show that, in addition to the pass and merit criteria, you are able to:
P1 demonstrate commitment to the development of performance skills through active participation in workshops and rehearsals **Assessment activity 1 page 166**	**M1** demonstrate a disciplined approach to the development of performance skills through focused participation in workshops and rehearsals **Assessment activity 1 page 166**	**D1** demonstrate self-management in the development of performance skills through thorough preparation and a determined participation in workshops and rehearsals **Assessment activity 1 page 166**
P2 respond positively to direction and corrections **Assessment activity 1 page 166**	**M2** respond positively to direction and corrections and successfully improve aspects of performance technique **Assessment activity 1 page 166**	**D2** respond positively to direction and corrections to improve performance and achieve high levels of technical proficiency **Assessment activity 1 page 166**
P3 demonstrate the application of physical and interpretive skills in performance, communicating the dance idea **Assessment activity 2 page 172**	**M3** demonstrate application of a range of physical and interpretative skills in performance, successfully communicating the dance idea and remaining focused and engaged in the dance **Assessment activity 2 page 172**	**D3** demonstrate application of physical and interpretative skills in performance, confidently and clearly communicating the dance idea and remaining focused and engaged throughout **Assessment activity 2 page 172**
P4 demonstrate an awareness of stylistic qualities in dance performance **Assessment activity 3 page 174**	**M4** show a clear sense of appropriate stylistic qualities in dance performance **Assessment activity 3 page 174**	**D4** show an excellent sense of stylistic qualities in dance performance, with confidence, interpretation and artistic flair **Assessment activity 3 page 174**
P5 review own technical performance, setting targets, with guidance. **Assessment activity 4 page 176**	**M5** review own technical performance setting appropriate and achievable targets with guidance. **Assessment activity 4 page 176**	**D5** thoroughly review own technical performance setting focused and challenging targets. **Assessment activity 4 page 176**

How you will be assessed

The tutor who normally teaches you will assess your work. They will deliver regular class, set you tasks to complete, and watch you as you learn and rehearse work for performance. Your work will be assessed in:

- practical class
- workshops
- technique class
- performances
- review and evaluation.

The work you produce for assessment will be practical for the most part, with other formally recorded information in addition to this. This may include:

- your work in class, rehearsals and performances (this is the most important)
- your dance diary or log
- reviews and evaluations of your progression through class and plans for improvement
- video/DVD recordings of your work
- feedback from your tutor(s) or peers.

Lee, 17-year-old dance learner

I was asked to dance in a music video for a Jay-Z track one of my friends at college was making. He needed a dancer to perform some choreography devised by another dance learner for her choreography unit.

The style was a mix of hip-hop, house and my own moves. I worked with the choreographer to produce a great combination, based on a motif, with some freestyle in the middle. In the end, we danced together in a rolling cannon – that's where you dance the same moves but one slightly after the other. We showed it to our dance tutor who helped us with a few rehearsals and gave us some ideas for developing the motif a bit more.

Although the project took a lot of my time – some of it spent looking at video clips on the internet to pick up new moves – our performance for the filming went really well.

Now it's over to the editors of the video to make it work on screen, but I am pleased with my performance. My tutor came to watch part of the filming and he said he thought my work was successful. I do need to work more on my turns to make them more accurate – I'll use spotting to prevent myself from getting dizzy.

Over to you

- How would you have responded if another dance learner asked you to learn and rehearse a dance like this?
- What sort of dancing do you like doing? Are you very good at a particular style, and would you like the chance to show off your skills?
- Would you give up the time to work in a team with other learners like Lee?

38.1 Be able to participate effectively in practical dance workshops and rehearsals

Setting your starting points

- Work with a partner on a short combination of movements, learned in regular class.
- Rehearse the combination.
- Watch your partner (one of you could film while the other dances), giving objective criticism and suggestions to help them improve.
- Swap roles.
- Perform for the group.
- Note down how you improved and developed your performance.

This is a good way for both you and your tutor to find out where you are at the start of the course. This will make both of you aware of your strengths and weaknesses.

This unit is designed to give you the experience of dance training and to provide you with an idea of the way professional dancers work. All dancers must constantly learn and master new skills, as well as keep up their basic fitness levels and technique, and you will follow that pathway.

To achieve the full unit, you will need to learn the key ingredients of at least two dance styles; this will mean mastering the particular ways the body is used to showcase the unique features of each style, such as pointed feet in ballet, and isolated head, hip and shoulders in jazz. Your tutor will lead regular class in whatever style you are working on. You will learn two of the following dance styles (some are more commonly taught than others): ballet, contemporary, jazz, hip-hop, rock 'n roll, folk, tap, African, South Asian, Latin, street.

Did you know?

Many styles of dance commonly performed today have their roots firmly in ballet. The terms and words used for steps and positions in classical ballet are often used elsewhere, such as in jazz.

38.1.1 Participation

The most important thing you can do is to attend class regularly. All professional dancers take regular class every day to keep up their skill and fitness levels; it is very hard to do this by working out at home. Many dancers go to more than one class a day where the focus is on different dance styles, or on building fitness and stamina. Many also attend a gym for strength and fitness and to work on associated disciplines such as Pilates, for alignment, posture and correcting faults.

Attending a gym can help dancers to build strength and fitness

Appropriate presentation

Your presentation in class tells your tutor, or a guest dance teacher, a lot about your commitment as a dancer. No serious dancer comes to class without the right dancewear and/or shoes. The right gear depends on the style of dance you are undertaking.

For contemporary dance, for example, you will need:

- a fitted top or leotard (so your tutor can see how you are moving)
- a pair of fitted sweat pants, leggings or tights
- socks or bare feet, or the correct dance shoe (if you are doing ballet, tap, jazz, street or hip-hop)
- warm-up clothes, such as a sweat top, leg-warmers and arm-warmers
- a dance belt (boys need this for support)
- a sport bra (some girls need this for support)
- no jewellery, including watches, as these can cause injury to others
- long hair tied back off your face
- deodorant (you will get hot).

In class, your tutor will normally follow a routine. Every style of dance has its own particular class structure, but most fit into a pattern that has been followed for years.

Focus and concentration

You must remain absolutely focused throughout class. You should:

- keep your eyes on the tutor when they are teaching
- watch yourself in the mirror (this is a good way to check positioning and body alignment)
- ask questions when you are confused or stuck – it is the only way to learn
- watch other dancers performing short combinations or solos, and learn from them.

Movement memory

The only way to develop movement memory is to practise your dancing over and over again. By doing this, dancers develop an incredible capacity to remember and accurately recall whole ballets, for example. With time, you will develop enough movement memory to perform long dance sequences accurately and exactly as you were taught or directed.

Did you know?

When dancers watch other dancers in action, the parts of their brain involved in their own movement become highly active. It is almost as though they are dancing the steps themselves.

Activity: Developing movement memory

Try to learn a new short dance combination every day for a week. You could:

- use some of the steps and moves taught in class
- make up some moves of your own
- watch a music video and try to learn the dance
- work with a partner to test out your memory.

Perform all your dance combinations at the end of the week.

Remember

Ensure you are warmed up before you attempt any difficult or very stretchy moves. This way you will avoid muscle strains.

Responding to direction

You will get a lot of practise working with your tutor in class and rehearsals. When you are preparing work for a specific occasion, such as a showcase, you must take and respond to direction. This means you must listen carefully to the criticism you receive and take action to improve your performance.

Make a note of feedback from your tutor or director, then set yourself some achievable targets to improve your dancing.

Assessment activity 1

Unit 38 **P1 M1 D1 P2 M2 D2** BTEC

Work with a partner on a short piece of learned choreography. Ask your tutor to give you notes on your work.

You can develop your work by being highly self-critical; this will mean watching yourself in the studio mirrors as you dance, as well as reviewing your dancing on video or DVD. It is useful to make a quick film of yourselves as you rehearse so you can check positioning, line, use of space and timing.

Your tutor will give you continuous feedback as you rehearse, and you must make sure you accept this objectively, not as personal criticism. Sometimes this is hard, but all dancers must take feedback throughout their career. You should try to take on board what your tutor says to you as you rehearse your dance.

Your partner will also be a source of support and help; this is part of the bargain you make when you agree to partner another dancer.

If you find that you cannot manage a particular step or movement as well as you would like, take a break and come back to it later.

Rehearse your dance and perform it to the group, asking for feedback.

Evidence

- your own and your group's observations
- films of the workshop and performance
- your log book where you record your ideas, responses to criticism and plans for improving your work
- tutor feedback.

Grading tips

M1 You must be disciplined and focused in class and participate fully in rehearsal.

D1 You must be a good self-manager as you develop performance skills. You are totally committed to your class and to rehearsing.

M2 You should respond positively to corrections and notes given to you by your director and your peers.

D2 You should take and use direction as a positive way of improving your performance, which will be technically excellent.

Functional skills

English: By observing peers and evaluating your own performance, you will be using your **speaking and listening** skills.

By evaluating your work in your performer's log book, you are using your **writing** skills.

38.1.2 Workshops

Most of the dance workshops you experience will be led by your tutor, so they will choreograph the dances you learn over time, you will become accustomed to their style of working and you may be able to anticipate what steps and moves they will use.

On some occasions, other learners will lead the class, sometimes with their own choreography. Take every opportunity to try out your own ideas on other dancers as this is an excellent way to expand your skills.

PLTS

By demonstrating commitment to the development of performance skills and improving performance through identifying your strengths and weaknesses, you will be developing your skills as an **independent enquirer** and **self-manager**.

By responding positively to direction and correction, and working and learning from other dancers, you will be developing your skills as a **reflective learner** and **effective participator**.

Professional repertoire

If you are lucky enough to have some classes with a visiting professional dancer or choreographer, you may be taught extracts from work danced by professional companies. This is challenging, but a great experience.

You can also achieve a lot by learning work from the repertoire on DVD/video. You can work with your tutor in reconstructing professional work.

Case study: Stella, a 17-year old dancer

Stella is studying BTEC National dance at a local FE college. Her tutor has taken the group to see one of the national contemporary dance companies which is performing at their local arts centre.

After the show, they are given the chance to ask the choreographer/director questions about his work.

The company sends their education officer to Stella's college so the BTEC dancers can learn some of the professional repertoire first hand.

The guest tutor teaches a warm-up first, then a section of one of the dances. This is a piece of choreography by Merce Cunningham, so the dance is very precise and difficult to grasp.

The following lesson, Stella and her group work on trying to master the steps of the piece. Their tutor asks them to develop a short sequence of their own from the learned choreography. This involves working the steps with their partner, making contact with them.

Stella works with Ammo; their dance uses the floor, they push each other into movements, a bit like in **contact improvisation**. The final sequence is more flowing than the original choreography, but works well. They decide, with their tutor, to work this piece up for their group-sharing showcase that Friday.

Over to you

- Choreography is not assessed in this unit, but taking a dance, and developing it, making it your own is a good way of building your dance skills. What work have you seen that you could use as a starting point for your own dances?

- Try to remember a dance sequence you have learned, and work with a partner to improvise your own dance, developed from the original choreography.

- Show this work to your tutor, rehearse it and perform it to the group.

Activity: Choreographer research

- Find out about some well-known choreographers, such as Merce Cunningham. He was a pioneer of contemporary choreography, and danced until he was an elderly man. Who did he train and dance with as a young man?

- What were some of his major dance works?

Key terms

Contact improvisation – improvised contemporary dance where the partners use each other's bodies to initiate and lead movements

38.1.3 Rehearsals

For every rehearsal you will need to:

- warm up, just like in regular class
- go over or learn dances; this will involve the introduction of new choreography, or the review of dance material you have been working on previously
- refine your dancing by listening carefully to your director's criticisms and responding to them; this is how your dancing is turned into performance
- pay strict attention to detail throughout the rehearsal, using your movement memory to help you reproduce every step and move accurately, and in time with the accompaniment, where there is any.

The dance class

Most dance classes take place in a studio. Yours may have a heated floor, mirrors and a barre.

Always try to be near the front so you will be able to see what your tutor wants you to do. However, a tutor may put a learner in a place they think is most suitable for their size, experience or concentration powers.

Every class must start with a warm-up, which will make your muscles and joints more flexible and comfortable to move. The warm-up will be style-specific; for jazz, for example, it will look something like this:

- **centre** – stretches, arms, torso, back mobilisation
- **isolation** – moving one body part at a time
- *pliés* – knee bends in different positions
- *tendus* – feet and leg stretches.

After that you might go into:

- centre work, where you perform a series of exercises to work on your body control and coordination
- floor stretches and work for your body's centre
- flexibility work, leg stretches, back extensions
- leg lifts and kicks
- **travelling steps** across the floor
- jumps.

Then you might learn a more complex **combination** of steps and moves that you perform as a group, in pairs or solo. After a dance session you must always cool down to allow your muscles to gradually lose heat and prevent aches the following day.

The style of dance you are working in will determine the dance vocabulary you will have to master. All dance styles have their own specific words; classical dance forms, such as ballet, and South Asian dance, for example **Kathakali** and **Bharata Natyam**, have whole dictionaries dedicated to them!

The costume is also an important part of the Bharata Natyam dance

Key terms

Centre – the part of your body around your belly button; it marks the place where your core strength lies, and controls all your movements

Isolations – the snappy rhythmic movements of separate body parts, such as head, shoulders and hands which is associated with jazz dance

Plié – controlled knee bend in set position with feet parallel or turned-out, to build control in legs and centre

Tendu – controlled stretch of the feet and legs, such as point-flex-point, to build control and strength in legs, hips and centre

Travelling steps – steps linked together, generally performed across the diagonal, or around the studio, to build up rhythm, coordination, style

Combination – a series of moves and steps joined together to make a short dance sequence.

Kathakali – a very old form of stylised dance drama, originally from Kerala, India

Bharata Natyam – an ancient traditional dance from Southern India, danced by both males and females

38.2 Be able to perform dances demonstrating application of physical and interpretive skills

38.2.1 Physical skills

You should strive to master the physical and interpretive skills of the dance styles you will be working in. Natural talent, such as an innate sense of rhythm and coordination, is obviously helpful but you can develop dance skills through hard work and commitment. For instance, you can improve your flexibility, balance, strength and control of movements. Physical and interpretive skills will develop over time. It is vital that you take any opportunity to try new styles, work with other people and see different forms of dance in performance.

Posture and alignment

In dance, your body is your work tool; how you hold yourself is vitally important as it shows how you feel.

Activity: Improve your posture and alignment

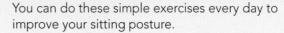

You can do these simple exercises every day to improve your posture and alignment.

- Stand sideways on to the mirror, feet together, relax your shoulders and arms.
- Think of your feet like two triangles and place your weight equally between the three points: heel, outer edge, ball.
- Make sure your ankles are vertical.
- Check your knees. Are they pulled up so your legs are stretched right up into the hips?
- What shape does your back make? There should be a pair of gentle curves, one outwards over the top of your back and in again at about the level of your shoulders; then another one coming outwards from the bottom of your waist. Your lower back should be straight.
- Stretch the space between the pelvis and the lower ribs; this way your stomach is held flatter.
- Do not allow shoulders to hang.
- Your head should sit comfortably on top of the spinal column with the chin more or less level.
- Arms hang comfortably by your sides.

If your body is slumped and your shoulders hang forward, you will not be able to move easily and this will put unnecessary strain on your back.

The way you align your body will affect the way you dance. Even hip-hop dancers have to have good alignment so they do not injure themselves dancing. Ask a partner to check your posture; a photo taken on your mobile phone should help you see just how good your natural alignment is. If you are not happy with it, practise in front of the mirror every day until you are. Your sitting posture is just as important.

Activity: Improve your sitting posture

You can do these simple exercises every day to improve your sitting posture.

- Sit on the floor in front of a mirror with legs out in front of you or crossed.
- Check you are on both sitting bones equally.
- Allow your spine to stretch up out of your pelvis.
- Keep your head level.
- Keep your shoulders relaxed.
- Check your alignment in the mirror.

If you can stand and sit with good posture, your alignment will automatically improve when you are working.

Coordination

Coordination is something that, to some extent, you are born with. However, you can improve it with some concentrated work. The more dance combinations you learn and master, the better your coordination will be.

Rhythm

Dancers must have a strong sense of rhythm. Rhythm is about being able to keep time during a movement, and dancers must work hard to develop this.

You can practise by listening to music and counting the beats. In class, always count the beats in your head. Most dancers count in rounds of eight beats.

Balance

Balance is not just about standing on one leg! All the exercises you carry out in class will help you improve your balance. Look back to the jazz dance warm-up (page 165). There were *tendus* and leg stretches, many of which are carried out on one leg. In ballet classes you will learn how to do an **attitude arabesque**. You will learn how to turn in most dance styles; hip-hop dancers sometimes turn on their head or hands. These moves all need a well-developed sense of balance and this comes with practice.

Strength and control

You will gradually build up strength and control throughout your course. You can help yourself by making sure you attend class very regularly, and/or by going to a gym.

Dancers tend to be strong because they work out so often in class, but to carry out some dance styles, such as street and hip-hop, requires extra strength. For example, to achieve some of the hip-hop turns dancers execute on their heads, your neck needs to be extremely strong. It takes time to build up this strength and you should not attempt to work on it without your tutor.

Much of your control as a dancer will derive from your centre, which is the abdominal area around the belly button. This central area must be toned and taut so you can move freely around it.

To achieve the kinds of turns you see in ballet, such as *pirouettes*, you will need to develop strong legs and ankles and be able to control your movements. Part of the control of turns comes from **spotting**.

Flexibility

You can improve your natural level of flexibility by working on stretching whenever you can. If you go into a working dance studio, every dancer who is relaxing will be stretching. They rarely stop unless they are actually in class or rehearsal.

Key terms

Attitude – a standing position, on one leg, the other raised in a bent position up at the rear, arms in fourth position

Arabesque – similar to attitude, but with leg and arms outstretched, one forward, one to the side, slightly back

Activity: Improve your flexibility

You can do these simple exercises every day to improve the flexibility in your legs and hips.

- Do a warm-up (follow the one on page 65 if you are not sure how).
- Lie on the floor on your back; raise one knee and unfold it upwards towards the ceiling. You can bend the other knee and keep that foot on the floor if you find this difficult.
- Holding behind the raised knee, gently pull back on the leg to stretch out the hamstrings.
- Change legs and repeat.
- Sit up, legs wide apart, feet pointed; make sure your posture is correct (see page 169).
- Sitting tall, arms out to each side, reach up through the top of your head and bend forward, keeping your back very straight; hold for four counts.
- Repeat with feet flexed; hold for four counts.
- Repeat with an even curve forward in your back, to take your head down towards the floor, feet pointed; hold for four counts.
- Repeat with feet flexed; hold for four counts.

Spatial awareness

As your dancing improves, you will become increasingly sure of yourself and where you are in space. Dancers have an innate sense of space, making the most of what they have to move around in. When dancing with a partner, you must forget about keeping a comfortable distance between you, especially if either of you is lifting the other, or you are working on contact improvisation.

Awareness of other dancers

Most of the time you will be working with other dancers, so you need to develop awareness of them as you rehearse and perform. You will work alongside your group right through the course, and like a professional company, you will find ways of dancing together.

The next step in building this awareness comes when you start to work on ensemble dances. You might have to dance next to, near, around or at a distance from others. As you begin to acquire choreography, you will learn how to do this. It is useful to develop an ability to use peripheral vision as you work. You cannot turn your head to see how close you are to another dancer, unless that is part of the choreography; you must sense where others are.

38.2.2 Interpretive skills

Timing, musicality and phrasing

These areas are linked, and relate directly to the style of dance you are learning. Where contemporary dancers perform in silence, for instance, they must count for themselves in their head. You will become good at this, as you will learn how counting works when your tutor counts you in for your class exercises.

Working with accompaniment helps you with timing, but you will still need to develop your own sense of timing so that your work sits comfortably alongside other dancers on stage with you. When your tutor is directing, they will show you where you need to place particular emphasis within the choreography. This might be where a particular step has a lively or springy quality, for instance, or how a sequence of steps can be performed smoothly and fluently.

Activity: Timing and phrasing

- Take a short section of choreography that you have learned; this could be a short combination your tutor has used during regular class.
- Now try using a piece of music that has a completely different tempo, that is, faster or slower.
- Try dancing it without music, counting for yourself.
- Phrasing is the way you link your dance steps together to create a seamless dance.

Projection and focus

Any performer has to accept that, at some point, their work must be ready to 'give away' to their audience; it must be communicated to them. You can develop this performance skill by working to project what you are dancing to an imaginary audience in class. This will make your work focused.

You can also use focus when you are carrying out a tricky step or move, such as a spin. Ensure your focus is very much on the successful execution of the move.

Facial and bodily expression

A common fault is when a dancer appears to be dancing the steps, but without any sense that they really 'mean it'. For example, a group of street jazz dancers might have little or no expression in their work, blank faces and obviously low energy levels. Yet street jazz is a style that must have attitude for it to work.

You must gauge the expression level to fit the style of the dance you are working on and performing. That does not necessarily mean putting a smile on your face. If you are dancing a piece of lyrical classical ballet, for example, the expectation is that your whole being is intent on expressing the grace and fluency of the dance.

Do they look like they 'mean it'?

Key terms

Pirouette – a ballet turn on one leg with the other foot placed just below the knee of the supporting leg, in a turned-out or parallel position

Spotting – this helps prevent dizziness in turns. As you start to turn, fix your eyes on a spot just in front of you at eye height; keep your gaze there as long as you can during the turn; flick your head around as you turn to prevent losing sight of your point

Assessment activity 2

BTEC

Practise two of the combinations you have learned in class; make sure they are in different styles, such as jazz and contemporary.

In a small group, work out the dances to some musical tracks. Rehearse the dances so that one dance leads into the other. Work on your focus and concentration.

Evidence

- perform your work to the group.

Grading tips

M3 You must show how well you have mastered the physical and interpretive skills of at least two dance styles. Your dance idea should be clearly communicated, so if the piece is high energy, make sure you communicate that feeling.

D3 Your dancing should be clear, focused and interpreted so that your ideas are clearly communicated to your audience.

PLTS

By applying and developing physical and interpretative skills in performance, you will be developing your skills as a **creative thinker** and **self-manager**.

By working on group dances, you will be developing your skills as a **team worker**.

Functional skills

English: By sharing movement ideas with others, you are using your **speaking and listening** skills.

38.3 Be able to perform dances demonstrating the application of appropriate stylistic qualities

38.3.1 Dances

This unit requires you to master and perform at least two different dance styles. You may be introduced to more than this, and many centres will give you opportunities to try several styles.

You will probably be better at one than the other, but few dancers make their living through just dancing one style. Be bold and push yourself to develop your skills in several.

Activity: Different dance styles

Find out about each of the styles listed below:

- Jazz
- Hip-hop
- Rock 'n roll
- Folk
- Tap
- African
- South Asia
- Latin.

Consider the following questions:

1   What are the main features of these styles?
2   Are there any you need a dancing partner to take part in?
3   Where do they come from?
4   Who dances them?
5   Do they have a social purpose, such as getting to know other people or celebration?

Select your favourite dance style from those listed above and make up a short sequence in that style.

Now, working with a partner:

- dance it as a street piece with some isolated head and shoulder twitches and rolls, spins and hand gestures
- take out all the gestures, and dance it smoothly and fluently like a piece of contemporary jazz ballet.

Ask your partner to assess how you are doing.

Key terms

Dynamic range – the quality of energy and drive that a dancer uses, how strong their movements are

38.3.2 Stylistic qualities

Technical and physical features of the dance style

How you hold yourself and what you do with your limbs is the basis of any dance style. For example, if you are dancing Latin style, you must draw your torso up very straight with your shoulders back and chin up. Elbows tend to be held away from the body slightly, whereas in ballet elbows are also held away from the torso, but arms are always held in a curve, away from the shoulders, so that the hands flow behind when the arms move.

Each dance style uses space in a particular way. Release uses the floor as a tool to propel the movements around it. Tap obviously uses the floor as part of the noise-making equipment of the dancer, but tap dancers do not always move across the floor, as they can do steps on the spot.

Expressive features

These encompass the dancer's focus, **dynamic range** and facial expression, and are closely related to the physical and interpretive skills.

How do breakdancers make use of the floor?

173

Musical accompaniment

Your tutor will probably teach you work that relates very closely to music or accompaniment. Practise your work both with and without music or accompaniment, as this helps you develop your timing and the essential skill of counting in your head.

Some dance is choreographed in a 'call and response' format, specifically to answer the call of a particular phrase in music; some dance tries to visualise the music very clearly. Choreography can be closely related to the timing of the music, but not always. For example, most rock-jazz dance works with the rhythm of its backing music, known as 'direct correlation', whereas ballet choreography rarely pays much attention to it. Ballet producers often aim for their choreography to sit independently alongside the music.

The choreographer Merce Cunningham created work independently from the composer who was creating the accompaniment for the piece. Often the dancers had never heard the music until the first performance, and sometimes interesting correlations happened when the dance was performed to the music. Anne Teresa De Keersmaeker's *Mozart Concert Arias* are an interesting example of how choreography works with the timing of the music, and also demonstrates disassociation; some of the arias were choreographed in association with the music, and some were deliberately disassociated from it.

Activity: Ballet and music

Explore some of the dances in a major ballet, such as *Swan Lake*. How much does the dancing correspond with the timing or style of the music? Who crafted the choreography?

Assessment activity 3

 BTEC

Watch a dance on a music video. Working with a partner, try to learn a section of the dance.

Work on creating an interpretation of the music. You could use the choreography as a starting point, making it your own by adapting it to suit your skills.

When interpreting music you must make sure you really listen to it carefully. Once you have found out how the music is phrased, through verses and choruses, you can use this structure to bring variation into your dance. For example, you could repeat the same choreography through each verse and different steps through each chorus.

The style of the dance in the music video will give you an idea of how the original choreographer wanted to interpret the sounds. You might take this further by adding some moves of your own in the same style, or by using a completely different style.

Keep it simple and work on perfecting how you dance the steps.

Rehearse your dance, film a rehearsal on DVD and watch it to make sure your work is successful.

Evidence

- DVD recording

Grading tips

M4 You must use the stylistic qualities of your chosen style in your dance. These should be clear for your audience to see.

D4 Your expression of the style should be clear and confident, so your audience get a real sense that you can dance the style with ease.

PLTS

By exploring new styles, techniques and skills for dances, you will be developing your skills as an **independent enquirer**.

Functional skills

English: By sharing movement ideas with your partner, you will be using your **speaking and listening** skills.

38.4 Understand how to improve dance for performance through evaluation and review

Your tutor will provide evidence for assessment through their observations and statements. There will also be evidence on DVD/video of you at work in rehearsal or performance. Writing is not an important part of this unit and you will not be asked to prepare essays or extended pieces of written work. However, you should keep a dancer's log, showing how you review your dancing, evaluate your performance and plan for improvement. This does not necessarily need to be written, but could be recorded by audio or visual means on tape, MP3 player, computer, blog, or phone, and stored carefully on a computer or your centre's virtual learning environment.

You might use a self-assessment and target-setting worksheet or write up your reviews and evaluations more formally. You can also provide peer and witness observation reports or statements on paper, recorded on DVD or by audio means. This will help you to achieve the last learning outcome.

38.4.1 Review

You must review your own work throughout the course. You can self-review, or ask your tutor or a fellow student to review it. The results of this review must be recorded so you can use it to make plans to improve your dancing.

Reviews must be objective, which means you do not look at a DVD recording of your work in rehearsal and think, 'I look fat!' It is more useful to think about how well you have mastered the style and qualities of the choreography, how expressive you are, and how good your timing is.

38.4.2 Evaluation

Evaluation is the process of closely identifying your strengths and weaknesses, then setting targets you can achieve that will still stretch and improve your dancing.

38.4.3 Improvement

Improvement in your dancing is the end point of review. You must get used to accepting criticism from tutors and directors as this is an essential ingredient in the life of every dancer. Constructive criticism is also something you can give your classmates. This will help you all set achievable, but challenging targets. These targets are useless without careful thought and planning; they must be specific. For example, where a dance has a lot of spins and turns, you might set yourself the following target:

- Practise spotting so my *pirouettes* and spins are better.

When you have set your target, you must think about how to implement it, and how to review your progress, for example:

- I will spend time in the studio practising a range of turns, *pirouettes*, spins, jazz turns, single leg runs, two leg turns, inward turns and outward turns.
- I will review my work by recording my practice on DVD.

Finally, you must re-evaluate your work at points during the learning and rehearsal process. Try not to get despondent when moves seem too difficult; always ask for help to relearn them.

Practising the steps together is key to improving

Assessment activity 4

Write a list of questions to ask yourself during the rehearsal process and after performance. For example:

- How well are your rehearsals going?
- Which pieces do you think you are dancing well and which not so well?

Explain why.

- What plans will you make for the next workshop or rehearsal?
- How did you perform in your final performance? What were your strengths and weaknesses?

Ask a friend to ask you the questions and film the interview.

Make a plan for future work based on your responses.

Evidence

- recorded notes in a journal
- filmed interview

Grading tips

M5 You should accurately review your work through all processes of the activity. You should pinpoint the strengths and weaknesses in your dance technique, and set yourself targets for improvement.

D5 You should thoroughly review your work throughout the activity. Focus on your technical abilities and how well you perform the work. You should set challenging and achievable targets to ensure your dancing improves.

PLTS

By improving your performance through identifying your strengths and weaknesses, and setting smart, challenging targets, you will be developing your skills as an **independent enquirer**, **reflective learner** and **self-manager**.

Functional skills

English: By evaluating your own performance in your 'interview', you are using your **speaking and listening** skills.

By evaluating your performance in your journal, you are using your **writing** skills.

Danni
Professional dancer

Danni trained at her local dance school. Then, at 16, she won a place at the London Studio Centre, where she extended the range of her dancing from classical ballet, jazz and contemporary to more recent styles like street and hip-hop.

She has started to build a portfolio of work by auditioning for contracts in dance schools and academies. She is now preparing herself to try for a contract in a major London dance school, to choreograph the end of year showcase for their dance learners.

How did you find out about the job?

Danni: I saw an advertisement in one of the professional dance papers and I applied. They want me to come with some dance ideas and talk them through my work.

What sort of dance will you be taking there?

Danni: I have some ideas for a variety of dances: one is a short ballet, one a more freestyle piece of street jazz, and another a contemporary piece.

How will you convince the panel you are the right dancer for the job?

Danni: I'm going to show them! I've learned some short dances that will showcase some of my ideas. I've made a recording of a mix of four music tracks and I'm going to perform my dance ideas. If I can, I'm going to teach some of my ideas to a group of their learners too, to show how well I can choreograph for other dancers. Wish me luck!

Think about it!

1 During your work for this unit, what skills have you learned that Danni should be using?

2 How could you prepare work to take to an audition like this?

3 What styles of dance would you want to showcase to an audition panel?

Just checking

1 Are there any sections of regular class that you find particularly tricky? Always ask your tutor to show you steps and moves again so you can get them right.

2 Are you taking time out of your schedule to stretch and exercise outside of class? This is essential if you want to build and maintain strength, flexibility, stamina and technique.

3 Are you taking note of the criticism or notes your tutor has given you in class and rehearsal? Remember, this is the way to plan for improvement.

4 Are you keeping up your dancer's log and ensuring you are recording your progress in your dancing? Is this helping you? If not, change the way you use it.

edexcel :::

Assignment tips

- You must make sure you dance at least a little every day. This way you will build and maintain your fitness, stamina and technique.

- Try to find other classes outside your centre. If this is not possible, run some yourself. Do not forget to ask your tutor if this is allowed in your centre.

- Try to arrange regular showcases of your work, maybe during a lunch break.

- Watch dance on TV and on the internet; there are lots of dance clips (of all styles) on websites to help you find out which style of dance you really want to pursue.

- Be helpful to your fellow dancers; give and accept constructive and objective criticism after rehearsals and during feedback times.

- Practise your dances over and over again before any performance, even ones you do for the group.

- Use different ways of keeping up your dancer's log, such as recording your voice on your phone and transferring it to the centre's VLE, writing a blog, filming yourself being interviewed by a friend or keeping an e-diary.

PROJECT 1: Creating and Delivering a Successful TiE Project

Theatre in education (TiE) has been a popular and successful style of live performance since the late 1960s. TiE performances incorporate elements of education and entertainment. They are mostly performed in schools and colleges but can be shown in any venue or establishment for audiences that might benefit from watching the show.

Many professional companies choose TiE as their main focus because it allows them a certain amount of artistic freedom: they can produce original work for specific audiences.

In this project you will work as a member of a TiE company, creating from scratch a TiE project or performance. Your tutor may adapt the examples given in this project for your school or college.

The focus of this project is to produce a 30-minute performance for your target audience. It must be both educational and entertaining, and can include some interactive elements if you wish. You will take on at least one role within the TiE company: you can perform, design, or take on responsibilities as part of the production team, as well as taking an active role in the organisation of the production.

Learning outcomes

After completing this project you should be able to achieve the following learning outcomes:

Unit 9: Devising Plays

1   Know how to use stimulus material
2   Know how to develop and shape ideas
3   Be able to rehearse for a devised performance
4   Be able to perform devised drama.

Unit 10: Theatre in Education

1   Know how to research and select suitable ideas for a TiE project
2   Be able to develop an educational performance project
3   Be able to contribute to the realisation of a TiE project.

179

Assessment and grading criteria

This table shows you what you must do in order to achieve a pass, merit or distinction, and where you can find activities in this book to help you.

To achieve a **pass** grade the evidence must show that you should be able to:	To achieve a **merit** grade the evidence must show that, in addition to the pass criteria, you should be able to:	To achieve a **distinction** grade the evidence must show that, in addition to the pass and merit criteria, you should be able to:
Unit 9: Devising Plays		
P1 respond to a range of stimuli, revealing creative ideas **Assessment activity 1 page 183**	**M1** respond to a range of stimuli, revealing awareness of their suitability for devising and performance **Assessment activity 1 page 183**	**D1** respond to a range of stimuli with imagination, revealing a clear and creative grasp of their suitability for devising and performance **Assessment activity 1 page 183**
P2 develop chosen ideas and materials for devising **Assessment activity 1 page 183**	**M2** develop chosen ideas for devising, using insight and imagination to demonstrate a detailed response **Assessment activity 1 page 183**	**D2** develop chosen ideas and materials for devising in a perceptive and comprehensive manner, demonstrating a thoroughly considered, insightful response **Assessment activity 1 page 183**
P3 demonstrate cooperation with other members of the company, making contributions to the group process **Assessment activity 3 page 186** **Assessment activity 4 page 188**	**M3** demonstrate cooperation with other members of the company in the devising process, making useful contributions **Assessment activity 3 page 186** **Assessment activity 4 page 188**	**D3** demonstrate a high degree of positive cooperation with other members of the company in all aspects of the process **Assessment activity 3 page 186** **Assessment activity 4 page 188**
P4 develop devised performance through rehearsal, with support and guidance **Assessment activity 3 page 186** **Assessment activity 4 page 188**	**M4** develop devised performance through rehearsal, with minimum support and guidance **Assessment activity 3 page 186** **Assessment activity 4 page 188**	**D4** develop devised performance through rehearsal, with thoroughly imaginative and independent application **Assessment activity 3 page 186** **Assessment activity 4 page 188**
P5 perform a devised theatre piece that communicates ideas to an audience. **Assessment activity 6 page 192**	**M5** perform a devised theatre piece that accurately communicates its intentions to an audience and shows awareness of its style. **Assessment activity 6 page 192**	**D5** perform a devised theatre piece that accurately communicates its style and intentions, fully engaging with the audience. **Assessment activity 6 page 192**
Unit 10: Theatre in Education		
P1 describe ideas for a TiE project that meet the educational needs of the targeted audience **Assessment activity 2 page 184**	**M1** explain the suitability of ideas for a TiE project that meets the educational needs of the target audience **Assessment activity 2 page 184**	**D1** analyse and justify ideas for a TiE project that meet the educational needs of the targeted audience **Assessment activity 2 page 184**
P2 develop ideas for a TIE project that would entertain and educate **Assessment activity 3 page 186**	**M2** develop ideas for a TiE project that would entertain and educate with skill and confidence **Assessment activity 3 page 186**	**D2** develop ideas for a TiE project that would entertain and educate with flair and imagination **Assessment activity 3 page 186**
P3 apply organisational skills competently **Assessment activity 5 page 191**	**M3** apply organisational skills efficiently **Assessment activity 5 page 191**	**D3** apply organisational skills with foresight and attention to detail **Assessment activity 5 page 191**
P4 apply performance and/or production skills competently. **Assessment activity 4 page 188** **Assessment activity 6 page 192**	**M4** apply performance and/or production skills confidently and proficiently. **Assessment activity 4 page 188** **Assessment activity 6 page 192**	**D4** apply performance and/or production skills with flair and imagination. **Assessment activity 4 page 188** **Assessment activity 6 page 192**

How you will be assessed

This project will be assessed as an internal assignment that will be designed and marked by the staff at your centre.

You will be assessed on your ability to take an active role in the development and organisation of the production, ensuring that the production is performed to relevant audiences, as well as your performance and/or production role.

The work you produce may include:
- a TiE overview document
- a creative log book that consists of:
  – research material
  – notes of the devising process and developmental ideas
  – records of your organisational role and responsibilities
- recordings of milestone rehearsals
- a recording of one of your performances
- observation statements from your tutor(s)
- any relevant feedback from the audience or audiences.

Paven , 18-year-old acting learner

We created a piece about taking care of the environment. We were inspired by a TiE show that visited our college, performed by the Big Fish Theatre Company.

We decided to do a tour in our local area, going to schools and community centres. The performance had something for everyone; it wasn't only aimed at young people but at parents and older people, too. We live in a town with the countryside nearby but some people don't seem to care that much, and there is a lot of rubbish about. So we wanted to create a piece of work that would highlight how important it is to take care of our surroundings, and to think of ways of preserving it for the future.

As well as creating and performing in the show, I was given the responsibility of Production Assistant. I had to find contact details for selected schools, phone them and tell them about our show, and try to negotiate performances. I had to be professional and polite when communicating with the school staff – I wanted to make a good impression!

The tour went really well, although we had some very early starts. Travelling in the minibus and spending so much time together helped us bond as a group. We were proud of our work and wanted to show it to as many people as possible. We had some brilliant feedback including one school that sent us some poems that they had written after seeing the show.

Over to you
- What issues and topics would you be interested in developing as a TiE performance?
- What type of work do you think would be suitable for a TiE piece for people in your area?

Theatre in education

Theatre in education is a piece of theatre for a specific audience that must:

- entertain – contain elements of drama and performance and use theatrical techniques
- educate – provide accurate and factual information on a particular subject/issue.

TiE is unlike other forms of performance because:

- you can specify who the audience should be
- you need only to perform to your chosen audiences and do not have to promote the work to the general public
- you can gauge feedback from your audience, and do further work/exploration of themes with them
- you can find out if your aims and objectives have been met, for example:
  - have the audience learnt something about the subject matter?
  - what did they think of the work?

TiE background

Theatre in education began in the mid-1960s as a project by the Belgrade Theatre in Coventry. They were reacting to developments in society at the time, including information on how people learn and changes to the education system. They perceived the role of theatre as a method of influencing change in society.

Those involved created a manifesto, or set of rules, that provided a framework for the productions they were doing:

1 The performance did not stand alone, but was part of an educational package.
2 There would be a preview and a discussion with the teachers.
3 There would be pre-performance work in the classroom.
4 The TiE company would often make more than one visit.
5 Classroom work would take place between the performance(s).
6 Follow-up work would be carried out in the classroom after the theatre company had finished its involvement.
7 The TiE company's work would often last a full term.

The work was a success, and theatre in education became more popular through the 1970s and the following decades. It is now a prescribed element of Personal, Social and Health Education in the national curriculum and there are lots of different theatre companies that specialise in TiE productions.

Activity: TiE companies

Select a TiE company to research and discover what they do. (The University of Exeter's Department of Drama includes a list of TiE companies on its website. To access this website, please see the Hotlinks section on page ii.)

Most companies have websites, and you can contact them to request further information and examples of the type of work they do.

If possible, watch a TIE performance by your chosen company.

Answer the following questions, and share your findings with your group.

1 What kind of subject(s) does the TiE company focus on?
2 Is there an artistic or company policy?
3 Who and where are their audiences?
4 Who do they employ and what jobs/roles do they have?
5 What types or styles of theatre do they use in their performance?
6 What resources do they have? Do they receive any funding?

Choosing the topic and subject matter of your TiE piece

When deciding on the topic and subject matter of your TiE piece, you can either first choose the topic and then use it to influence who you perform it to, or you can first choose the target audience and then use that decision to influence the topic/subject matter.

There are a number of ways to choose the subject matter for your TiE piece. You could:

- decide through group discussion
- brainstorm issues and topics
- bring in stimuli to discuss and work with, e.g. a song dealing with a particular theme, or a newspaper article about an important issue

- choose to work on topics on the national curriculum, e.g. Key Stage 3, Key Stage 4, PSHE Citizenship
- tie in with current national campaigns, e.g. the national Anti-Bullying Week
- ask your target audience what they want – try contacting teachers and students of local schools, or local organisations such as scouts/guides groups, youth groups, community groups and workshops, or hospices.

Key terms

Stimuli – anything that can have an impact or influence

Assessment activity 1

Unit 9   P1 M1 D1 P2 M2 D2    BTEC

When choosing the topic that your TiE project will address, you need to produce a record of your individual and group responses to each piece of stimuli – so make sure you make a valid contribution to the process.

This record can be called a 'creative log book'. The best way to keep your creative log book up to date is to complete it after each session. You can use the questions below as a guide.

What **stimuli** did you find and bring to the group?

- Who came up with ideas? What ideas did you have?
- What practical exercises did you take part in? Did you suggest any?
- What other suggestions did you make?
- What ideas didn't work? Do you know why?
- How did you contribute to/help decide/develop the final topic?

- What is the final topic? Are you happy with this choice?

Evidence

- creative log book (which can be written or an audio/visual recording)

Grading tips

M1 M2 Make sure you use your imagination when developing your ideas. Some ideas won't work (some members of your team might not like them) but that is all part of the creative process, and should not be ignored in your creative log book.

D1 D2 Experiment with lots of different ideas. Give reasons why ideas were either suitable or didn't work.

PLTS

Coming up with creative ideas for your project will demonstrate your skills as an **independent enquirer** and **creative thinker**. Your skills as a **reflective learner**, **team worker** and **self-manager** will be on display as you work with the rest of your group and give and receive feedback.

Functional skills

English: By writing documents, including extended writing pieces, communicating information, ideas and opinions, effectively and persuasively, you will be using your **writing** skills.

Choosing the target audience for your TiE piece

You can choose the target audience using different factors or categories: For example, you might choose to target people according to their:

- age group, e.g. children, 14–19 year olds, adults, pensioners
- type, e.g. single parents, the unemployed, factory workers, young offenders, or people with specific learning needs.

Suitability of topic for your target audience

Once the topic has been decided, you will need to confirm that it is suitable for the target audience and,

if it is, how to communicate your ideas to them in an effective and suitable manner.

For instance, you may want to focus on bulimia as your topic – but would this topic be suitable for young children? If you don't think it would be suitable, choose an audience that may need advice on this subject (Year 10 and 11 students might benefit from this kind of topic).

For advice and guidance, you could contact people who work with or support your potential audience, or those who specialise in the topic that you wish to cover.

See the *Organising the show* section, starting on page 189, for tips on effective communication.

Assessment activity 2
Unit 10  **BTEC**

Produce an overview of your piece to be used in a variety of ways. It can be used as an information sheet for the company (when contacting potential venues, audiences, group leaders, etc) and in an education pack for the audience/tutors/group leader.

It should state:

- the '**working title**' of your piece
- your company name – this will probably be the name of your centre, but you may wish to give your group an 'identity' (more on this is in the *Organising the show* section starting on page 189)
- the audience that will watch/take part in this show – age group, type, locations and venues
- the educational needs of the audience – what you think they need to learn, what they will learn, i.e. 'at the end of this show the audience will know more about …'
- the entertainment elements – how are you going to tell the story? Will you use any particular styles, e.g. pantomime, masks, forum theatre?

Evidence

- TiE overview document
- creative log book – research notes

Grading tips

M1 You will need to explain how you are going to go about producing the booklet, and why it is important the audience need to know this information.

D1 Include references to research you have done to justify your decisions. For example, if you are working on road safety you could refer to information produced by charities, road-safety organisations, etc.

PLTS

By generating ideas and exploring possibilities for you performance promotion, you will be using your skills as a **creative thinker**.

Functional skills

English: By writing a theatre programme, a booklet or preparing a press release, you will be using your **writing** skills.

The devising process

Developing and creating the TiE piece

In your TiE production, you can work as a performer and/or a member of the production team.

Production team responsibilities could focus on a particular element, such as set design and construction, costume design and creation, or lighting design and operation. For details of roles and responsibilities, look at the *Organising the show* section starting on page 189.

There are lots of different ways of working as part of a group when devising a piece of theatre. You can use some of the following suggestions, or find your own ways to develop the work:

- Verbally – through discussing ideas, brainstorming, and taking part in debates and forum theatre.
- Physically – by creating tableau and still life, body sculpting and role-play.
- Visually – through creating diagrams, making video recordings, adapting and including artwork and photos, filming and incorporating projections.
- Aurally – with creative use of sound effects, performing live music or selecting recorded music.

Working with others when devising can be difficult at times: tempers can get frayed, personality clashes may occur, and it can be hard to consider and incorporate all ideas and suggestions. The following ground rules will help you avoid these problems:

- Take responsibility rather than blame others.
- Try to be cooperative and supportive of the other people in your group.
- Let others take their turn to lead, direct and make decisions.
- Listen to others and expect to be listened to.
- Be flexible and don't be selfish: sometimes you might need to go with someone's idea for the sake of group harmony.

Activity: Ground rules

It might help to set some ground rules. You could use the ones listed above, or make your own.

You might decide to use a conch shell or some other 'speaker's symbol' which is held by the person speaking, and no-one else is allowed to speak until they have the conch. This approach can be very useful in group discussions.

When shaping material, apply your ground rules and keep your creative log up to date with how you coped as a group when completing the following tasks:

- adapting scripted material
- blocking and directing (taking responsibility and making decisions)
- selecting and rejecting material
- scene ordering
- deciding on the project name and character names
- including sound effects and soundtrack
- choosing your design requirements, e.g. set, costume, props.

Experimenting with theatrical techniques

Here are some examples that you could include:

Narration	Song
Thought tracking	Masks
Improvisation	Puppetry
Physical theatre	Dance
Live musical performance	

There are decisions to be made on the *style*, *shape* and *structure* of the overall production. Here are some suggestions – epic, naturalism, physical theatre. You can mix and match elements to suit the needs of the audience, the subject matter, and your skills and creativity.

Did you know?

Forum theatre was created by theatre practitioner Augusto Boal. It provides everyone, regardless of status or position, with an opportunity to express how they feel about the performance work they have watched, or about more general issues in their society.

A rehearsed and structured performance can be dissected and analysed by the audience, who have the opportunity to interact and re-direct the work. One actor is appointed as MC or 'Joker', responsible for leading the workshop and allowing all audience members the chance to participate.

Activity: Audience participation

As a group, decide whether there will there be audience participation and/or interaction? If so, when will this happen and what format will it take?

- Before the show? You could send the audience work or research to do in preparation for the performance. Or you could decide to do some pre-show.

- During the show? You could use the techniques of forum theatre to ask the audience what they think and allow them to take part in revising the work or specific scenes, etc. Or you could give the audience a role, eg the jury, witnesses, schoolchildren, etc.

- After the show? You could get the audience to discuss the outcomes of the work, hold a question and answer session, use forum theatre, hold workshops on themes and ideas, or use follow-up activities in the days/weeks to come, with evaluation and questionnaires.

Assessment activity 3

Unit 9  **P3 M3 D3 P4 M4 D4** **BTEC**

Unit 10 **P2 M2 D2**

For this activity, you must take an active role in your group's development of its TiE project.

You must choose and agree your primary role, e.g. performance or production.

You will also need to accept a role in the organisation and administration of the production.

Ensure you have a clear focus for the TiE project, i.e. the educational and entertainment elements.

You will need to develop the work using drama techniques and styles. You could choose at least one technique (e.g. thought tracking, narration, or mime) and include it with a scene. Experiment with new ideas.

You will also need to keep a record of the progress made (and your own contribution) during rehearsals; you can do this in your creative log book. You may also find you need to set targets for future rehearsals.

Make sure that you work cooperatively with others to progress the work and maintain a positive attitude within the group.

Evidence

- tutor observations
- creative log book, which includes ideas and a progress diary
- audio/visual recordings of rehearsals

Grading tips Units 9 and 10

M2 M3 M4 You should demonstrate your performance and devising ability with confidence and skill.

D2 D3 D4 You should use imagination (be creative and experiment with ideas) and flair to develop your work, being positive and co-operative.

By planning and carrying out research to develop performance ideas, you will be using your skills as an **independent enquirer**.

By generating ideas and exploring possibilities for performances, you will be using your skills as a **creative thinker**.

By collaborating with others to produce a devised performance, you will be using your skills as a **team-worker**.

Functional skills

English: By planning activities and evaluating work, you will be using your **speaking** and **listening** skills.

Set yourself some milestones

It's important to have milestones or targets to work towards. You can assess your progress against them and work out how much you have still to do.

Here are some milestones you can use, or you can create your own that are specific to your project:

- All scenes blocked
- First performance off book
- Costume, props and sound (no lighting)
- Technical rehearsal.

Create an education pack

Providing the audience (or more specifically the group leader/tutor) with an education pack can be beneficial for you and your audience. You can use it to:

- provide them with follow-up exercises
- give them information about the subject matter
- provide information about you, your theatre company, and your aims and objectives
- act as a reminder of the strengths of your work
- demonstrate good customer care, leaving a positive lasting impression.

POLKA THEATRE — World-class theatre for children

Illustration by Chris Garbutt

Activity Pack
The Monster under the Bed

Polka Theatre's *Monster Under the Bed* Activity Pack

Rehearsing the show

While working through this section, some of the evidence that you produce may also cover aspects of Unit 5&7: Rehearsing and Performing, page 65.

The rehearsal period requires dedication, stamina and a mature attitude. The creative process is now secondary to these qualities. You will also need to demonstrate reliability, use of rehearsal schedules, and physical and mental preparation.

Reliability includes turning up on time for rehearsals, meeting any required deadlines (e.g. for learning lines and finding props), bringing your costume to rehearsals.

Using rehearsal schedules means being involved in the creation and management of the rehearsal schedule (e.g. updating it with new information, amending it as appropriate, meeting relevant deadlines).

Physical and mental preparation focuses on getting early nights, having a good diet, practising acting techniques outside the rehearsal schedule (e.g. vocal warm-ups)

Be prepared to:

* wear clothing suitable for rehearsals
* receive and provide constructive criticism
* not give or take criticism personally
* be involved in scenes you are not in
* be flexible with rehearsals as they may overrun
* sit and watch others rehearse when you are not involved.

Assessment activity 4

Unit 9 P3 M3 D3 P4 M4 D4 **BTEC**

Unit 10  P4 M4 D4

Your TiE project may have two production elements to rehearse:

* the TIE performance itself
* the workshop following the performance.

The TiE performance will need to undergo the same rehearsal process as any other performance, including technical and dress rehearsals.

The rehearsal of the workshop will depend on a number of factors:

* its aims and objectives
* the content
* the time length of the workshop
* how many workshops are planned
* who will lead and assist; allocate per workshop
* any props, costumes, music needed.

Evidence

* tutor observations
* recorded milestone performance(s)
* log book

Grading tips Units 9 and 10

M3 M4 Be confident and demonstrate relevant skills to develop your work.

D3 D4 Ensure that you cooperate positively with the group. Being cooperative means contributing to the group and having your say, but also listening to other team members' ideas. Do show your imagination, try new ideas and techniques. Reliability means turning up on time and contributing to the rehearsal process.

Organising the show

Designating roles

Deciding on role(s) within the company should be done as soon as possible. It may be that you are required to take on more than one role. The different roles that are involved in staging a production are discussed in more detail in Unit 3: Performing Arts Business (see page 21).

Performance roles

As well as taking part in the selection of subject matter and the devising process, performers will be required to work as part of the team to create the structure of the piece, rehearse the work, and perform in all shows.

You may act as director and provide guidance for others in rehearsals. You will be involved in casting, blocking, scriptwriting, character development, and putting rehearsal techniques into practice.

Most professional TiE company members will also take on other roles, such as production assistant, stage crewmember, lighting or sound operator, minibus driver, etc.

Production roles

You will be responsible for the design, operation and/or creation of lighting, sound, costume, props, and/or sets. If acting as stage manager, you will create the prompt copy, called 'the book', keep notes on developments in the overall production and rehearsals, and manage and implement the rehearsal schedule.

Organisation and administration roles

The production manager is responsible for coordinating and recording the performance dates, venues and audiences. This role could be taken by your tutor or allocated to responsible members of the group.

The production assistant is responsible for researching and arranging the performance dates, venues and audiences; this role is normally divided between the production team.

Activity: Selecting roles

Work out your own strengths and those of the others in your group. Then, using the questions below, discuss the roles and responsibilities in your group.

You might find that others volunteer for things they feel confident with, are interested in, or have special skills in. You could make a questionnaire to figure out who is best suited to particular roles.

You may find that, for a variety of reasons (e.g. illness, the size and scale of the role), job roles change during the cycle of rehearsing and performing.

Multi-tasking is an important skill for any member of a TiE company.

Here are a few resource considerations for you to think about. These might influence the kind of role(s) you end up with.

- Do you know how to write a business letter?
- How are your presentation skills? Do you have a good telephone manner?
- Can you move sets? Can you follow lighting cues?
- Can you find out what facilities are available for you to use at the venues?
- Do you know how to work out how much performance space is needed, and where the audience is seated?
- How do you hire a CD player if there isn't one at the venue?
- Do you know how to set up and use a portable lighting rig?
- Can you find a suitable sound effects CD?
- Can you find good costumes within a week?
- Can you contribute to the content of the education pack, or develop the resources for workshops?

Professional identity

Why not give your production company a name and an identity?

When you did your research into professional TiE companies, you may have noticed the name of some companies more than others. It probably indicates the kind of work they do, or is memorable for some other reason.

Activity: Company name

Choose a name for your production group. This can be used to publicise your work, and provides a professional touch. It will should also give you an identity and provide a group focus.

Your group name and identity can be developed by, among other things:

- designing a logo, publicity materials, and even T-shirts for the production team
- writing an artistic policy, including the aims and objectives of the production.

Communicating effectively with potential venues and audiences

It is very important to make a good impression when discussing the production with people in the industry who you might contract to work for your show. They are your customers, so you need to 'sell' them the show and make sure they understand the exact details.

Here are some tips on how to communicate your ideas effectively on the phone.

- Be polite – remember your manners and show respect.
- Have the correct names and job titles of relevant contact people handy.
- Have a pen and paper ready to take notes.
- The Production information sheet will be required for facts about your work (see below for details).
- Be confident and prepared to demonstrate your knowledge of your show.

Have a list of statements and questions prepared, but remember to be flexible and respond to any comments or questions they may make. You might want to cover the following things.

- "Would you be interested in watching [give play title] by the … [name of your production company]?"
- "We are students on a BTEC National in Performing Arts at … [name of your centre]."
- "The play deals with … [name the issues covered]."
- "It lasts … [length of time]."
- [If applicable] "There is a workshop that … [mention what the workshop covers]."
- "Would you be interested?"
- [If they answer 'yes' to the above question] "When would you like us to visit?"
- "Would you be able to provide us with the following resources? … [Go through the technical facilities required, eg a CD player, chairs.]

Plan for any follow-up calls that you may have to make, ie by asking them to give a time when it is convenient for you to ring them back. (Teachers are in the classroom for most of the day and may not be available after 4pm.)

During the research and development period, you will need to delegate responsibility for speaking to contacts on the phone and/or writing emails and letters.

The information gathered during the conversations will need to be passed on to the rest of your group; this can be done by updating the **programme schedule**.

Remember

These documents are valuable during the whole process. They will contain all the information you need. Keep them up to date, and don't lose them.

Key terms

Programme schedule – contains all information on props and technical requirements, and contributions from all the people involved in booking performances

Production information sheet

Title of piece:
Theatre company 'name' and centre details:
Production manager/company manager name and contact details:
Number of performers:
Dates and times available for performances:
Target audience profile – age group, numbers:
Overview of piece – issue, performance time:
Interactive/workshop elements (if appropriate):
Teachers'/education pack details (if appropriate):
Requirements from venue – e.g. chairs, tables, flats, plug sockets, CD players, changing facilities, audience position, performance space:
Arrival and departure times:
Transport details:
Get in/strike details:
Lighting/sound equipment/requirements:

Managing the programme schedule

The programme schedule should be managed by one person: the production manager. It should include:

- names and contact details of all centres that have been contacted/will be contacted/have booked
- an up-to-date calendar with latest bookings
- schedules and deadlines for rehearsals and performances.

Health and safety

It is very important to consider the health and safety implications of the performance, for both the audience and the performers. Discuss the staging and physical elements of the production with your tutor.

Speak with your tutor about the possibility of conducting risk assessments in the venues before your performances.

Assessment activity 5 Unit 10 P3 M3 D3 BTEC

You should try your hand at other production roles and responsibilities in the organisation of your TiE project. For example, you could consider the role of production manager, assistant, or maybe stage crew.

Chose one of these roles and make a list of the all responsibilities that you might be charged with while doing this particular job.

This list will be helpful when you are part of the production team for your TiE project.

Evidence

- keep a contribution diary in your creative log book

Grading tips

M3 Think of the best methods of planning that will help you be confident when you will actually do the job.

D3 Be imaginative when devising the list. Try to consider any problems that might occur. You should in terms of being prepared for anything!

PLTS

By organising time and resources and prioritising actions through the rehearsal process and by working on the development and production of a TiE project you will be using your **self-manager** skills.

By reviewing and reflecting on the performance work and acting on the outcomes to modify and progress, you will be using your skills as a **reflective learner**.

Functional skills

English: By producing scripts and/or support materials for a TiE project, you will be using and developing your **writing** skills.

Presenting the TiE work to an audience

The preparation is over, the organisation and administration has run smoothly. Now the work will be shown to audiences!

Whether you are performing or are a member of the production team, now is your opportunity to educate and entertain.

Remember

Adopt a professional attitude when visiting the venues. You are a representative for your project team and your centre.

Assessment activity 6

Unit 9 Unit 10  **BTEC**

Take part in the performances, either as a performer or a member of the production team. You will be required to demonstrate your skills and techniques to the audience.

The most important thing is to ensure that the audience understands the message and meaning of your play, and this will be done through your successful performance.

Be confident: the audience will learn a lot more about the subject matter if they trust that you aren't going to forget your lines, or miss a cue. You don't want them to be concentrating on any mistakes; you want them to understand and appreciate the story and subject matter.

Evidence

* recording(s) of the performance(s)
* tutor observations
* audience feedback

Grading tips for Units 9 and 10

M4 **M5** Demonstrate that you can be focused and be determined to get the message across clearly and effectively.

D4 **D5** You will need to be fully engaged in the performance, whether on stage or behind the scenes. Engagement means that you are committed to the work, supportive of others, and focused on entertaining/instructing the audience.

After the show is over ...

Here are a few things to consider once the performance has ended.

- Curtain calls: how will you line up, who will lead with the bow, how will you exit the stage or move back from the bow into neutral positions?

- Make sure that the venue contact has the education pack and your follow-up details.

- Striking the set: getting out of the venue should be done swiftly and professionally. Leave the venue with a good impression of the production team.

Knowing how to greeting the audience at the end will add to a good impression

Just checking

1 Can you define what an explorative strategy is and give a few examples?

2 What is the purpose of your Theatre in Education piece? Do you have a target audience?

3 Can you name a few of your sources of inspiration while developing your TiE project ideas?

4 What kind of information should be included in your Creative Log book?

5 What is the purpose of the Production Information Sheet? When could it be used to develop and shape initial ideas even further?

6 Can you think of different ways of structuring ideas to bring them closer to a form that can be played?

7 Can you describe the different ways of working when devising your TIE piece?

8 What kind of responsibilities will you be expected to carry out as a performer in a TiE show?

edexcel

Assignment tips

- Your group is there to help you, and you are there to help your group. Remember to be confident, contribute and listen during the devising and rehearsal process.

- Always try to link your ideas back to the reasons why you are developing and performing this piece, i.e. to the needs of your targeted audience.

- Being organised means keeping your creative log book up-to-date as well as meeting all your deadlines and commitments.

- Rehearsing the work is incredibly important for your own development as a performer, for the other members of your production company, and especially for the audience.

- Try to keep some form of record in your creative log book for every stage in the process. They could be photos, videos, notes, costumes and/or drawings, and provide evidence of your research, the development of your work, and your contribution to the process.

- Using stimuli that interest and excite you will help you to be more creative when devising your play. Aim for a variety of stimulus material to help you generate ideas, from music to photos and objects, from books to TV programmes.

- Involvement in a run of shows is an invaluable experience – it can affect your performance/production skills, allowing you to develop and nurture your techniques.

PROJECT 2:
An Evening of Showtunes

Competition for jobs in the performing arts industry is often tough, so the ability to sing is an important addition to the many of skills required by actors and dancers. This project will allow you to apply the singing skills you have developed during Unit 14: Musical Theatre Performance and Unit 30: Singing for Actors and Dancers to the preparation of a concert of showtunes.

The rehearsal and performance of songs from the musical theatre repertoire must consider the issue of building a character as well as the musical elements of that character. This project will give you the opportunity to develop and demonstrate your vocal skills whilst preparing a solo piece in a style suited to your vocal ability and range, as well as performing in a vocal ensemble.

Learning outcomes

After completing this project you should be able to achieve the following learning outcomes.

Unit 30: Singing Skills for Actors and Dancers

3   Be able to rehearse sung musical material

4   Be able to perform sung musical material using characterisation

Unit 14: Musical Theatre Performance

2   Be able to apply the appropriate performance skills

Assessment and grading criteria

This table shows you what you must do in order to achieve a **pass**, **merit** or **distinction** grade, and where you can find activities in this book to help you.

To achieve a **pass** grade the evidence must show that you are able to:	To achieve a **merit** grade the evidence must show that, in addition to the pass criteria, you are able to:	To achieve a **distinction** grade the evidence must show that, in addition to the pass and merit criteria, you are able to:
Unit 30: Singing Skills for Actors and Dancers		
P4 take part in rehearsals of musical material **Assessment activity 1 page 204**	**M4** take part in rehearsals of musical material responding to direction appropriately **Assessment activity 1 page 204**	**D4** take part in rehearsals of musical material responding to direction and working with confidence and attention to detail **Assessment activity 1 page 204**
P5 perform sung musical material in character using physical and vocal expression **Assessment activity 2 page 205**	**M5** perform sung musical material in character with confident use of physical and vocal expression **Assessment activity 2 page 205**	**D5** perform sung musical material in character with imaginative and inventive use of physical and vocal expression **Assessment activity 2 page 205**
Unit 14: Musical Theatre Performance		
P2 use the appropriate skills and techniques with support and guidance **Assessment activity 1 page 204**	**M2** use the appropriate skills and techniques with minimal support and guidance **Assessment activity 1 page 204**	**D2** use the appropriate skills and techniques autonomously **Assessment activity 1 page 204**
P4 use performing skills competently to create a performance that communicates an interpretation to an audience **Assessment activity 2 page 205**	**M4** use performing skills effectively to create a performance that communicates a considered interpretation to an audience **Assessment activity 2 page 205**	**D4** use performing skills confidently to create a performance that communicates a detailed and imaginative interpretation to an audience **Assessment activity 2 page 205**

How you will be assessed

This unit will be assessed by an internal assignment that will be designed and marked by the staff at your centre. You will be assessed on your ability to rehearse and perform material for a concert of classic musical theatre songs.

The evidence you produce during your work on this project may include:

- a process log, including notes taken during rehearsals
- recordings of rehearsals
- recordings of performances
- observation reports from your tutor(s).

Hayley , 17-year-old dance learner

I found this unit both challenging and rewarding. Although I am studying for a performing arts BTEC, I have always considered myself a dancer rather than a singer or an actor. This unit initially scared me as I have not sung in front of anyone before. Our teacher was really good at putting us all at our ease and, in the end I really enjoyed both the solo and the ensemble work we did. I now see myself as a dancer who also sings.

Over to you

In terms of performance do you class yourself as:

- a dancer?
- an actor?
- an all-rounder (actor who sings etc)?

How do you feel as you approach this project?

Activity: Why are some singers good?

Divide into small groups and think of singers you admire.

- What vocal qualities does the singer have that you think makes them particularly good?
- Make a list and return to the main group to collate and discuss your thoughts.

Your brief

You are required to work as a company to develop a programme of songs for 'An Evening of Showtunes'. Each member of the company should prepare a solo and should also be included in at least two ensemble pieces. You should work together to decide on the programme for the show and work under the direction of your tutor to rehearse the selected pieces. The concert should be performed to an audience.

Warm up

Kay Smythe : Professional singer

I graduated from university with a degree in Performing Arts in 1996 and have been working as a jobbing singer ever since. Although I like to think of myself as a full-time professional, like most singers, I do need to supplement my income by teaching private students and running singing workshops in schools and colleges. The singing work I do ranges from full-scale musicals and operettas to concerts and very occasional recording work.

In many ways, the concert work I do is the most rewarding and challenging. It is rewarding as I often get to choose the repertoire I sing. This means I can perform my favourites and I can also choose pieces that I might never get to sing in the context of a full production. Concerts are also challenging for a singer. Without the costumes, scenery and other effects you can feel very exposed as a performer. Venues are sometimes quite small, so you might be very close to the audience. These types of intimate performances require careful preparation.

Choosing your repertoire

Unlike an assignment that requires you to perform a full musical, where some will be cast in large roles and others will be in the chorus, this project gives everyone in your class the opportunity to experience a 'leading role' for at least one song from a musical. It is a great chance to shine and play to your strengths. However, before you dive into your tutor's songbooks there are a number of factors you must consider when choosing pieces for a concert performance.

or simply a piano. This must be taken into account as you choose pieces for your concert. Pieces in a pop or rock style may not sound very impressive with a piano accompaniment. If you opt to use backing tracks bear in mind that some may not be readily available.

Before you make any definite choices about the solo you would like to perform, check whether the accompaniment is available and what it might sound like.

Accompaniment

A full musical performance may be accompanied by a large band or orchestra. In a concert, however, you may be accompanied by a much smaller ensemble

Vocal range

The vocal range of a singer is a term used to describe the notes he or she can comfortably sing. Male and female voices are divided into six different types (see opposite).

Types of male and female voices			Approximate Vocal Range (middle C = C4)
Female Voices	High	Soprano	C4 – C6
	Medium	Mezzo Soprano	A3 – A5
	Low	Alto (or Contralto)	G3 – E5
Male Voices	High	Tenor	C3 – A4
	Medium	Baritone	A2 – F4
	Low	Bass	F2 – E4

Activity: Finding your vocal range

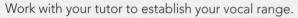

Work with your tutor to establish your vocal range.

This can be done by beginning with a midrange note and working up the scale to find the highest comfortable note that can be sung. The process can then be repeated singing down the scale to find the lower end of the vocal range.

NB This process must be undertaken when the voice is fully warmed-up. (Ideas for warm-ups can be found in the next section).

Make a note of the lowest and the highest notes you can comfortably sing.

A note for male singers
A young man's voice can break at anytime between the ages of 12 and 16. When this happens the voice usually drops an octave and for a time it may be difficult to control. Newly broken voices should be treated with care. If your voice has broken recently (i.e. in the last 6 months), it's fine to sing but now is not the time to try for very high notes. Top notes will come as your voice matures.

Working to your vocal strengths

Musical theatre songs can be written in a range of different musical styles, from light operatic to rock. Some songs require a well-developed vocal technique, whilst others are semi-spoken and can be performed successfully by an actor with only a reasonable singing technique. Here are some examples of different types of musical theatre songs for male and female performers:

Songs for Males	Vocal Style
'Music of the Night' from *The Phantom of the Opera*	Light Operatic
'Reviewing the Situation' from *Oliver*	Half sung – half spoken
'Heaven on their minds' from *Jesus Christ Superstar*	Rock
Songs for females	Songs for Males
'Poor Wand'ring One' from *The Pirates of Penzance*	Light Classical
'When you're good to Mama' from *Chicago*	Jazz/Blues

For a successful performance the quality of the vocal must match the style of the music and, in order to work to your own vocal strengths, you must consider your choice carefully. When selecting an appropriate song, you must think about what kind of singer you are and be realistic about your strengths and weaknesses.

Consider:

- **Tone & Timbre**: how does your voice sound? The following words may help you describe the quality of your voice: thick, thin, shrill, soft, mellow, strident, harsh.

- **Strength**: where in your range is your voice most and least powerful? eg high voice, medium voice, low voice.

Think about the qualities of your voice and consider which styles of song will suit your vocal abilities and which will not.

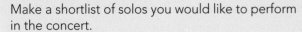

Activity: Decisions decisions!

Make a shortlist of solos you would like to perform in the concert.

Work with your tutor to choose an appropriate solo from your list that will suit your vocal range and ability.

Ensemble pieces

An important part of the performance you are working towards will be the ensemble pieces you choose to present.

You may wish to perform large chorus numbers or smaller ensemble pieces eg duets, trios or quartets. Your tutor will be able to guide you in your choices to ensure the pieces selected are suitable and achievable.

Rehearse

Warm-ups

Every vocal rehearsal must begin with a warm-up to protect the voice from damage. Most warm-ups include a series of vocal exercises.

For example:

1 **Voice Production: Obtaining a forward tone**.
Sing the scales very slowly. On each note sing 'mm' with the mouth closed. When you feel the vibration on your lips and face open the sound into a vowel eg 'ay'. Try to keep the sound forward as you open your mouth. Repeat using other vowel sounds eg 'mm-ee', 'mm-ah', 'mm-ooh' etc.

2 **Voice Production: Maintaining a forward tone**
Repeat the first exercise more quickly, singing up the scale on a single vowel prefixed with an 'mm' sound. Try to keep the production of the voice forward. If you feel it dropping back into your throat, stop and begin again. Repeat the exercise beginning on different notes.

3 **Flexibility**
Sing arpeggios (**broken chords**) on each vowel sound (again beginning with 'mm'.) Repeat the exercise beginning on different notes.

4 **Flexibility and Stamina**
Sing the sequence using an 'mm-ah' sound. Repeat using different vowel sounds.

5 **Consonants and attack**
Sing the following patterns on the same repeated note:

'Koo koo koo koo koo …'

'Tay tay tay tay tay …'

'Paa paa paa paa paa …'

'Bee bee bee bee bee …'

Key terms

Forward tone – where the voice resonates off the cavities of the face rather than resonating in the throat

Broken chords – notes from a chord that are played one after another

Musical sentences – a musical phrase

Musical material

Just as dancers need to work to improve their movement memory, singers must develop their musical memory in order to learn materials quickly and accurately.

Learning a song

A song consists of three elements:

1 **Lyrics (the words)**
Memorising words is much like learning lines from a script. The more times you repeat them, the more you will remember. However, songs are much more unforgiving of memory lapses than dialogue. Forget a line in a play and you may be able to cover with a reflective pause or be helped out by a fellow performer. But a musical accompaniment will not stop while you try to think of what comes next. This is why it is vital that you are fully secure with any lyrics you have to perform.

2 **Rhythm**
Difficult rhythms should be clapped until they are securely learnt. Also try saying the lyrics in time with the rhythm.

3 Melody

Listen carefully to the melody whilst it is being played or sung by your tutor, who will break it into short phrases. Join in and only repeat when you are ready. Sing to 'lah' to begin with so you can concentrate on the tune without worrying about the words.

Did you know?

For dancers: it can be helpful to choreograph moves to help remember and consolidate a difficult rhythm, eg *West Side Story*, 'America'

stamp clap clap

stamp clap clap

stamp clap

stamp clap

stamp clap

Putting the three elements together

Music is always divided into phrases (like **musical sentences**). Songs are most easily learnt a phrase at a time and your tutor will probably break a song into phrases to teach it to you. Phrasing is important in performance, as poor phrasing can obscure the meaning of the lyrics. Phrases will also dictate where you breathe whilst singing. Generally speaking, it is a bad form to breathe midway through a phrase.

Activity: Phrasing

Write out the lyrics of a song you are working on and mark the beginnings and ends of the phrases. Now put 'ticks' at the places where you should breathe.

Practise the piece, paying particular attention to the phrasing.

Did you know?

Speaking phrases naturalistically, as you would when preparing a script, will help you to find the best spots to breathe.

Ensemble work

Whether you are performing in a small group or as part of a larger ensemble, there are certain skills you must develop.

Blending with other voices

A vocal group will sound at its best if all the voices are well matched. The members of an ensemble must listen and be aware of the vocal qualities of singers in the group so that they can blend their voice with the other voices. If you sing too loudly, your voice will stand out too much. If you hold back too much, your voice may get lost and contribute too little.

Ideally, you should work with a musical director, who will listen critically to the sound the group makes and give direction to the ensemble as a whole, and sometimes to individual singers.

Activity: Singing in unison

Divide into groups of 4-6 to practise singing a familiar song in unison.

Concentrate on blending your voices and ensuring the **intonation** of the group is accurate.

If possible, record a performance and listen back to it. Discuss the 'sound' your group made and how successfully you managed to blend your voices.

- Can you hear individual voices at certain points of the song?
- Are all the voices starting and finishing phrases at the same time?
- Listen particularly carefully to long, sustained notes as these can be tricky to maintain at a steady pitch.

Key terms

Unison – when everyone sings the same melody

Intonation – the rise and fall of the voice when speaking

Singing a harmony line

One of the skills you may need to master when tackling ensemble singing is harmonising with other voices. Singing a harmony line tends to be more difficult than singing the melody. When learning a harmony part, try to think of your line as a melody in it's own right. Learn to sing it alone and make sure you can do so securely and confidently before trying to combine it with the main melody line.

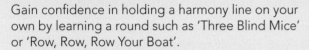

Activity: Singing in harmony

Gain confidence in holding a harmony line on your own by learning a round such as 'Three Blind Mice' or 'Row, Row, Row Your Boat'.

Once it has been learnt, divide into small groups and try it with one singer per line.

Presentation skills

Presentation and performance skills are just as important when you are performing in a vocal group as they are when you are working as a soloist. When performing in an ensemble, it is vital that you remain focussed at all times. You may feel rather anonymous in the backline of a 20-strong chorus but any fidgeting or looking around is sure to draw the audience's attention and spoil the effect of the group's performance. Depending on the type of vocal performance being undertaken, you may also need to combine movement or dance with singing skills eg if you are performing a chorus number for a musical or as backing vocalists in a pop or rock group.

Activity: Ensemble singing

Prepare an ensemble piece for a 'performance' that will be filmed.

Watch your performance back and consider how well the group:

- maintained their focus and concentration throughout
- communicated the mood and emotion of the song through vocal expression
- blended their voices together
- performed with good intonation.

Working on your solo

A singer performing as a soloist has nowhere to hide. The vocal technique should be strong and the song should be delivered in a confident manner. As the solo you have chosen for this performance is from a musical you should prepare to perform the song, not as yourself, but as the character from the show the song is taken from.

Background information

When preparing a song from a musical, it is a good idea to find out as much as you can about the show. You should know about the composer and the lyricist and find out about the setting of the show.

It is also vital that you are familiar with the plot of the musical. This can be done by reading the libretto or synopsis, or by watching a video of a performance.

Activity: Researching the musical

Create a fact sheet about the musical your chosen song is from.

Include information about:

- the composer and lyricist
- the setting of the show
- when and where it was first performed.

Also include a brief synopsis of the plot.

Activity: Character sketch

You will next need to investigate the character that sings the song you have selected. You should consider what happens to them during the musical and their relationships with other characters.

Create a character sketch or '**role on the wall**' for the character.

Key terms

Role on the wall – a blank template of a person is filled in with information about a character eg their personality traits, relationships with other characters etc

Presentation of the song

Next consider the context of the song itself. You could begin this process by considering the following questions:

- At what point in the story is it being sung?
- What has just happened to the character?
- What does he/she want or hope for at this point?
- What is he/she feeling?
- Who else is on stage?

Activity: Presentation

Now, taking into account all the information you have gathered, consider how you are going to present the song in terms of vocal performance and use of movement and gesture. Consider how the character would act and react during the song. Are their any changes in mood eg reflective then angry? How will you show these changes?

Write out the lyrics to your song, leaving a double space between each line.

Use the gaps between the lines to write information about what the character is thinking and feeling during the song.

Expression

Expression is a vital element in any performance of a song from a musical. A song might be sung with a beautiful tone, secure intonation and excellent diction, but if the performance lacks expression, the audience may be left cold.

An expressive performance should draw the audience into the moment, involving them in the emotions and feelings the singer is expressing.

Word painting

Composers help singers to express the emotions of a song by using a technique called word painting. This is where the music reflects the meaning of the words. For example, sad, reflective emotions may be expressed through a slow, quiet melody. Hightened emotions like anger, despair or excitement may be expressed through more strident melodies and a louder accompaniment.

Activity: Word painting

Listen to a song from a musical and discuss how the composer has used word painting to express the meaning of the lyrics.

Good examples to listen to include:

'Hopelessly Devoted to You' from *Grease*

'Wishing You Were Somehow Here Again' from *The Phantom of the Opera*

'Soliloquy' from *Carousel*

'Gethsemane' from *Jesus Christ Superstar*

Assessment activity 1 Unit 30 P4 M4 D4 Unit 14 P2 M2 D2

Take part in rehearsals for *An Evening of Showtunes*

- work on your solo as well as the ensemble pieces you are involved in
- respond to direction from your tutor in an appropriate manner
- use the appropriate vocal skills and techniques.

Evidence

- a log book with your activities
- recording of your rehearsal sessions
- tutor observation records

Grading tips for Unit 30

M4 You should demonstrate that you are able to focus and concentrate to ensure that the musical material is learnt accurately. You will be able to consider the use of characterisation in performance through vocal and movement work. You will also work cooperatively with your tutor to develop an understanding of the music and lyrics.

D4 You will be able to work with your tutor to shape the content and structure of the musical material in order to make the most of its creative possibilities. You will be fully engaged with the musical material and be able to work with confidence and attention to detail.

Grading tips for Unit 14

M2 You should be able to apply previously learnt skills (ie those learned in previous work for units 5&7) to the rehearsal of materials with only some guidance from your tutor. You will be prepared to work, during rehearsals and individually, to develop new skills and improve existing ones.

D2 You will be able to use your skills confidently and will apply them to the context of the work being undertaken for this project. You will take responsibility for your own improvement and will use the direction given by your teacher to improve and develop your skills.

PLTS

By taking part in sustained practice sessions to improve technique, you will be developing your skills as a **reflective learner**.
By colloborating with others to rehearse an ensemble piece for performance, you will be developing your skills as a **team worker**.
By taking part in rehearsals of musical material, you will be developing your skills as a **self-manager**.

Functional skills

English: By responding to direction during rehearsals, you are using your **speaking** and **listening** skills.

Performance

Final preparations

As the evening of the show approaches, there will be much to do in terms of final rehearsals and other preparations.

During performances it is vital that you:

- **Perform with musical accuracy**
  Getting the notes right is obviously vital, so performing with a secure sense of pitch and rhythm should be a priority. Listen to the feedback from your tutor during rehearsals and always correct mistakes immediately.

- **Maintain focus and concentration at all times**
  Concentration must be sustained throughout the piece. Be especially aware of your focus during ensemble pieces. One person fidgeting in a chorus line can be very distracting for the audience.

- **Perform with confidence**
  A performer who is obviously nervous will make an audience feel uncomfortable. Confidence comes from knowing you are fully prepared, so do not cut corners during rehearsals and individual preparations.

- **Communicate the mood, meaning and emotion of the songs you are performing**
  Characterisation is key to the successful performance of a musical theatre piece. 'Sell' your song to the audience through your use of vocal and physical expression.

- **Communicate with other performers where appropriate**
  Be aware of other performers when performing ensemble pieces. If movement and gesture are involved, ensure that you are fully aware of how your performance relates to what others are doing.

- **Blend with other voices in ensemble work**
  Listen to yourself and how your voice blends with others. For example, you may need to hold back if you are performing with someone who does not have a voice as powerful as yours.

> **Unit 5&7: Rehearsing and Performing, page 65** will offer more information on how to prepare for a performance and the skills you need to acquire to perform in front of an audience.

Activity: Dry run of solo pieces

Undertake a dry run of the solo pieces for the show.

Give each other feedback, making constructive comments about:

- musical accuracy
- focus and concentration
- confidence in presentation
- communication of mood, meaning and emotion.

PLTS

By performing musical material in character using vocal and physical expression, you will be developing your skills as a **creative thinker**.

By performing a role to an audience and ensuring that cues are responded to on time and that any props or costume are being used correctly, you will be developing your skills as a **self-manager.**

Functional skills

English: By responding to direction during rehearsal, you will be using your **speaking** and **listening** skills.

Assessment activity 2   Unit 30   P5 M5 D5   Unit 14   P4 M4 D4   BTEC

Take part in the performance of *An Evening of Showtunes*

- performing in character using physical and vocal expression
- using your skills to create a performance that communicates an interpretation of the material to the audience.

Evidence

- the video recording of the show

Grading tips for Unit 30

M5 Your performance should be secure in terms of accuracy of pitch and rhythm, with some attention to phrasing and use of vocal and physical expression

to communicate the meaning of the song.

D5 Your performance should show a high degree of confidence. As a soloist, try to express the meaning of the song with flair and commitment. As an ensemble singer, you should act as an anchor to the group.

Grading tips for Unit 14

M4 Your performance will be consistently watchable and will have memorable elements.

D4 You will be able to communicate an interpretation of the material with a complete sense of ease, commitment and imagination.

Just checking

1 What vital skills must an actor who sings have? What is it that makes then so good?

2 When singing, do you know what your strengths are?

3 Do you know what a forward tone is?

4 Can you think of the best way of braking up a song so you can breathe properly? What is the technique called?

5 When singing together with other people, can you think of the best things to do to help you blend your voice with the group?

6 Do you know what a 'role on the wall' is?

7 What are the best ways to prepare and present a song with confidence?

edexcel

Assignment tips

Success in this project will be achieved through hard work and perseverance. Focus and concentration will be vital in rehearsals and during performances. Individual practice and preparation outside timetabled sessions will also be crucial. When learning new material, set yourself small achievable goals and always respond to the feedback you get from your tutor in a positive manner to ensure you reach your targets.

Although much of the evidence for work completed for this project will come from practical activities it is still worth keeping a portfolio that logs your activities. Your log should include details of:

• progress you made when working on particular pieces

• decisions made with regards to choices of repertoire and vocal and physical interpretation of songs

• notes from your tutor and plans for how to respond to feedback.

PROJECT 3: Children's Theatre Festival

Children are the most difficult yet the most rewarding of audiences. When they are engaged in a performance they are fully engaged. However, when they are bored they will let the performers know.

This project will allow you to become involved in what might be a young person's first experience of live performance work. You will be required to form a children's theatre company and prepare work for a performance festival for children that combines traditional storytelling techniques and theatre. You will need to work as a team to address all aspects of the preparation process, from researching appropriate material to devising and shaping work for performance.

Learning outcomes

After completing this project you should be able to achieve the following learning outcomes:

Unit 11: Theatre for Children

1 Know how to research, select and refine suitable material for children's theatre
2 Be able to devise and shape material for children's theatre
3 Be able to perform in children's theatre.

Unit 28: Storytelling as Performance

3 Be able to use storytelling techniques

Assessment and grading criteria

This table shows you what you must do in order to achieve a pass, merit or distinction, and where you can find activities in this book to help you.

To achieve a pass grade the evidence must show that you should be able to:	To achieve a merit grade the evidence must show that, in addition to the pass criteria, you should be able to:	To achieve a distinction grade the evidence must show that, in addition to the pass and merit criteria, you should be able to:
Unit 11: Theatre for Children		
P1 describe the suitability of material for a children's audience **Assessment activity 1 page 213**	**M1** explain the potential and suitability of material for a children's audience **Assessment activity 1 page 213**	**D1** analyse appropriate material for children's theatre, with creative ideas for developing its potential **Assessment activity 1 page 213**
P2 develop and shape material for children's theatre, responding to ideas offered **Assessment activity 2 page 215**	**M2** actively shape and develop material for children's theatre, offering creative, realistic and appropriate ideas **Assessment activity 2 page 215**	**D2** shape with commitment the material for children's theatre, showing an appreciation of what can be effective and appropriate for performance **Assessment activity 2 page 215**
P3 perform a role in a piece of theatre for children using performance or production skills competently. **Assessment activity 3 page 217**	**M3** perform a role in a piece of theatre for children using performance or production skills confidently. **Assessment activity 3 page 217**	**D3** perform a role in a piece of theatre for children using performance or production skills with confidence, interpretation and flair. **Assessment activity 3 page 217**
Unit 28: Storytelling as Performance		
P1 show evidence of research into source material used for a story **Assessment activity 1 page 213**	**M1** show evidence of detailed research into source material used for a story **Assessment activity 1 page 213**	**D1** show evidence of comprehensive research into source material used for a story **Assessment activity 1 page 213**
P4 demonstrate a degree of control over storytelling techniques **Assessment activity 3 page 217**	**M4** demonstrate control over storytelling techniques, with occasional lapses in consistency **Assessment activity 3 page 217**	**D4** demonstrate full control over storytelling techniques, with complete consistency and confidence **Assessment activity 3 page 217**

How you will be assessed

This unit will be assessed by an internal assignment that will be designed and marked by the staff at your centre. You will be assessed on your ability to create material for a children's theatre festival, working as a team to:

- explore a range of materials and make choices about it's suitability
- develop and shape chosen material
- rehearse and perform a role in a piece of children's theatre
- demonstrate storytelling techniques in an appropriate manner.

The evidence you produce during your work on this project unit may include:

- research notes and a summary of your findings
- a process log book, including notes taken during development activities and rehearsals
- recordings of rehearsals
- recordings of performances
- observation reports from you tutor(s).

First experiences of theatre

Think back to an early experience of live theatre. It may have been a family trip to a pantomime or a school visit to the theatre. Perhaps you remember a theatre company visiting your school. You may have seen a professional or amateur production.

Over to you

- Try to recall the experience. What was particularly memorable? Do any details stand out, eg the lights, the music or the story? How did you feel before, during and after the performance?
- Write up your recollections as a brief monologue.
- As a class, or in small groups, share your monologues with each other.
- Discuss any common themes, eg anticipation, excitement etc.

Your brief

You are required to develop ideas and write a script for a radio drama lasting at least ten minutes. It should have at least two, but no more than six, speaking characters.

Your radio drama must appeal to an audience of young adults, and should therefore be based on a topic that will interest the age group.

The finished plays will be recorded, and you will be expected to perform in plays written by others in your group as necessary.

Getting started: the key features of children's theatre

Before beginning to develop a piece of theatre for children it is important to consider the features of the genre.

Plot

A good story is vital to any piece of theatre for children. A typical story will include twists and turns that lead to a final positive resolution. Common structures for the plots of children's stories include:

- **The quest**: a character in search of something overcomes **adversity** to reach his/her goal. For younger audiences, this his will often include a magical journey, eg *The Wizard of Oz*.

- **Good triumphs over evil**: wicked plans are **thwarted** by the hero, e.g. *Sleeping Beauty* or *Snow White*.

- **Repetitive plots**: episodes within the story are repeated a number of times, eg *The Three Little Pigs*.

- **Cumulative plots**: the plot is based on a simple idea that is extended each time it is repeated, eg *Henny Penny*, *The Enormous Turnip*.

- **Cautionary plots**: a story that warns of danger. Many fables and fairy stories are cautionary in their content. A **prohibited** activity is stated eg don't tell lies, don't wander away from the path, don't go into the dark woods. The central character of the tale ignores this advice and performs the 'prohibited' act. The character suffers or narrowly escapes a terrible fate, eg *Goldilocks and the Three Bears*.

- **Be careful what you wish for**: these plots involve people being granted a wish or a certain number of wishes. Those granted the wishes waste them by asking for selfish things or set off a chain of events that lead to terrible consequences, eg *King Midas*.

David Wood, playwright and director, explains that a vital ingredient of good children's theatre is the "suddenly". In his book, *Theatre for Children*, 'suddenlies' are described as the things in a story that cause an audience to pay attention – the shifts or surprises. They draw the audience in, leaving them unable to take their eyes from the stage in case they miss something (Wood D and Grant J – *Theatre for Children* (Faber and Faber, 1997) ISBN: 9780571177493).

Characters

The typical children's story often includes a range of easily recognisable characters, including heroes/heroines, villains and wise 'older' people. The central character(s) is usually someone children can identify with, often another a child, eg Charlie in *Charlie and the Chocolate Factory* or Max in *Where the Wild Things Are*. Animals and even **inanimate** objects can, however, also make good central characters, eg Woody in *Toy Story*.

Stylistic features

The use of humour can be a vital element in theatre for younger children. Audience participation might also be central to a show aimed at the younger child. However, productions for teenagers and young adults can also employ audience participation, for example, through **thought tracking** or **forum theatre**. Music can also be a key element in the form of songs and/or incidental music.

Key terms

Adversity – difficulty or hardship

Prohibited – forbidden, banned

Thwarted – ruined, spoiled

Inanimate – not alive

Thought tracking – actors will pause the action to speak their current thoughts and/or feelings aloud. Or they may ask audience members to speak their thoughts/feelings for them; in other words the audience decide what that character is thinking/feeling at that point.

Forum theatre – a type of theatre created by the practitioner Augusto Boal. Actors pause the action and ask audience members to suggest what they should do next. The audience have a direct influence on what they will see next and the outcomes of a piece.

Production features

Some productions for children include lavish sets and costumes. It should be remembered, however, that younger children in particular have a wonderful capacity to imagine. Therefore, minimal sets and costumes can be used to good effect if you can create a magical atmosphere through words and actions.

Activity: Watching Children's Theatre

Watch a piece of theatre or film for children on DVD or video and discuss the use of plot, characters and stylistic elements.

Note the age of the target audience. How does this affect the content and form of the pieces?

The following DVDs would be useful for this activity:

The Gruffalo (Universal Pictures Video)

Chuckle Brothers Pirates Of The River Rother'(Liberation Entertainment).

Puppetry shows often keep children glued to the performance

Thinking about your audience

It is important that you begin by considering the target audience for your festival. The needs of 12–14 year olds will be very different to those of 4–6 year olds so, before you begin to research and develop material for the festival, you must decide on the age group you intend to target.

Finding suitable material for performance

The choice of performance pieces used by professional children's theatre companies will depend on a range of factors. Companies may have a mission statement or series of aims that their work must conform to, or a particular company style, eg the use of puppets, music or physical theatre.

Many companies use and adapt existing materials such as:

Myths

Myths are explaining stories. They often provide explanations of concepts that are difficult to understand, describing the origins of creatures, customs and even life itself.

Legends

A legend is typically the story of an individual character who triumphs over evil or adversity. Legends can often have an element of truth about them, for example the central character may be based on a real person. The story, however, is likely to have been embellished and exaggerated over time.

Fairy stories

Fairy stories are tales that include some elements of magic or the supernatural. The stories commonly include characters like fairies, goblins, elves, giants, witches and wizards. Although commonly associated with children, the original versions of many traditional fairy tales often include adult themes. Unlike legends, which are set in a specific country at a specific time in history, fairy stories are more likely to be set 'once upon a time' in a land 'far, far away'. Many of the fairy stories we are familiar with today were collected and published by brothers Jacob and Wilhelm Grimm. The brothers were German historians who researched medieval folklore. Their tales include *Snow White*, *Cinderella*, *Rapunzel*, *Rumplestilskin*, *The Frog Prince* and *Hansel and Gretel*.

Fables

Fables are brief stories that have a moral message. The central characters of a fable are often animals, plants or even forces of natures that are given human characteristics. Probably the best-known writer of fables is Aesop, a slave and storyteller who lived in ancient Greece. His fables include *The Hare and the Tortoise*, *The Fox and the Grapes* and *The Boy Who Cried Wolf*.

Children's literature

There are many excellent classic and contemporary children's stories that could be used as a starting point for a piece of performance. However, copyright issues should be taken into account when adapting the work of a specific author, rather than a traditional story.

Historical and biographical material

True stories can be a good source of inspiration for children's theatre.

When considering the potential and suitability of any type of material for a children's audience, two key considerations are:

- is it a subject the children might care about?
- can it be approached from the child's point of view?

Assessment activity 1

Unit 11 Unit 28 BTEC

Research a range of material to assess its suitability for a children's audience.

You should investigate materials from different sources, eg myths, legends, classic stories.

You should look for:

- material that could be developed into a theatrical performance
- material that could be performed by an individual storyteller.

Remember to take into account the needs of your target audience.

Having conducted your investigation you should present your findings to your group, explaining the reasons for your choices.

Evidence

A portfolio of evidence containing materials such as:

- research log & notes
- summary of findings in the form of a presentation.

Grading tips for Unit 11

M1 You must consider the potential of source material you investigate, explaining why it would be suitable for development into a theatrical performance and how it could meet the needs of the target audience.

D1 You should evaluate source material investigated, making imaginative suggestions for how it could best be developed into a theatrical performance to meet the needs of the target audience.

Grading tips for Unit 28

M1 Your research will result in a detailed account of the ways in which the material might be used by an individual storyteller.

D1 Your research will be wide-ranging and will result in you being able to fully assess the potential of materials, discussing why certain material is suitable and how it might be used by an individual storyteller.

PLTS

By researching source material and considering the suitability and potential of that material for children's theatre, you will be developing your skills as an **independent enquirer**.

By selecting appropriate material for children's theatre, you will be developing your skills as a **creative thinker**.

Functional skills

English: By effectively presenting your ideas and research findings to your group, you are using your **speaking and listening** skills.

By investigating, selecting and comparing possible sources of material that material, you are using your **reading** skills.

Case study: Polka Theatre

Polka Theatre is one of the many theatre companies in Britain that specialises in producing work specifically for children. Polka Theatre began in 1967 as a touring company but, since 1979, they have performed in their own venue in Wimbledon

– the UK's first performance venue specially dedicated to children's theatre. The venue has two performance spaces as well as a café, play area, toyshop and exhibition spaces.

Each year Polka Theatre creates seven productions, as well as providing a venue for touring children's theatre companies. The company's work includes adaptations of classical and contemporary children's stories, the staging of historical and biographical material, and original pieces.

For more information on Polka Theatre go to the Hotlinks section on page XX and follow the instructions.

Shaping the material for the theatre piece

Now you have come to a decision about the material you will use as the basis of your theatre piece you will need to begin to shape the material.

During the shaping and devising process you should:

- consider dramatic techniques you could use to bring the story to the stage.
- think about the style of presentation and methods can you use to make the piece interesting.
- think about how the techniques you've explored in other units of the course (eg Devising or Physical Theatre) might be used in this project.

Activities during this stage of the project could include:

- identifying the key moments in the story you are developing and writing them as a series of bullet points
- presenting the plot as a series of still pictures with narration
- using improvisation to develop the scenes of the piece

- exploring the characters and their relationships with each other
- exploring ways of including audience participation by having some of the class act as audience members
- exploring ways of including some of the key elements of children's theatre, eg 'suddenlies' or 'it's behind you' moments
- producing ideas and/or sketches of costumes and props
- producing a plan of the set.

It is vital that you always keep your target audience in mind as you are working. You will need to consider what their attention span might be like and work on ways of keeping them engaged in the action. You will also need to think about the language used, particularly if you are developing a show for the very young. You must ensure that they will be able to understand the dialogue and follow the plot.

Assessment activity 2

Under the guidance of a director (your tutor) you will develop your chosen material into a performance piece for an audience of children. Your piece should last 35-45 minutes. You should respond to ideas offered by the director and other members of the company and, where possible, contribute creative and realistic suggestions of your own. This will involve you working as a class, in groups and individually.

As you work take the following factors into consideration:

- The story and structure of the piece should be suitable for the target audience, ie it should be understandable and should hold their interest.

- Children must be able to identify with the characters.

- The use of humour and audience participation should be included where appropriate.

- The production features (eg the use of costumes and sets) should be suitable for the audience.

During this process you will be allocated a role as a performer and/or a member of the production team. You role may involve a number of duties including:

- Devising and rehearsing

- Designing sets, props and/or costumes.

Evidence

- your production log book

- tutor observation records

Grading tips

M2 An active contribution to the process must be made. Ideas offered should be inventive and practical and should be suitable for the needs of the target audience and help to shape the key features of the piece.

D2 You must make an enthusiastic and focused contribution to the development process. Ideas and suggestions should be imaginative and inventive and should show a firm understanding of the key elements of children's theatre and the needs of your target audience.

PLTS

By creating a story that is suitable for your target audience, you will be developing your skills as a **creative thinker**.

By organising your time and resources as you develop your piece, you will be developing your skills as a **self-manager**.

By making a contribution to the performance of a piece of children's theatre, you will be developing your skills as a **team worker**.

Functional skills

English: By selecting scripts and/or stories for use, comparing and understanding them, you are using your **reading** skills.

By discussing the potential and suitability of source materials for children's theatre with others, you are using your **speaking and listening** skills.

Developing storytelling techniques

The storytelling sessions will be an important part of your festival and you will need to develop the necessary skills to allow you to present your chosen story in an appropriate manner. The art of storytelling is more complex than it may seem. The role of the storyteller is to recount the tale to their audience. They must guide them through the highs and lows of the story, allowing

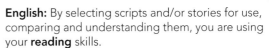

them to create mental images to match the words they hear and the movements and gestures they see.

Vocal Work

Storytelling is often a solo art form. The storyteller must work without the support of other performers or the help of complex sets, costumes and lighting effects. He or she must play the part of narrator and portray all of the characters in the story. The voice is the storyteller's main tool in this process.

Activity: Voices

The storyteller will need a range of voices for the different characters in the stories he tells.

Choose three of the characters listed and develop a 'voice' for each one. Think carefully about the pitch and tone you use for each.

• Kind old lady	• Kindly father
• Haughty princess	• Sly fox
• Wise owl	• Fearless hero
• Wicked stepmother	• Plucky servant girl

The Face

Storytelling is often an intimate art form, with the storyteller working in close proximity to their audience. This gives the storyteller the opportunity to use facial expression to a much greater degree than an actor might.

Gesture

Gesture is an important part of the art of storytelling. Gestures can be used to add expression, meaning or emotion to a word or phrase. Depending on the situation, the storyteller may use small subtle gestures or large exaggerated ones.

Movement

The amount of movement incorporated in the performance of a story will depend on its style and content and the nature of the performance space.

If the story is being told in an intimate setting, eg a small space with the audience (a group of young children) sitting on the floor, the amount of movement would be minimal.

Activity: Embodiment

Having found a voice for your three characters in the previous activity, now move on to developing some facial expressions, movement patterns and/or gestures that the character might use, eg smile/frown, a walk, a way of sitting/standing. Practise moving from character to character.

Considering the target audience when telling a story

As with any performance piece, the style of presentation used to tell a story must take account of the intended audience. What suits an audience of adolescents will not be appropriate for an audience of pre-school children.

Building a relationship with the audience

The storyteller must engage with the audience and draw them into the story. They must ensure that the audience cares about the characters in the story and what happens to them. This engagement comes from the relationship between storyteller and audience.

Reading the audience

Many storytellers use some degree of improvisation within their storytelling. Rather than sticking to the 'script', they may alter the delivery of certain sections of the story in response to the audience's reactions and the performance's progression.

Audience participation

Some storytellers include some degree of audience participation or interaction in their performances. This might include asking them to help in the telling of the story by creating sound effects, allowing them to ask questions or asking them to suggest solutions to problems (eg what should the character do next?).

Engaging with an audience made up of children

Activity: Space Jump

This is a game that explores the way in which storytelling techniques are altered to take into account the needs of the target audience.

One person should be the 'storyteller' and the rest of the group the audience. The storyteller should have prepared a story to tell to the group.

The storyteller begins their story. From time to time, the tutor should shout 'space jump…' then indicate the age and type of audience the storyteller is working with. For example:

- "Space Jump…pre-school children"
- "Space Jump…businessmen at a meeting"
- "Space Jump…college students"
- "Space Jump…13 year olds"

The storyteller must immediately alter the way in which he/she presents the story to suit the needs of the new audience.

Assessment activity 3

Unit 11 Unit 28

During final preparations and rehearsals for the festival you should carry out your allocated role within the production and/or performance team to the best of your ability.

This may involve:

- taking part in final rehearsals for the festival, eg the technical and dress rehearsals
- performing a role in the show, responding to and communicating with the audience
- performing your chosen individual story to an audience.

Evidence

- your production log book
- recording of your performance in the show and during your solo storytelling performance

Grading tips for Unit 11

M3 You should demonstrate a secure and assured use of appropriate skills during the children's show.

D3 You should demonstrate proficient and creative use of performance skills and should show imagination and a feel for the nature of the piece.

Grading tips for Unit 28

M4 You should show a good degree of control over storytelling techniques. Any lapses in consistency will be infrequent and will not detract from the overall presentation of the story.

D4 You should demonstrate full control over storytelling techniques and you should perform with flair and ease.

PLTS

By making a contribution to the performance of a piece of children's theatre, you will be developing your skills as a **team worker**.

By considering the skills you have developed during this project unit and other parts of the course as you enter final preparations and rehearsals, you will be developing your skills as a **reflective learner**.

Functional skills

English: By performing your role and watching others perform theirs, you are using your **speaking and listening** skills.

Just checking

1 What kinds of plots are commonly found in children's theatre?
2 What kinds of characters are commonly found in children's theatre?
3 Describe some activities that might be used to help shape a piece of devised children's theatre.
4 What kinds of audience participation techniques might be included in a piece of children's theatre?
5 How might gesture and movement be used by a storyteller?

edexcel ▦

Assignment tips

- Use a range of sources when researching suitable material (not just the internet) for your target audience. Try to undertake some primary research by speaking to younger brothers, sisters or cousins.

- Get to know your audience by reading books and watching TV programmes designed for the age group you will be performing to. This will allow you to develop an understanding of the target audience that will stand you in good stead when developing and shaping material.

- Focus is vital to success in the development phase of the project. This includes being supportive of others in your group and being a team player.

- Audiences of children are difficult to perform to. They are unforgiving of performances that are not of a good standard. Rehearsals and individual practice will be vital to the success of final performances, so make sure you make good use of the time you have.

PROJECT 4:
End of the Pier Show

This project will be a chance to develop original work for a performance to a live audience, one with very specific needs and wishes. People visit piers for entertainment, usually on holiday or for the day, so the audience will want to enjoy themselves. The work you create and perform should suit the needs of this audience. Your work will not need to be serious in content but should be of a high standard. Bear in mind that audiences can be tough to please, particularly when they are hoping to be entertained and amused.

The work you produce for this project may contribute towards your assessments for Units 15 and 47. This example focuses on tutor-devised choreography; and for this project you will need to know the key features of the styles being used and rehearse to develop a polished performance. Your tutor may adapt the examples given in this project to your school or college. During the rest of your BTEC course, you may be given other opportunities to learn different jazz dance styles and familiarise yourself with their particular stylistic features – you may use different accompaniment and perform to new audiences. By carrying out your own research into performances made for a range of different audience types, you will have a variety of material to add to your portfolio.

The particular focus of this project is to learn and perfect performance material. Therefore, you will need to know about several different styles of work. The rehearsals for the project will be detailed and give you the opportunity to hone your skills, not only in dance, but also in the art of rehearsal itself.

You will be working in a prescribed genre, or performance style, with other performers so you will have to be ready to give and take, compromise and be a true professional in the way you approach the project.

Learning outcomes

After completing this project you should be able to achieve the following learning outcomes:

Unit 15: Variety Performance

3   Be able to rehearse material for a variety act
4   Be able to perform a variety act or turn.

Unit 47: Jazz Dance

2   Be able to demonstrate key features of jazz dance styles
3   Be able to perform combinations within the jazz style.

Assessment and grading criteria

This table shows you what you must do in order to achieve a Pass, Merit or Distinction, and where you can find activities in this book to help you.

To achieve a pass grade the evidence must show that you should be able to:	To achieve a merit grade the evidence must show that, in addition to the pass criteria, you should be able to:	To achieve a distinction grade the evidence must show that, in addition to the pass and merit criteria, you should be able to:
Unit 15: Variety Performance		
P4 use appropriate skills and techniques to rehearse material for a variety performance, with support and guidance **Assessment activity 2 page 227**	**M4** use appropriate skills and techniques to rehearse material for a variety performance, with minimal support and guidance **Assessment activity 2 page 227**	**D4** use appropriate skills and techniques to rehearse material for a variety performance independently **Assessment activity 2 page 227**
P5 use performing skills competently to produce a performance that communicates to an audience, with only occasional lapses of concentration. **Assessment activity 3 page 229**	**M5** use performing skills effectively to produce a performance that is focused and engaged with the material and the audience much of the time. **Assessment activity 3 page 229**	**D5** use performing skills confidently and imaginatively to produce a performance that remains focused and engaged with the material and the audience throughout. **Assessment activity 3 page 229**
Unit 47: Jazz Dance		
P3 reproduce the key features of a specified jazz dance style with some level of skill **Assessment activity 1 page 224** **Assessment activity 2 page 227**	**M3** reproduce the key features of a specified jazz dance style with aptitude **Assessment activity 1 page 224** **Assessment activity 2 page 227**	**D3** reproduce the key features of a specified jazz dance style demonstrating high levels of skill and accomplishment **Assessment activity 1 page 224** **Assessment activity 2 page 227**
P4 utilise rehearsal process, working with a sense of self-discipline **Assessment activity 2 page 227**	**M4** utilise rehearsal process effectively, working with self-discipline **Assessment activity 2 page 227**	**D4** work with dedication during the rehearsal process, demonstrating self-discipline throughout **Assessment activity 2 page 227**
P5 execute a jazz dance performance with evidence of expression, interpretation and sense of style. **Assessment activity 3 page 229**	**M5** execute a jazz dance accurately with appropriate use of expression, interpretation and sense of style. **Assessment activity 3 page 229**	**D5** execute a jazz dance accurately with highly effective use of expression, interpretation and sense of style. **Assessment activity 3 page 229**

How you will be assessed

Your work will be assessed in several ways, through performance, workshops and rehearsals. The evidence for assessment may include:

- **tutor observations:** you will be observed during workshop sessions and in rehearsals as you work in the studio, devising and developing your jazz dance, and as you independently improve and hone your dance skills.
- **your log book:** you will need to keep a portfolio, or dancer's log book, to record your thoughts and working practices as you go through the project.
- **presentations/workshops/seminars:** your tutor may ask you to make presentations or run a workshop or seminar to explain the progress of the work.
- **witness statements:** other dancers, tutors or invited professionals might be asked to provide evidence of how well you work. Your audience may also be asked to respond to the work and how well it suits the style of this variety performance.

Nova, 17-year-old jazz dance learner

This is what I've done for Project 4 so far:

- I found out about some dancers from the Victorian era, so I could use what I knew about them in my work. I found out that the music hall ballet was a very hard way of earning a living and dancers often got injured. They weren't always very well respected and girls had to be careful coming and going to the theatre, in case they were accosted by over-friendly men.
- I've been taking jazz dance class regularly at college, along with classical ballet. This has helped me to master some of the techniques you need for both styles.
- I choreographed a short dance combination based on what I found out about the music hall dancers. I developed the combination into a modern piece of lyrical jazz dance, put to modern music, but I wore a calf-length dress that looked a bit like a ballet dress. I danced this for my show audition and got a lead role!
- The end of the pier show involves a lot of performers; I will be in the music hall jazz ballet. We will be dancing a modern version of what the music hall dancers used to perform. Our work will be an interlude between the other variety acts and should be a break from the audience for comedy acts, jugglers, magicians and sketches.
- The show has given me a chance to polish my jazz skills and I am now much more flexible, have loads more stamina and energy, and have mastered a lot of tricky steps that I never thought I could to pick up.

Over to you

- How much of your dancing is really stretching your technique?
- Do you take class regularly so that you are constantly improving your dancing?

Try to use every class as an opportunity to stretch yourself even further: learn a new step, fit in one more turn or jump higher and land better.

Your brief

Your tutor will give you a detailed assignment brief for this project and you must ensure that you read and absorb all of the information. The brief will detail all of the activities you will have to undertake, the way you will be assessed and some helpful tips on how you can achieve your best.

More about this project

- There will be a range of other performers in your act, but you will be responsible for learning and developing your part in it.

- You will not have to make up the dance material yourself, your tutor or choreographer will be responsible for that.

- You will have to audition for a part then, once your part has been decided, you will be taught the dances for the show. The audition will provide the opportunity for you to show that you can learn choreography, master it quickly, and then perform it to a panel. This will provide practical evidence for parts of both Unit 15 and Unit 47. Evidence for assessment will come from tutor observations, your own and your peers' observations, and DVD/video recordings.

- Workshops will allow you to learn dances and make up your own. They will provide evidence for Unit 47 Jazz Dance, as you will reproduce key features of the particular style your tutor has chosen.

Evidence will be gathered for assessment through observations, recordings and entries in your log book.

- The rehearsals will see you developing your own work to a high level and improving your basic technique in jazz dance. Listen to any criticism you are given in rehearsals and use it to further your work. The rehearsals will contribute to both units and evidence will be gathered through tutor observations, your own and your peers' observations, your log book, DVD/video recordings of rehearsals and witness statements from any visiting professionals or experts.

- In the performance you must express the dance material you have rehearsed to the audience; communicating with them and, hopefully, giving them some enjoyment. Performance will count for both units and evidence will come from observations and recordings. Audience feedback could also provide useful evidence.

Incorporating jazz dance and variety performance

Popular seaside resorts with piers, like Brighton or Eastbourne, are places people visit for a holiday or day out, to spend money they have saved up, to eat and drink but, most importantly, to have fun.

Your group has been asked to perform in an end of the pier show for an audience of young people. There will be a number of acts in the show – you will be performing a jazz ballet as part of a 21st century music hall tribute act.

You will be part of a dance company called the *Music Hall Jazz Ballet* – a contemporary version of the Victorian music hall ballet.

You will have to audition for a dance part in the jazz company – this will decide which role you will be playing. You will be given instructions for the audition on what to wear, where to go and what you will have to perform.

When you have been cast in your role, you should attend workshops where your tutor will teach you the choreography. There will be several dances to learn.

The rehearsal period will last for several weeks and you will learn and master the dances in the chosen style. The rehearsals will culminate in technical rehearsals to run through and polish your work on stage, lights and sound. There will be dress rehearsals and, finally, the performance itself.

Things to find out

It is always a good idea to carry out some research at the start of projects. Here, research should help you to find out more about the history of end of pier shows, what they involve and the styles of performance used. You should also think about what will you will be expected to do for this project. Here are some research questions to get you started:

- What are piers? Where are they found and what are they really for?
- What types of entertainment do the piers offer?
- What kinds of performers are involved in pier variety shows?
- What is a music hall act? When did this style of performance have its heyday?
- Can you name any well-known music hall players/dancers?
- What was the music hall ballet? You will be performing an up-to-date, jazz version – what might this involve?

Sources of information

- You can find out about the original version of the music hall ballet online and by looking at dance textbooks such as: Carter A – *Dance and Dancers in the Victorian and Edwardian Music Hall Ballet* (Ashgate Publishing Limited, 2005, ISBN 9780754637363).
- For these units it is important that you know what the function of the dancers in the music hall was. The modern equivalent of the music hall would be a variety show. Use the internet, books and any video footage you can get hold of to find out:
  - the names of some original music hall personalities
  - how they compare with modern-day stars of stage and musical theatre.
- Cara Tranders, danced at the Empire Palace of Varieties in London from 1892-1899. See what you can find out about her:
  - what sort of training did she have?
  - what kinds of dances did she perform?
- The following textbook may be useful: Carter A (Ed) – *Rethinking Dance History: A Reader* (Routledge, 2003 ISBN 9780415287470).

Timetable

Your tutor will decide what kind of timetable you will follow. The basic structure will probably be:

- assignment given out; discussion and brainstorming
- preparations for the audition
- learning the audition: jazz dance combinations
- rehearsing the combinations
- audition time
- casting
- workshops to learn the choreography
- rehearsals
- **get-in**
- technical and costume rehearsals
- performance
- evaluations.

Key term

Get-in – moving the set and other equipment, including technical equipment, into the performance space before the technical rehearsal

Activity: **What is variety theatre?**

See what you can find out about variety theatre. You can use the internet but might also have to visit the library.

Note down answers to the following points:

- What is the function of a variety show? Try to list a few.
- Who goes to them today?
- What sort of artists put on acts in variety shows?
- List some well-known variety artists.
- Write a profile of a variety artist – describe their work, who they perform to and the key features of their act.

Assessment activity 1

Imagine you have been asked to attend a jazz dance audition. Just like in a professional audition, your tutor will teach you a combination of steps and give you some time to learn and practise them.

Then you will need to prepare for the audition itself. Make sure you turn up on time, you are in the right place, and you have the correct dance kit.

For example, a jazz ballet gear is made up of leotard and tights, leotard with fitted trousers or a flared jazz skirt and tights; jazz shoes/bare feet, depending on the choreography.

- Learn the combination.
- Rehearse the combination. Ask a dance buddy to watch you; use the mirror to check your alignment, placing and style.
- Practise. Remember: you are showing how you use the skills of jazz dance and this will contribute to assessments for grading criteria 3.
- Warm up before the audition.
- Perform at the audition. This can be nerve-wracking – it is so for every dancer, regardless of how experienced they are. If you are taking part in a group audition, stand as near to the front as possible. You want to be seen. If you are dancing solo, take your time, get your music sorted out and start when you are ready.
- Ask for feedback so you can plan to improve your work in the future.

Evidence

- your observations
- your group's observations
- films of the workshop and performance
- your log book where you record your ideas, responses to criticism and plans for improving your work
- tutor feedback

You should keep all of this in your portfolio.

Grading tips

(M3) You must make sure you go to class regularly in order to get to grips with the style you are working in. When you perform your audition piece, really try to get across the key style features, such as isolated head, shoulder, and hip movements.

(D3) Your use and expression of the key style features should be clear and obvious. For example, where you are using hands, they will reflect the strength of the movement. In a lyrical piece, they would be soft, in a rock jazz dance, they would be strong and directed.

PLTS

By joining in rehearsals and helping others, you will be developing your skill as an **effective participator**.

By exploring and developing your own work, you will be developing your skills as a **self-motivated learner**.

By finding your own ways of recording your dance steps and moves, you will be developing your skills as an **independent enquirer**.

Functional skills

English: By making a range of contributions to discussions and making effective presentations in a wide range of contexts, you will be using your **speaking and listening** skills.

By researching different jazz dance styles, you will be developing your **reading** skills.

Remember

To help you remember your steps, try making a record of the combination. You could film yourself or a friend dancing.

Labanotation

This is an example of *Labanotation*; a way of writing down dance steps. It is a very complicated method but is still used to record dance movements very accurately.

The columns on the diagram opposite represent parts of the body. The centre columns are the feet, which are together at first, then move forward. The dark blocks are the arms, which are held low. This is a very short piece of Labanotation for a very short dance! It shows two light steps forward from a starting position with arms down, danced to a marching rhythm: 2/4 beat.

You won't be expected to learn how to write notation like this – it takes years to master. But you would be advised to try and make up a way of recording dance steps and moves that you can easily read back and refer to. That way you won't forget your dances and, when it comes to evaluating what you have done, you will easily be able to recall your work.

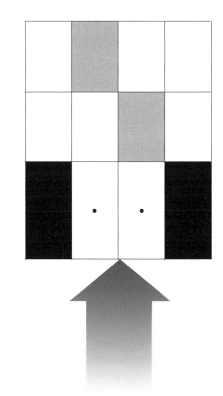

2
4

Case study: Mark, magician

Mark is a magician. He works part-time at clubs, summer shows and parties.

"I started learning to become a magician when I was about 10 years old. I just saw someone doing magic at a party and was hooked. I bought some books and began to teach myself. I practiced all the time and drove my mum and brothers mad trying out tricks on them.

It was great for parties though and everyone loved it when I performed magic tricks at birthdays and Christmas.

I got my first gig when I was 18 – I was a student and the gig was at the Student Union. My act went down a storm and, since then, I have got an agent who finds me work. There's not a lot of work around, but I really enjoy doing it when I can. It's not my main money earner, I'm also a teacher in a primary school. My pupils think my magic is great!"

Over to you

- Think about little things that you can start to teach yourself. Have you ever thought of yourself as a self-starter?

The audition

At an audition, you must dance to the best of your ability. You will find out whether or not you have a lead or chorus part either then and there, or when the director has seen everyone.

You will probably be expected to dance a short jazz combination; maybe more than one, depending on the show. You may only have one chance to get yourself the part you want.

Now, you've got the part!

Congratulations, you have a part in the show!

The next thing will be workshops for learning the choreography. Your tutor or a guest choreographer will teach you the dances. In these workshops you must try hard to learn and absorb the choreography quickly, so you can repeat it accurately, every time. You could write down the steps to help you remember them, maybe using a system similar to Labanotation.

The music hall jazz ballet

This will be part of a music hall tribute act in the show. What do you think the style might be like?

What is jazz ballet?

Jazz ballet is a form of stage jazz dance that was developed in the 1940s and 1950s. Most good jazz ballet dancers began their training in classical ballet, then branched out.

See if you can find out about one key practitioner.

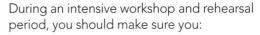

Activity: Jazz ballet terms

Find out the names of jazz ballet steps and exercises used in regular class; make a list; practise them every day.

Structure of a jazz ballet class

The basic jazz ballet class is often structured like a classical ballet class with the following:

- warm-up stretches
- barre work

- centre practice
- travelling steps
- jumps
- combinations and sequences.

This may seem like a lot for a dance class, but it's a minimum if you are serious about raising the level of your basic technique. Dancers who are successful jazz ballet dancers also have very strong ballet technique, as well as mastery of several styles of more modern dance. Jazz ballet sometimes includes styles like street, but has at its foundation the basic foot and leg positions found in classical ballet.

During the workshop period you will need to attend every class. Make sure you keep a diary telling you where you should be and at what time. Directors get frustrated with performers who are late or absent from workshops and rehearsals.

Remember

During an intensive workshop and rehearsal period, you should make sure you:

- get enough sleep
- eat properly
- drink enough water to stop you becoming dehydrated in the studio
- turn up on time for every session
- keep an open and creative mind so you can accept direction positively
- take criticism objectively – this is a fundamental part of the dancer's life
- practise in your own time and get used to costumes and shoes.

Remember

While you are learning your choreography, you should be making contacts with the relevant project personnel, such as the publicity organisers, and the technical director if you are designing or recording your group's musical accompaniment.

Activity: Jazz ballet class

- Stretch yourself out by lying on the floor and stretch from your head to your feet.

- Run through some isolations to ensure you are warmed up and ready for action.

- Barre work; you will need to run through *pliés* in turned out foot positions and parallel.

- *Tendues*: feet and leg stretches that work the muscles of the whole leg, as well as the toes, foot arches and heels. They also work the centre, as you have to hold yourself firmly to stop your hips

moving when you stretch your leg. Do these in first, second and fifth foot positions.

- Try some: *plié (demi* and *grand)*; **battement** *(tendu,* **glissé** and **fondu***); rond de jambe (à terre* and *en l'air)*; **développé**; **grand battement** – these will work your centre, back, legs and feet.

- Centre practice, such as *developpé en l'air, rond de jambe à terre* and *en l'air, attitude, arabesque*.

- *Grand battements*, jumps.

- Then practise some dance steps and moves.

Assessment activity 2

Unit 15 P4 M4 D4

Unit 47 P3 M3 D3 P4 M4 D4

BTEC

Rehearse your dances, working closely with the team or independently, as appropriate. Use your technique creatively in every rehearsal.

Ensure you master the style of the dances, putting across the key features, like isolations and quick, accurate turns – use your spotting technique to ensure turns are accurate.

Evidence

- tutor observations during rehearsals
- peer observations
- witness statements from other professionals
- DVD recordings of workshops and rehearsals

You should keep all written evidence in your portfolio.

Grading tips Unit 15

M4 Use you skills carefully in rehearsals to ensure your work progresses; try to work independently.

D4 Work independently to ensure your work improves, ready for performance.

Grading tips Unit 47

M3 Make sure you master the key features of the jazz ballet style and accurately reproduce them every time.

D3 Your skills must be at a high level so you will need to show energy and commitment in all of your dancing, during both rehearsals and performances.

M4 You must be self-disciplined throughout rehearsals: always on time, working through tiredness when necessary, showing commitment throughout.

D4 You must be dedicated to the success of not only your own work, but that of the whole enterprise. This must show on every occasion, even when you are tired.

Key terms

Battement – beating the foot or leg to front, side or back

Grand battement – a sharp raise of the leg extending the foot as high as possible without losing placing of the centre and hip alignment

Glissé – sliding the foot through the movement

Fondu – on a bent supporting leg

Rond de jambe – taking the leg in a circular motion either, à terre, with the foot sliding along the ground or en l'air, with the leg raised

Développé – raising the leg in an unfolding motion to front, side or back

The performance itself

The final stage of this project is the performance. This will be a complicated one, with lots of other performers alongside you, the dancers. Try to watch the other groups in rehearsal so you get an idea of what the whole show will be like.

You will need to focus on the following skills:

- *Movement memory training:* practise; discipline; repetition and recall
- *Accurate performance combinations:* body management and core stability; alignment of limbs; spatial awareness; shape; rhythmic accuracy
- *Performance skills:* appropriate use of contrasting dynamics; projection; focus; style and interpretation of mood, theme or intention

The time you have spent in rehearsals will now pay off because you will have developed the necessary movement memory to recall and perform all of your dances accurately. You will also have developed a level of fitness and stamina that you can make use of to ensure you have the ability to keep on dancing at a high level.

You must focus your performance on your audience, too, so pay particular attention to communication:

- maintaining focus and concentration
- vocal and physical projection
- communication of mood and emotion
- achieving an appropriate response from the audience
- 'working' the audience where and when appropriate
- maintaining energy levels
- communication of intended outcomes.

You will not be using vocal skills here, as you are a member of the jazz ballet company, but you must communicate through your dancing to achieve a response from your audience.

Assessment activity 3

Take part in the performance as a key member of the dance group within the music hall tribute.

You will be in costume, working with and for the success of the whole piece.

You must ensure that you have all of your costumes and shoes ready, that you are there on time and you really know your dances.

Evidence

- tutor observations during performances
- peer observations
- witness statements from other professionals
- DVD recordings of workshops and rehearsals
- audience statements

You should keep all written evidence in your portfolio.

Grading tips Unit 15

M5 Your performance must engage the audience; this means you need to communicate with them. Where the work is funny, make sure they understand how funny it is.

D5 Your performance must be imaginative, really grabbing the audience's attention throughout.

Grading tips Unit 47

M5 Your work must be accurate and well expressed, interpreting the moves well and in the correct style.

D5 Your jazz performance must be highly accurate with no mistakes, plus it will be expressive and the style totally accurate.

PLTS

By taking part with great enthusiasm, you will be developing your skill as an **effective participator**. By being ready, prepared and on time, you will be developing your skills as a **self-manager**.

Functional skills

English: By discussing musical structures, key features and stylistic qualities prior to the rehearsal, you will be developing your **speaking and listening** skills.

Neither of the units asks you for formal evaluations, but your tutor will expect you to engage with this. You must use your dancer's log book regularly to note your areas for development and act on them. Alternatively, ask your tutor to film rehearsals right through to the performance so you can follow and note down thoughts on your progress.

Remember, it is difficult to reach distinction in the pure dance units; natural talent and experience comes into play. If you haven't had much dance training before you started your BTEC, it will be difficult to get to that level. You must be realistic about your work – the world of professional dance is tough.

Just checking

You must maintain the build-up of your evidence base throughout the project. You will find your log book a useful place to record your thoughts and plans; you can note down areas you need to hone and improve, rehearsal notes from your tutor and what other dancers said about your work. Your bank of evidence should include the following:

- tutor observations
- peer observations
- witness statements from the audience
- DVD recordings of workshops, rehearsals and performance
- DVD recordings of performances
- audience feedback and responses
- log book – regularly kept up.

edexcel

Assignment tips

- Your dedication can be demonstrated by your commitment in rehearsals; make sure you always turn up on time and make sure you have everything you need.

- The more you understand your chosen style, the better you will be able to communicate it to an audience.

- The most successful dance students will ensure they take regular class, often in different styles, so that they maintain their technique and their levels of fitness and stamina.

- If you are offered an opportunity in rehearsal, take it – lead roles are often swapped and you might be offered one if your work is good enough and you maintain the right attitude.

- Watching other performers at work is always useful. You could watch live or recorded performances, go and observe fellow students in class or rehearsals and look out for dance on TV.

- Try to keep up your interest in these suggested ways and always strive to improve your technique, range and expertise through every dance opportunity.

PROJECT 5: Contemporary Dance Showcase

This project will help you accomplish two important goals. Firstly, you will develop your own choreography by taking opportunities to design dances for a particular purpose. Your tutor might decide on the nature and level of the challenges you could face, the target audience, the timescale, the numbers of dancers who will be performing, and the venue.

But you will also have to be adaptable, as with all professional choreographic projects and assignments where choreographers have designed their work suitable for more than one place and time. With a few notable exceptions, very little dance work is put together specifically for one exact time and location – in the main, dances are designed to be performable in a range of spaces and to different audiences.

Secondly, this project will help you develop your own contemporary dance technique. You may be advised to choose a particular style, or you can make the choice on your own. Regardless, you should take the chance to design new dances that really stretch your skills towards new levels of expertise. Dancers/choreographers are generally happy to expand the bounds of their existing movement and style repertoire. They take the opportunity of a new commission to extend their skill set and experience into new areas.

Learning outcomes

After completing this project, you should be able to achieve the following learning outcomes:

Unit 45: Developing Contemporary Dance Technique

2   Be able to improve physical and interpretative skills

3   Be able to absorb and reproduce sequences of movement in class.

Unit 39: Choreographic Principles

1   Be able to apply compositional structures and devices in the creation of dance work

2   Know how to respond to, and work with, different stimuli

3   Be able to work effectively with dancers.

Assessment and grading criteria

This table shows you what you must do in order to achieve a **pass**, **merit** or **distinction** grade, and where you can find activities in this book to help you.

To achieve a **pass** grade the evidence must show that you are able to:	To achieve a **merit** grade the evidence must show that, in addition to the pass criteria, you are able to:	To achieve a **distinction** grade the evidence must show that, in addition to the pass and merit criteria, you are able to:
Unit 45: Developing Contemporary Dance Technique		
P3 demonstrate the application of physical skills in the execution of movement phrases **Assessment activity 1 page 235** **Assessment activity 3 page 241**	**M3** demonstrate the consistent application of physical skills in the execution of movement phrases **Assessment activity 1 page 235** **Assessment activity 3 page 241**	**D3** demonstrate the competent use of physical skills in the execution of movement phrases with correct alignment **Assessment activity 1 page 235** **Assessment activity 3 page 241**
P4 apply interpretative skills to the performance of class work **Assessment activity 1 page 235** **Assessment activity 2 page 237**	**M4** apply appropriate interpretative skills to the performance of class work **Assessment activity 1 page 235** **Assessment activity 2 page 237**	**D4** confidently apply appropriate interpretative skills to the performance of class work **Assessment activity 1 page 235** **Assessment activity 2 page 237**
P5 demonstrate technical phrases with only occasional errors in action, dynamic, rhythmic or spatial content **Assessment activity 1 page 235** **Assessment activity 3 page 241**	**M5** demonstrate technical phrases demonstrating an awareness of action, dynamic, rhythmic and spatial content **Assessment activity 1 page 235** **Assessment activity 3 page 241**	**D5** demonstrate technique phrases accurately and confidently **Assessment activity 1 page 235** **Assessment activity 3 page 241**
Unit 39: Choreographic Principles		
P1 create dance material which demonstrates the use of compositional structures and devices **Assessment activity 1 page 235** **Assessment activity 2 page 237** **Assessment activity 3 page 241** **Assessment activity 4 page 242**	**M1** create dance material which demonstrates a comprehensive use of compositional structures and devices **Assessment activity 1 page 235** **Assessment activity 2 page 237** **Assessment activity 3 page 241** **Assessment activity 4 page 242**	**D1** create innovative and well-structured dance material which demonstrates a thorough use and effect of compositional structures and devices **Assessment activity 1 page 235** **Assessment activity 2 page 237** **Assessment activity 3 page 241** **Assessment activity 4 page 242**
P2 explore the potential of stimuli, demonstrating appropriate responses **Assessment activity 1 page 235** **Assessment activity 2 page 237** **Assessment activity 3 page 241** **Assessment activity 4 page 242**	**M2** explore the potential of stimuli, demonstrating appropriate and developed responses **Assessment activity 1 page 235** **Assessment activity 2 page 237** **Assessment activity 3 page 241** **Assessment activity 4 page 242**	**D2** explore the full potential of stimuli, demonstrating complex and developed responses **Assessment activity 1 page 235** **Assessment activity 2 page 237** **Assessment activity 3 page 241** **Assessment activity 4 page 242**
P3 demonstrate a working method with dancers showing an awareness of their needs and abilities, when creating dance material **Assessment activity 2 page 237** **Assessment activity 4 page 242**	**M3** adapt choreographic intentions to the capabilities of dancers when creating dance material **Assessment activity 2 page 232** **Assessment activity 4 page 242**	**D3** work with dancers to fully communicate choreographic intentions that are successfully realised in performance **Assessment activity 2 page 232** **Assessment activity 4 page 242**

How you will be assessed

The assessment of your work will involve a variety of means and forms of evidence.

- Tutor observations will form a large part of the assessment evidence. You will be observed as you work in the studio on devising and developing dance choreography. You will also be observed as you improve and hone your own dance skills, both during workshop sessions and in rehearsals.
- You will keep a portfolio, or dancer's log, to record your thoughts and working practices.
- Your tutor may ask you to make presentations, and/or run workshops/seminars, to explain the progress of the work.
- Other dancers, tutors, and/or invited professionals might be asked to provide witness statements as evidence of how well you work as a choreographer.
- Choreographic workshops and rehearsals/performances may be digitally recorded and used as assessment evidence.

Darshana, 16-year-old dance learner

My two pieces of choreography for our showcase were very different. The first one was just me, in a solo. I worked out a piece that used an idea I had seen in a contemporary dance performance by a visiting company at the college. It was a piece where a dancer kept trying to dance a **motif**, but every time she did it, something didn't quite work out. She kept trying it in different ways until she finally finished it. The whole piece was very funny and quite challenging.

I choreographed a short sequence of release, using the floor for lots of falls and turns. My own dance involved turns and jumps that I kept getting slightly off. I repeated the sequence over and over, varying it until I got it 'right'. I didn't use any music or accompaniment.

My second dance was to a piece of **Bhangra** music. My group of four dancers each brought along four movements that they liked. Each one had to have a hand gesture, a turn, a jump and a fall. I put them together into a sequence that we repeated in canon, very quickly one after another, simultaneously. We repeated it in pairs, in a circle and one by one.

We rehearsed the final dance over and over, which was hard work for a couple of the dancers who were not used to my style of dancing.

The performances went well and I have since reviewed the DVD of my dances and used this to evaluate my work. I did improve my technique during my solo work especially, as I had to work hard on getting my movement sequence absolutely right for each part of my dance. The group work taught me a lot about working with other dancers and how much you have to develop your ideas to suit everybody in the group. You have to be patient!

Over to you

- Which styles of dance that you use might work in a scenario like Darshana's?
- Try to work out some choreography for yourself, based on something you already know. See if you can develop it by changing one of its characteristics, like its speed or dynamics.

Your brief

The project will involve creating a dance for the purpose of a showcase performance. Since dance is a growing and changing performance form, your tutor may not give you any more details in terms of a vocational setting for your work. However, they might ask you to develop work for a particular audience, venue, or purpose. Where this is the case, your work should be appropriate and fulfil the needs of the brief.

In this showcase, you will be asked to create and perform two dances for an evening of contemporary dance for a mixed audience. The audience will consist mainly of adults and other learners.

The project demands that you create two short pieces of original, contrasting choreography, in a contemporary dance style (or styles) of your choice. You will perform in at least one of your pieces, and at least one must be choreographed for a group. The other may be a solo, duet or group piece. Your own performance should come from some intensive activity in the dance studio, where you can show your technique growing and improving. This will help you to be assessed for Unit 45: Developing Contemporary Dance Technique. You should show that you understand and deliver what is required of you when you collaborate with your colleague dancers on their own choreography.

The choreography should be a showcase of your skills, so the contrasting nature of the two works must be clear. For example, one piece may be a solo for yourself, or another dancer you will work closely with to ensure that the work 'fits' them. When you are choreographing for a group or more than one dancer, you must work with their abilities and talents in mind. There is little point creating a dance that only you can accomplish if the piece has other dancers in it.

The choices are:

- one group piece plus a solo
- one group piece plus a duet
- two duets

Did you know?

Some choreographers have created dance works specifically for a purpose or venue and they make use of the place's features. These dances are called site-specific.

- one duet plus a solo
- two group pieces.

The choreography will be developed from two different stimuli. The first will be based on the idea of changing shape. The second stimulus will be chosen by you, from one of the following:

- *chance* – see Assessment activity 4 on page 242
- *improvisation* – see Assessment Activity 2 on page 237

You can use these ideas to get you thinking about developing dance. During the project there will be opportunities to use material, such as pictures or stories, as ways of giving you ideas for your choreography. Music is the most obvious choice of ways to get you dancing, but just looking at a photo could give you a shape to begin with, or a mood to get you going. You can then take movements from the starting point, perhaps to help you develop a short sequence that can then be repeated or developed further.

Assessment activity 1 will help you to get started on your main pieces; in fact, you might decide to use your ideas as starting points for your main works. Many choreographers use previous work to help them develop their dance into more complex pieces.

Assessment activity 1

Unit 45 P3 M3 D3 P4 M4 D4 M5 D5

Unit 39 P1 M1 D1 P2 M2 D2

BTEC

Explore a stimulus by taking an idea from a picture, newspaper story or image.

Think of ways to create a short solo dance in a contemporary style of your choice that explores an idea suggested by the stimulus you have chosen.

Choreograph the short dance, rehearse it and perform it to the group.

The dance may be performed to accompaniment of your choice.

Evidence

- your observations
- your group's observations
- films of the workshop and performance
- your log book where you record your ideas, responses to criticism, and plans for improving your work
- tutor feedback

Grading tips Unit 45

M3 You should show that you can apply the physical skills of your chosen style during your work.

D3 Your dancing should be correctly aligned as you accurately reproduce your choreography in performance.

M4 You should interpret the choreography clearly.

D4 Your interpretation should be confident.

M5 Technique should be used effectively, using the correct dynamics, rhythm and space.

D5 Technique should be used accurately and with confidence.

Grading tips Unit 39

M1 Compositional structures and devices, such as logical sequencing, canon and repetition, should be used comprehensively.

D1 Composition should be complex and developed, such as through reversal, dynamic variation and contrast.

M2 Your work should show that you have explored the possibilities of the stimulus.

D2 Your work should show how thorough you have been in your responses. You should have experimented, explored, rejected and chosen material carefully.

PLTS

By exploring the possibilities of different groupings and stimuli and the opportunities these offer for choreography, you will be using your skills as a **creative thinker**.

By coping with the pressure of producing dance material in time for a scheduled performance, you will be using your skills as a **self-manager**.

Functional skills

By reading research information about individual choreographers researching stimulus material, you are developing your **reading** skills.

Activity: Choreographers today

See what you can find out about the work of one of the leading practitioners working in the field of dance today. For example, have a look at the work of Wayne McGregor who has choreographed pieces for many of the major dance companies today, such as his own company Random Dance, the Royal Ballet, and for Rambert Dance Company.

Try to find out about his working methods, how he comes up with his ideas and how he transposes these ideas on to the bodies of the dancers who will be performing them.

Choosing an accompaniment – or not!

You must decide whether or not you are going to create dance to music, to sound or to nothing at all. This choice will be crucial, as it will affect how your audience will receive and understand your work.

When you watch dances that are performed to a specific musical accompaniment you are instantly affected by the sounds you are hearing. Many of the great pieces of classical dance would not possess the romance they clearly have without the melodic strains of the orchestral music. A good example of this would be the ballet Swan Lake, performed to the music by Tchaikovsky.

Some contemporary dance makers do not use music at all: work is danced in silence or to recorded sounds. See if you can find out about any of these works.

You can choreograph you dance directly to the music, to the beat, following the natural patterns in the music. An example of this would be 'Dance of the Cygnets' from Swan Lake. Generally choreographers do not make their steps relate very directly with the rhythm of the accompanying music, preferring their dance to sit alongside the music.

Choosing your company

Your tutor may split you into groups for working, to suit your ability levels. Or you may choose your own dancers for any group or duet choreography. When working with other dancers, choreographers often try to use the talents and skills of their dancers, carefully creating movement that fits in with their experiences and possibilities.

When you have made your decisions about who you will be choreographing work for, watch them in class to familiarise yourself with how they move and what can they do well.

Going for it – using your talents

Activity: Music or not?

Take a known short piece of dance, such as the one you choreographed for Assessment activity 1.

Try re-enacting it on a piece of music; afterwards try dancing the piece without music. What are the effects the music have on the way you dance? How is the dance without music?

Assessment activity 2

Create a simple motif – a series of steps and movements that you can repeat and show to your group.

Teach it to the group and ask them to work on it but to also improvise, adding some stresses or accents that make it their own. These can be a particular way of using the hands or head, doing a turn, or maybe using a flexed foot where your original sequence required a pointed foot.

Watch the group as they run through the motif, and notice the subtle changes they have introduced through improvisation, eg working with different speeds.

Take the ideas away with you and think about them.

Work on a new version of the sequence, using the ideas generated in the group improvisation workshop.

Go back to the group and re-choreograph the sequence, using the new modifications.

You can repeat this over and over again until you have the whole piece worked out.

Finalise the sequence, rehearse it, and then perform it.

Prepare a short lecture/demonstration to show the class what you have done and how the group's improvisations helped you get to your final ideas.

Evidence

- your observations
- your group's observations
- films of the workshop and performance
- your log book where you record your ideas, responses to criticism, and plans for improving your work
- tutor feedback

Grading tips Unit 45

M4 You should interpret what your group has developed, using appropriate dynamics, stresses and accents, focus, phrasing, and emphasis on chosen steps and movements.

D4 You should interpret the ideas of the group with confidence, using the skills of emphasis, accent, phrasing and accenting of movements.

Grading tips Unit 39

M1 You should use a range of compositional structures in your dance, such as variation and development.

D1 You should capitalise on the work of the group by formulating new ideas, based on their development of the motif.

M2 You should show you have developed your own response to the group's ideas.

D2 You should have taken the group's ideas and made a new work of your own.

M3 You should use a range of compositional structures in your dance, such as variation and development.

D3 You should successfully realise your intentions by communicating your ideas successfully, and your choreography should work on the bodies of your dancers.

PLTS

By carrying out research to generate stimulus material, you will be using your skills as an **independent enquirer**.

By experimenting with movement, timing, dynamics, space and relationships and by adapting and modifying movement phrases, you will be using your skills as a **creative thinker**.

By discussing issues related to the choreographic process and positively seeking solutions, you will be using your skills as an **effective participator**.

Functional skills

English: By having in discussing choreographic ideas, discussing the development of stimulus material and making suggestions for improvement, you will be using your **speaking** and **listening** skills.

Working on your own technique

The specification for Unit 45: Developing Contemporary Dance Technique asks that you show your own technique improving gradually, as you progress through the unit. In particular, you must show improvements in the following elements of technique:

- *Physical skills*: posture; alignment; balance; co-ordination; flexibility; strength; stamina; body awareness; extension; contraction; rotation; ability to reproduce movement accurately; whole body participation and/or isolation; application of dynamic range; placement of the feet; awareness of centre

- *Interpretative skills*: projection; focus; phrasing; emphasis; rhythmic awareness; quality; musicality; dynamics; facial expression; timing; use of breath; use of gravity; **suspension**.

Every time you approach class, workshop or rehearsal activities, you must bear in mind that your tutor will be watching these elements of technique. You will be expected to develop them through working on this project.

Use you dancer's log to help record your progress and meet your own smart targets for improvement. The table below shows an example of a self-development plan.

High level of technique is needed to execute this simultaneous *grand jete*

You can create your own development plan to build on areas of perceived technical weakness. Remember to ask your tutor for help with this. He or she will evaluate you at the beginning of the course and give you ideas for where you need to go next.

You should record your ideas for choreography in your dancer's log book or with a digital camera.

Exercise or move	Evaluation	Development task	Desired outcome	Evaluation
Turns, single, double	Not always precise. I do not make enough use of spotting	Practise spotting every time I use turns	Turns are precise and on the spot where necessary	Turns more precise
Use of parallel	My feet are not always fully parallel	Work on hip location to allow feet to remain parallel		

Remember

Always keep records of your work safe!

Key terms

Suspension – giving a sense of weightlessness in space.

Symmetry/asymmetry – movements of dancers that are in balance (symmetry) or not (asymmetry)

Inversion – when a movement is repeated the other way around, backwards or on its head

The unit specification for Unit 39: Choreographic Principles asks you to work with other dancers. This means both as a choreographer and as a fellow dancer. How you go about this will determine your success as a choreographer. Most successful professional choreographers are thoughtful, good listeners, highly observant, and realistic about what other dancers can achieve. You must be able to work with other dancers:

- *Work with at least two of the following*: solo, duo, trio, small groups, larger groups
- *Establish good working relationships*: co-operation; listening; valuing the work of others; organisation; focus.

Did you know?

Your communication skills are important in getting across your choreographic ideas. For example, when the choreographer Christopher Wheeldon worked with the Russian company the Bolshoi Ballet, he had enormous trouble getting his ideas across in the way he usually likes to work. None of the dancers spoke English, so it took the intervention of accompanying friends Michael Nunn and William Trevitt, known as 'the Ballet Boyz', to help him use dance to physically communicate.

The final stages of the project is to complete your choreography and teach it to your group of dancers. This might be another dancer, a pair or a group.

This gives opportunities to develop your choreography through compositional structures.

Dance duos have specific features, such as:

- ability to contrast movements
- mirror movements
- follow each other
- support, lift or catch each other
- possibility of **symmetry**, **asymmetry**, **inversion**.

Dance trios have specific features, such as:

- a dancer can go between the other two
- arms can be linked to make shapes
- possibility of repetition
- possibility of canon
- lifts are possible
- spacing can be developed
- dance can involve logical sequencing, unity, symmetry, asymmetry, inversion.

Dance groups have specific features, such as:

- opportunities for proportion and balance, logical sequencing
- interesting shapes
- canon, instant and logical sequence
- supports, lifts and carrying
- complicated motif development.

They all have the possibility for you to try experimentation, selection and rejection, manipulation of the stimulus, and the development of your ideas. No choreographer just comes up with an idea, teaches the dancers, then rehearses and performs it. There is always a long process of trial and error, rejection of ideas and motifs, selection of the most successful sequences, and final decisions.

See page 240 for ideas on dance compositions.

An arresting performance by Panchenko, Michael Nunn and William Jrevitt

The following sequence might give you an idea of how you can structure your dance.

Project 5: Contemporary Dance Showcase

Assessment activity 3

Unit 39 

Unit 45 

BTEC

Create a piece of dance for yourself. This dance must last at least a minute and you can use it to explore the idea of changing shape.

Choose your accompaniment from samples of recorded natural sounds, created by a learner in your centre who is studying music or supplied by your tutor.

Using two of the following choreographic devices, create your dance: repetition, dynamic variation, contrast.

Using one of the following two structures: **theme and variation**, **abstract**, choreograph and present your final ideas to the group.

Evidence

- your observations
- your group's observations
- films of the workshop and performance
- your log book where you record your ideas, responses to criticism, and plans for improving your work
- tutor feedback

Grading tips Unit 39

M1 Your work should use the compositional structures and devices with imagination.

D1 Your dance should be original and show your understanding of how devices and structures give shape and meaning to a dance.

M2 Your presentation of the dance should show how much you have explored the stimulus.

D2 You should have fully explored the stimulus showing this through varied and interesting responses.

Grading tips Unit 45

M3 Your movement should be created through physical skills that are applied consistently.

D3 All your movement should be aligned correctly.

M5 You should be able to repeat your work without errors, using the same dynamics, rhythm and space.

D5 Your dance should be accurate every time and be performed confidently.

PLTS

By adapting movements learnt to a new facing or timing, you are using your skills as a **creative thinker**.

By coping with the pressure of producing dance material in time for a scheduled performance, you will be using your skills as a **self-manager**.

Key terms

Theme and variation – this is a sequence that forms around an idea, such as movements rising and lowering, and is developed and changed as the dance goes on.

Abstract – when there is no obvious storyline, narrative or any particular idea prominent in the piece

Functional skills

English: By discussing choreographic ideas, you will be using your **speaking** and **listening** skills. By updating the choreographic log (reflective journal), you will be using your **writing** skills.

Assessment activity 4 — Unit 39

P1 M1 D1 P2 M2 D2 P3 M3 D3   BTEC

You have chosen the dancers you wish to work with for the final dance piece you are going to showcase. You have also chosen to use *chance* as your starting idea. The piece will be called *Chance Factor* and will be danced to music of your own choosing.

- Watch the group in class to determine where their strengths and weaknesses lie.

- Create a set of chance cards for your dancers; they might have words like *shocked, tentatively, dominating, timidly, speedily* and *diminishing* written on them. These will denote the quality you want each dancer to use in their movement.

- Ask the dancers to create a short sequence that they think shows off the best in their technique. Watch each sequence.

- Hand each dancer a chance card and tell them to repeat their sequence, using the word on the card to change the quality of their movement.

- Teach the group a short motif that you have choreographed.

- Start the piece with the group motif in unison, followed by the same thing danced using the qualities each dancer has been given.

- Combine the five sections: group motif in unison; group motif with qualities; individual motifs; individual danced solo motifs with qualities, while other dancers are still; and group motif in unison.

- Work on the spacing of each dancer, exploring where each will be on stage, and whether there will be entrances and exits.

- Choose costumes, rehearse on the showcase stage, and perform to an audience.

Evidence

- notes and ideas in your dancer's log book
- recordings of choreographic workshops and rehearsals
- evaluations by your group and your tutor
- self-evaluation as the process has gone on
- a recording of the final performance itself

Grading tips

M1 Your dance should use compositional structures with confidence and show you have considered overall shape and how the whole piece works together.

D1 Your work should be individual and imaginative, working well as a whole dance.

M2 Your chance stimulus should be explored effectively and the work should develop ideas arising from this.

D2 Your responses should be complex, taking the original ideas beyond the obvious.

M3 Your intentions should take the other dancers into account and you should adapt ideas to suit them.

D3 Your ideas should be well communicated to your group and be shown in a successfully realised performance.

PLTS

By experimenting with movement, timing, dynamics, space and relationships adapting and modifying movement phrases, you will use your skills as a **creative thinker**.

By considering other dancers in the space during technique classes and by reviewing work with other learners and agreeing ways of improving collaborative work in the future, you will be using your skills as a **team worker**.

Functional skills

English: By having in group discussions and peer conversations on strengths, weaknesses and areas for improvement, you will be using your **speaking** and **listening** skills.

The Company Albermarle are a small touring dance company that originated at the university where its founder members first met.

Their work is generally contemporary and they usually dance pieces created by members of the company. Occasionally, they have had the chance to work closely with visiting choreographers.

Recently they created a work with an experienced choreographer, based on the ideas of Pina Bausch.

They took the notion of choreographing movement for dancers across a wide age range, and used invited dancers who were untrained to work with them on the project.

The choreographer asked the dancers to talk about a key event in their lives, then to try to encompass that in a short movement phrase. They grouped the performers together according to age.

Each small group produced a motif made up of their own movement phrases. The choreographer then worked each group's sequence up into a rolling cannon, where groups came and went across the stage, throughout the work.

The music used was a mix of tunes from the radio of the last 30 years, although the dancing was disassociated from it. The dancers wore costumes of varying shades, pale for the older dancers, dark colours for the younger ones.

The set was totally bare but lighting created shaded zones and very bright areas.

Overall, the work was very touching and created an atmosphere of emotion and thoughtfulness in the audience.

Think about it!

1 How would you go about creating a work for dancers with different abilities?

2 Try out some of your ideas on non-dancers. This is how Pina Bausch sometimes worked to create some of her most celebrated dances.

Just checking

1 Have you tried out a range of different choreographic methods and styles? It would be more difficult to find out how best you work if you don't do that.

2 Try to really experiment with your ideas. Don't just take the first one without challenging yourself to develop it. Remember, you need to be able to discard ideas that aren't going anywhere just as effectively as you keep those that are.

3 When you have finished a piece of choreography, check that the end is as interesting as the start. Very often, learner dances fade out because the choreographer ran out of ideas before the end.

4 Check your work by asking someone neutral to have a look at it and ask them what they think you were getting at.

5 Remember to pay attention to what other people are working on in the studio. The way others move around the space can stimulate ideas for new choreography.

edexcel

Assignment tips

- Keep your dancer's log book up to date.

- Use methods to record your thinking that work for you, eg diagrams, notes, mind maps, sketches, digital recordings of your choreographic ideas.

- Use other people to watch your ideas as they develop, and ask them for their opinions.

- Go to see performers of all styles of dance at work; this is always useful. You could watch live or recorded performances.

- Sit in to watch fellow learners in class or rehearsals.

- The most successful dance learners will ensure they take regular contemporary dance classes, so that they maintain their technique and their levels of fitness and stamina.

- Practise your choreography be setting yourself problems to solve, such as, 'How can I develop this movement sequence further, to bring out a different meaning or aspect of it?'

- Try to keep up your interest and always strive to improve you technique, range and expertise through every dance opportunity.

PROJECT 6: Performing in a Contemporary Play

As an actor, you are responsible for transforming the words of the playwright into a performance. To make this transformation, you can be influenced and guided in different ways.

You might study and interpret the play with the guidance of the director, or you might use the methods and techniques of a particular theatre practitioner, such as Konstantin Stanislavski, Bertolt Brecht or Antonin Artaud.

As an actor, you will study a script and apply your acting skills to bring the character(s) to life. You will need to be imaginative and let go of your inhibitions. You will need to develop techniques and skills that will allow you to perform the role before an audience, to a high standard, as many times as required.

Naturalistic acting is the most popular style of performance and the one used most in theatre, film, television and radio performance. But there are many other styles of acting and we are going to look at some of these in this project.

This project will guide you through the process of researching, interpreting, and performing extracts from contemporary plays. In this example you will be required to work as a part of an ensemble, taking part in research and analysis of a non-naturalistic play/characters, practical exploration of the themes and background of a play and development of non-naturalistic performance skills.

Learning outcomes

After completing this project you should be able to achieve the following learning outcomes.

Unit 13: Contemporary Theatre Performance

1. Be able to research contemporary texts
2. Be able to interpret and realise contemporary texts
3. Be able to rehearse contemporary texts for performance
4. Be able to perform contemporary texts

Unit 20: Applying Acting Styles

2. Be able to develop and rehearse material using different acting styles
3. Be able to perform as an actor using different acting styles

Assessment and grading criteria

This table shows you what you must do in order to achieve a Pass, Merit or Distinction, and where you can find activities in this book to help you.

To achieve a pass grade the evidence must show that you are able to:	To achieve a merit grade the evidence must show that, in addition to the pass criteria, you are able to:	To achieve a distinction grade the evidence must show that, in addition to the pass and merit criteria, you are able to:
Unit 13: Contemporary Theatre Performance		
P1 research contemporary texts to provide ideas for their interpretations **Assessment activity 1 page 251** **Assessment activity 2 page 253**	**M1** research contemporary texts, selecting features for their interpretation **Assessment activity 1 page 251** **Assessment activity 2 page 253**	**D1** research contemporary texts, selecting detailed features for their interpretation **Assessment activity 1 page 251** **Assessment activity 2 page 253**
P2 realise characters and meet demands of the texts in relation to the interpretations (partial) **Assessment activity 3 page 256**	**M2** realise characters with skill and imagination, meeting the demands of the texts in relation to the interpretations (partial) **Assessment activity 3 page 256**	**D2** realise characters with discipline, skill and imagination, meeting the demands of the texts in relation to the interpretations (partial) **Assessment activity 3 page 256**
P3 develop performance through rehearsal, with guidance **Assessment activity 3 page 256**	**M3** develop performance through rehearsal, with independent application of direction and creative autonomy **Assessment activity 3 page 256**	**D3** develop performance through rehearsal, with imaginative and independent direction and highly creative autonomy **Assessment activity 3 page 256**
P4 perform roles from contrasting contemporary texts, showing differences in characterisation. **Assessment activity 4 page 257**	**M4** perform roles from contrasting contemporary texts, showing effective and distinctive differences in characterisation (partial). **Assessment activity 4 page 257**	**D4** perform roles from contrasting contemporary texts, showing expressive and imaginative differences in characterisation (partial). **Assessment activity 4 page 257**
Unit 20: Applying Acting Styles		
P1 develop characterisation as an actor with guidance **Assessment activity 2 page 253**	**M1** develop characterisation as an actor with skill and a degree of imagination **Assessment activity 2 page 253**	**D1** develop characterisation as an actor with skill, insight and imagination **Assessment activity 2 page 253**
P2 develop and rehearse material using contrasting acting styles with guidance (partial) **Assessment activity 3 page 256**	**M2** develop and rehearse material using two contrasting acting styles, responding appropriately to direction and demonstrating a degree of creative autonomy (partial) **Assessment activity 3 page 256**	**D2** develop and rehearse material using two contrasting acting styles, responding imaginatively to the text and demonstrating complete creative autonomy (partial) **Assessment activity 3 page 256**
P3 perform as an actor using contrasting acting styles (partial). **Assessment activity 4 page 257**	**M3** perform as an actor using contrasting acting styles with skill and a degree of imagination (partial). **Assessment activity 4 page 257**	**D3** perform as an actor using contrasting acting styles with focus, engagement and imagination (partial). **Assessment activity 4 page 257**

How you will be assessed

This project will be assessed as an internal assignment that will be designed and marked by the staff at your centre.

You will be assessed on your ability to research contemporary texts, make decisions on interpretation, develop a character using your imagination and skills, rehearse your work, and perform to an audience.

The evidence for assessment may include:

- research notes and findings
- a process log that charts the development of your role, including details of interpretation and annotated scripts
- a recording of a milestone rehearsal
- a recording of one of your performances before an audience
- observation statements from your tutor(s).

For both units (13 and 20) you will be required to study and perform at least two plays, or extracts from plays. This project focuses on one play.

Julia, 16-year-old acting learner

In a group of four, we are performing in an extract from Steven Berkoff's *Metamorphosis*.

We will perform in a non-naturalistic way – we are like puppets, with mechanical movements and symbolic gestures. We will demonstrate the characters rather than 'become' the characters. There is a definite distance between the actor and the character.

The script requires us to perform as narrators/storytellers; most of the words are directed at the audience, rather than other characters. Costumes, make-up, props, lighting and sound all combine to demonstrate and underpin this type of non-naturalistic performance.

These are the acting techniques that we will use are imagination, elongation of words, repetition, still images and tableaux, exaggerated gestures, stylised/slow pace, mime and rhythmical movements.

This style of acting seemed so complicated and difficult in theory, but when we started rehearsing with the script it all began to make sense. It reminds me of performing in a pantomime, with exaggerated movements and speech directed at the audience. I'm looking forward to seeing how the audience reacts to our piece. The work we have done in rehearsals so far might shock them and make them laugh but we want to make sure that we don't confuse or frighten them too much.

Over to you

- As an actor, what challenges do you think you would face in rehearsing and performing in a contemporary play?

Researching a contemporary text

For the purposes of this project, a contemporary play text is anything written from 1930 up to the present day.

Choosing your play

- It could be that you are presented with an extract from the play.
- You might be studying a particular period of theatre history, performance style, theatre practitioner, or playwright.
- You decide which play, or extract, you would like to perform.

Context

It is important to understand the context of the chosen play when developing it for performance. Only then can you make informed decisions about interpretation and performance style.

The play could be:

- influenced by a particular theatre practitioner or style of theatre
- a response to a political situation, eg war
- a reflection of a society – a class system, a type of community, types of employment (and unemployment), family life
- capturing a snapshot of a particular time – when and where the play was written, or when the play is set
- a reflection of cultural influences and trends – types of music, literature, fashion, cultural movements or technological developments
- a response to the economic impact on theatre – how money affects lifestyle, or the   amount of money that is spent on theatre by the government or audiences
- a reflection of morality and ethics – how people thought, behaved and judged each other in a particular time and place.

Activity: The context of the play

Find out what you can about why the play was created.

How you can find this information?

The play script might contain an introduction and/or background notes by the playwright. Some plays have study guides written especially for them. You may be able to get a copy of a programme for a production of the play, or find reviews and articles about the play, the playwright or the theatrical genre.

PLTS

By researching the context of the play text, you will be developing your skills as an **independent enquirer**.

Functional skills

ICT: If you use the Internet to research the context of the play and evaluate the usefulness of the information you find, you will be developing your ability to **find and select information**.

Subject matter

Find out the following:

- when your play was created
- where it has been performed/types of audiences
- If there has been any censorship/criticism of the subject matter – consider how references to sexuality and sexual practice, politics, social and cultural taboos, the monarchy, establishment figures and laws and legislation might be viewed and understood by different types of people.

Theme

Understanding the themes of the play can help you to develop your interpretation and performance. In Jim Cartwright's *Road*, one of the major themes explored is working class life in northern England in the 1980s, including the impact of mass unemployment and the changes in traditional working life (people stopped working in factories and moved into services industries, such as call centres.)

Equus: The play is about a boy's obsession with horses and the crime he commits towards them

There might be clues and indicators about the meaning or themes of the play in the title, as shown in these examples:

- *Endgame* (Samuel Beckett) – the last part of a chess game, where one person wins and the other loses.
- *Death and the King's Horseman* (Wole Soyinka) – set in Nigeria, 1944. If the king of a region died, his horseman would be expected to commit suicide after celebrating the king's life for one month.
- *Equus* (Peter Schaffer) – equus is Latin for horse.

Activity: Themes of the play

How does the playwright treat the themes of the play?

Discuss why you think the playwright has chosen to present them to the audience in this way.

Notice how the playwright might include the themes in the following:

- the title of the play
- the plot and action
- the names of the characters
- the language used by the characters
- the stage directions
- the setting and location.

Treatment of themes and issues

The playwright might use particular devices to tell the story. Presenting a difficult or controversial issue in a stylised play can help overcome problems in staging, as in the following examples:

- *The Love of the Nightingale* (Timberlake Wertenbaker): uses ancient myths and classical stories to explore ideas of female oppression and enforced silence. The play includes brutal violence, but it is represented in tapestry, puppetry and mime.
- *Metamorphosis* (Steven Berkoff): takes the symbolism of Kafka's original story and presents it literally. The surreal imagery of a man turning into a beetle is recreated in a highly physical play.

Aesthetics

Aesthetics are the artistic qualities of the work.

The playwright will use, or refer to, any of the following elements when writing the play:

- how the themes and issues are treated
- the style, form and structure of the play
- the design and any specialist requirements.

Style, form and structure

A play is a story. The playwright makes decisions on how to tell the story to the audience. The play will be constructed of the following elements:

Act divisions

In most plays, there are separate acts. This might be to allow a change in time, setting, and/or characters.

For example, in *The Three Lives of Lucie Cabrol* (Théâtre de Complicité), there are two parts (acts); the second part moves forward 40 years.

Shifts in time and setting will impact on your performance. Make notes on how this might happen in your chosen play and how you will deal with it. For example, you might think about how you will show the audience the changes that have occurred to your character – the character might move from child to adult, and you could show this change in your posture, how you speak, and costume or make-up.

You can also think about design and production elements that would signify differences in time and setting, for example changes in costume, lighting, sound, makeup or setting.

Scene structure

When telling the story, a playwright will usually follow the accepted conventions and structure, i.e. introduction, development of **plot** and character, and **dénouement**. Each scene has a narrative driving the story, with dramatic tension created as the action unfolds. There are some playwrights that break these conventions and rules in order to have a particular effect on the audience, for example, Bertolt Brecht created plays that give the audience a summary of the scene about to happen. In epic plays such as *Mother Courage and her Children* (written in 1941) and *The Life of Galileo* (1943), the audience is told the date, the country or situation, and the most significant element of action in the scene.

Fiona Shaw as Mother Courage

Does telling the audience what will happen before they watch the scene remove tension?

The audience will watch the scene differently, concentrating on the technique, the interaction between the characters, and how the story unfolds.

It's like watching a recorded game of football when you already know the final score – you watch to see how the result is shaped, formed and decided, how individuals work (or don't work) together, who is at fault, who instigates the moves.

Knowing the result of a scene allows the audience to take a different role – if you know the answer to the dramatic story, you can observe.

Brecht called this technique 'verfremdungseffekt'; known in English as the 'alienation effect'.

Key terms

Plot – is the main story that runs throughout the play

Dénouement – conclusion

Sub-plot – is a minor story or stories that do not necessarily alter, or affect, the main story

Assessment activity 1

Unit 13 (working towards)

After deciding which play you are going to stage, read through the script in your group.

You could take it in turns to play characters.

If the play is well written, it shouldn't be too difficult to grasp the plot, the characters and their relationships.

Make sure you understand what is happening and what all words and references mean.

After each scene, section or act, summarise the action.

Discuss the plot and characters: what you think and know about them so far.

As you read, consider what might happen next in the story and to the characters.

After you have read the play, you are going to create a short summary of the plot, which will include a list of the themes, the main plot, and any **sub-plots**.

Evidence

- notes on the plot – summary of plot (main plot, any sub-plots), list of themes

Grading tips Unit 13

M1 Add a description of the subject matter and your personal feelings about the story and characters.

D1 You can also provide an outline of how you see the play being performed to an audience.

PLTS

By researching characterisation, you will be developing your skills as an **independent enquirer**.

Functional skills

English: By contributing to discussions about text interpretation and performing lines, you are using your **speaking and listening** skills.

Design and specialist requirements

The playwright might have stated particular requirements regarding furniture, props, stage directions or lighting/sound details in the main body of the script or in production notes.

Samuel Beckett has very specific staging requirements and, as part of the performance license, stipulates that changes cannot be made to his instructions.

Other playwrights may have included detailed design requirements but not made them compulsory.

Does your play have particular design requirements? Do you think that including design elements would help you with your interpretation of the story?

Consider how you will design the following for your play:

- set
- performance space
- lighting
- costume
- sound
- props
- makeup.

Using non-naturalistic production elements

Rather than using realistic design elements, you could *represent* objects and scenes. For example, you could use soft materials, such as sheets, cloth, blankets and ribbons. They can be used to represent environment (a river), as props (a baby), as clothing (a shawl), etc.

You might incorporate blocks/shapes to represent furniture, interiors or doorframes.

Music, sound effects and lighting can represent environments or emotions.

Case study: Design in practice

The practitioner/style of performance could dictate the content of the design. In this example, a group of students are involved in a production of Brecht's *Good Person of Szechuan*, using elements of the Epic Theatre style. Here, a learner describes the setting for this production:

Set: Box theatre, end on staging

- 2 white flats, 7ft x 3ft each, upstage left and right
- wooden boxes used to create different settings, eg desks, shop serving area, etc.

Actors sit on wooden boxes, in horseshoe shape, round performance space. They watch performance as 'actors', not as characters.

Banners/signs carried/held/positioned by actors; used to:

- summarise scenes – date, place, summary of action
- introduce characters – an arrow pointing downwards with the name of a character
- describe situation and environment – shop names, signposts.

Props: Each actor has one prop that defines character/s, and keeps it with them at all times.

Costumes: Designed to represent elements of the character and their situation. The costumes are kept in a trunk on stage. The actors get changed in performance space.

Lighting: one red wash, three spots, one blue wash, one general wash. two portable lighting racks on stage.

Sound: Eno/Bowie tracks CD; Cartoon sound effects CD; Weather/environment CD

Performers relationship to/with audience

As a performer, you need to identify how you want to communicate with the audience, based on the 'instructions' of the playwright.

- In your play, has the playwright stated or indicated characters stepping out of role or speaking directly to the audience? Or does it seem realistic?
- Are the audience required to take on a role? Is there audience interaction?

Specific techniques of movement/voice required by style of text

The performance techniques required for your work will be determined by the style and content of the text. For naturalistic acting, refer to Unit 19: Principles of Acting for guidance (see page 121 for further information and techniques on naturalistic acting.)

For non-naturalistic plays you might be required to use your voice and body to express abstract emotions and concepts in sound and rhythm.

Activity: Non-naturalistic acting

Try experimenting with your voice and body to 'capture' the sounds and movements of the following:

- weather conditions (light rain, a clear blue sky, freezing fog)
- types of environments (a forest, a busy high street, a rubbish dump)
- machinery (a washing machine, a tractor, a toaster)
- animals (a swan, a wasp, a whale)
- musical instruments (a flute, a triangle, a trombone)
- abstract emotions (desire, jealousy, pride).

Brecht developed the concept of 'gestus', meaning both gist and gesture. Actions and gestures are 'shown' by the actor rather than 'felt', with a certain attitude expressed. The actor doesn't have to feel the emotions and psychological state of the character with 'gestus', they can *demonstrate* them. For example, instead of weeping in a naturalistic way (sobbing noises, tears, slouching of shoulders etc), the cry becomes an elongated wail. It still sounds realistic (the character appears to be in emotional pain) but the performance has been reduced to a simplified sound and movements. The audience will still understand the intention (the character is upset), but will not experience the realistic portrayal of the emotion.

Assessment activity 2

Unit 13 (P1) (M1) (D1)   BTEC
Unit 20 (P1) (M1) (D1)

You are going to choose a 10-15 minute extract from a contemporary play that will allow you to perform using non-naturalistic techniques.

Was the playwright influenced by certain styles of performance, eg **Commedia dell'Arte** or **Melodrama**?

You must present your initial ideas, including details of:

- the play and playwright
- a summary of the play
- any themes and issues that you find interesting and make the play relevant to a modern audience
- why you have chosen this extract
- which theatre practitioner you will use as an influence
- ideas on how the extract will be presented to the audience.

Evidence

- research notes and ideas
- annotated version of the script
- presentation notes and ideas (eg DVD, powerpoint, essay).

Grading tips Unit 13 and Unit 20

(M1) You will provide details of the performance styles and techniques you are going to use.

(D1) You will include your ideas on the design elements of the work and the relationship between the audience and the performers.

PLTS

By considering production style in the light of research into the play text and characteristaion, you will be developing your skills as an **independent enquirer** and **reflective learner**.

Functional skills

English: By making an effective presentation, you are using your **speaking and listening** skills.

By understanding your text and selecting an appropriate extract for performance, you are using your **reading** skills.

ICT: By using the internet for research purposes and selecting significant information that is fit for purpose, you are demonstrating your ability to **find and select information**.

Key terms

Commedia dell'Arte – Translated as 'comedy of art', the Commedia dell'Arte began in Italy in the 15th Century. Its key features include the use of masked character 'types' and (usually) unscripted, improvised performance. Pantomine and Punch and Judy puppet shows both have their origins in this style of theatre.

Melodrama – A genre of theatre that uses stereotypical and one-dimensional characters (heroes, villains etc) to control an audience's emotions. The entrance of a 'good' or 'bad' character will be marked with a piece of music suited to that character type.

Case study: Julia, 16 year-old acting student

In our project we are going to perform an extract from *Metamorphosis* by Steven Berkoff.

I will be playing Greta Samsa. The play is about a man (Gregor, Greta's brother) who turns into a beetle. It is a very unusual play – not only because of the 'metamorphosis' from human to insect, but also because the style of acting used is very technical and expressive. The movements are highly choreographed.

There is nothing naturalistic or realistic about this play; it is all about representing characters rather than being them.

We are going to use a combination of techniques based on the theories of Brecht and Berkoff. Berkoff provides very specific stage directions, including character movements, descriptions of music and lighting cues, as well as information on how some lines should be spoken (what the lines mean, rather than the motivation for saying them.)

We are going to perform the scene that begins with Mr Samsa finding a job through to Mr Samsa attacking Gregor with the apples. We have made a few decisions about the design elements, including the following:

Lighting – we want a bright white light, used in an aggressive way. Not subtle and faded but snapped on and off.

Hair, make-up and costume – we are going to base these elements on Edwardian (beginning of 20th century) fashions but in an exaggerated, expressionist style.

Setting – three stools for the family, a ramp, and a simple climbing frame.

Interpret and realise contemporary texts

After completing your analysis of the text, you can put your ideas into practice and make decisions about your chosen interpretation and performance style.

When using an extract from a full-length play you must ensure that it makes sense as an independent piece. Read the play, understand the requirements, then make decisions on what you want the audience to see, hear and experience.

The way language is used in some plays is essential to performance. For example, performing in a Beckett play is like playing music; the words act as a score. Beckett includes very specific stage directions and descriptions of the performance in the script – and if you don't perform them in the correct way, following Beckett's intentions, the meaning will change completely.

Did you know?

In *Metamorphosis*, the characters let the audience know they are telling a story. Instead of speaking realistically, they talk about themselves in the third person, for example 'he said' (rather than 'I said').

Activity: The language

Investigate the language in your play and see how the characters communicate with each other.

Are the conversations realistic? Has the playwright written the language using recognisable words, phrases? Do they use everyday words and sentences? If the sentences aren't complete, the playwright might be trying to capture a natural way of conversing.

Is technical language used? A character might speak with words and phrases from a particular profession, eg medical language.

Do characters interrupt/talk over each other? Does the playwright indicate pauses? Pauses might be stated or indicated with '…'

Do any characters have soliloquies or talk directly to the audience?

Is there a narrator? Do any characters speak thoughts out loud?

Is it prose? Or verse?

Rehearsing contemporary texts for performance

Have a look at unit 5&7: Rehearsing and Performing (pages 65–86) for advice on rehearsal skills, which includes personal management, listening and response, growth and development.

When researching and developing a character for a non-naturalistic performance, there are many different approaches you can use. You can rely both on your own experiences as a performer and on performance work you have seen. You could also use the experience, behaviour and physicality of people or animals you observe in your eveyday life to help you understand and develop your character.

You can use the Animal study activity on the next page to help you experiment with different ways of portraying a character.

Remember

Be brave, put your preparation to good use.

In the words of Franklin D Roosevelt "The only thing we have to fear is fear itself".

Activity: Animal study

This exercise can be physically and mentally demanding (if approached with the right intentions.)

Everyone in the group will complete an animal study, based on analysis of the text and character.

The study could be through observation (a pet, a trip to a farm, wildlife park or zoo) or watching nature programmes or films.

For this activity, don't tell anyone in your group which animal you are.

Perform a short piece: show your animal entering the space, moving around its environment, feeding (or whatever you observed or think suitable to perform), and leaving the space.

Pay attention to the following:

- The use of the spine, holding the head, how the animal looks at things, eg constantly observing for fear of attack/ focus and concentration on prey/ ignorant of surroundings.

- The use of the eyes – perception, awareness, front or side of head.

- State(s) of tension: feeding, relaxing, hunting, thinking.

- Tempo-rhythm of the animal in different states: the speed of action, movement.

- The essence of the animal: capturing its relaxed state (the instantly recognisable image) – its natural posture and 'average' position and stance

- The sound of the animal – communication through voice or other parts of the body, eg the beating of wings, cricket legs, horses hooves, the snap of a crocodile bite.

The following are examples of ideas about portraying an animal.

Chimpanzee – strong arm movements, strong facial expressions, human-like behaviour, very emotive.

Swan – the grace and tranquillity in water, the waddling beast on land, its vicious side (hissing).

Consider how you can incorporate these ideas into your characterisation: it might be that for a non-naturalistic role, the animal is just below the surface!

Assessment activity 3

Unit 13  P2 M2 D2 P3 M3 D3

Unit 20 P2 M2 D2

Explore and develop your characterisation in the rehearsal process.

Using your ideas on the interpretation, bring the character to life using vocal and physical expression.

Evidence

• actor's log
• audio/visual recordings of observations of others, rehearsals

Grading tips Unit 13 and Unit 20

M2 **M3** Be responsible for the development of your character; don't wait for your director to help you, make decisions on your own.

D2 **D3** You must be as creative and independent as possible. Take the initiative at all times.

PLTS

By exploring and developing characterisation, you will be developing your skills as a **creative thinker** and **reflective learner**.

Functional skills

By using your ideas on the interpretation of your character to perform lines, you are using your **speaking and listening** skills.

Keeping a log book

It is always a good idea to keep a log of your progress and development during the rehearsal process. Use a dedicated notebook (your log book) to jot down notes. You can focus on any of the following elements:

• development of vocal technique, including daily or weekly exercises to practise
• development of physical technique, including decisions about movement, posture and gesture for your character
• character development, with details of status and relationships with others
• director's notes and guidance, including extra rehearsal activities, research, and performance feedback
• understanding of the play, with notes on how your understanding of the play might change through the rehearsal process
• staging and production style and requirements, with details of any props and costumes you need to find, or ideas for music and sound effects.

Performing your work

The most important element of performance work is the marriage of character development and performance technique.

You have developed and rehearsed the work; you now have to perform it to the audience, using physical and vocal expression.

In Unit 5&7: Rehearsing and Performing (pages 65 to 86), there is lots of advice on performance technique in a naturalistic performance; if you are performing a non-naturalistic work you must adapt the principles according to:

• the demands of the text
• the interpretation of the character by you and/or the director.

Assessment activity 4

Unit 13 (working towards) **P4** **M4** **D4**

Unit 20 (working towards) **P3** **M3** **D3**

When performing your work to an audience, you need to incorporate the following elements.

Physical Expression

Posture: the stance, positioning and movement of your character

Gesture: the physical expression of the character and physical communications with others

Physical presence; use of space on stage: tension, height, openness, space, eye contact

Tempo-rhythm and appropriateness of energy: the speed and rhythm of your character.

Vocal Expression

Range and use of vocal instrument: the type of character (age, background) shown through your voice

Projection: volume and clarity of your voice

Register: the tone and frequency of your voice

Vocal characteristics; inflection, musicality, expression and diction

Speech characteristics: pace of speech, idiosyncrasies, diction, accent and dialect.

Grading tips Unit 13

M4 Communicate the character effectively and imaginatively.

D4 You must use all your physical theatre skills in rehearsal to imagination.

Grading tips Unit 20

M3 You must make thoughtful links between the rehearsal process and performance by successfully refining and adjusting work as you go through the process.

D3 Express the character with confidence, skill and clarity.

PLTS

By performing to and communicating effectively with an audience, you will be developing your skills as an **effective participator**.

Functional skills

By giving a successfuly performance, you are using your **speaking and listening** skills.

Endgame, a Théâtre de Complicité production of Samuel Beckett's play

Audience

Your relationship with the audience is key to the success of the performance work.

The audience will respond in different ways to the work. You can try to predict when they will laugh, or when they will be silent, or when they will applaud, but you cannot guarantee their reactions. This is what makes live theatre performance so rewarding and so difficult.

Just checking

1 Do you know and understand the context of the play?

2 Make sure you research your play and understand its characters and the messages it may contain.

3 Why was the play writen? Did anything influence the writer? Knowing the context of the play will help you to translate it to the audience.

4 Discuss the differences in the performance demands of the two different plays you have worked on.

5 Which elements and techniques are unique to contemporary plays?

edexcel :::

Assignment tips

- You will be making decisions when interpreting the play – be sure to make notes on whether you have been influenced by any practitioners or styles of performance.

- Be clear about what you need to achieve and stay in control of the process: know your timescales, share responsibilities, keep track of the evidence you need to produce for assessment, eg a log book and recordings of your rehearsals/performances.

- Try to keep a record of your involvement in the creative process, and what decisions you and others have made to progress the work.

- Combine the skills and techniques you have learnt with your own imagination when developing your work.

- Don't rely on others to build and shape the work; take responsibility and lead by example.

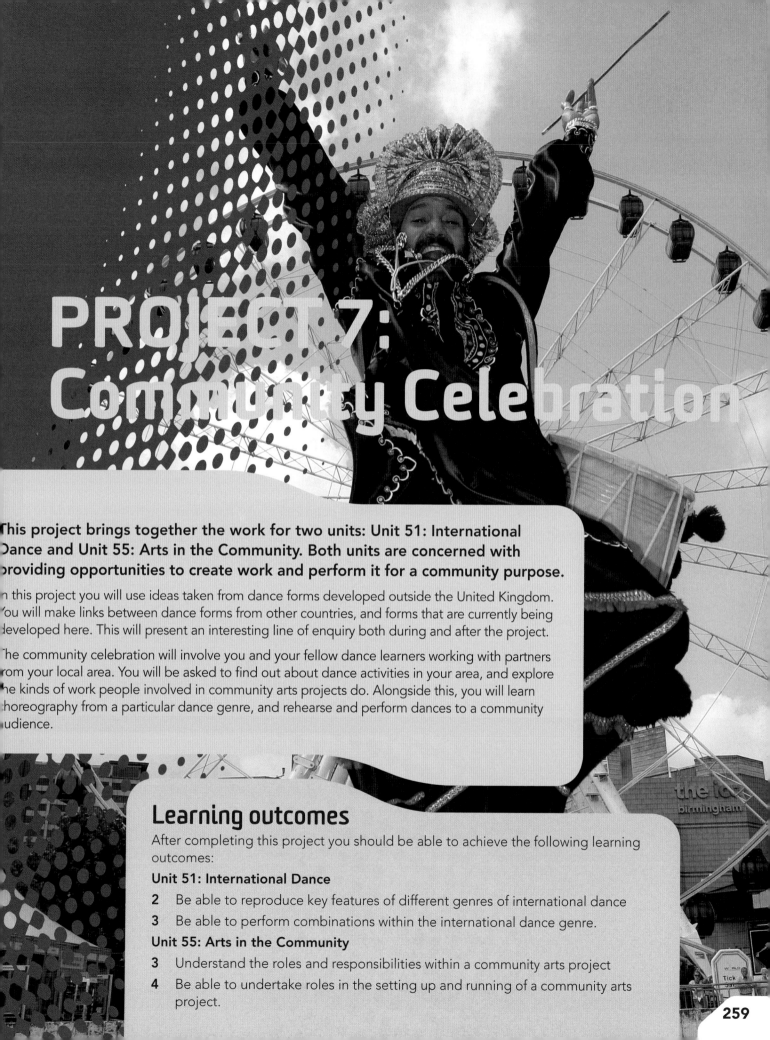

PROJECT 7: Community Celebration

This project brings together the work for two units: Unit 51: International Dance and Unit 55: Arts in the Community. Both units are concerned with providing opportunities to create work and perform it for a community purpose.

In this project you will use ideas taken from dance forms developed outside the United Kingdom. You will make links between dance forms from other countries, and forms that are currently being developed here. This will present an interesting line of enquiry both during and after the project.

The community celebration will involve you and your fellow dance learners working with partners from your local area. You will be asked to find out about dance activities in your area, and explore the kinds of work people involved in community arts projects do. Alongside this, you will learn choreography from a particular dance genre, and rehearse and perform dances to a community audience.

Learning outcomes

After completing this project you should be able to achieve the following learning outcomes:

Unit 51: International Dance

2   Be able to reproduce key features of different genres of international dance

3   Be able to perform combinations within the international dance genre.

Unit 55: Arts in the Community

3   Understand the roles and responsibilities within a community arts project

4   Be able to undertake roles in the setting up and running of a community arts project.

259

Assessment and grading criteria

This table shows you what you must do in order to achieve a **pass**, **merit** or **distinction** grade, and where you can find activities in this book to help you.

To achieve a **pass** grade the evidence must show that you are able to:	To achieve a **merit** grade the evidence must show that, in addition to the pass criteria, you are able to:	To achieve a **distinction** grade the evidence must show that, in addition to the pass and merit criteria, you are able to:
Unit 51: International Dance		
P2 demonstrate the key features of specified traditional dance genres with some level of skill **Assessment activity 2 page 265** **Assessment activity 3 page 266**	**M2** demonstrate the key features of specified traditional dance genres with aptitude **Assessment activity 2 page 265** **Assessment activity 3 page 266**	**D2** demonstrate the key features of specified international dance genres demonstrating high levels of skill and accomplishment **Assessment activity 2 page 265** **Assessment activity 3 page 266**
P3 utilise the rehearsal process, working with a sense of self-discipline **Assessment activity 4 page 267**	**M3** utilise the rehearsal process effectively, working with self-discipline **Assessment activity 4 page 267**	**D3** work with dedication during the rehearsal process, demonstrating self-discipline throughout **Assessment activity 4 page 267**
P4 execute international dance performances with evidence of accuracy, expression, interpretation and sense of style. **Assessment activity 5 page 268**	**M4** execute international dance performances accurately with appropriate use of expression, interpretation and sense of style. **Assessment activity 5 page 268**	**D4** execute international dance performances accurately with highly effective use of expression, interpretation and sense of style. **Assessment activity 5 page 268**
Unit 55: Arts in the Community		
P3 discuss the roles needed to run a community arts project, with some detail of the responsibilities of each one **Assessment activity 1 page 263**	**M3** explain the roles needed to run a community arts project with some reference to relevant examples, detailing the main responsibilities of each one **Assessment activity 1 page 263**	**D3** analyse the roles needed to run a community arts project with full reference to relevant and well-chosen examples, considering fully the responsibilities of each one **Assessment activity 1 page 263**
P4 undertake a role in the running of a community arts project with support and guidance. **Assessment activity 5 page 268**	**M4** undertake a role in the running of a community arts project with minimum support and guidance. **Assessment activity 5 page 268**	**D4** undertake a role in the running of a community arts project, working independently. **Assessment activity 5 page 268**

How you will be assessed

This project will be assessed through evidence that you will gather as you progress through it.

This may include:

For Unit 51: International Dance

- feedback from your tutor
- feedback from your peers
- your log book
- video/DVD recordings of rehearsals and performances.

For Unit 55: Arts in the Community

- your job description
- your research log, a presentation
- minutes of meetings
- planning documents
- your blog/your diary
- witness feedback
- feedback from the audience.

Alice, 16-year-old Bhangra dancer

I am studying for a BTEC National in Performing Arts (Dance) at my local college. The group is a real multi-cultural mix, including many learners from South Asian families, learners from Eastern Europe, some from Africa and one from the USA.

We are dancing in a festival to celebrate our community and my group are performing in a Bollywood scene. I am taking part in the Bhangra dances. We are performing to a song by Malkit Singh. There is a lot of call and response in the song and our dance reflects that. We dance a motif and then another group responds to the motif.

The dance is very rhythmical and funky, with clapping and chanting. I like the fact that it's upbeat and positive.

Over to you

- What styles of dance are you familiar with – do you know any styles that are non-western, like Bhangra or African dance? See what you can find out about the style you will be using for the Community Celebration.

- Find out about the props and costumes that are used in your community style.

- Find out about the music or accompaniment used for your community style.

Your brief

Your centre has decided to take part in a local community celebration of dance. You will perform some dances at a gathering of dance groups from schools, colleges and clubs.

Your centre has chosen to produce two dances in the hybrid South Asian style of Bhangra dancing. You will play a role in organising your centre's contributions. The position you are given will depend on your knowledge and understanding of the roles taken within a community arts project; you will apply for a post and interview or audition for it. How you carry out your assigned role will be vital in your assessments for Unit 55: Arts in the Community.

Your assessments will take place throughout the project, but there will be a particular focus on the setting up and running of the project, the rehearsals and the performances.

Warm up

Bhangra dance

See what you can find out about Bhangra dance. Look at video clips and read articles on the internet. Try to listen to some music in this style.

- Where does this style originate?
- Who dances it and why?
- What occasions are used for performing Bhangra dances?
- What sort of costumes do Bhangra dancers wear?

The first part of this project will require you to find out about the nature of the community celebration, for example what kind of project it will be and who the key players will be, so you must be very organised from the start.

Key terms

Répétiteur – the person who schedules and organises rehearsals for a show and who teaches the repertoire

CV – Curriculum Vitae; a document listing all your personal details, such as name, date of birth, address and contact details, relevant training received, qualifications and previous experience

Young girl dancing

Assessment activity 1

1 Make a list of roles and responsibilities within your organisation for the community celebration project. This will allow you to explore the roles taken when schools/colleges and clubs come together.

2 Make a list of administrative roles, such as: programme planner; marketing assistant; public relations assistant; tour planner; risk assessor; *répétiteur*. Summarise each job and the main areas of responsibility, making reference to your community celebration project.

3 Make a list of the creative roles, such as: actor; dancer; choreographer; director; musical director; costume designer; sound designer/technician; lighting designer/operator.

4 Choose a role you wish to be considered for.

5 Write your **CV**. Remember to include a photo and your experience to date, stating why you think you should be considered for the job. Submit your application online to your tutor or project director. Make sure it is submitted on time and in the correct format.

Evidence

- your job lists with role descriptions at your centre and at the venue
- your list of administrative roles
- your CV and job application in relation to the community celebration project
- your log book where you record your ideas, responses to criticism and plans for improving your work
- feedback from your tutor

Grading tips

M3 You must describe the main functions of a range of roles, making reference to your own project and job choice.

D3 You will analyse the roles, using your own choice of job as a well-informed example that covers all the major areas of that role.

Functional skills

English: By researching for a community project, you are using your **writing** skills.

PLTS

By planning to develop a community project, you will be developing your skills as an **independent enquirer**. By generating ideas and exploring possibilities for a community project, you will be developing your skills as a **creative thinker**.

When the job choices have been made, you must start by drawing up a timetable like the example below:

My role	Essential tasks	Date	Description of activity	Next steps
Publicity officer	Speak to organiser about project style and artwork.	02.09.2010	Email organiser's office to request sample materials.	Meet media group to discuss design of our publicity.

Now make yourself a 'contacts' chart like this one:

Publicity officer				
Name of group taking part	Number of performances	Style(s) of dance	Music	Contact name and date of contact

You might want to explore an African dance

Activity: **Your community**

Investigate the community you will be entering for the project.

- What kind of community will you be celebrating?
- Who lives there?
- What are the cultures of the people who live there?
- What are the main forms of dance performed in the community?
- Are there any cultural issues that might impinge on your work, such as taboo over females and males dancing together?

Be able to reproduce key features of different genres of international dance

Learning about international dance forms

The next step will be acquiring and learning the choreography. Bhangra dancing is a South Asian form with roots going back to India and Pakistan. It used to be danced at celebrations, such as weddings. When India and Pakistan were divided as countries, their dance forms developed in separate ways and became influenced by the areas in which their people lived. Their music and dance evolved and today Bhangra is a *hybrid form*, one that encompasses different styles of dance within it.

Although Bhangra music was traditionally based on the folk instruments of the Punjab, it has developed extensively and now incorporates all the contemporary western instruments that are used in popular music. This music and dancing can be seen in many films that are produced in India today.

Bhangra music has the following features:

- It is danced in single gender or mixed groups.
- It is danced to music performed using traditional instruments, but often mixed with modern music forms, such as hip-hop and reggae.
- There is a lot of call and response in the music.
- Traditionally, men wear Punjabi suits with colourful turbans, women wear loose trousers, a salwar kameez (tunic and trousers) or a ghagra (a long skirt), and a scarf around the neck.
- There are many forms of traditional Bhangra, for example Daankara is performed at weddings and Kikli is performed by women.
- Contemporary forms mix up the traditional styles, and dancers wear a variety of South Asian costumes in performance.

Assessment activity 2

Research the main characteristics of Bhangra dancing.

Bhangra is a folk-type dance with origins in the Indian province Punjab which has become very popular in Britain since the late 1960s and early 1970s. It was brought here by Indian migrants with a strong sense of cultural identity and the rhythms resemble those of reggae. The accompanying songs are traditionally related to current issues that the singers face, and provide a way of communicating what they really think. Bhangra music aims for a higher level of complexity than Punjabi folk and is mainly instrumental.

1   Give the names of some Bhangra dances.

2   What are the differences between the way males and females dance?

3   What instruments commonly feature in the music?

4   What costumes do dancers traditionally wear?

5   List some characteristic moves and steps, including facial expressions, alignment of limbs and use of rhythm.

6   Practise a short sequence you have learned in class and try to add some appropriate dynamic development using a different piece of music. Rehearse your combination and perform it to the group.

Evidence

- your feedback
- feedback from your peer(s)
- feedback from your tutor
- video/DVD recordings of workshops and performances
- your log book where you record your ideas, responses to criticism and plans for improving your work

Grading tips

M2 You will demonstrate key features of Bhangra dance in your workshop, rehearsals and performance.

D2 You will be highly competent in the way you demonstrate the key features of the dance style.

PLTS

By researching the origin and development of international dance genres, you will be developing your skills as an **independent enquirer**.

By learning, rehearsing and performing international dance genres, you will be developing your skills as an **effective participator**.

Functional skills

English: By researching international dance styles, you are using your **reading** skills.

Key features

When working on a new style of dance, you should always have an open mind. Try hard to take on the key features that mark this new style out from others. Think about:

- appropriate posture; alignment; balance; co-ordination; elevation; stamina; strength; flexibility; use of torso/individual body parts; musicality; timing; relationship between performers; use of space; dynamic range; facial expression.

Make a list of the key features you find difficult, for example:

- posture and alignment – how to hold the head and arms high
- singing and yelling at the same time as dancing
- dancing closely to the beat
- dancing in a skirt or costume.

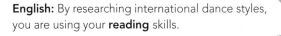

You can find more information and guidance on all of these key features in Unit 38: Dance Performance, pages 161–178.

Assessment activity 3

Unit 51 **BTEC**

1 Working with a partner or in a small group, work out a short dance, based on your own or another learnt choreography.

2 Choose some Bhangra music.

3 Rehearse the dance, using the studio mirrors to help with alignment and positioning. Record rehearsals so you can see how to improve.

4 Choose costumes, eg loose trousers under tunics.

5 Plan a short performance or seminar to explain the key features of your dance.

6 Perform to the group.

Evidence

- feedback: your own, from your partner/group, from your tutor

- video/DVD recordings of workshops and performances

- your log book where you record your ideas, responses to criticism and plans for improving your work

Grading tips

M2 You will show and clearly explain the main features of the style.

D2 Your skills will be highly accomplished and the style clearly explained through demonstration of good examples in your performance or seminar.

Functional skills

English: By having verbal discussions about international dance styles, you are using your **speaking and listening** skills.

PLTS

By engaging in group work during the rehearsal process, you will be developing your skills as a **team worker**. By learning, rehearsing and performing international dance genres, you will be developing your skills as an **effective participator**.

Activity: Make a 'to do' list

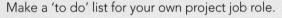

Make a 'to do' list for your own project job role.

You could adapt this activity for any of the other production roles that might apply to you personally. For example, the costume designer would:

- discuss costume ideas with the show director

- design ideas for costumes and show them to the director, with costings and estimates worked out

- meet with individual performers to arrange measuring, making and fittings

- try out costumes in rehearsal

- store costumes; prepare to move them to venue.

Remember

While you are learning your choreography, you should be making contacts with the relevant project personnel, such as the publicity organisers, and the technical director if you are designing or recording your group's musical accompaniment.

Working safely

For every project, a series of risk assessments must be carried out to ensure the legal safety requirements of schools and colleges are met. Ask your tutor to show you some risk assessments they have carried out for the course you are taking.

Someone in your group may have been given the job of carrying out the risk assessment for your project performance, or you may have to do this yourself to gain experience.

To carry out an effective risk assessment, make a list of all the activities undertaken throughout the project, eg: making contact with host venue; visiting venue; getting in to venue; setting up sound and lighting effects (potential technical hazards); transporting performers to venue; carrying out rehearsals; carrying out technical rehearsals; carrying out performances; getting out of venue.

Activity: Risk assessment

Design an appropriate document to help you analyse and deal with possible risks associated with the project. Below is an example of a risk assessment prompt sheet.

Activity	Possible hazards	Averting the risks	Contingency plan	Effect
Visit to venue	Journey, synchronisation with host venue leader.	Ensure travel is well-organised, permissions received from parents/carer, travel documents in order.	Provide emergency call number and funds.	Visit carried out effectively and arrangements made.

Assessment activity 4

Unit 51 **P3 M3 D3** BTEC

1 Rehearse each of your dances; run through the dances on your own or with a partner.

2 Check each other to ensure accuracy of steps and moves.

3 Use the relevant accompaniment.

4 Focus on dynamics, projection, focus, expression and communication.

5 Record your work.

6 Evaluate the results.

Evidence

- feedback: your own, from your partner/group, from your tutor

- video/DVD recordings of workshops and performances

- your log book where you record your ideas, responses to criticism and plans for improving your work

Grading tips

M3 You will show self-discipline in your rehearsals, tackling each area of difficulty with objectivity and persistence.

D3 You will show considerable dedication, often planning your own rehearsals.

Functional skills

English: By having verbal discussions about international dance styles, you are using your **speaking and listening** skills.

PLTS

By learning, rehearsing and performing international dance genres, you will be developing your skills as an **effective participator**. By observing your own execution of key features and making appropriate improvements, you will be developing your skills as a **reflective learner**.

Final stages

The final stages of any project are the technical rehearsals, the get-in, the performance and the get-out.

Technical rehearsals

Technical rehearsals involve the whole company of performers getting together in the performance space; this includes the show's director, the lighting and sound designers, the stage manager and anyone else involved in the project.

As a performer, you will be asked to run through your dances on stage and sometimes in costume. Your performance may be interrupted as sound and lighting are adjusted. These rehearsals can be rather lengthy. Performers must be patient and understanding throughout.

The performance

The day of the performance will be exciting and challenging and you must be well-prepared and organised. Here are some useful tips:

- Get a good night's sleep beforehand.
- Prepare your make-up and any costumes.
- Arrive at the venue on time.
- Eat and drink enough to get you through the event.
- Be supportive and positive to other group members.

> **Further information on physical and interpretive performance skills are included in Unit 38: Dance Performance page 161.**

Assessment activity 5 — Unit 51 — Unit 55  — BTEC

You must perform your role on the day of the event to the best of your ability, so that the project is successful.

You will need to perform the Bhangra dance pieces as faultlessly as possible, and complete any other production roles efficiently.

Evidence

- your feedback
- feedback from your group
- feedback from your tutor
- feedback from the audience
- video/DVD recordings of the performance
- your log book where you record your ideas, responses to criticism and plans for improving your work

Grading tips Unit 51

M4 Your work will be full of expression and a true sense of the style needed in Bhangra. Your steps and movements will be accurately executed.

D4 You will use expression very effectively, interpreting the style highly accurately.

Grading tips Unit 55

M4 You will undertake your role with little support from your tutor.

D4 You will work independently throughout the project.

Functional skills

English: By recording ideas, responses to criticism and plans for improvement in your log book, you are using your **writing** skills.

PLTS

By learning, rehearsing and performing international dance genres, you will be developing your skills as an **effective participator**.

Azeez
Community arts project officer

Azeez works in a community arts centre in London. He was trained in performing arts at his local FE college and then went on to university where he studied Community Arts and Performance. He got his job by attending an interview and an audition, both of which were very daunting.

How did you find out about your job?

Azeez: I saw an advert in *The Stage*, one of the professional newspapers dancers have to read to keep up with what's going on.

How did you plan for your audition and interview?

Azeez: I kept going to class to keep up my technique, then when I knew what they were going to ask me to do, I choreographed a short sequence of dance and worked on my presentation.

What did you have to do in the audition?

Azeez: I had to perform a solo and then explain what kind of project I could run for a group of local dance clubs. I had already done some projects like this when I was at uni, so I used ideas I had already tried out.

How did the audition and interview go?

Azeez: It went really well! The panel loved my ideas and my style of dancing, so I got the job and now I am in the middle of running a community project involving ten dance clubs!

Think about it!

1 What kind of work would you produce for an audition and interview like this. Try to work out a short solo dance just like Azeez had to.

2 How would you present an idea for a community project to a prospective client?

3 Find out what community arts projects are going on in your local area.

Just checking

1 Make sure you explore the style you are using in your dances. This could mean researching on the Internet for examples of dancers working in your style. Try to see any live performances of the style you are using.

2 Ensure you have a good understanding of the extent of the role you are playing in the project, as well as what other roles and responsibilities are needed for the project to run smoothly.

3 Check what skills and processes are required to run a large project and bring it to fruition. This project is complex and many roles interlink – make sure you carry out your duties to the full.

4 Make sure you have knowledge of the community in which you will be performing.

edexcel :::

Assignment tips

- Be open to new and challenging dance forms, don't be put off by something that challenges you.

- Keep exploring dance styles and genres.

- Be really well organised when working on a large group project.

- Keep up regular dance class throughout the project so your dance technique continues to improve.

- Keep your planning and evaluations up-to-date throughout the project.

- Ask your tutor how well you are doing. Regular feedback will help you plans ways of improving your work.

- Keep up your minutes of all production meetings.

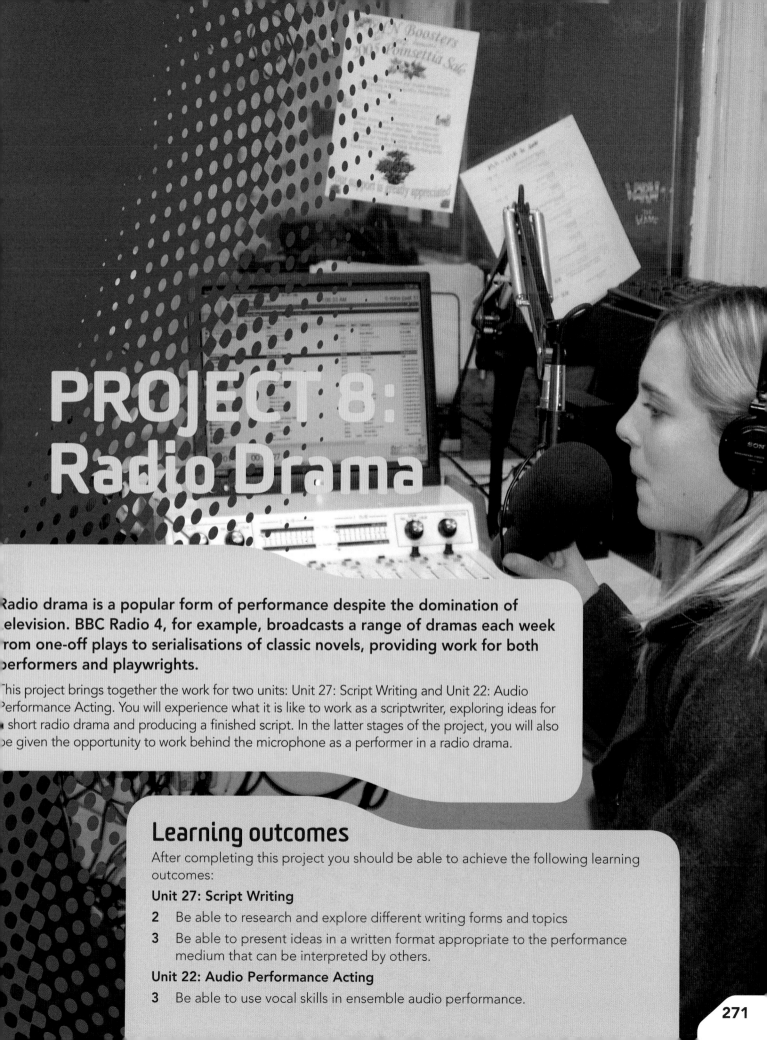

PROJECT 8: Radio Drama

Radio drama is a popular form of performance despite the domination of television. BBC Radio 4, for example, broadcasts a range of dramas each week from one-off plays to serialisations of classic novels, providing work for both performers and playwrights.

This project brings together the work for two units: Unit 27: Script Writing and Unit 22: Audio Performance Acting. You will experience what it is like to work as a scriptwriter, exploring ideas for a short radio drama and producing a finished script. In the latter stages of the project, you will also be given the opportunity to work behind the microphone as a performer in a radio drama.

Learning outcomes

After completing this project you should be able to achieve the following learning outcomes:

Unit 27: Script Writing

2   Be able to research and explore different writing forms and topics

3   Be able to present ideas in a written format appropriate to the performance medium that can be interpreted by others.

Unit 22: Audio Performance Acting

3   Be able to use vocal skills in ensemble audio performance.

Assessment and grading criteria

This table shows you what you must do in order to achieve a pass, merit or distinction, and where you can find activities in this book to help you.

To achieve a **pass** grade the evidence must show that you are able to:	To achieve a **merit** grade the evidence must show that, in addition to the pass criteria, you are able to:	To achieve a **distinction** grade the evidence must show that, in addition to the pass and merit criteria, you are able to:
Unit 27: Script Writing		
P2 research and explore ideas and topics for scripts **Assessment activity 1 page 277**	**M2** research and explore ideas and topics for scripts using a variety of imaginative approaches **Assessment activity 1 page 277**	**D2** research and explore ideas and topics for scripts using imaginative and highly creative analytical approaches **Assessment activity 1 page 277**
P3 revise ideas to form a working script using script writing skills **Assessment activity 2 page 279**	**M3** revise ideas with creativity to form a working script using script writing skills **Assessment activity 2 page 279**	**D3** continually revise ideas with creativity and independence to form a working script using script writing skills **Assessment activity 2 page 279**
P4 present a script that is appropriate to the medium. **Assessment activity 2 page 279**	**M4** present a script that is sensitive to the medium and communicates meaning. **Assessment activity 2 page 279**	**D4** present an original script that is highly appropriate to the medium and effectively communicates meaning. **Assessment activity 2 page 279**
Unit 22: Audio Performance Acting		
P3 present ensemble audio performance work using appropriate vocal skills. **Assessment activity 3 page 280**	**M3** present ensemble audio performance work using a range of appropriate vocal skills, demonstrating some versatility. **Assessment activity 3 page 280**	**D3** present ensemble audio performance work using a wide range of appropriate vocal skills, demonstrating versatility. **Assessment activity 3 page 280**

How you will be assessed

This project will be assessed through an internal assignment that will be designed and marked by the tutors at your centre. You will be assessed on your ability to produce a script for a short radio drama, working as a team to:

- research and explore topics for a radio drama
- develop and revise ideas for a working script
- present a finished script
- present an ensemble performance of a radio script.

The work you produce may include:

- research notes and ideas
- a draft version of a script
- a finished script
- audio recording(s) of performance(s)
- observation reports from your tutor(s).

Neil, 18-year-old drama learner

I wasn't really aware of radio drama before doing this project. I watch plenty of stuff on TV but the radio shows I listen to tend to be music-based. During the early stages of the project we listened to some different examples of radio plays and I was really surprised at how much I enjoyed them. There is something about radio drama that requires you to use your imagination and I really liked this. Because you can't see any of the characters or locations, you have to create pictures in your head, deciding what people and places might look like.

When it came to creating my own script, it was great to have the freedom to set the play in any location. The beauty of radio drama is that the action can take place absolutely anywhere as you are free from the financial and logistical constraints that apply to TV or film drama.

Over to you

- In what ways is having 'the freedom to set a play in any location' an advantage to the writer of a radio play?
- Might there be any disadvantages?

Your brief

You are required to develop ideas and write a script for a radio drama lasting at least ten minutes. It should have at least two, but no more than six, speaking characters.

Your radio drama must appeal to an audience of young adults, and should therefore be based on a topic that will interest this age group.

The finished plays will be recorded, and you will be expected to perform in plays written by others in your group as necessary.

Warm up

Radio drama

Listen to a radio play. (Radio 4 transmits a 45 minute play each weekday afternoon at 2.15 p.m. These can be accessed via the internet using Radio 4's listen again facility – go to the Hotlinks section on page ii and follow the instructions there.

Discuss the following:

- the structure of the play
- the settings/locations used
- how music is used
- the use of sound effects.

Despite the popularity of television, people are really enthusiastic about radio plays

Radio plays are different from other forms of dramatic performance in that the meaning of the drama must be communicated to the audience entirely through the medium of sound. The playwright and the performers must ensure that listeners know about the locations used and understand the action of the piece without the help of sets or the physical expressions of performers. The lack of visual performance can be an advantage for the playwright as the type and number of locations is not restrained. Settings and effects that would be prohibitively expensive on television or film are easily used in a radio production. The drama can move through time and space using fantastic and unusual locations, if required. Douglas Adams' sci-fi classic *The Hitchhiker's Guide to the Galaxy*, for example, began life on radio in 1978. Having gained popularity, it was later adapted for television and was eventually released as a feature film.

A successful radio drama will include the following features:

- **Characterisation:** strong characterisation is vital to a successful radio drama. The listener must be able to understand the actions of the characters and the dramatic journey they undertake during the drama.

- **Plot:** a strong story is essential. It must hold the listener's attention from the beginning to the very end of the piece, and must be easy to understand.

- **Dialogue:** the quality of the dialogue is vital as it conveys the twists and turns of the plot. As the performers are not able to use physical expression, dialogue allows them to communicate effectively to the listeners. Dialogue is also used to make the listener aware of the presence of a character in a sequence.

- **Sound effects:** these are essential to radio drama. They help the listeners to picture the location and what the characters are physically doing during a section.

- **Music:** music can be used to create an atmosphere. Short musical tracks can also punctuate the various sequences in the piece, to show the passage of time or change of location.

Case study: *The Archers*

The Archers is Britain's longest running soap opera, having been broadcast on Radio 4 since 1950. Set in Ambridge in the fictional county of Borsetshire, it tells the story of the ups and downs of a rural community.

The six 13-minute episodes that are broadcast each week are written by a team of nine writers. The episodes are recorded – three to six weeks prior to transmission with a month's worth of episodes recorded in just six days at BBC Pebble Mill in Birmingham.

Over to you

Listen to an episode of *The Archers*. Go to go to the Hotlinks section on page ii and follow the instructions there.

Compare what you hear with a television soap such as *EastEnders* or *Coronation Street*. What are the similarities and differences?

Activity: Sound and music

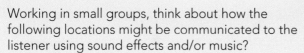

Working in small groups, think about how the following locations might be communicated to the listener using sound effects and/or music?

- a smart restaurant
- a busy city street
- an office
- a nightclub
- a stately home in the late 19th century
- a family kitchen
- in the countryside
- inside a spaceship

Consider how any suggested sound effects might be made, that is, with live effects or recordings.

Did you know?

In 1938, a radio drama of the H.G. Wells classic novel *The War of the Worlds* directed and narrated by Orson Welles was so realistic that many Americans panicked, believing that an actual invasion from Mars was taking place.

Research and explore writing forms and topics

Research

Any play, whether it is written for television, radio or the stage, begins with an idea. You might create a piece of radio drama about a topic or issue that is relevant to your target audience. You might base your drama on a true story, or adapt an existing short story. Your drama could be a comedy or a tragedy, or in the style of a documentary or piece of epic drama. With such an open brief, you must generate and then explore ideas in detail to assess their suitability.

Further guidance on researching material for performance is included in Unit 1: Performance Workshop (LO1).

Explore

Many successful plots begin with a central character known as a **protagonist**. The protagonist is facing a problem or a challenge. This may be caused, or made worse, by an **antagonist**. The protagonist must face the challenge and solve the problem so that order can be restored.

Outline and plot synopsis

You can create an outline plot for a drama by using a flow chart. The flow chart illustrates the key points in the plot.

Key terms

Protagonist – the principal character in a play or story

Antagonist – an opponent

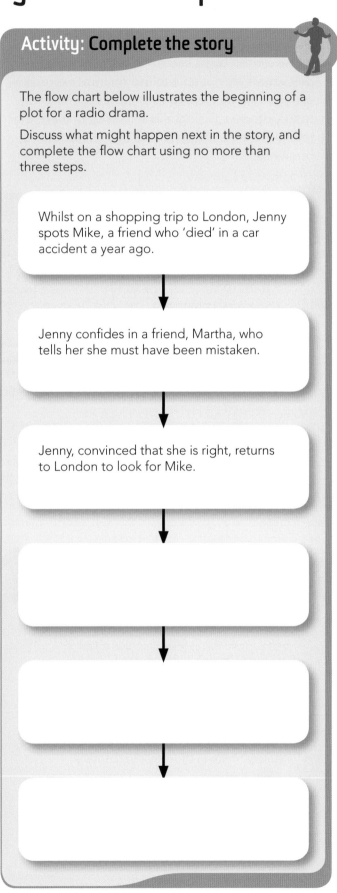

Activity: Complete the story

The flow chart below illustrates the beginning of a plot for a radio drama.

Discuss what might happen next in the story, and complete the flow chart using no more than three steps.

> Whilst on a shopping trip to London, Jenny spots Mike, a friend who 'died' in a car accident a year ago.

> Jenny confides in a friend, Martha, who tells her she must have been mistaken.

> Jenny, convinced that she is right, returns to London to look for Mike.

Experimenting with character

Making characters real is a challenge for any writer. Remember that all people have both positive and negative personality traits. An essentially 'good' character who is hardworking and selfless will appear more authentic if they have some personality quirks or flaws, such as a morbid fear of water. Creating a back story for your character that explains their personality traits may add depth and realism to the character, for example that the fear of water is a result of capsizing in a rowing boat as a child.

Activity: Creating characters

Look back at the flow chart completed in the previous activity. How might the story change if:

- the main character, Jenny, was a passenger in the car crash that 'killed Mike', and has suffered from flashbacks ever since.
- Jenny blames herself for the accident because of an argument with Mike prior to him getting in the car and driving off?

Assessment activity 1

Unit 27  BTEC

Investigate a range of topics that might interest young adults (aged 16–24); for example you may research a social issue such as knife crime or a topic such as 'celebrity'.

Use your investigation to develop an idea for a plot for a short radio play.

Evidence

A portfolio of evidence containing materials such as:

- analysis of the topics considered, and justification of decisions made
- a flow chart of the proposed plot.

Grading tips

M2 You will carry out your research in a creative and imaginative manner. You must show that you are able to analyse the topics considered, and provide a clear justification for the selection or rejection of ideas.

D2 You will show good levels of independence in your research. You will undertake an in-depth analysis of the topics considered to ensure your final decisions have been developed from a solid base.

PLTS

By generating ideas and exploring possibilities for scripts, you will be developing your skills as a **creative thinker**.

By carrying out research to develop ideas for your own script, you will be developing your skills as an **independent enquirer**.

Functional skills

ICT: By using the internet to find and select information, you are using your **ICT** skills.

English: By developing your ideas for plot, analysing topics considered and putting together a flow chart, you are using your **writing** skills.

Rough drafts

Once you have created an outline for your story, you are ready to produce the first draft of your script. When producing your draft, consider the following:

- Do not include too many characters in a single scene. This can be confusing for the listener who might lose track of who is who.
- Think in sound, not pictures. The listener will not know that a character is present in a scene unless they speak or are referred to by name by another character.
- Choose sound effects sparingly and use them sparingly. They are important, but too many may confuse the listener.
- Do not include stage directions. They are not needed in radio drama.
- Try speaking dialogue out loud. This is the best way to check if what you have written sounds natural.
- Get on with it. You can redraft what you are not happy with later so do not spend too much time at this stage agonising over each sentence.

When setting out your script, you should:

- use capitals for sound effects and other technical information so they are not confused with dialogue.
- clearly separate characters' names from the dialogue.

The best source of inspiration for script writing is listening to radio drama

For further advice on the layout of radio scripts, including examples from a range of writers, go to the Hotlinks section on page ii and follow the instructions there.

The following extract is an example of how this might be done:

```
        SCENE 2 JENNY'S OFFICE

    SOUND OF PHONES RINGING AND
            GENERAL CHAT

JENNY   It was such a shock Martha. I
        just froze.

MARTHA  But you must have been
        mistaken Jenny. It was just
        someone who looked like Mike.

JENNY   But he was as near to me as
        you are now. I know it was
        him.

MARTHA  But how could it have been?
        He's dead, we all went to the
        funeral.

JENNY   (FRUSTRATED) I don't know...I
        don't know.

MARTHA  Look Jenny, you've been
        through a lot. I'm not
        saying you imagined it but...
        there has to be a simple
        explanation. Some guy who
        looked like Mike...

JENNY   (ANNOYED) No it was him I tell
        you...it was him.
```

Redrafting

Most writers redraft their work a number of times for the following reasons:

- In response to feedback from an editor.
- To ensure the length of the play meets required timings.
- To simply improve the piece.

Once you have completed the first draft of your script, read it from beginning to end before making any necessary changes. Remember to keep a copy of your first draft.

Assessment activity 2

Unit 27 P3 M3 D3 P4 M4 D4   BTEC

Revise your ideas to form a working script for your radio play.

Evidence

- all drafts of your script including notes about changes made
- the final draft of your script

Grading tips

M3 Your drafts and your notes must include detailed evidence of where and why changes have been made.

D3 You will be continually revising your work, only stopping when deadlines are approaching.

M4 You will present your script using the conventions of radio drama in a sensitive way. It will show that you have been responsive to the way in which radio drama can be presented.

D4 Your script will be imaginative and will use the conventions of radio drama in an effective and interesting way.

PLTS

By reviewing and reflecting on your script writing and research work and acting on the outcomes to modify and improve your work, you will be developing your skills as a **reflective learner**.

By trying out alternative ways of revising drafts, following ideas through to complete a script, you will be developing your skills as a **creative thinker**.

Functional skills

English: By revising your ideas into a working script, you are using your **writing** skills.

Recording your play

Rehearsals

Just like in the theatre the first rehearsal of a radio play will be a read-through with the cast and the director. Further rehearsals may be required, but the absence of movement means the rehearsal process is a lot simpler and quicker than it would be for a theatre piece or a film. There is no need for the actors to commit the dialogue to memory, but it is advisable for them to spend time practising lines.

While many sound effects are pre-recorded, some are created live in the studio. Actors must be aware of any sound effects used, so they can react to them appropriately.

Vocal skills

Without movement, gesture and facial expression, the radio actor's only means of expression is the voice. The use of vocal techniques to create a character and communicate meaning is therefore vital in radio drama.

The actor must make use of:

- volume (loudness, softness)
- vocal inflection (pitch, modulation, variety)
- changes in tone (hard, soft)
- pace (fast, slow).

The actor must also work with the microphones (closeness and distance from them) to achieve the best sound.

Activity: Using microphones and sound effects

Experiment with recording equipment, microphones and sound effects to create the following scenes:

- An intimate conversation, such as two characters talking quietly in an enclosed space.
- A chance meeting, such as a character calling to another across a busy street.
- A dinner party, such as a group of people having dinner in a noisy restaurant.
- A telephone conversation, such as one character 'live', the other at the end of the phone.

Recording

Time in a recording studio is expensive and therefore very precious. The more 'takes' needed to record a scene, the more expensive it is, so it is vital that actors and studio personnel are fully prepared for each session and make best use of the time available.

Key terms

Dramaturg – a person who is a specialist in dramatic composition and theatrical representation

Assessment activity 3

Unit 22 **P3** **M3** **D3** **BTEC**

Taking part in recordings of the group's radio plays using vocal skills and responding to the recording environment in an appropriate manner.

Evidence

- recordings of rehearsals
- recordings of final performances

Grading tips

M3 You should use vocal skills in a competent manner to express the meaning of the piece(s) being performed.

D3 You should use vocal skills in an imaginative and creative manner to fully communicate the intentions of the piece(s).

PLTS

By taking responsibility for your own role in group recordings, you will be developing your skills as a **team worker**.

By communicating effectively to a targeted audience, you will be developing your skills as an **effective participator**.

Functional skills

English: By participating in recordings that involve other performers, you will be using your **speaking and listening** skills.

playwright

'I write plays – for theatres, festivals, schools, one-off events, for friends and for myself. I've written my own original plays, and adapted/translated plays by Euripides and Wedekind. I've recently started to write screenplays.

I've previously worked on education projects, going into schools and universities to run workshops, and participate in student productions of my work. I've also acted as an adviser, or '**dramaturg**', to assist with dialogue or storytelling on other people's plays. I'm sometimes commissioned to edit a classical text for production, or help skew it towards the vision of the director.

The most rewarding aspect of what I do is seeing the play with an audience. You don't always get the expected response, but having a whole theatre laugh or cry at something you've written is a wonderful feeling.

Perhaps even more enjoyable is the rehearsal stage, which is really just an organised form of playing – spending all day doing something you love with like-minded people.

The hardest part of my job is the disappointment when something doesn't work. You can invest so much time and hard work in a project and never see it come to fruition. A writer's success relies on other people – mainly directors and producers – having faith in your work and having the capacity to produce it. As such, networking is very important, a task that requires skills I don't naturally possess. Another downside can be the money – when I started out, it was far from a steady income.

I got into writing plays by accident. I went to art school to study photography and had to take some compulsory creative writing classes. I found I enjoyed writing more than photography and have been doing it ever since.

I have a Bachelors degree in Cultural Studies and a Masters degree in Creative Writing. I think practical experience, however, is just as valid as any qualification; an MA isn't really necessary but it has undoubtedly helped me to develop my skills as a writer and make contacts in the industry.'

Think about it!

1 What does 'commissioned' mean in relation to writing?
2 What do you think the playwright might contribute to the rehearsal process?
3 What is 'networking'? Why do you think it is important to a playwright? What skills might be involved?

Just checking

Assessment activity 1

There are many ways to present evidence of research. You could, for example:

- create a large spider diagram
- keep a scrap book of clippings from newspapers and magazines
- create a research log that gives details of websites visited.

Annotate these materials to show evidence of your decision making.

Assessment activity 2

Keep all drafts of your script, labelling them clearly (Draft 1, 2, 3...).

Your final script should be typed onto A4 paper using double spacing. Include the title of the play and your name on a cover sheet. It is also good practice to include a brief synopsis of the plot (no more than half a side of A4) with the script.

Assessment activity 3

This activity will be evidenced through recordings of rehearsals and performances. Written portfolio work is not required.

edexcel

Assignment tips

- Become a consumer of radio drama. The more you listen to it, the more familiar you will become with the genre, and that will help you when you are creating a play of your own.

- Consider at least two or three ideas for your play. Test your ideas out by discussing them with other members of your group as well as your tutor. Consider the strengths and weaknesses of each idea.

- Do not agonise over your first draft of your script. The important thing is to get something down on paper. You can revise it later.

- Remember that team work is essential in this project. Treat other group members with respect when performing in their plays.

- Many writers carry a notebook at all times to record ideas that may come to them on the go.

- There should be a distinct difference between the first and final drafts of your play. You should include notes explaining why changes have been made. Where material is rejected, you must say why.

- Your final script should be presented in a professional manner. It should be free from spelling mistakes and grammatical errors. Ask a friend to proofread your final version as they are more likely to spot errors.

- Your work in the studio should show that you are fully engaged with the project, and that you are as committed to others' scripts as your own work. You should think about the vocal work undertaken in other units of the course and how you can transfer these skills to this new context.

PROJECT 9: Physical Theatre Performance

Performing physical theatre gives performers the opportunity to use and combine many techniques to express themselves, not solely through acting or dance, but through a diverse range of art forms. This is a multi-layered genre that includes movement, mime, acrobatics and clowning, as well as all the more traditional forms of acting.

Dance and acting both require the performer to consider the use and place of movement in relation to the character or style of choreography. Different genres of performing arts dictate the type of movement to be used in diverse ways. Movement is used very differently by a performer in a classical ballet compared with how it is used by an actor in a Greek chorus.

This project brings together the work for two units: Unit 33: Applying Physical Theatre and Unit 50: Movement in Performance. You will develop a role for a site-specific performance, rehearse it and perform it.

You will work with your group in the studio, and your tutor will direct your work. In a series of workshops, you will experiment with different ways of creating a role or character using physical theatre skills. The focus will be on using dance and movement to create meaning, and your tutor will expect you to learn and reproduce sequences that have been taught to you, just as a professional performer does when working with a director. You will learn how to apply your skills in rehearsal, gradually building up towards the final performance.

Learning outcomes

After completing this project you should be able to achieve the following learning outcomes:

Unit 33: Applying Physical Theatre

2   Be able to use physical theatre skills to develop a role/character in rehearsal

3   Be able to perform role/character using physical theatre skills.

Unit 50: Movement in Performance

2   Be able to reproduce movement phrases within a performance

3   Be able to apply movement skills in rehearsal

4   Be able to apply movement skills in performance.

Assessment and grading criteria

This table shows you what you must do in order to achieve a **pass**, **merit** or **distinction** grade, and where you can find activities in this book to help you.

To achieve a **pass** grade the evidence must show that you are able to:	To achieve a **merit** grade the evidence must show that, in addition to the pass criteria, you are able to:	To achieve a **distinction** grade the evidence must show that, in addition to the pass and merit criteria, you are able to:
Unit 33: Applying Physical Theatre		
P2 apply physical theatre skills in rehearsal to develop a role/character **Assessment activity 1 page 289** **Assessment activity 2 page 291** **Assessment activity 3 page 292**	**M2** apply physical theatre skills in rehearsal to develop a role/character with sensitivity, creativity and commitment **Assessment activity 1 page 289** **Assessment activity 2 page 291** **Assessment activity 3 page 292**	**D2** apply physical theatre skills in rehearsal to develop a role/character with sensitivity, highly developed creativity and imagination **Assessment activity 1 page 289** **Assessment activity 2 page 291** **Assessment activity 3 page 292**
P3 perform a physical theatre role/character that communicates an appropriate interpretation to an audience. **Assessment activity 1 page 289** **Assessment activity 3 page 292**	**M3** perform a physical theatre role/character that fully communicates the intentions of the interpretation. **Assessment activity 1 page 289** **Assessment activity 3 page 292**	**D3** perform a physical theatre role/character that makes a significant and imaginative contribution to the interpretation. **Assessment activity 1 page 289** **Assessment activity 3 page 292**
Unit 50: Movement in Performance		
P2 reproduce movement phrases, showing evidence of movement memory **Assessment activity 1 page 289**	**M2** reproduce movement phrases accurately, showing competent use of movement memory **Assessment activity 1 page 289**	**D2** reproduce movement phrases with attention to detail, accuracy and assured confidence **Assessment activity 1 page 289**
P3 attend workshops and rehearsals with evidence of responding to instruction and contributing ideas **Assessment activity 1 page 289** **Assessment activity 2 page 291**	**M3** attend workshops and rehearsals regularly with evidence of effective response to instruction and appropriate contribution of ideas **Assessment activity 1 page 289** **Assessment activity 2 page 291**	**D3** fully engage in the rehearsal process, responding consistently well to instruction and providing a valuable contribution of ideas **Assessment activity 1 page 289** **Assessment activity 2 page 291**

How you will be assessed

This project will be assessed through evidence that you will gather as you progress through it.

This may include:

- feedback from your tutor(s)
- feedback from your peers and audience
- your log book
- video/DVD recordings of rehearsals and performances.

You must keep up your self-evaluation, recording the notes and comments you receive from your tutor in both the workshops and rehearsals, and after the performance itself. This will be essential to you doing well in both units, particularly Unit 50: Movement in Performance, where you have to produce evidence of linking the process of rehearsal to the improvements you make in your contribution to the whole piece.

Paul, physical theatre performer

I performed in a physical theatre piece in one of the regional theatres. The work was a reinterpretation of *Grimm's Fairy Tales*. I played several roles, all of them using my dance experience and acting skills to the full. In some scenes I was an animal, like a tiny mouse, and in others I was a tree or a bird. There were loads of fast costume changes and the set was incredibly complex with some moving sections and a revolve. You had to be very careful during every part of the performance that you were in exactly the correct position, or else you might end up falling through the trap door!

There were several weeks of rehearsals beforehand where we worked with the director and choreographer to develop the movement style and all the sequences to represent the different stories within the tales. Then we got together for general blocking rehearsals, followed by more general rehearsals.

The technical rehearsal was nightmarish and we all thought the set might not work, but it did. The audience of mainly parents and children seemed to really enjoy the performance.

I think physical theatre is a brilliant way of showing an audience a whole range of places, objects and characters. Each one of us played at least four roles during the show.

Over to you

- What other stories might work well as a basis for some physical theatre?
- Using a story you know, work out the opening scene to a physical theatre version.
- Take a story from the newspaper and work out a physical re-interpretation of the key moments in the story.

Your brief

The work you carry out will lead to a site-specific physical theatre performance, designed for an audience of drama and dance learners.

You will be expected to develop the necessary skills to take part in a work about the life and ideas of an arts practitioner; one that has had an important influence on the way theatre is made today. The final piece will be called *The Troubled Life of Antonin Artaud*.

The style and scope of the piece will be dictated by the individual abilities of the group, which may be made up of both dance and drama learners, as well as the site itself. All learners will be expected to be involved in the whole performance: it will encompass movement and physical drama.

The tutor/director will lead the piece, but each learner is expected to bring ideas to the workshop and to contribute to the shaping and rehearsal of the work.

The most appropriate type of space for this project would be a small studio theatre.

Warm up

Antonin Artaud

Antonin Artaud was born in Marseille in 1896. As a young boy he was placed in a sanitorium, or clinic, where he sleepwalked, had bouts of depression and, even though he was cared for, he did not get better.

He was a troubled man who suffered from psychological problems from early childhood. Even when he was conscripted into the army during the First World War, he was discharged for sleepwalking too much. He was a drug addict but very well read, and he became extremely important in the history and development of modern theatre. He died in Paris in 1948.

Using this information, create a simple movement sequence showing support, where each partner takes it in turns to move and support the other. The person being moved should also convey a sense of being asleep.

Antonin Artaud

Activity: Exploring movement

Look back at the Antontin Artaud warm up activity above. You could develop it further by each taking a role; one the carer, one the boy. The carer always tries to be positive in their movements while the boy is less so.

- Film a run-through of your sequence and watch it.
- Rehearse and perform the sequence to the group.
- Ask your tutor and group for feedback,

The first part of your physical theatre piece will be called 'Early ideas'. Artaud started his professional life working with the surrealists, a group of *avant-garde* artists. You will need to find out what kind of movement surrealism was.

Key terms

Automatic writing – a form of writing in which the actions of the hand alone produce a message, with no input from the mind

Activity: Your community

Find a surrealist picture and some details about the artist who painted it. You might choose one by Salvador Dali, or Henri Magritte, both well-known artists of this genre. What kind of work is this? Is it naturalistic? How real is it?

Try to use your answers when you are working on the Artaud project as this will give you a sense of the style of work being produced around him during his lifetime.

Main events in the life of Artaud

Use the timeline below to help you place the ideas of Antonin Artaud in context.

- Writing and performing career: at the age of 24, Artaud lived in Paris; he wrote poetry and essays and performed in *avant-garde* theatre.

- In 1925, he took over the surrealist movement, running their bureau of research; they worked on the idea of **automatic writing** and trying to understand dreams.

- He developed an interest in cinema, writing the first surrealist film *The Seashell and the Clergyman*, directed by Germaine Dulac. He also acted in several films.

- He ran the Alfred Jarry Theatre, directing his own plays and those by several other writers, such as Strindberg.

- In 1931, he saw a troupe of Balinese dancers at the Paris Colonial Exhibition, which made a deep impression on him. He published his first ideas for a Theatre of Cruelty in *La Nouvelle Revue Française*. This later formed part of his book *The Theatre and Its Double*.

- In 1936, he went to Mexico where he became interested in ancient civilisations and local tribes. He also became addicted to drugs and he suffered greatly with this addiction throughout his life.

- In 1937, back in Paris, he acquired a walking stick that he thought had belonged to St Patrick, patron saint of Ireland. He travelled to Ireland to return it, but unable to be understood and without any money, he spent his time in a hotel room. He returned to France.

- In1938, he published his most famous book, *The Theatre and Its Double*. This was the manifesto for the Theatre of Cruelty.

- Following long stays in psychiatric hospitals, Artaud saw an exhibition of paintings by Vincent Van Gogh and he was inspired to write about him. He also wrote performance material for radio, some of which was considered too anti-religious, too wild and too difficult. There were lots of animal noises, grunts and screams. Although a group of very celebrated French and international artists, writers and journalists thought his work should be broadcast, this did not happen until much later.

- He died in 1948 in a psychiatric hospital, suffering from cancer. It is said that he died alone, sitting on the end of his bed, holding his shoe.

- Thirty years later, French radio broadcast his play *Pour en Finir avec le Jugement de Dieu*.

Artaud thought that theatre was about physicality, not just words. He believed theatre should be unique and truly connected with human existence. He rejected any kind of discipline, and so created a theatre that was about chaos, where the audience was pushed right into the centre of the action, completely exposed and forced to take part. This was what he meant by cruelty.

Movement memory

Developing movement memory is all about learning, retaining and then reproducing phrases of movement; this is something performers are always working on. There are several ways of breaking this down.

Technical accuracy – you will have to learn and recall movements very accurately, using a range of different techniques. For example, you might have to remember exactly how to reproduce a tumbling movement, during a scene.

Timing – your timing will be vital, for instance, when you are working on a fast piece of comedy, you will have to be exactly in the right place, at the right time, or the scene may not work.

Rhythmic control – this is about keeping to the rhythm of the accompaniment or the piece itself.

Spatial control – you must make sure you reproduce your movements in exactly the same space and place, in every rehearsal and in performance.

Dynamics – this is an element of every piece of movement and refers to the energy you use within it: slow, fast, relaxed, tense, loose, controlled, for example.

Relationships – this is about whom you are working with. Pairs might have to work closely, for example; your performance must be carefully controlled so it fits in with those of others.

Projection – you must ensure your work always reaches out to the audience so the meaning comes across.

Interpretation- as you work through a piece, you will develop meaning from the stimulus you started with; for example, you might be creating a new version of an old tale – this is an intepretation.

Using physical theatre skills

Assessment activity 1

Unit 33 P2 M2 D2 P3 M3 D3

Unit 50 P2 M2 D2 P3 M3 D3

BTEC

In a small group, improvise the main sequence of events in the life of Artaud, starting with his early life spent in psychiatric clinics. Other events that may be interesting to explore include:

- his love of surrealist works
- his exposure to the Balinese dancers
- the walking stick and his fateful trip to Ireland
- one of his plays that was too extreme to be broadcast
- his lonely death, sitting on the end of a bed, holding his shoe.

1   You could use sound and movement to enact these key moments. Choose a style of movement that suits this activity, eg contact improvisation.

2   Ensure you tackle the specific requirements of the unit: adapting and developing your personal technique through repetition of exercises, accurate recreation of movement, voice and action; accepting criticism and moving forward; using self-appraisal and objectivity.

3   Make sure your character or role embodies what it needs to; this might include working with costume and props.

4   Make sure your work allows the audience to be involved; this is key to Artaud's work.

5   Express all your ideas directly to the audience.

6   You might perform within the audience and around them, or even address the audience directly.

Evidence

- feedback from your tutor, peer(s) and the audience

- video/DVD recordings of workshops, rehearsals and performances
- your log book with records of your ideas, responses to criticism and plans for improving work

Grading tips Unit 33

M2 Use sensitivity by making sure your work corresponds to others'. Be committed to the whole piece.

D2 You must be highly sensitive to the needs of the piece, and use your imagination both in the workshop and in rehearsal.

M3 You must make sure all your intentions and ideas are communicated to the audience.

D3 Your personal contribution must be significant to the success of the whole group's performance.

Grading tips Unit 50

M2 You must reproduce all movement accurately in rehearsal, using movement memory to help you.

D2 You must accurately reproduce, detail and confidently perform all movements.

M3 You must make sure you are at every workshop and rehearsal. You must contribute ideas freely and accept criticism and instruction objectively.

D3 You must participate fully in the rehearsal process, giving and accepting ideas consistently, thus adding value to the piece.

Functional skills

English: By evaluating your work in your performer's log book, you are using your **writing skills**. By proposing ideas for performance, you are using your **speaking and listening** skills.

PLTS

By performing a role or character in a complex movement piece and confidently presenting an appropriate interpretation to an audience, you will be developing your skills as an **effective participator**. By developing your role and character for performance, you will be using your skills as an **independent enquirer** and **creative thinker**.

Using physical theatre skills to develop a role/character in rehearsal

Performance space

As the final piece will be site-specific, you must familiarise yourself with the performance space. This will mean visiting the space to make sure you understand how your own contribution, and the work as a whole, will be performed in this space. Your tutor will give you opportunities to do this.

PLTS

As you make links between rehearsals and performance, you will use your skills as a **reflective learner**. As you try to work out each movement sequence in a different space, you will be stretched as a **creative thinker**.

Activity: Experiment in the performance space

Perform a short section of movement you have already learned in some different spaces.

- Try the movement with performers on different levels.
- Try the work in smaller and larger spaces.
- What difference does performance space make to you as well as to an audience?
- How does this type of activity apply to the ideas of Artaud?
- Remember to make the most of your movement memory including technical accuracy, timing, rhythmic control, spatial control, dynamics and relationships.

Exploring the performance space first will help you focus on your role later

Assessment activity 2

Unit 33 Unit 50  BTEC

Using the work created and learned for Assessment activity 1, your group will take it apart, plan and rehearse each section for a number of different performance spaces. Try to find out the very specific thing that marks out each new space.

- Explore the suitability of each space: its size, objects to avoid, hazards, levels, doorways and windows.

- Block out the piece, section by section.

- Ensure you tackle the specific requirements of the unit: using the performance space; scenic elements; entrances and exits; use of resources, such as props, lighting, sound, costume; effects.

- Rehearse the sections, then film and watch each part to see how well it works in its new venue.

- Evaluate the success of the whole piece in its new site-specific format.

Evidence

- feedback from your tutor
- feedback from your peer(s)

- video/DVD recordings of workshops, rehearsals and performances

- your log book where you record your ideas, responses to criticism and plans for improving your work

Grading tips Unit 33

M2 You must use your skills throughout rehearsals, developing your role sensitively and with commitment.

D2 You must use your imagination and creativity to develop your role through rehearsal.

Grading tips Unit 50

M3 You must respond well to the challenges of the new venues, instruction and criticism, contributing ideas throughout the process.

D3 You will participate fully in the rehearsal process, contributing ideas and responding well to instruction.

PLTS

By engaging in the rehearsal process effectively and making perceptive judgements about your work and setting targets for improvement, you will be developing your skills as a **reflective learner**.
By giving and taking ideas in discussions during the rehearsal process, refining work and responding to criticism where necessary to improve it, and recording ideas in the performer's log book, you will be developing your skills as a **self-manager**.
By using ideas and resources to shape an appropriate form, you will be developing you skills as an **independent enquirer** and **creative thinker**.

Functional skills

English: By evaluating your work in your performer's log book, you are using your **writing** skills. By orally evaluating the success of your work, you are using your **speaking and listening** skills.

When you get to the final rehearsals, your tutor will ensure that you have been taught all the choreography you will be using and any lines you will be speaking, and that the work fits the site-specific space that the performance has been designed for. You must do the following:

- Turn up at every rehearsal, well prepared for the challenges each one brings.

- Ensure your log book is up-to-date and you have sorted out any issues that came up during the previous rehearsal.

- Make sure you have an open mind, and are ready to use your creativity and imagination to contribute to the final work.

Assessment activity 3

You will take part in rehearsals for the final performance of *The Troubled Life of Antonin Artaud*. You must:

- show development of movement ideas; give and take ideas; work cooperatively with others; respond to instructions; take part in warm-ups; take part in rehearsals

- identify targets; make adjustments; practise sequences; analyse; review; repeat accurately

- reproduce ideas; respond to other performers; project and communicate ideas through movement; use performance elements, e.g. space, props, costumes

- share ideas; respond to others; demonstrate good time management, personal organisation, group organisation, goal setting, physical and mental preparation

- attend technical rehearsals and dress rehearsals

- communicate with other performers and the audience through your character; tackle visual and vocal qualities; understand the content of the piece, e.g. its meaning, story, theme, ideas

- identify your strengths and weaknesses; make suggestions for improvement; consider audience reaction; assimilate the views and opinions of others.

Evidence

- feedback from your tutor
- feedback from your peer(s)
- video/DVD recordings of workshops, rehearsals and performances
- your log book where you record your ideas, responses to criticism and plans for improving your work

Grading tips Unit 33

M2 You must use your full range of physical theatre skills in rehearsal to develop a role/character with sensitivity, creativity and commitment.

D2 You must use all of your physical theatre skills in rehearsal to develop a role/character with sensitivity, highly developed creativity and imagination.

M3 You must perform a physical theatre role/character that fully communicates the director's interpretation.

D3 You will perform a physical theatre role/character that makes a significant and imaginative contribution to the interpretation.

Grading tips Unit 50

M4 You must make thoughtful links between the rehearsal process and performance by successfully refining and adjusting work as you go through the process.

D4 You must make significant links between the rehearsal process and performance by refining and adjusting the work with skill and expertise.

M5 You must perform a role, showing movement skills that accurately convey the character, mood or intention of the material.

D5 You must perform a role, showing confident movement skills with a real sense of style; you will easily communicate the character, mood and/or intention to the audience.

Functional skills

English: By sharing ideas and having discussions during the rehearsal process, then making any adjustments to work, as well as planning rehearsals, you are using your **speaking and listening** skills.

By evaluating your work in your performer's log book, you are using your **writing** skills.

PLTS

By planning a suitable and useful rehearsal schedule and making perceptive judgements about your own work, setting targets for improvement where necessary, you will be developing your skills as a **reflective learner**.

Sally McDowel
Physical theatre peformer

Sally is a performer, currently working with a touring company. Her training is in dance and drama and she works with a lot of companies that use her skills in physical theatre.

What are you working on at the moment?

Sally: I am currently in a show about work and the way it has developed through the ages, from agriculture, to industry, to offices, to virtual work, where people often work from home again, like they did when they were farmers or, say, weavers or something like that.

We are performing in a regional tour to audiences that mainly consist of students. I'm using my physical skills and this means I have to lift and take weight and balance on scenery and props to create the places the narrative runs through.

The piece is hard and quite gruelling at times, but it's absolutely amazing to watch.

The director has worked hard with us to produce a piece which uses very few real objects to suggest what we are doing, we just have ourselves.

At the end of the show we have a half-hour audience Q&A session, where the audience can ask us how we created the piece. This can leads to us showing how we manage some of the lifts. The students usually love it.

Think about it!

1 What sort of physical theatre work do you like watching?

2 Try to work out how performers create meaning from their bodies to suggest places and objects. Have you used this in your own work?

3 Develop a workshop you and a group could produce to show younger learners in your centre what this project is all about. What could the theme be?

Just checking

1 Make sure you understand the requirements of the piece, as well as the intentions of your director. If you do not, then ask.

2 Research background material on the project, such as the life and writings of Artaud.

3 Keep your personal log book up-to-date with plans for future improvement to your work.

4 Make sure you are ready for any challenge your director throws at you.

5 Contribute ideas confidently throughout the workshop process.

6 Learn your movements, steps and any lines you are given.

7 Work on your role or character in your own time.

8 Review your work by watching yourself on video/DVD.

9 Take criticism objectively; it is part of learning how to become a performer.

10 Keep up your regular dance/drama class to maintain your skill level.

edexcel

Assignment tips

- Ensure you address the specific requirements of the unit: adapting and developing your personal technique through repetition of exercises, accurate recreation of movement, voice and action; accepting criticism and moving forward; using self-appraisal and objectivity.

- Keep up your self-evaluation, recording the notes and comments you receive from your tutor in both the workshops and rehearsals, and after the performance itself.

- Make sure you turn up at every rehearsal, well prepared for the challenges each one brings.

- Maintain a good level of discipline in rehearsals. Contribute in a positive manner, being supportive and respectful of others and responding to direction in an appropriate way.

PROJECT 10:
Moving On

What do you want to do after you have completed your BTEC National in Performing Arts course? What are the options if you want to continue to study or work in the performing arts? What must you do to get a job as an actor?

This project brings together the work for two units: Unit 17: Developing Voice for the Actor and Unit 18: Auditions for Actors. You will select and prepare a portfolio of speeches that can be used to enter education and training, ie, drama school or higher education establishments.

You may also be able to adapt and use these speeches to enter employment, such as working in theatre, film/television/radio performance and advertising, or the leisure industries.

You must be able to show that you know why the material chosen is suitable for use in particular auditions.

You will have the opportunity to develop your vocal and physical performance techniques throughout the project. You will take part in mock auditions, receiving feedback and guidance from your tutors and peers.

Learning outcomes

After completing this project you should be able to achieve the following learning outcomes:

Unit 17: Developing Voice for the Actor

3   Be able to demonstrate vocal technique in performance.

Unit 18: Auditions for Actors

1   Know how to select suitable audition material

2   Be able to relate vocal and physical performance technique to character and style

3   Be able to use vocal and physical technique in performance.

Assessment and grading criteria

This table shows you what you must do in order to achieve a pass, merit or distinction, and where you can find activities in this book to help you.

To achieve a **pass** grade the evidence must show that you are able to:	To achieve a **merit** grade the evidence must show that, in addition to the pass criteria, you are able to:	To achieve a **distinction** grade the evidence must show that, in addition to the pass and merit criteria, you are able to:
Unit 17: Developing Voice for the Actor		
P5 demonstrate competently the application of vocal technique in performance. **Assessment activity 4 page 306**	**M5** demonstrate a skilled and confident application of appropriate vocal technique in performance. **Assessment activity 4 page 306**	**D5** demonstrate a comprehensive and fully appropriate application of vocal technique in performance, with confidence, ease and fluency. **Assessment activity 4 page 306**
Unit 18: Auditions for Actors		
P1 describe the suitability of chosen audition material for audition contexts **Assessment activity 1 page 302**	**M1** explain the suitability of chosen audition material for audition contexts **Assessment activity 1 page 302**	**D1** analyse the suitability of chosen audition material for audition contexts **Assessment activity 1 page 302**
P2 develop vocal and physical performance technique, responding to character and style of audition text **Assessment activity 2, 3 page 304**	**M2** develop vocal and physical performance technique, showing control and thoughtfulness in response to character and responding to style of audition text **Assessment activity 2, 3 page 304**	**D2** develop vocal and physical performance technique, showing consistent control, physical ease and an imaginative response to character and responding to style of audition text **Assessment activity 2, 3 page 304**
P3 demonstrate vocal and physical technique in an audition situation. **Assessment activity 4 page 306**	**M3** demonstrate competent vocal and physical technique in an audition situation. **Assessment activity 4 page 306**	**D3** demonstrate effective and confident vocal and physical technique in an audition situation. **Assessment activity 4 page 306**

How you will be assessed

This project will be assessed through an internal assignment that will be designed and marked by the tutors at your centre. You will be assessed on your ability to select suitable material for auditions, and the way you develop your vocal and physical technique. You will take part in mock and/or real auditions.

The work you produce may include:
- an analysis of your chosen audition material
- an actor's log that shows progress with developing your characters
- annotated versions of your chosen scripts
- a recording of the preparatory or mock auditions
- observations from your tutor(s)
- feedback from your audience(s) and peer(s).

Ryan, 18-year-old actor

I am applying to a couple of drama schools and some universities. I can't really afford to go to drama school but I hope to get a scholarship, so my audition pieces are especially important.

I have three contemporary speeches I like. The Oggy Moxon speech from *Teechers* (John Godber): it's written to be played by a girl, and is an exaggerated, big character. It is a bit rude, and I hope it will make the panel laugh and see that I can play a comic role. The other two speeches are more serious and naturalistic: a speech from *The Accrington Pals*, (Peter Whelan), and one from *Equus* (Peter Shaffer), playing Alan. *The Accrington Pals* speech allows me to show off my attempt at a Lancashire accent, and Alan in *Equus* is a confused, angry lad, unable to cope with his own behaviour.

For the classical speeches I am going to choose between *Titus Andronicus* (William Shakespeare) – it's a brilliant speech, filled with passion and despair – and Giovanni from *'Tis Pity She's a Whore* (John Ford). He is a complex character who is in love with his sister. I found it quite difficult to understand the classical pieces at first. Watching a performance of *Titus Andronicus* really helped me see that the language used is quite straightforward and can sound realistic. There are lots of speeches for Giovanni and I need to choose one that will contrast well with my contemporary piece.

Over to you
- What type of training would you like to undertake after your BTEC course?
- What sort of pieces would be suitable for you, allowing you to show your skills as a performer?

Your brief

You are required to prepare two contrasting monologues for auditions to drama school or a higher education establishment.

Know how to select suitable audition material

Research and planning

Drama schools and higher education establishments

Most learners on a BTEC National in Performing Arts course will want to continue their education and training at drama school or a higher education establishment.

Some drama schools and HE establishments will provide you with a list of suggested audition speeches or characters. Some will tell you which ones not to do – they may decide that there are too many interpretations of particular characters, or that a monologue is too popular or over-familiar and appears in too many audition collection books.

For the audition and interview process, you should be prepared to:

- perform two contrasting pieces to an audition panel, sometimes in front of other candidates
- perform your speech(es) with a new or different context
- take part in a solo or group improvisation or workshop
- discuss your speeches, and take part in a more general interview about your ambitions and aims.

Although you may need to prepare auditions for employment purposes in the future, the focus of this project is auditioning for further and higher education.

Key terms

Typecasting – playing roles close to your own personal type, especially physical appearance. This might result in not having the opportunity to show different types of characterisations and roles.

Understanding your own profile

Your own strengths and profile will influence your choice of material for your auditions.

These are things to consider:

Your age: finding roles that are suitable for your age. Your age range is the minimum and maximum character ages for you.

Your physical appearance: for example, your hair colour, height, body shape.

Your vocal range: for example, your ability to recreate regional accents, or speak in higher and lower registers.

Your acting style(s): for example, playing comic characters, serious drama, stereotypes, your physicality, **typecasting**.

Activity: Skills audit of your strengths and profile

In your audit, include your answers to the above strengths/profile points, and the following details:

Performance experience: (list in this order) title of play; character name; director; performance venue; date of performance

Qualifications to date

Work skills and interests, for example, driving licence, hobbies, e.g. waterskiing

Performance skills, such as acting, acrobatics, juggling, dancing, singing (do not lie as you may be required to prove that you can juggle or water ski (or do both simultaneously).

Casting type: if you had to fit into a type, what would it be? What kind of roles would you apply for?

Selecting your audition material

Building a repertoire of audition speeches will be useful for applying to drama school and university. It will also provide you with a selection of speeches that you can choose from when you need to demonstrate, for example, your ability to play different types of characters, perform particular accents, and your specialist skills.

There are various ways of choosing your audition materials:

Your own experiences as a performer:

- Think about characters that you played in previous productions.
- Consider roles you did not play; there may be a character that you would like to perform.

Productions you have seen:

- You might have seen a play or film with a character that made an impression on you, or one that would be a challenge (if using a film, make sure there is a stage version).
- Consider roles played by actors of a similar age to yourself.

Advice and guidance from your tutor:

- Ask your tutor which would be suitable characters for you to try.

Plays you have read:

- You might have studied a particular play, or scenes from a play, and would like to explore it further.
- You could investigate the work of a playwright that you like.

Using compilation books:

- You are relying on someone else to choose the speech and provide you with a summary of the play and character.
- Use the book as a starting point, and if you like the speech, read the play.
- Make up your own mind about the summary of the plot and character; you may also find more appropriate speeches to choose from.
- Drama schools may disapprove of speeches taken from audition compilations as they are used many times in auditions; they may send you details of speeches to avoid.

Drama school/HE establishment prospectus audition requirements:

- Investigate what kind of performance material is acceptable at your chosen establishment. They may provide you with a list of suggested speeches. Drama schools often focus on particular acting styles. Investigate the types of actors that graduated from the school in recent years.

Why you need contrasting pieces

Presenting different (contrasting) pieces will show your range of skills and techniques and demonstrate that you:

- are comfortable speaking **verse** and **prose**
- can play differences in characters, for instance, in age, social status, physicality, objectives and motivations
- can perform in a serious drama but also as a comic character
- are comfortable in a realistic role and also playing a stylised Brechtian-type performance
- can play characters that are close to type or away from type.

Key terms

Verse – a type of poetry; it has a regular meter in each line and can be rhyme (blank verse does not rhyme)

Prose – is writing that resembles ordinary, everyday speech

Monologue – a solo speech that is either lifted directly, or adapted, from a full-length play

How to choose your monologue

Some playwrights create monologues or soliloquies for their characters.

You might see an opportunity to create your own monologue by removing other characters' lines in a scene. Make sure that the context of the character remains the same, and seek the advice of your tutor to help and guide you with this task.

Remember

It is vital that you:

- read the entire play
- make sure you understand all the words, references, themes and ideas of the play.
- understand what happens to your character and how it happens.

Case study: Michaela, age 17

I have two speeches that will show my ability to do accents – both girls are working class, both are really lovely, honest and kind. Louise from *Road* (Jim Cartwright) is a Sheffield girl and is quite understated during the play, but grows in strength during her speech. Karen in *Essex Girls* (Rebecca Pritchard) is really outspoken, rude and funny, but completely loving and supportive towards her friend. I've got Pearl from *House and Garden* (Alan Ayckbourn) as a more realistic character, too.

My classical speeches are Goneril from *King Lear* (Shakespeare) - I have removed Oswald's lines in Act 1, Scene 3 and made it into a continuous monologue. She is a really manipulative character and it is good to play someone with such high status and self-importance.

In contrast, I have a speech from *Saint Joan* (George Bernard Shaw). She is earnest but another very powerful character, able to fight like a soldier and lead an army.

Over to you

- Have you chosen contrasting speeches?
- What are the differences between your speeches? What skills do they showcase?

Activity: Choose monologues from contemporary and classical plays

As a general rule, a play is defined as 'classical' if written before the 1930s.

A contemporary piece should be taken from a play written from 1930 onwards, although this may vary as some people see late 19th-century work as contemporary.

Make a shortlist of potential monologues from both classical and contemporary plays. You can include different styles of performance, characters, or even a wildcard choice (find something that is obscure, bizarre or challenging).

Activity: Preparing your audition material

Read all your selected plays, and discuss the themes with others to share opinions and ideas. Your tutor might act as director and provide you with an interpretation for the work.

You should consider possible interpretations of the role, or whether there are any famous performances that you can refer to.

In your audition, you are likely to be asked about your interpretation. Be ready to discuss the decisions you have made on your characterisation.

Activity: Produce a character overview

Find the following facts about your characters:

- life; relationships; job; social status; likes and dislikes; where they live; when they live (the year(s) when the play is set); how they live

- physical appearance; dress; eating and drinking habits; exercise

- personality traits: where do your characters stand in terms of happiness and misery? Are they shy or show-offs? Do they remain calm or are they on the point of madness?

How original is your performance piece? Is it heavily influenced by the work of others or is it truly innovative?

Note what other characters say about you and act towards you, and what you say about others.

Be prepared to explain the background and summarise the plays whether you have chosen obscure pieces, contemporary texts or well-known pieces.

Deconstruct the scripts

Find out your characters' desires and dreams, their intentions by analysing the subtext: this is a Stanislavski technique and is suitable for most plays.

Decide the units and objectives of each line, each scene, each act, and the super objective of the play (see page 118 for more information and guidance).

Did you know?

Shakespeare uses iambic pentameter; this means that there are five stressed and five unstressed syllables in each line.

Here is an example from *Taming of the Shrew*, where the second syllable is stressed.

Act 3, Scene 1:

KATE: 'No **shame** but **mine**, I **must**, for**sooth** be **forc'd**

To **give** my **hand**, op**pos'd** ag**ainst** my **heart**...

Make the scripts work for you

- Underline or highlight stresses and rhythms in your lines.
- Indicate where you think a pause should occur.
- Write in stage directions and moves.
- Note where you want to interact with the audience.

Jude Law sees the script as a map to unlocking the emotional journey of a play

Assessment activity 1

Unit 18 **P1** **M1** **D1** **BTEC**

Once you have selected two contrasting audition pieces, you will need to explain the reasons for doing so and analyse the following.

1 The purpose, content and context of the speeches.
   - Who is being addressed in the speeches? (eg the audience, yourself, other characters, an object).
   - What are the speeches about? (the purpose, themes, ideas, emotions).
   - Why is your character speaking? (the motivation for expressing the words, the characters spoken to, and the relationships between them).

2 Why you chose these speeches.
   - What is the style and content?
   - What do they offer you as a performer?
   - What is interesting or challenging about them?

3 Which plays the speeches come from.
   - Give a summary of the plots.
   - Describe the themes.
   - Explain your characters.
   - Describe the context of the speeches.
   - Give details of the playwrights.
   - Describe the historical backgrounds.

4 The speeches you disregarded in your shortlist.
   - Explain why you did not use them.

5 The contrasting qualities of the speeches; use the examples below or include your own.
   - Classical/contemporary
   - Naturalistic/stylised

- Serious/comic
- For older/younger character
- For character who is extrovert/introvert.

6 The establishments and courses you have applied for, and the reasons for choosing them.

7 The suitability of your speeches for your chosen establishments or employment.

8 Why your speeches are suitable for you as a performer.
   - What is your vocal range? (accents, clarity, range)
   - What is your physical ability and acting style(s)? (for example comedy/comic characters, serious drama, physicality)
   - How suitable are they for your age?

9 How you will prepare and rehearse for the auditions.

Evidence

- annotated scripts
- the actor's log

Grading tips

M1 You need to provide an explanation, rather than a description, of why you have chosen your pieces.

D1 You need to analyse your choices, reflecting on your own abilities and the effectiveness of your choices.

PLTS

Analysing your reasons for choosing your audition pieces will allow you to develop your skills as a **creative thinker.**

Functional skills

English: Your work in preparing audition materials will demonstrate your **reading** abilities. You will need to **select** suitable scripts, **compare** and **understand** the content to form your **ideas** about how they should be performed.

Be able to relate vocal and physical performance technique to character and style

Unit 19: Principles of Acting (page 113) will provide you with guidance and exercises for analysing and developing your characters. Here are some further points to consider.

The age of the characters will have some impact on how you will use your voice and physicality.

You will need to decide how you will indicate age to the audience, especially as you cannot rely on make-up or costume to add (or remove) years to your appearance.

Try to show your work in progress to a friend, fellow actor or tutor. Feedback can be really valuable and help build your confidence. Working alone in rehearsing your work can result in a fixed interpretation, and most auditions require you to demonstrate that you can be flexible and modify your performance.

Focus on character development, by setting aside time for this daily or weekly. This work might include:

- reading, and rereading the plays
- experimenting with how you deliver lines, changing gestures or altering the tone of your voice
- changing the motivation of your characters
- experimenting with positioning, blocking and movement
- exaggerating your characters, then bringing them back to a realistic portrayal.

Vocal technique

Consider how different your own voice is from that of the characters. Using your analysis of the script and any stage directions and background information on the plays, make notes on the differences in the accent, the pitch, the volume, the rhythm and the use of **dialect**. What needs to change?

Activity: Vocal performance

Look for characters on TV, film and radio that you think have the accents or voice patterns of your characters. Listen to them and imitate their vocal patterns and styles.

Once you have decided on the motivations and emotions of your characters, think about how the voices will sound, for example, are your characters softly spoken? This could indicate weakness and low status, but it could also indicate security, authority, relaxation and lacking in tension.

Physical technique

Think about how much movement is in the piece, read the playwright's notes and decide on your interpretation.

You will need to decide how you will move and when you will move.

You may need to imagine furniture, doors and windows. If the speech is being directed at another character (who isn't actually there), you will need to consider where that character would be positioned. For example, maybe the character is in the same position as the panel – and that is where you will address you speech. Or maybe the other character is to one side of the panel?

There is no right or wrong way to do this, but some actors prefer to perform comic scenes directly to the audition panel (for example, the Benedick speeches in Shakespeare's *Much Ado About Nothing*), and tragic speeches in a more introverted manner.

Try rehearsing your scenes in a number of different situations, such as in traverse (with the audience either side) or with the audience 'in the round'.

Key terms

Dialect – a form of language spoken in a particular geographical area or by members of a particular social class or occupational group, distinguished by its vocabulary, grammar and pronunciation

Assessment activity 2
Develop characters and rehearse monologues

Unit 18  **:BTEC**

When developing each of your characters for performance, you need to work on the following elements.

What defines the character – age, status, relationships, personality and given circumstances.

What defines the performance – the style of the piece, the context of the scene and the play.

Your vocal and physical technique – the specific requirements of the text and character.

Your decisions as an actor – the decisions you make when bringing the character to life.

Evidence
- the actor's log
- tutor observations.

Grading tips

M2 You should experiment with your performance, pushing boundaries and not choosing obvious ways of expressing ideas.

D2 You will need to be highly creative in your interpretations, demonstrating confidence and ease with your physical and vocal technique.

Interpretation

The playwright may have specified in the stage directions or dialogue, the year, time of year, day, location, weather conditions, interior or exterior, and so on. Think about how you will show these elements without the use of lighting, set, costume and props.

If the writer has not been specific, you will need to make these decisions. You must also decide how to demonstrate them in your performance.

Remember

If you do not understand a word or reference in your speech, find out what it means. You could ask your tutor, friends or family, or refer to reference books or a reliable website. Understanding the meaning of words and references can have a significant effect on your interpretation and performance.

Assessment activity 3

Unit 18  **:BTEC**

Your actor's log should include the following information.

Character development
- Objectives and motivation for each role.
- Observation notes on other performers, real people, animals, and so on.
- Images, thoughts, ideas (such as costumes, historical background notes).
- Notes on vocal and physical decisions you have made.

Performance development
- Scripts with useful annotations, that is, marked with stresses and pauses, stage directions, and so on.
- Ideas and decisions you have made, according to the style of the chosen pieces.
- Details of vocal exercises.

- Details of physical exercises.
- Evaluative comments (daily or weekly progress, tutor feedback, self appraisal, target setting).

Evidence
- the actor's log

Grading tips

M2 Your evaluative comments should demonstrate how much attention you are paying to the development of your performances.

D2 You should be consistent and imaginative in your development of the performances.

Be able to use vocal and physical technique in performance

Auditions are concerned with potential; an audition is not a fully polished performance.

Be prepared to be flexible, to change your style of acting, to try new ideas and suggestions.

Choose monologues you enjoy performing and feel comfortable with.

Audition performance requirements (drama school and HE)

Behaviour

Arrive on time. Turn your phone off.

Wear clothing that is simple, comfortable, understated, and that allows you to move. Avoid anything too showy or obviously ridiculous.

If you have to watch others perform, be encouraging and show respect (your behaviour will be noted).

Demonstrate that you are able to learn, and are malleable, that is, you can be directed and moulded.

Introduction

Introduce yourself, the title of the play, the playwright, and the part you are playing. If this was chosen by you (rather than requested by the audition panel), a brief introduction may be required, for example: 'This is the scene where the character…'. Alternatively, you might be asked to enter the room, and complete the speech, without stating at the beginning 'Please imagine…' or ending with 'And cue blackout'.

Redirected audition

Be prepared to be challenged. You may be asked to perform the scene again, but set in a different context or environment, for example your character must maintain the level of anger, but you are not allowed to raise your voice.

If you are using verse, make sure you are comfortable with it. You may be asked to take part in a run-around and change direction on the thought, line or stress; therefore being familiar with the content and structure of the verse is very important.

You may be asked to change the motivation for your character, for example your character is lying rather than telling the truth.

Improvisations and exercises

This could be solo, with other people auditioning, or with members of the audition panel.

Listen to the panel's requests; if in doubt, ask them to clarify their instructions.

You may be asked to improvise in character or with other characters from the play. You may be given a new scenario (and new characters), or a situation your character might find themselves in.

It could be a whole day of activities, depending on where you are auditioning. The panel will be looking at your abilities; be natural and cooperative, and show your skills.

Sight reading or cold reading

This may not happen in every audition. If you are

required to read from a script, you would be given time to practise beforehand. If you are put in this position, ask questions to find out what they expect from you. Do not be afraid to say if you are not a confident reader.

Interview

Here are some examples of interview questions and topics:

- Your audition pieces: why did you choose the particular characters? What motivates the characters?

- Why did you choose the institution? Discuss the particular elements of this centre that are appealing.

- What are your strengths as a performer?

- What was your last performance role?

- Give an example of when you had to overcome difficulties with working with others.

- Give an example of overcoming problems in meeting deadlines.

- What aspects of your performance technique do you need to improve upon?

- What are your other interests and hobbies, apart from acting?

Did you know?

There are 19,000 members of the UK performers' union Equity, which lists acting as its main profession.

UK actors work professionally for an average of 11.3 weeks a year.

At any given moment, 92 per cent of UK-based actors are reckoned to be out of work.

52 per cent of Equity members earn less that £6,000 a year.

Sources: Spotlight/Equity; www.getintotheatre.org; Guardian

Assessment activity 4

Unit 18 Unit 17  **BTEC**

A mock audition can be an incredibly useful exercise as it allows you to practise your speeches in a more relaxed environment.

In small groups, set up audition panels.

Each audition panel will decide on improvisation exercises and interview questions. One person will be responsible for recording the audition.

Each person auditioning will introduce and perform the speeches, and be prepared to undergo redirection, improvisations in character, and a short interview.

After the audition, complete the following:

- Receive feedback from the audition panel.

- Carry out a self-appraisal of your performance skills, listening to your vocal performance and observing your physicality through recordings of your performance.

- Evaluate the success of your work, how you reacted to suggestions from the panel, and your

involvement in improvisations.

Were your responses to the interview questions believable and honest?

Evidence

- tutor observations

- peer assessment sheets

Grading tips

Unit 18 **M3** Unit 17 **M5** Demonstrate your skills with confidence in performance. Your technical skills will be secure and well executed.

Unit 18 **D3** Unit 17 **D5** Be positive, confident and courageous as a performer, ensuring that you demonstrate strong vocal and physical techniques in your work.

PLTS

Carrying out a self-appraisal of your performance skills and evaluating the success of your work will use your skills as a **self-manager**.

Functional skills

Maintaining an actor's log enables you to **communicate ideas** and **opinions in writing** about any choices you made when developing a character.

Thomas Aldridge is a professional actor whose theatre credits include *His Dark Materials*, *The Secret Garden*, *The Taming of the Shrew* and *A Midsummer Night's Dream*. Tom has also appeared on television shows such as *EastEnders* and *Primeval*.

Tom completed a BTEC National in Performing Arts before graduating from Mountview Academy of Theatre Arts.

Here are Tom's thoughts on drama school auditions:

'You need to show some 'castability' when up for a play. But when you are trying to enter drama school, you mainly want to show how good you are – you can have a little bit of free licence with drama college speeches. It's about

potential, and you have another three years before you are going to be cast in those roles anyway.

I have never had to do a speech at an audition in front of other actors except at drama school. In a drama school audition, the actors are in direct competition. In this situation, you have to show the other actors respect, and show that you can be cooperative. It's definitely noticed by the people that matter!

If I were to give one piece of advice to someone auditioning, I would say choose two pieces that you are completely confident and comfortable with. If you were asked to do one of them a different way, you would be happy to do so, completely flipping it on its head, you are that comfortable with it.

Also, audition for as many drama colleges that you can afford the audition fees for. Not only because of the greater chance of getting in somewhere, but because you have no idea what those colleges are like until you actually experience them. You may have had a dream of going to one college and find that you hate it when you actually audition there; there might be another that you had no intention of going to but you get a real feel for the place when auditioning. Every actor works better in particular environments and it is most important as an actor to be in the right drama school. You won't flourish unless you are around the kind of training that is going to suit you, and bring out the best in you.'

Think about it!

1 Have you decided which drama school or university course to apply for?

2 Have you read the prospectus and carried out any research for your chosen institutions?

3 Have you selected two pieces that you are confident and comfortable with?

Just checking

1 Make sure you have done your research into your chosen drama schools, colleges and universities and know what they offer.
2 Read the plays and get a thorough understanding of the characters.
3 Research the plays to ensure you know about the playwright and context of the work.
4 Have a suitable selection of pieces to showcase your skills.
5 Rehearse, prepare and experiment with your pieces.
6 Practise your interview technique.
7 Be prepared to experiment and change your rehearsed material in the auditions.
8 Be confident, be focused and prepare yourself for your auditions.

edexcel

Assignment tips

- Read your assignment brief.
- Understand the tasks.
- If in doubt, ask your tutor for advice and guidance.
- Know your deadlines.
- Make sure you know the plays.
- Choose your speeches carefully.
- Try to get feedback on your progress before the final assessment deadline.
- Consider your future – do you want to be an actor?
- Try to keep some form of record for every step of the process. It could be photos, videos, notes, and evidence of your research for the development of your characters. You could also keep prospectuses and guidance from different drama schools and HE establishments.

Glossary

Abstract – when there is no obvious storyline, narrative or any particular idea prominent in the piece

Adversity – difficulty or hardship

Antagonist – an opponent

Antic – a ludicrous or grotesque act done for fun or amusement

Arabesque – similar to attitude, but with leg and arms outstretched, one forward, one to the side, slightly back

Aside – a character speaking thoughts directly to the audience when other characters are present

Atmosphere – the tone or mood of a theatrical performance

Attitude – a standing position, on one leg, the other raised in a bent position up at the rear, arms in fourth position

Automatic writing – a form of writing in which the actions of the hand alone produce a message, with no input from the mind

Battlement – beating the foot or leg to front, side or back

Bharata Natyam – an ancient traditional dance from Southern India, danced by both males and females

Bigotry – the intolerance of a person who does not accept any opinions differing from their own

Black box studio – a large square room with black walls and a flat floor

Blocking – deciding on the general positions and spatial relationships for the actors on stage

Broken chords – notes from a chord that are played one after another

Canon – movements that are repeated by other dancers, sometimes simultaneously, sometimes following one another

Casting – the process by which the creative team decides who will undertake the principal roles in a show

Censorship – examination by an authorised person or organisation of publications, theatrical work, films, letters, and so on, in order to suppress those considered obscene or politically unacceptable

Choreography – sequences of steps or movements for a dance performance

Chorus – an ensemble of singers and dancers

Climax – the highest point of anything conceived of as growing, developing or unfolding

Combination – a series of moves and steps joined together to make a short dance sequence

Commedia dell'Arte – Translated as 'comedy of art', the Commedia dell'Arte began in Italy in the 16th Century. Its key features include the use of masked character 'types' and (usually) unscripted, improvised performance. Pantomine and Punch and Judy puppet shows both have their origins in this style of theatre.

Conventions – doing things in generally agreed upon ways

Contact improvisation – improvised contemporary dance where the partners use each other's bodies to initiate and marks the place where your core strength lies, and controls all your movements

Cultural taboo – Something that a certain cultural group considers to be unacceptable. Some taboos are shared by the majority of cultures, such as the view that intentional murder or cannibalism is wrong, whilst others are more culturally specific, for example in Japan it is seen as a cultural taboo to wear shoes indoors. Taboos can also be specific to a certain era or time period. For example, some things that were once considered taboo in the UK, such as divorce, are now much more widely accepted.

CV – Curriculum Vitae; a document listing all your personal details, such as name, date of birth, address and contact details, relevant training received, qualifications and previous experience

Dénouement – conclusion

Développé – raising the leg in an unfolding motion to front, side or back

Dialect – a form of language spoken in a particular geographical area or by members of a particular social class or occupational group, distinguished by its vocabulary, grammar and pronunciation

Dirge – a song or hymn of mourning composed or performed as a memorial to a dead person

Dramaturg – A person who is a specialist in dramatic composition and theatrical representation

Dynamics – the volume of the piece

Dynamic range – the quality of energy and drive that a dancer uses, how strong their movements are

Ensemble – the performing group

Entr'acte – a short piece of music played between an act or a scene

Equity minimum rate – the minimum rate of pay set by the actors trade union Equity

Expenditure – the act of spending money for goods or services

Fondu – on a bent supporting leg

Form – the design, structure and arrangement of performance work

Forum theatre – a type of theatre created by the practitioner Augusto Boal. Actors pause the action and ask audience members to suggest what they should do next. The audience have a direct influence on what they will see next and the outcomes of a piece

Forward tone – where the voice resonates off the cavities of the face rather than resonating in the throat

Genre – a category or type of performance; comedy and tragedy are broad genres

Get-in – moving the set and other equipment, including technical equipment, into the performance space before the technical rehearsal

Glissé – sliding the foot through the movement

Grand battlement – a sharp raise of the leg extending the foot as high as possible without losing placing of the centre and hip alignment

Headshot – a photograph of the head and shoulders only

Inanimate – not alive

Intonation – tuning; the rise and fall of the voice when speaking

Isolations – the snappy rhythmic movements of separate body parts, such as head, shoulders and hands which is associated with jazz dance

Isolations – moving parts of the body separately from others

Inversion – when a movement is repeated the other way around, backwards or on its head

Jacobean tragedy – a play with a tragic theme written in the Jacobean period (1603 – 1625)

Kathakali – a very old form of stylised dance drama, originally from Kerala, India

Manipulation – to handle especially skilfully; to manage or influence cleverly

Mannerism – a trait; a behavioural attribute that is distinctive and peculiar to an individual

Melodrama – A genre of theatre that uses stereotypical and one-dimensional characters (heroes, villains etc) to control an audience's emotions. The entrance of a 'good' or 'bad' character will be marked with a piece of music suited to that character type.

Monologue – a solo speech that is either lifted directly, or adapted, from a full-length play

Motif – A sequence of movement that is developed through repetition or change, throughout a piece

Motivate – to drive or compel a character to behave, speak, act and react

Musical sentences – a musical phrase

Note-bashing – a rehearsal where the musical director teaches a song to performers by bashing the melody out on

Octave – an interval of eight notes

Off book – able to perform the dialogue from memory

Operetta – a short, amusing opera

Pirouette – a ballet turn on one leg with the other foot placed just below the knee of the supporting leg, in a turned out or parallel position

Plié – controlled knee bend in set position with feet parallel or turned-out, to build control in legs and centre

Plot – is the main story that runs throughout the play

Practitioner – someone who creates performance work and a theoretical context for the work

Programme schedule – contains all information on props and technical requirements, and contributions from all the people involved in booking performances

Prohibited – forbidden, banned

Projection – a way of projecting the voice through driving the breath from the lungs (using the diaphragm), over the vocal chords and through the mouth

Prompt copy of script ('the book') – includes lighting and sound cues, stage directions

Protagonist – the principal character in a play or story

Proscenium arch theatre – a performance space with a stage set behind an arch which acts like a picture frame

Prose – is writing that resembles ordinary, everyday speech

Raga – traditional Indian melody made up of five or more musical notes usually associated with different parts of the day or various seasons

Raked stage – a tilt in the floor of the stage, usually from upstage to downstage, to improve the view for the audience

Répétiteur – the person who schedules and organises rehearsals for a show and who teaches the repertoire

Revenue – the entire amount of income before any deductions are made

Revue – a variety show

Role on the wall – a blank template of a person is filled in with information about a character e.g. their personality traits, relationships with other characters etc

Rond de jamble – taking the leg in a circular motion either, *à terre*, with the foot sliding along the ground or *en l'air*, with the leg raised

Satire – a literary technique of writing or art which principally ridicules its subjects

Show stopper – a musical number received by the audience with prolonged applause that literally

stops the show until it dies down

Site-specific – a performance made specially for a particular venue or place that utilises its features in performance

Sitzprobe – a seated rehearsal where the singers sing with the orchestra, focusing attention on integrating the two groups

Soliloquy – a character speaking thoughts aloud when alone on stage

Sponsorship – to provide support (usually financial) to a person, object, activity or company

Spotting – this helps prevent dizziness in turns. As you start to turn, fix your eyes on a spot just in front of you at eye height; keep your gaze there as long as you can during the turn; flick your head around as you turn to prevent losing sight of your point.

Stimuli – anything that can have an impact or influence

Sub-plot – is a minor story or stories that do not necessarily alter, or affect, the main story

Suspension – giving a sense of weightlessness in space

Symmetry/asymmetry – movements of dancers that are in balance (symmetry) or not (asymmetry)

Tableaux – the plural for 'picture' or 'image' in French. They were a popular form of entertainment before radio, film or television.

Tempo – usually a music term, meaning how fast a piece of music is to be played. It also means the pace at

Tendu – controlled stretch of the feet and legs, such as point-flex-point, to build control and strength in legs, hips and centre which an action or process occurs

Theatre practitioner – someone who creates theatrical performance and/or writes theoretical ideas and teachings

Theme and variation – this is a sequence that forms around an idea, such as movements rising and lowering, and is developed and changed as the dance goes on

Thought tracking – actors will pause the action to speak their current thoughts and/or feelings aloud. Or they may ask audience members to speak their thoughts/feelings for them; in other words the audience decide what that character is thinking/feeling at that point

Thwarted – ruined, spoiled

Travelling steps – steps linked together, generally performed across the diagonal, or around the studio, to build up rhythm, coordination, style

Unison – when everyone sings the same melody

Verse – a type of poetry; it has a regular meter in each line and can be rhyme (blank verse does not rhyme)

Vocal dynamics – The range of sounds the voice can make by using the vocal organs (vocal chords, mouth, throat)

Working title – a title that has not been confirmed yet and may change during the devising process

Zeitgeist – trend; the cultural spirit and mood of a particular time

Index